ODYSSEY

Homer

ODYSSEY

Translated by
Stanley Lombardo

Introduction by
Sheila Murnaghan

Hackett Publishing Company, Inc.
Indianapolis/Cambridge

Printed in the United States of America

06 05 04 03 02 01 00   1 2 3 4 5 6 7 8

For further information, please address
Hackett Publishing Company, Inc.
P. O. Box 44937
Indianapolis, Indiana 46244–0937

www.hackettpublishing.com

Cover design by Brian Rak and John Pershing

Interior design by Meera Dash

The Palace of Odysseus illustration on page xi adapted from *Homer's Odyssey: A Companion to the Translation of Richmond Lattimore* by P. V. Jones (Bristol: Bristol Classical Press, 1988) and reprinted by permission of Duckworth.

Library of Congress Cataloging-in-Publication Data
Homer.
    [Odyssey. English]
    Odyssey / Homer ; translated by Stanley Lombardo ; introduction by Sheila Murnaghan.
      p. cm.
    Includes bibliographical references and index.
    ISBN 0-87220-485-5 — ISBN 0-87220-484-7 (pbk.)
    1. Epic poetry, Greek—Translations into English.   2. Odysseus (Greek mythology)—Poetry.   I. Lombardo, Stanley, 1943–   .
II. Title.

PA4025.A5 L66   2000
883'.01—dc21   99-054175

The paper used in this publication meets the minimum requirements of American National Standard for Information Sciences—Permanence of Paper for Printed Library Materials, ANSI Z39.48–1984.

Contents

FOR

Zen Master Seung Sahn

&

IN MEMORIAM

Emmett Bienvenu, S.J.

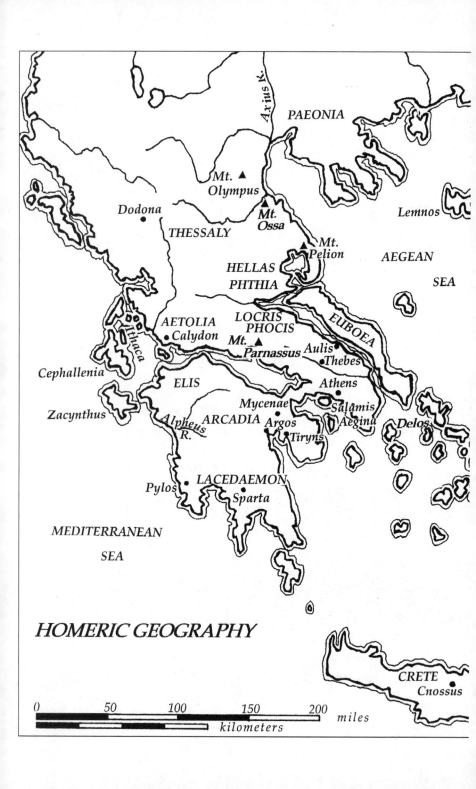

Axius R.

PAEONIA

Mt. ▲
Olympus

Dodona

THESSALY

Mt.
Ossa

Lemnos

Mt.
Pelion

AEGEAN

SEA

HELLAS
PHTHIA

AETOLIA
Calydon

Ithaca

LOCRIS
PHOCIS
Mt. ▲
Parnassus

EUBOEA

Aulis
Thebes

Cephallenia

ELIS

Athens

Zacynthus

Alpheus
R.

ARCADIA

Mycenae
Argos
Tiryns

Salamis
Aegina

Delos

Pylos

LACEDAEMON
Sparta

MEDITERRANEAN

SEA

HOMERIC GEOGRAPHY

CRETE
Cnossus

0   50   100   150   200   miles
                                      kilometers

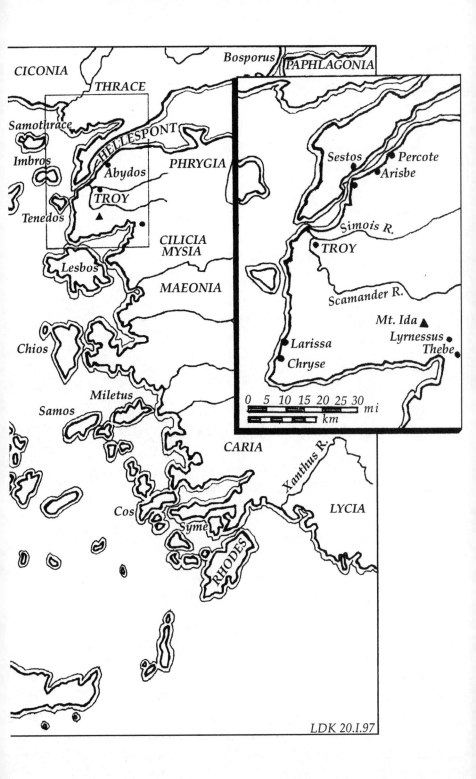

CICONIA

THRACE

Bosporus

PAPHLAGONIA

Samothrace

HELLESPONT

Imbros

Abydos

PHRYGIA

TROY

Tenedos

CILICIA
MYSIA

Lesbos

MAEONIA

Chios

Miletus

Samos

CARIA

Cos

Syme

Xanthus R.

LYCIA

RHODES

Sestos

Percote

Arisbe

Simois R.

TROY

Scamander R.

Mt. Ida

Lyrnessus

Thebe

Larissa

Chryse

0 5 10 15 20 25 30   mi

km

LDK 20.I.97

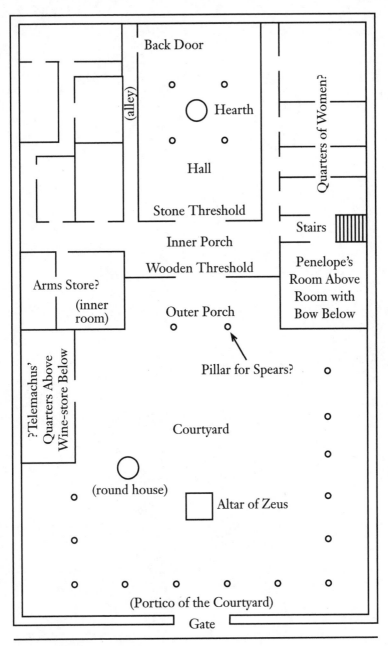

Back Door

(alley)

Hearth

Hall

Quarters of Women?

Stone Threshold

Stairs

Inner Porch

Wooden Threshold

Penelope's
Room Above
Room with
Bow Below

Arms Store?

(inner room)

Outer Porch

Pillar for Spears?

?Telemachus'
Quarters Above
Wine-store Below

Courtyard

(round house)

Altar of Zeus

(Portico of the Courtyard)

Gate

Road

Dung Heap?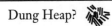

THE PALACE OF ODYSSEUS
(after J. Lazenby)

Introduction

The *Odyssey* is an epic account of survival and homecoming. The poem tells of the return (or in Greek, *nostos*) of Odysseus from the Greek victory at Troy to Ithaca, the small, rocky island from which he set out twenty years before. It was a central theme of the Trojan legend that getting home again was at least as great a challenge for the Greeks as winning the war. Many heroes lost their homecomings by dying at Troy, including Achilles, the greatest warrior of the Greeks, whose decision to fight in the full knowledge that he would not survive to go home again is told in the *Iliad*, the other epic attributed to Homer. Others were lost at sea or met disaster when they finally arrived home. The story of the returns of the major Greek heroes was a favorite subject of heroic song. Within the *Odyssey*, a bard is portrayed as singing "the tale / Of the hard journeys home that Pallas Athena / Ordained for the Greeks on their way back from Troy" (1.343–45), and we know of an actual epic, no longer surviving, that was entitled the *Nostoi* or "Returns" of the Greeks. The *Odyssey* is also a version of this story, and it contains accounts of the homecomings of all the major heroes who went to Troy. But it gives that story a distinctive emphasis through its focus on Odysseus, who is presented as the hero best suited to the arduous task of homecoming and the one whose return is both the most difficult and protracted and the most joyful and glorious.

In telling this story, the poet has also given the greatest weight, not to the perilous, exotic sea journey from Troy, on the west coast of Asia Minor (present-day Turkey), to the shore of Ithaca, off the west coast of Greece, but to the final phase of the hero's return, his reentry into his household and recovery of his former position at its center. As a result, the *Odyssey* is, perhaps surprisingly, an epic poem that foregrounds its hero's experiences in his home and with his family, presenting his success in picking up the threads of his previous life as his greatest exploit. The *Odyssey* charges the domestic world to which its hero returns with the same danger and enchantment found in the larger, wilder realm of warfare and seafaring. Seen from the perspective of his wanderings, Odysseus' home becomes at once more precious and more precarious. As he struggles to reestablish himself in a place that has been changed by his twenty-year absence, we are made to reconsider, along with him, the value of the familiar and the danger of taking it for granted.

A Tale of Homecoming

The *Odyssey* makes skillful use of the craft of storytelling to create this emphasis on the final phase of Odysseus' homecoming. Throughout the poem, Odysseus' story is set against that of another great hero of Troy, Agamemnon, whose own return failed just at the point when he reached his home. As the leader of the Greek expedition, Agamemnon seemed poised to enjoy the greatest triumph, and he was able to make the sea journey back to the shores of his kingdom without much trouble. But in his absence his wife, Clytemnestra, had taken a lover, Aegisthus, who plotted to kill Agamemnon on his return, cutting him down just when he thought he could relax his guard and rejoice in his achievement. This story has the status in the *Odyssey* of a kind of norm or model for what might be expected to happen, and it is brought up at strategic moments to serve as a warning to Odysseus and his supporters, a repeated reminder that simply arriving home does not mean the end of peril and risk.

The importance of this final phase is also conveyed by the intricate structure of the *Odyssey*'s plot, which places stress on Ithaca and on Odysseus' experiences there through the manipulation of chronology and changes of scene. The action of the *Odyssey* begins, not with the fall of Troy as one might expect, but just a few weeks before Odysseus' arrival at Ithaca ten years later. The poem opens with a divine council, in which the gods recognize that the fated time for Odysseus' return has finally arrived and take steps to set it in motion. In the human realm, the urgency of this moment is more acute on Ithaca, where events are moving swiftly in a dangerous direction, than on Ogygia, the remote island where Odysseus is trapped with a goddess, Calypso, in a suspended state of inactivity and nostalgia that has been going on for seven years and could continue indefinitely. The plan the gods come up with has two parts: Athena will go to Ithaca to prompt Odysseus' son, Telemachus, to useful action, and Hermes will go to Calypso and command her to release Odysseus; the poet chooses to narrate the Ithacan part first, giving priority to the situation and characters there. Thus, before we see Odysseus in action, we are introduced to Odysseus' household in his absence, where his long years away have created a difficult situation that is now heading toward a crisis.

All the young men of Ithaca and the surrounding region are trying to take over Odysseus' vacant position, staking their claims by setting themselves up as suitors to Odysseus' wife, Penelope. In this role, they spend their days feasting and reveling in Odysseus' house, steadily consuming the resources of his large estate. Unable to send them packing, Penelope has cleverly held them at bay for three years, but they have discovered her ruses and their patience is running out. Meanwhile, Telemachus is just reaching manhood. Until now, he has been too young to do anything about the suitors, but he too is getting impatient with the unresolved nature of the situation and the constant depletion of his inheritance. Athena's strategy is to spur him on to a full assumption of his adult role. She appears to him disguised as a traveling friend of his father's, Mentes, the king of the Taphians, and urges him to make a journey to the mainland, where he can consult two of the heroes who have returned from Troy, Nestor and Menelaus, in the hopes of finding out what has happened to Odysseus.

The aim of Telemachus' voyage is, specifically, information that might help to clarify and resolve the situation on Ithaca but, more broadly, education, the initiation into the ways of a proper heroic household that Telemachus is unable to find in his own fatherless, suitor-besieged home and an opportunity for him to discover and display his own inherent nobility. With the subtle guidance of Athena, who accompanies him, now in the disguise of Mentor, an Ithacan supporter of Odysseus, Telemachus first visits Nestor in Pylos and then Menelaus and his wife, Helen, in Sparta. From Menelaus, he receives the inconclusive news that Odysseus, when last heard of, was stranded with Calypso. But he also learns from both of his hosts about the homeward journeys of all the major Greek heroes, and hears reminiscences about the father he has never met. He gains a companion in Nestor's son Peisistratus and has the experience of being spontaneously recognized as Odysseus' son.

Thus the initial section of the *Odyssey*, which occupies the first four of its twenty-four books, is what is known as the "Telemachy," the story of Telemachus. It is only in the fifth book that we encounter Odysseus in person, as the poem begins again at the beginning, now offering an account of what has been happening to Odysseus during the same time. The scene returns to Olympus, and the other part of the divine plan is put into action. Hermes is sent to free Odysseus from Calypso, and a new eight-book section focused on Odysseus begins. This is a new beginning for Odysseus as well as for the poem: in the episodes that follow, Odysseus has to create himself anew, acquiring again all the signs of identity and status that were once his. With Calypso's reluctant blessing, he builds a raft and sets off across the sea, only to be hit with a storm by his great divine enemy, the sea-god Poseidon. He narrowly avoids drowning and manages to reach the shore of Schería, a lush, isolated island inhabited by a race of magical seafarers, the Phaeacians. At this point, he is in a state of naked homelessness, just barely holding on to life, a condition described in an extended comparison, or simile, as he burrows into a nest of olive leaves and falls into an exhausted sleep.

> *A solitary man*
> *Who lives on the edge of the wilderness*
> *And has no neighbors, will hide a charred log*
> *Deep in the black embers and so keep alive*
> *The fire's seed and not have to rekindle it*
> *From who knows where.*

> So Odysseus buried
> Himself in the leaves.
>   (5.493–500)

Through his encounters with the Phaeacians, Odysseus gradually recovers his former status. He gains the help of the Phaeacian princess, Nausicaa, who provides him with clothes and directions, and he makes his way to the court of their king, Alcinous, where he is welcomed and promised transportation back to Ithaca. At a great feast at Alcinous' court, he is finally ready to identify himself, and he gives an account of his adventures since leaving Troy. Thus the earliest part of the *Odyssey*'s story is actually narrated in the middle of the poem, in a long first-person flashback that occupies Books 8 through 12.

The experiences that Odysseus recounts are strange and fascinating: his visit to the land of the Lotus-Eaters; his risky confrontation of the one-eyed, man-eating giant, the Cyclops Polyphemus; his battle of wits with the enchantress Circe, who turns men into pigs with a stroke of her magic wand; his visit to the Underworld where he meets his mother, his comrades from Troy, and the prophet Tiresias, who tells him about a last mysterious journey before his life is over; his success in hearing the beautiful, but usually deadly, singing of the Sirens; the difficult passage between two horrific monsters, Scylla and Charybdis; and the ordeal of being marooned on the island of the Sun God, where his starving crew make the fatal mistake of eating the god's cattle. These famous stories have many parallels in widely disseminated folktales, with which they share an element of magic and an ability to convert basic human situations and concerns into marvelous plots. They are so well told that they enchant Odysseus' Phaeacian listeners, and they have come to dominate the later reputation of Odysseus, so that it is often a surprise to readers who encounter or re-encounter the *Odyssey* itself that those adventures actually occupy a relatively small portion of the poem.

The second half of the poem begins with Odysseus' passage from Schería to Ithaca in a swift Phaeacian ship. Again, the moment of transition is marked by sleep:

> So lifted the keel of that ship, and in her wake
> An indigo wave hissed and roiled
> As she ran straight ahead. Not even a falcon,
> Lord of the skies, could have matched her pace,
> So light her course as she cut through the waves,
> Bearing a man with a mind like the gods',
> A man who had suffered deep in his heart,
> Enduring men's wars and the bitter sea—
> But now he slept, his sorrows forgotten.
>
> (13.86–94)

As on the shore of Schería, Odysseus' sleep is the prelude to a new phase of action, and the rest of the poem is concerned with the process by which, having made it to Ithaca, he reclaims his position there and restores the conditions that existed when he left. Because of the danger posed by the suitors, who have already been plotting to murder Telemachus, this process has to be slow, careful, and indirect. Soon after he reaches the Ithacan shore at the beginning of Book 13, Odysseus adopts a disguise: with the aid of Athena, he is transformed into an old, derelict beggar. Before approaching his house, he goes for help and information to the hut of his loyal swineherd, Eumaeus, and there he is joined by Telemachus, as he returns from his journey to the mainland. At this point the two parallel strands of the plot merge, and the poem maintains from then on a consistent forward momentum toward the conclusion of the plot, in contrast to the more complicated structure of the first half. Odysseus reveals himself to Telemachus, and together they plot a strategy that will allow them to overcome the suitors, despite the suitors' reckless arrogance and superior numbers. Infiltrating his house in his beggar's disguise, Odysseus is able to exploit Penelope's decision that she will set a contest to decide whom she will marry, a contest that involves stringing a bow that Odysseus left behind when he went to Troy and shooting an arrow through a series of axe heads. Insisting on a turn when all the suitors have failed, Odysseus gains the weapon he needs to defeat his enemies. With the help of a small band of supporters, he takes on the suitors, and the house of Odysseus becomes the scene of a battle that is as glorious and bloody as those at Troy. With the skill and courage of a great warrior, Odysseus takes back his wife and his home, bringing his journey to a triumphant conclusion at last.

The *Mêtis* of Odysseus

Odysseus' triumph is possible only because of his exceptional nature, marked by a distinctive form of heroism. Like the other heroes who fought at Troy, Odysseus is physically powerful and adept at the arts of war, but what really distinguishes him is a quality of mind. In Greek, this quality is designated by the term *mêtis*, which denotes intelligence, cunning, versatility, and a facility with words. Odysseus is a master at assessing situations, devising plans, using language for his own ends, and manipulating the relations of appearance and reality. His skills extend far beyond those of the typical warrior to include, for example, craftsmanship, as when he builds his own raft with which to leave Calypso. His most characteristic and successful tactic is his use of disguises, which depends on a rare willingness to efface his own identity and a cool-headed capacity to say one thing while thinking another. Odysseus disguises himself at every stage of the *Odyssey*'s plot. In his early and defining encounter with the monstrous Cyclops, Odysseus overcomes his physical disadvantage through the brilliant trick of telling the Cyclops that his name is "no man" (a word that has several forms in Greek, one of which happens to be *mêtis*). After Odysseus succeeds in blinding the Cyclops and escaping from his cave, he would still be at the mercy of the Cyclops' neighbors if the Cyclops were not crying out to them that "No man is hurting me." When he washes up, dispossessed and shipwrecked among the Phaeacians, Odysseus shrewdly suppresses his identity until he can demonstrate his civility and distinction and win his hosts' support. And on Ithaca his success depends on his extended impersonation of an old, broken-down beggar. In pretending to be a beggar on Ithaca, Odysseus is repeating an old tactic, as we learn when Helen tells Telemachus how Odysseus once sneaked into Troy in a similar disguise.

Odysseus' use of disguise demands not only constant alertness and wit but a particular form of discipline, for the heroes of Homeric epic are animated by a constant drive to self-assertion. Their names are not just names to them but claims to high status and reputation based on their aristocratic heritage and their own impressive actions, and their relations with each other revolve around the giving and getting of recognition. It is clear from the *Iliad* that these heroes find any questioning or suspension of their identity intolerable. Warriors are stung to action if a peer questions their courage or compares them unfavorably to an ancestor. Living up to an illustrious name and the privileges that go with it is, for them, paramount. They risk their lives in the hopes of achieving something memorable enough to turn the honor they enjoy in their lifetimes into everlasting fame, or *kleos*. The plot of the *Iliad* turns on a quarrel between Agamemnon and Achilles, the best fighter in the army, when Agamemnon loses one of the war prizes—in this case a captive woman—through which status is expressed. When he tries to compensate for that loss by taking a prize of Achilles', the result is a bitter and deadly conflict that reveals how impossible each of them finds it to do without such markers of heroic identity.

For Odysseus to voluntarily suppress his famous name, to actively embrace the identity of "no man," and to adopt the persona of such a social nonentity as a homeless beggar involves a form of self-denial that most heroes could not tolerate. And he, of course, only does tolerate it as a means to ultimate self-disclosure and recognition, which are as important to him as to any other hero. When he has succeeded in outwitting the Cyclops and is sailing away from his island, Odysseus must have the satisfaction of shouting out his real name to him. This irresistible self-assertion has terrible and far-reaching consequences, since the Cyclops is then able to call on his father, Poseidon, to punish Odysseus:

> Grant that Odysseus, son of Laertes,
> May never reach his home on Ithaca.
> But if he is fated to see his family again,

And return to his home and own native land,
May he come late, having lost all companions,
In another's ship, and find trouble at home.
                                        (9.524–29)

When Odysseus is with the Phaeacians, his prolonged exercise of discretion and reserve only serves to heighten the moment of dramatic revelation when, secure in their high regard and assured of their gifts and transport home, he begins his long narrative with a ringing self-introduction:

I am Odysseus, great Laertes' son,
Known for my cunning throughout the world,
And my fame reaches even to heaven.
                                        (9.21–23)

And his impersonation of a dishonored beggar on Ithaca is a strategy that makes possible the stunning moment when he surprises the suitors with the truth of his real identity, throwing aside his rags as he shoots his bow, no longer through the axe heads but now—to their stupefied horror—at them. It is one of many paradoxes about Odysseus that he embraces obscurity and dishonor in order to claim the greatest possible glory.

In this way, the *Odyssey*'s hero embodies one of its central themes, which is that the capacity to defer satisfaction and endure suffering is as necessary for success as the ability to perform brilliant feats. The rewards Odysseus enjoys are bound up with hardship and delay, as is clear from the opening lines of the poem, where he is identified as "the wanderer, blown off course time and again," and where a main subject of the poem is defined as "the suffering deep in his heart at sea." As vital to Odysseus' defeat of the suitors as his dazzling archery is his ability to accept the verbal and physical abuse they subject him to in his beggar's disguise, and he must repeatedly resist the impulse to react before he is in a position to crush them. His ability to resist provocation is matched by an ability to resist pleasure as well, to defer the gratifications of food, sex, and beautiful music. Many of the stories that make up his adventures are concerned with such temptations, and, in the end, Odysseus' self-control allows him to survive when none of his companions do. This is shown definitively in the final adventure, which involves the cattle of the sun.

Warned by Circe and Tiresias that eating those cattle would be fatal, Odysseus instructs his men to leave them alone, but when they find themselves stranded and facing starvation, they give in to their hunger and are lost at sea as a punishment.

This distinction between Odysseus and his companions is expressed in many ways throughout the adventures. In one episode, Odysseus has to drag a contingent of them away from the land of the Lotus-Eaters, where "Whoever ate that sweet fruit / Lost the will to report back, preferring instead / To stay there, munching lotus, oblivious of home" (9.94–96). The obliviousness brought by the delicious lotus makes clear the link between this quality of self-control and memory, specifically the memory of home. Odysseus succeeds where others fail because he never forgets his goal and never loses sight of his desire for it, even in the face of the greatest temptations.

The contrast between Odysseus and his men plays out somewhat differently in the episode involving the seductive enchantress Circe. When Circe tries to overcome him with her magical potion, Odysseus retains his self-possession and forces her to swear she will not harm him; just before that, however, she easily transforms his companions into pigs. Here, in a typical Homeric situation in which divine favor marks and enhances a human's intrinsic superiority, Odysseus' ability to withstand Circe's designs stems from a protective magic plant, the *moly*, which he has been given by Hermes. In this episode we can also see the way in which Odysseus' superiority allows him, at times, to get away with the enjoyment of dangerous pleasures that might be the undoing of ordinary mortals. Having assured himself of Circe's good will, Odysseus climbs into bed with her, and he stays with her for a year, feasting and recuperating from his travels until—in a somewhat inconsistent reversal—his men recall him to his purpose: "Good god, man, at long last remember your home" (10.493).

Another adventure in which Odysseus is able to taste pleasure without succumbing to it is that of the Sirens, in which his companions are again his saviors as well as his inferiors, and in which the danger comes not from sex or food but from poetry. The Sirens are female monsters who lure seafarers to shipwreck and death with their exquisite singing. Following a plan supplied by Circe, Odysseus blocks his men's ears with wax and has them tie him to the mast of his ship, charging them not to untie him however urgently he pleads. In this way he survives a temptation that no one else could handle, hearing the Sirens' song but also leaving it behind, continuing on his journey thanks to the strenuous rowing of his crew. From the brief, teasing few lines of the Sirens' song that we hear, it seems that its attraction includes the pleasure of learning the events of the past: "For we know everything / that the Greeks and Trojans / Suffered in wide Troy / by the will of the gods" (12.197–98). Odysseus must withstand not only the beauty of the song but the impulse it inspires to linger in the past, to take pleasure in a story, the story of the Trojan War, that he still needs to bring to conclusion.

After the adventures have been weathered and the companions have been lost, a similar contrast is drawn between Odysseus and his Phaeacian hosts. The land of the Phaeacians is a site of otherworldly pleasure—an opulent, hyper-civilized community whose inhabitants have no experience of strife or hardship. Life with the Phaeacians also represents a temptation for Odysseus, as Alcinous encourages him to marry Nausicaa and settle down among them. But he keeps his sights set on Ithaca and on Penelope, insisting politely but determinedly that the Phaeacians keep their promise to take him home. While the Phaeacians are not lost in the way the companions are for their enjoyment of all the pleasures that lie before them, that is because they are not trying to get anywhere, and they are cut off from life in the world to which Odysseus belongs. As in the episode of the Sirens, this contrast is developed in relation to the enjoyment of poetry. Song is one of the chief pleasures of the Phaeacians' life, the perfect complement to their elegant feasts, and their bard, Demodocus, sings several songs during Odysseus' visit in what may be an internal representation of the kind of occasion on which poems like the *Odyssey* itself were performed. Launching into his own story during a banquet at which Demodocus has already sung, Odysseus begins with an encomium of song as the sweetest of pleasures.

> My Lord Alcinous, what could be finer
> Than listening to a singer of tales
> Such as Demodocus, with a voice like a god's?
> Nothing we do is sweeter than this—
> A cheerful gathering of all the people
> Sitting side by side throughout the halls,
> Feasting and listening to a singer of tales . . .
>   (9.2–8)

And yet Odysseus is unable to join his hosts in their detached delight at the songs Demodocus sings about the great events of the Trojan War: while they relax and rejoice, he weeps. His own, still unconcluded involvement in the events being told keeps him from enjoying what song has to offer, just as it keeps him from taking Alcinous up on his offer to stay. For him song does not yet serve the function that Homeric poetry claims for itself of converting suffering into a source of pleasure and offering, through the memories of the past, forgetfulness of the cares of the present. Odysseus is in an extraordinary position in that, unlike most Homeric heroes, he has survived his own exploits to the point at which he can hear them sung about in song, experiencing the fame that others die for but never actually taste. But he cannot yet enjoy that experience of fame; pleasure in the recounting of his achievements must wait until his reunion with Penelope, when husband and wife are able to spend a long night exchanging stories.

Odysseus' grief at what delights the Phaeacians is described most pointedly in a simile that occurs just after Demodocus recounts, at Odysseus' own request, Odysseus' greatest exploit, his taking of Troy through the trick of the wooden horse. The response of this hero who is still caught up in the struggle to survive the war is compared to the pain of war's most wretched survivor.

> And Odysseus wept. Tears
> Welled up in his eyes and flowed down his cheeks.
>
> *A woman wails as she throws herself upon*
> *Her husband's body. He has fallen in battle*
> *Before the town walls, fighting to the last*
> *To defend his city and protect his children.*
> *As she sees him dying and gasping for breath*
> *She clings to him and shrieks, while behind her*
> *Soldiers prod their spears into her shoulders and back,*
> *And as they lead her away into slavery*
> *Her tear-drenched face is a mask of pain.*
>
> So too Odysseus, pitiful in his grief.
>
> (8.564–575)

The victor of Troy is more like his own most piteous victim than like his carefree hosts; the simile identifies Odysseus with pain, defining this moment in his journey as one at which his struggles are still far from finished and, at the same time, pointing to an essential feature of his makeup.

The Man of Pain

Between the end of his adventures and his arrival on the Phaeacian shore, Odysseus meets a greater temptation than any of those that distract his companions: the temptation of immortality. The storm that drowns his companions lands him with the beautiful nymph Calypso, who feeds and cares for him, takes him as her lover, and offers to make him immortal if he will stay with her. Calypso's island cave dwelling is a paradise of ease and beauty, lovely enough to delight even a god, as we see from Hermes' appreciative appraisal when he arrives to deliver his message. And yet our first view of Odysseus is of him "sitting where the breakers rolled in. / His eyes were perpetually wet with tears now, / His life draining away in homesickness" (5.150–52). Odysseus gives voice to his rejection of Calypso's offer when she comes to tell him that she will let him leave. She makes one last pitch by suggesting that if he only knew the trouble ahead he would surely stay with her; and she adds that, as a goddess, she undoubtedly outshines his mortal wife, Penelope. He answers:

> Goddess and mistress, don't be angry with me.
> I know very well that Penelope,
> For all her virtues, would pale beside you.
> She's only human, and you are a goddess,
> Eternally young. Still, I want to go back.
> My heart aches for the day I return to my home.
> If some god hits me hard as I sail the dark purple,
> I'll weather it like the sea-bitten veteran I am.
> God knows I've suffered and had my share of sorrows
> In war and at sea. I can take more if I have to.
> (5.215–24)

Odysseus does not just endure the sufferings that come his way, he actively accepts them as the cost of his homecoming. And he does not just long for his home on Ithaca, he prizes it above even the paradise of Calypso's island. Odysseus' speech suggests the characteristically human motive behind this seemingly perverse choice: the love that people have for what is their own simply because it is theirs. Here that love is associated with Penelope, but at other points in their respective journeys both Odysseus and Telemachus express a similar devotion to Ithaca itself, despite the fact that it is a small and stony island, not particularly good for pasturing horses and cattle. Or, as Odysseus puts it simply in his great speech at Alcinous' court, recalling his resistance to both Circe and Calypso:

> But they could not persuade me or touch my heart.
> Nothing is sweeter than your own country
> And your own parents, not even living in a rich house—
> Not if it's far from family and home.
>
> (9.36–39)

An additional reason for Odysseus' choice is encoded in Calypso's name, which in Greek means "concealer." The life that Odysseus has with Calypso is endless and carefree, but it is entirely cut off from the world of mortals, where his fate is unknown and he is in danger of being forgotten. Escape from the trials of mortal life would also mean the death of his aspirations to eternal fame among the human generations to come. As a mortal, Odysseus is not only consigned to human suffering but also committed to human goals, to pursuing the consolations that human beings find for the brevity and difficulty of their lives in their relations with one another and in the prospect of glory.

In the *Odyssey*, death is not experienced only as looming prospect, as an inevitable finality shadowing every life. Among Odysseus' adventures is an actual visit to the realm of death, a journey to the edge of the Underworld involving a series of encounters with the dead that gives him—and us—a concrete sense of what death is like. The Homeric afterlife is a place of relentless dreariness and gloom in which people continue on and on as lifeless ghosts, endlessly trapped in old worries and old grudges, cut off from any sense of purpose or any knowledge of what has happened since they died. The awfulness of this state is famously expressed by the ghost of Achilles, when Odysseus tries to cheer him up by pointing out how much honor he has among the dead.

> Don't try to sell me on death, Odysseus.
> I'd rather be a hired hand back up on earth,

Slaving away for some poor dirt farmer,
Than lord it over all these withered dead.
                  (11.510–13)

Briefly animated by their encounter with Odysseus, the ghosts
that he meets tell him their stories, but cannot really make contact
with him, as is most evident when Odysseus unexpectedly finds his
mother among the dead, sent there by grief at his long absence from
Ithaca.

Three times I rushed forward to hug her,
And three times she drifted out of my arms
Like a shadow or a dream. The pain
That pierced my heart grew ever sharper,
And my words rose to my mother on wings:

'Mother, why do you slip away when I try
To embrace you? Even though we are in Hades,
Why can't we throw our arms around each other
And console ourselves with chill lamentation? . . . '
                  (11.206–14)

Odysseus' journey to the Underworld reinforces the joy of survival,
the pleasure of returning to the familiar world of action and light,
but his meetings there also deepen his experience of the particular
bind of the survivor, of the way in which the satisfaction of living on
is accompanied by sorrow and guilt at outliving so many beloved rel-
atives and friends. His homecoming, as it turns out, will not be a
return to both of his "own parents."

Like Calypso's, Odysseus' name is significant, and its meaning
points to his association with pain. The name Odysseus is connected
(in the poetic tradition, if not in actual linguistic history) to a Greek
verb, *odussomai*, which means "to suffer pain." Several times in the
Odyssey that connection is exploited to create puns on Odysseus'
name; these puns give pointed expression to his identity as a hero
who both has to endure and can endure an exceptional measure of
suffering—and they also provide a special challenge to the translator.
Thus Athena, in the initial council on Olympus, trying to get Zeus
to do something about Odysseus' stalled homecoming, asks him why
he causes Odysseus so much trouble: "Why is Odysseus so odious,

Zeus?" But, as scholars who have studied this wordplay have pointed out, the verb *odussomai* can mean to inflict pain as well as to suffer it, and Odysseus' name describes an active as well as a passive relationship to suffering. He is given his name by his grandfather Autolycus, whose own name means something like "the wolf himself," and who connects his grandson's name to his own tough and tricky nature:

> I come here as one who is odious, yes,
> Hateful to many for the pain I have caused
> All over the land. Let this child, therefore,
> Go by the name of Odysseus.
> (19.445–48)

The determination and self-control that allow Odysseus to survive when others are lost are linked to a readiness to cause pain when necessary. Odysseus does not shrink from violence, as when he plunges a sharpened olive stake into the Cyclops' only eye, or from taking advantage of others, as when he manipulates the Phaeacian princess, Nausicaa, into helping him by playing on her thoughts of marriage. Once on Ithaca, he is brusque with his son and his old nurse when their many questions delay his plans and, encountering his wife and old father while in disguise, he is capable of observing the grief they experience in his absence without letting on that he is home. His revenge against the suitors is bloody and thorough; he does not give in to special pleas and is not interested in making fine judgments of relative guilt. The *Odyssey* does not conceal the ruthlessness that is a necessary element in the success of its cool-headed and resourceful hero.

Olympian Friends and Enemies

Extraordinary as Odysseus may be in his versatility and self-reliance, he can by no means achieve his homecoming alone. He relies on a range of helpers, both divine and human, whose relations with him help to define who he is and to articulate the central values of the poem. Of these, the most powerful is his divine patron, the goddess Athena. Not only is Athena Odysseus' ardent champion, but she actively supervises and directs the action of the *Odyssey*, which is, in a sense, her personal project. The action begins when she intervenes on Olympus to turn her father Zeus' attention away from the family

of Agamemnon to the plight of Odysseus. Athena gets things mov-
ing on Ithaca by stirring up Telemachus, and she accompanies him
on his actual journey disguised as Mentor. When Odysseus himself
arrives on Ithaca, the final, most intense phase of the action begins
with an encounter between Odysseus and Athena, in which she
appears to him openly, assures him of her support, and gives him his
disguise. Just as she opens the action of the poem, Athena also shuts
it down. Having slaughtered the suitors, Odysseus has to contend
with their relatives, who swarm his estate in a vengeful crowd. War-
fare is just beginning between this group and Odysseus and his sup-
porters, when Athena, with Zeus' blessing, intervenes to insist that
they make peace. In the final lines of the poem, Athena swears both
sides to binding oaths that will assure amity and prosperity among
the Ithacans.

Athena's support tells us a lot about Odysseus and the meaning of
his *nostos*. Its very intensity marks him out as unlike other heroes,
who could not achieve what they do without divine help, but whose
access to it is never so open or so steady. Athena's partiality is related
to the other qualities that set Odysseus apart, especially his *mêtis*. She
says as much herself when they meet on the Ithacan shore and the
goddess and her mortal favorite act out the qualities that underlie
their partnership. This meeting is their first face-to-face encounter
since Troy, and it signals that the final phase of Odysseus' return has
begun. Athena approaches Odysseus as gods normally approach
mortals, through devices that put them at a disadvantage. She covers
his familiar home with a mist, so that he imagines his Phaeacian
hosts have betrayed him and he has landed once more on unfamiliar
terrain, and she appears to him in a disguise, in this case the disguise
of a young shepherd. But Odysseus is instinctively wary, even when
the supposed shepherd tells him that he is on Ithaca, and he responds
to her with a deception of his own, spinning a misleading tale of his
origins and history, the first of many such false tales that he will tell
on Ithaca. Athena is delighted and rewards him with an open epiph-
any, transforming herself into her truest form, a tall, beautiful, and
skillful woman, and laying out the basis of her devotion.

> Only a master thief, a real con artist,
> Could match your tricks—even a god
> Might come up short. You wily bastard,
> You cunning, elusive, habitual liar!

Even in your own land you weren't about
To give up the stories and sly deceits
That are so much a part of you.
Never mind about that though. Here we are,
The two shrewdest minds in the universe,
You far and away the best man on earth
In plotting strategies, and I famed among gods
For my clever schemes.

(13.299–310)

Athena is Odysseus' divine counterpart, a figure who similarly represents a combination of martial abilities and intelligence. She is the daughter of Zeus and of the goddess Metis, the personification of cunning. Born from Zeus' head after he swallowed Metis, Athena is Zeus' ever-loyal daughter, a perpetual virgin who never leaves her father, and she stands for both military power and cleverness as they are subordinated to Zeus' authority and regulation of the universe. She is a military goddess who is associated especially with just causes and civilization, and a crafty goddess whose intelligence inspires expert craftsmanship—the metalworking and shipbuilding of gifted men and the fine weaving of gifted women—as well as clever plans. Her sponsorship of Odysseus, with the carefully sought blessing of Zeus, indicates that his cause is seen among the gods as just, and Odysseus is unusual among Homeric characters for the gods' clear endorsement of his cause, as well as for the steadiness of their support. Zeus' favor is clear from the divine council with which the poem opens. Although he seems to have forgotten about Odysseus at that point and has to be reminded by Athena, his mind is on the terrible crime and just punishment of Aegisthus, the figure in the Agamemnon story who provides a parallel to Penelope's suitors. Before the suitors are even mentioned, then, they are cast by analogy into the role of villains and Odysseus into the role of divinely sanctioned avenger.

The point at which the *Odyssey* starts is, in fact, the moment in Odysseus' story at which Athena can first hope to get Zeus to grant Odysseus his full attention and support. Their conversation takes place at a time when the sea-god Poseidon is away from Olympus, feasting with the far-off Ethiopians. Poseidon, as the poet tells us, is the only god who does not pity Odysseus, and throughout his adventures Poseidon is opposed to Athena as Odysseus' bitter adversary.

The immediate cause of his enmity is anger on behalf of the Cyclops, who is Poseidon's son, and who calls on Poseidon to avenge him after he has been blinded by Odysseus. More generally, as the god of the treacherous and uncertain sea, Poseidon represents all the challenges of the wild realm between Troy and Ithaca that Odysseus must first negotiate before he can face the problems that await him on land. Further, behind the particular story of Odysseus lie the perennial divine struggles that determine the nature of the cosmos. In cosmic history, Poseidon is Zeus' brother, who has received the sea as his not-quite-equal portion in a division of the universe in which Zeus gained the superior portion of the sky and a third brother, Hades, the Underworld. As a consequence, Poseidon is constantly jealous of his prerogatives and sensitive to any diminution of his honor, and he is in a recurrent state of opposition to Zeus' favorite, Athena, an opposition that in part symbolizes a conflict between untamed wildness and civilization. The best known expression of this opposition is their competition to be the patron deity of the city of Athens. This competition is won by Athena when she produces an olive tree—the plant sacred to her—and it is judged to be more useful to civilization than a spring of salt water produced by Poseidon.

Odysseus' success in surviving his adventures at sea and reaching Ithaca, where he restores the civilized conditions that have been eroded in his absence, represents another version of Athena's victory, but it cannot occur until Poseidon has had his due. Odysseus has had to endure all the perils of the sea, its adverse winds, raging storms, sudden rocks, and engulfing whirlpools, and he has had to contend with its island settlements, places where the strangeness of the sea extends to its inhabitants and the normal rules of ordinary human civilization do not apply. In the Cyclops Odysseus meets a monster who scorns the rules by which humans live and, as he gobbles down Odysseus' men, thumbs his nose at the rules of hospitality that Odysseus expects him to follow. While Odysseus contends that his punishment of the Cyclops is just revenge for the Cyclops' monstrous incivility, he is nonetheless made to suffer for it through the Cyclops' curse, which activates the enmity of Poseidon. It is Poseidon's anger, along with that of the Sun God whose cattle are eaten, that causes the death of Odysseus' companions. And even though Poseidon's absence among the Ethiopians allows Athena to set Odysseus' return in motion, Poseidon's anger still remains an important element in the story. As he returns to Olympus, Poseidon sees Odysseus on his raft and blasts him with the terrible storm that he barely survives to wash up on the Phaeacian shore. And when the Phaeacians transport Odysseus back to Ithaca, Poseidon is so outraged that he declares he will end their role of conveying men across the sea, smashing their ship and hemming their city in with a mountain. Zeus soothes his wounded pride and suggests he simply turn the ship into a rock; he does, and it is left uncertain whether or not he encloses the city.

Only when Odysseus has reached the dry land of Ithaca and a society with familiar rules is Poseidon no longer an obstacle to Odysseus' return, and this is signaled by the way Athena's support, which is muted and indirect even while he is among the Phaeacians, now becomes open and assured. But even then Odysseus' need to come to terms with Poseidon has not ended, and he remains affected by his dealings with a wilder world even as he settles back into his peaceful and orderly home. One of the most important things he learns from Tiresias in the Underworld is that even after he regains Ithaca, he will still need to take one last journey.

> . . . when you have slain
> The suitors in your hall, by ruse or by sword,
> Then you must go off again, carrying a broad-bladed oar,
> Until you come to men who know nothing of the sea,
> Who eat their food unsalted, and have never seen
> Red-prowed ships or oars that wing them along.
> And I will tell you a sure sign that you have found them,
> One you cannot miss. When you meet another traveler
> Who thinks you are carrying a winnowing fan,
> Then you must fix your oar in the earth
> And offer sacrifice to Lord Poseidon,
> A ram, a bull, and a boar in its prime.
> Then return to your home and offer
> Perfect sacrifice to the immortal gods
> Who hold high heaven, to each in turn.
> And death will come to you off the sea,
> A death so gentle, and carry you off
> When you are worn out in sleek old age,
> Your people prosperous all around you.

(11.117–35)

Much about this prophecy is mysterious, but it seems that Odysseus must undertake a final mission in service of Poseidon, extending Poseidon's worship into a place where he is unknown, and that the result may be reconciliation between them. Assuming that the proper conditions are successfully fulfilled—a question that Tiresias leaves open—Poseidon's element, the sea, will become no longer the harsh force against which Odysseus must contend but the medium of a gentle death, the best end a mortal can hope for.

The support that Odysseus has from Athena and especially from Zeus is not based solely on favoritism, but also on his association with justice. In overcoming the suitors' challenge, Odysseus is not only seeking personal vindication; he is also punishing their assaults on the most highly valued and sacred principles of his culture, the rights and obligations surrounding hospitality. The need to turn to strangers for shelter, food, and help with the next stage of a journey is a constant feature of life in the *Odyssey*, experienced alike by those who are temporarily away from home, like the fully credentialed prince Telemachus, and by those who have no home, like the roving exiles of Odysseus' false tales or the down-and-out beggar of his disguise. Among highly placed aristocrats like Odysseus and the heroes Telemachus visits on his journey, reciprocal hospitality is a way of forming and maintaining important political alliances, which are cemented by the guest-gifts that hosts present to their visitors. In extending hospitality, a host mitigates a stranger's foreignness, incorporating him for a time into his own household; he expresses a sense of universal human kinship based on a common subjection to fortune, which can drive anyone from home, and on common needs, above all the relentless demands of the belly, which override and banish all other concerns. As Odysseus puts it to Alcinous when he first appears at his court in a condition of utter neediness,

> I could tell you much more, a long tale,
> Of the suffering I've had by the will of the gods,
> But all I want now is to be allowed to eat,
> Despite my grief. There is nothing more shameless
> Than this belly of ours, which forces a man
> To pay attention to it, no matter how many
> Troubles he has, how much pain in his heart.
>   (7.226–32)

In the *Odyssey* upright characters show their virtue by honoring their obligation to provide hospitality, a point which is stressed in the extended portrayal of the courteous treatment that Odysseus as the beggar receives from the humble swineherd Eumaeus and in the dismay of Telemachus when the conditions of his household prevent him from being a proper host to Theoclymenus, a wandering prophet who joins him at the end of his journey. The suitors, by contrast, reaffirm their lawlessness through their repeated rudeness to the disguised Odysseus.

In dishonoring the beggar among them, the suitors are recapitulating their original offense against the rules of hospitality in the form of their unwanted trespass in Odysseus' house. If hosts have obligations, so do guests, who must not abuse the generosity that is owed to them. Above all, guests must remember that they are not at home and cannot treat their host's possessions as their own. In this way, the rules of hospitality dovetail with the strong sense of a householder's rights to his own property that is also a fundamental principle of Homeric society. The Trojan War itself has its origin in a guest's abuse of hospitality, when the Trojan prince, Paris, visits Menelaus and steals his wife, Helen. Paris' crime is echoed in the transgression that troubles Zeus at the opening of the *Odyssey*, Aegisthus' seduction of Clytemnestra, which leads to his murder of Agamemnon and seizure of Agamemnon's house. As Zeus' concern here indicates, the gods of the *Odyssey* back up the rules of human society and take note of violations against them; they support human beings in their efforts to soften the sufferings that the gods themselves impose. Zeus is evoked throughout the poem as the special protector of strangers and beggars, and in his exasperation with Aegisthus, he makes it clear that trangressions against the rights and obligations of the household meet with divine punishment. As he puts it, by ignoring the common rules of human culture, humans bring on themselves "more [troubles] than they were destined for" (1.39), an extra measure of suffering beyond that which the gods impose on everyone.

Fathers and Sons, Master and Slaves

In the world of the Homeric epics, the help of the gods is not a randomly bestowed benefit, but an advantage that expresses and reinforces a mortal's inherent qualities and his or her ability to command the help of other mortals. For all the divine favor he enjoys, Odysseus must also rely on key mortal supporters in order to achieve his aims. In particular, he must rely on the members of his household, who create and preserve the position at its center that he hopes to reclaim. The success of his return depends on the reconstitution of a series of relationships that define both his own identity and the social order in which it is meaningful. In the second half of the poem, those relationships are mapped out in a sequence of reunions that punctuate the narrative of Odysseus' homecoming: with Telemachus in Book 16, with his old nurse Eurycleia in Book 19, with Eumaeus and another loyal servant, the herdsman Philoetius, in Book 21, with Penelope in Book 23, and finally with his father, Laertes, in Book 24.

The device of disguise, which provides an index to Odysseus' character and a strategy for his defeat of the suitors, also creates opportunities for episodes of recognition in which Odysseus' identity as father, son, master, and husband is declared and accepted. Each encounter renews a mutually beneficial bond, to which both parties make significant contributions, and each encounter involves recognition on both sides. Odysseus acknowledges the identity and loyalty of his supporters as they acknowledge his identity and continued right to the privileges and possessions that are bound up with it. As he sheds his disguise of old age and low status to reveal that he is home, his supporters respond by shedding similarly constraining states of weakness and despair brought about by Odysseus' absence, and each is restored to a state of flourishing strength by the presence of the other.

This mutuality is reflected in the tokens Odysseus uses to prove his identity, which express the nature of the characters to whom they are displayed as well as Odysseus' own nature. His nurse, Eurycleia, knows who he is when she notices a scar on his thigh. This scar was received in a fight with a boar that was Odysseus' first adult exploit, a defining rite of passage. That fight was undertaken as part of his relationship with his grandfather Autolycus, the master trickster who gave Odysseus his significant name. But, as the poet pauses to fill in the history of the scar, he also elaborates on Eurycleia's role in Odysseus' naming, noting that she was the one who asked Autolycus to name the baby and thus identifying her as a kind of surrogate mother for Odysseus. Odysseus convinces his father, Laertes, by identifying a series of trees on the family estate; in the process, he recalls the time when Laertes gave those trees to him, evoking his father's role in passing on their ancestral possessions. What convinces Penelope is Odysseus' knowledge of a secret built into their marriage bed, something that is meaningful as a token only if it is shared between them.

Odysseus' first reunion is with his son, Telemachus, who becomes his most trusted ally, and this, along with the prominence given to Telemachus in the opening sequence of the narrative, shows how vital to Odysseus' success is the presence of his son. In the aristocratic world of the Homeric hero, the legacy of power and prestige passed on through the male line is an essential element of selfhood. Heroes are constantly identified by patronymics, as sons of their fathers, and they become who they are by living up to their paternal heritage. And their own accomplishments are fully satisfying only if that heritage can be passed on to a son who will preserve and extend it. The individual hero's life is only fulfilled if he has reason to hope that, after his death, he will be replaced by a son of equal stature and ability, that he will live on in his lineage as well as in his reputation.

When Odysseus makes his extraordinary journey to the Underworld, he is not only able to gain knowledge for himself that mortals normally have no access to, but he also brings with him knowledge of which the dead are normally deprived. He is able to offer Achilles some cheer by reporting to him about the achievements of his son Neoptolemus. Sadly, Odysseus is unable to bring a similar joy to Agamemnon, although Agamemnon's son, Orestes, has in fact distinguished himself as an ideal son, avenging his father's murder and restoring his father's lost honor by killing Aegisthus and Clytemnestra. While Orestes' action is still unknown to Odysseus, it is famous among the Achaeans in Greece, and Orestes with his exemplary loyalty and initiative comes up a number of times as a possible model for Telemachus.

The first such mention of Orestes comes in Book 1, when Athena visits Telemachus and prompts him to take his own journey, in part by urging him to be more like Orestes. Telemachus' journey has the effect of bringing him to a state of self-fulfillment in which he is identified by himself and others as a worthy successor to Odysseus. Part of this process involves literal identification, both in the sense that he is seen doing some of the same things his father does and in the sense that he is identified as Odysseus' son. When he visits the court of Menelaus and Helen he behaves in a way that anticipates his father's behavior among the Phaeacians. Because the rules of hospitality prohibit asking a guest's identity until his essential needs have

been taken care of, both father and son are entertained by their hosts
while remaining unknown. In parallel episodes, Telemachus and
Odysseus give signs of their unusual identities when they react dif-
ferently from the rest of the company to a story that is being told: in
Telemachus' case, Menelaus' reminiscences of the Trojan War and
especially of Odysseus; in Odysseus' case, the formal song of the
Phaeacian bard, which also concerns the Trojan War. Both father
and son respond to these songs with weeping, which they try to hide
with a cloak. In the case of Telemachus, this curious weeping leads to
the striking moment when Helen breaks out with her spontaneous
suggestion that he must be the son of Odysseus:

> I have never seen
> Such a resemblance between any two people,
> Man or woman, as between this man
> And Odysseus' son—as I imagine him now—
> Telemachus . . .
>
> (4.146–50)

When Telemachus returns to Ithaca, he has entered fully into his
role as Odysseus' son and the continuer of Odysseus' heritage. But,
by the time he does so, Odysseus has managed to return himself and
Telemachus does not actually need to play that role. Unlike his Tro-
jan comrades, Odysseus has evaded death and need not gain satisfac-
tion only from the thought of his son carrying on without him.
There is a certain tension between the two strands of the *Odyssey*'s
plot that corresponds to the psychological tension experienced by
fathers and sons as they manage the tricky but inevitable process by
which the son replaces the father. This tension is expressed at certain
moments of the narrative but is also resolved as the Telemachus plot
is folded into the Odysseus plot and Telemachus is enlisted in his
father's cause as his indispensable but subordinate lieutenant. One
manifestation of this tension is Odysseus' rather harsh manner dur-
ing their recognition scene in Book 16. Because Odysseus left Ithaca
when Telemachus was still a baby, the two have a relationship that is
not based in common experience and there is no token by which
they might recall a shared past as with Odysseus' other supporters.
Instead, Odysseus establishes his identity through the assurance with
which he asserts his paternal authority. Since Odysseus discloses
himself through a sudden transformation out of his beggar's disguise,

effected by Athena, Telemachus is understandably wary and thinks Odysseus must be himself a god. Odysseus' response is impatient and somewhat belittling.

> Telemachus, it does not become you to be so amazed
> That your father is here in this house. You can be sure
> That no other Odysseus will ever come.
> But I am here, just as you see, home at last
> After twenty years of suffering and wandering.
>
> (16.215–19)

A role is created for Telemachus as Odysseus' equal and future heir but not yet quite his replacement, and this is dramatized most explicitly in the climactic episode of the contest with the bow. Before the suitors have their turn, Telemachus himself makes an attempt. He is on the verge of succeeding, of doing what otherwise only Odysseus himself can do, when Odysseus gives him a significant nod and he withdraws. This willing withdrawal accomplishes Telemachus' smooth relegation to second place for the time being, and it is in a sense justified in the ensuing battle in which, skillfully as he fights, Telemachus does make a strategic error, leaving open the door to a storeroom where weapons are kept, which allows the suitors to arm themselves. Smoothly as this is accomplished, however, there is a sense beneath the surface of the plot that Telemachus' own growth is hampered by his father's return, his story foreshortened by that of Odysseus' unexpected return. This is manifested in part in Telemachus' somewhat tense relations with Penelope, whose determination to hold out for Odysseus' return makes it harder for Telemachus, now that he is grown, to resolve the situation and take charge of his inheritance. There are even moments in the poem at which Telemachus' interests and those of the suitors seem to be more congruent than opposed.

One of several ways in which Odysseus' return occurs just in the nick of time is that he is able to reassume his position at a point in his life when his son is just mature enough to guarantee the future but is not yet able to eclipse him. At the same time, Odysseus' replacement of his own father is complete, as can be seen from Laertes' somewhat peripheral role in the plot. Laertes has assumed a literally marginal position, leaving the main house for a farm at the edge of their holdings and a state of deathlike destitution. Odysseus only makes contact with him at the end of the story, after his defeat of the suitors, in an episode that seems so much like an afterthought that some have believed that it was not originally part of the *Odyssey*. The lateness of this reunion can be understood as telling us more about the independence and self-reliance that Odysseus enjoys in the prime of life than about the history of the poem's composition: Laertes' legacy may be essential to Odysseus' success in his greatest trial, but his actual presence is not. At the same time, it is significant that once Odysseus has recovered his house, he does need to reconnect with his father and his base of power in the land before he can deal with the suitors' relatives. Reanimated by Odysseus' return, Laertes becomes once again the warrior he was in his youth and fights with equal vigor beside Odysseus and Telemachus, picking off an enemy leader before Athena calls a halt to the hostilities.

As three generations of the same house form together a victorious fighting force, the poem ends with a kind of pageant of the aristocratic family, in which power and prestige are transmitted in an unbroken succession through the male line. Just before the fighting begins, there is a brief, revealing bit of dialogue among the three. Odysseus warns Telemachus not to shame his ancestors; Telemachus assures him, just a bit testily, that he certainly will not; and Laertes rejoices: "What a day, dear gods! My son and grandson / Going head to head to see who is best" (24.534–35). The rivalries among the generations have been finessed, subsumed into useful competition as the family presents a united front against the outside world.

The three successive heads of Odysseus' family are supported at this point by a small band of loyal servants: the swineherd Eumaeus, the cowherd Philoetius, Dolius, a loyal servant attached to the farm, and Dolius' sons. In describing the loyalty of these figures, the *Odyssey* takes on and attempts to resolve other tensions within the aristocratic household, those that involve figures who are in a condition of servitude or even actually slaves. In order to maintain the wealth of his household, the master has to depend on the labor of those who are in a position of inequality, a situation that raises difficult questions both about whether they can really be counted on to view their master's interests as their own and about whether their radical inequality is really justified. In its exploration and celebration of the extended household, the *Odyssey* exemplifies several of the somewhat tangled and contradictory ways of dealing with those questions that run through ancient Greek culture. Ancient discussions of slavery tend to turn on the issue of whether slavery is a natural state—the proper position in the social hierarchy of the naturally inferior—or an accidental one—a stroke of bad fortune—and both views were supported by the actual conditions of the ancient world, in which some people were born into slavery and some became slaves through capture in war. The *Odyssey* approaches this issue through its own central organizing principle, the rightness of Odysseus' claims to his household. The slaves in the household are divided into good ones and bad ones depending on their loyalty to his cause. The bad ones are those who serve the suitors willingly, especially those female slaves who sleep with the suitors, exemplified in particular by Melantho, who is the lover of their ringleader, and whose evil nature is expressed in her nasty jibes at Odysseus when he is in the role of a beggar. These disloyal slaves display the moral inferiority that later theorists would invoke as a justification for slavery, and they receive harsh punishment for their disloyalty: after the suitors have been killed, the maids are forced to clean up the mess and then Telemachus takes them to the courtyard and subjects them to a painful death by hanging.

The surprising violence of this punishment testifies to the unease created by the need to depend on slaves, especially if they are viewed as inherently depraved. A contrasting solution to that problem is offered though the portrayal of the good slaves of the household, the ones who remain loyal to Odysseus, most prominently Eumaeus and Eurycleia. Eumaeus, in particular, is given a large role in the plot as he welcomes and entertains Odysseus in his hut. During the several conversations between Eumaeus and the disguised Odysseus, Eumaeus displays his inherent virtue through characteristics that are understood to be related: his courteous observation of the laws of hospitality, even when his guest is a broken-down nonentity, and his unwavering loyalty to Odysseus and his family. Eumaeus is an ideal slave, then, in the sense that he adopts his master's interests as his own, but he does not easily fit the image personified by Melantho of slaves as naturally inferior and untrustworthy. The *Odyssey* manages this contradiction by portraying Eumaeus as not really being a slave. When he and the beggar exchange life stories, it turns out that he is actually an aristocrat by birth, the son of a king who was kidnapped and sold into slavery by a faithless female slave. And his relations with his owners are made to seem more like family relations as he describes how he was raised by Odysseus' mother along with Odysseus' sister.

In general, the *Odyssey* presents the good slaves of the household—never as actual family members—but as somehow comparable to family members. As mentioned already, Eurycleia functions as a kind of surrogate for Odysseus' mother, Anticleia. Eumaeus stands in a relation to Telemachus like that of a surrogate father, as is suggested by a simile expressing his joy on Telemachus' return from his journey.

> *And as a loving father embraces his own son*
> *Come back from a distant land after ten long years,*
> *His only son, greatly beloved and much sorrowed for—*

> So did the noble swineherd clasp Telemachus
> And kiss him all over—
>
>   (16.19–23)

When, just before the bow contest, Odysseus reveals himself to Eumaeus and Philoetius, he acknowledges their fidelity by promising them a status that, again, resembles incorporation into the family: "I will give you each a wife, property, / And a house built near mine. You two shall be / Friends to me and brothers to Telemachus" (21.221–23).

The Fame of Penelope

But the most important relationship through which Odysseus establishes and maintains his identity is with his wife, Penelope. One of the most impressive features of the *Odyssey* is that, despite its portrayal of a male-dominated world and its allegiance to its male hero, Penelope turns out to be fully as important and interesting a character as Odysseus—a feature of the poem that is apparent in recent criticism, which has been intensely concerned with Penelope and the interpretive issues raised by her role. The poem's domestic focus gives prominence to the figure of the wife, whose activities are confined to the household, and to forms of heroism other than the physical strength and courage required on the battlefield or on the high seas, qualities of mind that a woman could possess as much as a man. Penelope is Odysseus' match in the virtues that the *Odyssey* portrays as most important: cleverness, self-possession, and patient endurance. Her *mêtis* is revealed in the famous trick with which she keeps the suitors at bay for several years leading up to the time of the *Odyssey*'s action. Telling them that she cannot marry any of them until she has woven a shroud for her father-in-law, Laertes, she weaves by day and secretly unweaves at night. This trick, which works until she is betrayed by those disloyal female slaves, is a brilliant use of the resources available to her in a world in which women's activities are severely restricted and closely watched. She uses both the woman's traditional activity of weaving and the woman's traditional role of serving the men of her family to her advantage.

The marriage of Odysseus and Penelope is based, then, in like-mindedness, a quality designated in Greek by the term *homophrosynê*, which suggests both a similar cast of mind, in this case a similar wiliness, and a congruence of interests, in this case a similar dedication to the cause of Odysseus' return. Odysseus celebrates *homophrosynê* in one of his most eloquent speeches, when he meets the Phaeacian princess, Nausicaa, on the shore of Schería and approaches her with flattering words. He concludes by wishing her a successful marriage:

> And for yourself, may the gods grant you
> Your heart's desire, a husband and a home,
> And the blessing of a harmonious life.
> For nothing is greater or finer than this,
> When a man and woman live together
> With one heart and mind, bringing joy
> To their friends and grief to their foes.
> (6.183–89)

The *Odyssey* celebrates this vision but also shows how hard it is to fulfill. For Nausicaa, it will not come true with the alluring stranger who describes it, however much both she and her father may be struck by Odysseus' suitability as a husband for her. Odysseus' heart is set on returning to Penelope, but re-creating the harmonious life he has shared with her is a far from straightforward undertaking. The very cautiousness that unites Odysseus and Penelope makes them unusually wary of one another, keeping them at a distance during much of the *Odyssey*'s narrative. Odysseus brings to his treatment of Penelope a suspicion of women in general that transcends her particular and highly virtuous character and reflects a hero's unsettling dependence on his wife. A hero's honor is affected not only by his own actions but by what he can less easily control, his wife's fidelity. The Trojan War itself is undertaken to defend the honor of a

Greek leader, Menelaus, whose honor is compromised when his wife, Helen, goes off with the Trojan prince, Paris. The ambitions of those who follow him not only to win glory in the war there but to return home as well depend on the cooperation of a wife who will maintain that home, seeing to their affairs and keeping open a place for her husband to return to. The importance of this is expressed in the terrible counter-example of Clytemnestra, Helen's sister, whose infidelity has led to Aegisthus' murder of Agamemnon and usurpation of his kingdom.

The male heroes of the *Odyssey* view Clytemnestra's behavior as an expected norm and a reason to mistrust all women, as Agamemnon makes clear when he sees Odysseus in the Underworld and warns him not to fall into the same trap. And, however faithful she may be, Penelope does expose Odysseus to danger through the attraction she holds for the suitors, the opportunity she provides for his rivals to take control of his house. This pervasive anxiety about women is fully expressed in the more fantastic realm of Odysseus' adventures. There he has to combat a range of female monsters: the huge, voracious queen of the cannibal Laestrygonians; the deadly, disgusting alternatives of Scylla and Charybdis; the devious Sirens, who lure sailors to death with beautiful songs. And he has to overcome the seduction of female figures who threaten to deflect him from his course, such as Circe, Calypso, and the Phaeacian princess, Nausicaa. Yet one of Odysseus' many gifts is his rapport with women, and he succeeds because he is able to convert potentially destructive female figures into his helpers, often with the help of Athena, a figure who herself represents female power used to uphold male endeavors.

Despite Penelope's virtue, Odysseus approaches her with great caution, disguising himself from her as carefully as from the suitors. The result is an extended stretch of narrative in which husband and wife deal with each other indirectly, each testing the other in conversations that are tailored to his ostensible identity as a wandering beggar, especially in a meeting by the fire late in the evening before the contest. A strong sympathy develops between them, as he recounts a meeting he supposedly once had with Odysseus and she describes the difficulties of her situation, tells him of a dream that seemingly foretells the defeat of the suitors, and confides her intention of setting the contest of the bow. Throughout this episode it remains unclear how we should understand Penelope's state of mind as she responds to the stranger with increasing openness and makes the crucial decision that allows him to succeed. A number of critics, bearing in mind Penelope's own intelligence and the many hints Odysseus gives, have concluded that she must realize, or at least suspect, who he really is. Others see her as finally bowing to the pressures around her at just the moment when the husband she has been waiting for is finally home.

The question of whether or not Penelope recognizes Odysseus before he reveals himself cannot be conclusively answered, and that in itself is significant: the poem replicates for its audience the sense of uncertainty about what a woman is really thinking that was, for the male heroes of the Homeric world, a constant source of anxiety. And the interactions between Odysseus and Penelope while he is still in disguise are revealing about both of them. For Odysseus, maintaining his disguise in the face of Penelope's anguish and uncertainty is the greatest test of his self-control and the clearest demonstration of his protective hardness of heart. Moved by the supposed beggar's false tale of having seen Odysseus, Penelope breaks down in tears, but Odysseus stays in his role.

> So her lovely cheeks coursed with tears as she wept
> For her husband, who was sitting before her.
> Odysseus pitied her tears in his heart,
> But his eyes were as steady between their lids
> As if they were made of horn or iron
> As he concealed his own tears through guile.
> (19.224–29)

As she weeps at the thought of her absent husband and gives voice to her feelings, we gain a deeper understanding of what Penelope has had to contend with. In particular, she reveals a wrenching conflict between her roles as wife of Odysseus and mother of Telemachus. As long as Telemachus was small, those roles were congruent, but now that he has grown, his interests are no longer supported by her determination to hold out against a new marriage. She describes this sense of conflict through a simile that is also an allusion to a surprisingly violent myth: the myth of the nightingale, who killed her own son.

> . . . at night, when sleep takes hold of others,
> I lie in bed, smothered by my own anxiety,

Mourning restlessly, my heart racing.
Just as the daughter of Pandareus,
The pale nightingale, sings sweetly
In the greening of spring, perched in the leaves,
And trills out her song of lament for her son,
Her beloved Itylus, whom she killed unwittingly,
Itylus, the son of Zethus her lord—
So too my heart is torn with dismay.
Should I stay here with my son
And keep everything safe and just as it is,
My goods, my slaves, my high-gabled house,
Honoring my husband's bed and public opinion—
Or should I go with whoever is best
Of all my suitors, and gives me gifts past counting?
And then there's my son. While he was young
And not yet mature, he kept me from leaving
My husband's house and marrying another.
But now that he's grown and come into manhood,
He begs me to leave, worried because
These Achaean men are devouring his goods.

(19.563–84)

Odysseus' refusal to end her uncertainty is certainly cruel, and per-
haps needlessly so, but it does allow the poem to show how much
Penelope has suffered at home during Odysseus' long years away.
Penelope's experience, too, supports the *Odyssey*'s claim that the
rewards of a happy ending are deepened by the many trials that must
be endured before it can come true.

In the end, Penelope proves even more cautious than Odysseus
about embracing those rewards—and certainly more cautious than
Odysseus himself expects her to be. The *Odyssey*'s plot takes an unex-
pected turn when Odysseus, having dispatched the suitors,
announces his presence to Penelope and she refuses to recognize
him, claiming she is unsure that he is really Odysseus. For a hero
who has so carefully planned and controlled the scenario of his
return, this is a startling and frustrating development. By withhold-
ing her acknowledgment, Penelope shows that she is as self-con-
trolled as Odysseus and exercises her control over Odysseus' home-
coming just at the point when he thought it was assured, in a response
that reminds us how much his success has depended on her all along.

And she only grants that acknowledgment after she has provoked him into losing his own self-control, devising a brilliant test of his identity that brings their long-suspended marriage back to life.

When Odysseus has finally given up hope and asks for a bed to be made up so he can get some sleep at last, Penelope seizes this opportunity, slyly commanding Eurycleia to move their marriage bed out into the hall. At this, Odysseus breaks down. It turns out that he built that bed himself when he built his house and used a rooted olive tree as one of the bedposts. For it to be moved would have involved not only Penelope letting someone else into the bedroom but a feat of superhuman strength from a successful rival: the suggestion is a devastating threat to his honor and his identity. As he bursts out with an account of how he made the bed, he confirms that identity, through his knowledge of the secret, through his account of himself as an expert craftsman who has shaped both his physical surroundings and his fate, and through the passion of his reaction. By using the bed as her test, Penelope also reveals her own fidelity, for it would be useless as proof if she had let any one else in on the secret. The marriage bed then becomes the symbol and the means of restoring a marriage that is equally constructed by a powerful husband and a powerful wife. The rooted nature of the bed expresses not only the permanence of the marriage despite their long separation but also the continuity of the property which they both share and she has helped to protect.

The shared love behind the equally important but different roles of Odysseus and Penelope in keeping their marriage alive is expressed in a simile that marks the moment when Penelope finally lets down *her* guard and accepts Odysseus' return.

And as he wept he clung to his beloved wife.

Land is a welcome sight to men swimming
For their lives, after Poseidon has smashed their ship
In heavy seas. Only a few of them escape
And make it to shore. They come out
Of the grey water crusted with brine, glad
To be alive and set foot on dry land.

So welcome a sight was her husband to her.

(23.239–46)

The trials that Penelope has weathered at home are identified with Odysseus' adventures at sea.

The importance of Penelope's role is confirmed again in the last book of the *Odyssey*. There the scene shifts once more to the Underworld, where the ghosts of the dead suitors arrive with the news of Odysseus' triumph. Agamemnon, who has played the role of Odysseus' foil throughout the poem, offers a final comment on how differently Odysseus' story has turned out, and he attributes this—not to Odysseus' extraordinary talents and efforts—but to his success in winning a good wife.

> Well done, Odysseus, Laertes' wily son!
> You won a wife of great character
> In Icarius' daughter. What a mind she has,
> A woman beyond reproach! How well Penelope
> Kept in her heart her husband, Odysseus.
> And so her virtue's fame will never perish,
> And the gods will make among men on earth
> A song of praise for steadfast Penelope.
>
> (24.199–206)

Agamemnon here comes close to saying that Penelope, not Odysseus, is the real hero of the *Odyssey*, the one who makes its happy ending possible and the one who earns the reward of undying celebration in song.

The Limits of Heroism

The *Odyssey* never loses its focus on the heroism of its central character, on the exceptional achievement of a man who resembles the gods in his ability to evade death and overcome the passage of time, who succeeds miraculously in achieving his desires and solving his own and others' problems. But Agamemnon's tribute to Penelope is one example of the several ways in which the poem also gives credit to those who are Odysseus' inferiors in gender, age, breadth of experience, and social status. In doing so, it opens up a challenge, not only to Odysseus' individual claims to greatness and autonomy, but also to the ideology of aristocratic, male superiority on which those claims partly rest. The *Odyssey* brings in the voices and outlooks of these other characters, letting us see that there are other stories to be told than the one that it itself has chosen. The loyal characters are portrayed as having the same interests as Odysseus and therefore happy to cooperate in his return, but we do get hints of a point of view from which being an accessory to Odysseus' success might not be altogether desirable: in indications that Telemachus' development is thwarted by Odysseus' return; in the glimpses Penelope gives of how much it has cost her psychologically to remain forever faithful; in Nausicaa's unfulfilled fantasies of having Odysseus marry her and settle down in Phaeacia; in Calypso's bitter disappointment when she learns she has to let Odysseus go. While failing to wish for Odysseus' return is presented as unforgivable disloyalty, we see the outlines of other possible solutions as Telemachus and Penelope begin to figure out what to do if Odysseus does not come back. We can detect, under the surface, the possibility of another perspective, according to which it might not be so terrible for these characters to get on with their lives. At times, even the suitors, with their hopes of succeeding to Odysseus' seemingly abandoned prerogatives, seem not to be altogether unreasonable, and they are not all made to appear as reckless and vile as their ringleaders.

With the *Odyssey*'s stress on domestic life comes an interest in the lives and activities of ordinary people, such as the swineherd Eumaeus. In this way, the poem departs a little from the assumptions of heroic epic and looks forward across many centuries to the modern novel, in which people of no particular distinction claim attention as the heroes of their own lives—the preeminent example being Leopold Bloom, who takes over the role of Odysseus in James Joyce's *Ulysses*. This can be seen even in connection with Telemachus, whose experiences are much more humdrum than Odysseus', involving mostly a brief trip to the mainland and a series of social interactions with old family friends, but are presented as comparable to Odysseus' and also worthy of interest. With Penelope, whose actions are few and whose trials are largely psychological, the poem hints—most explicitly in the simile quoted above—that the inner life of feelings might be as compelling and significant as the external arena of male heroic actions.

As Odysseus' home becomes a prize that must be won with the utmost skill and daring, the ordinary objects and experiences that are to be found there take on a special power and value. The routine activities of a household become important moments in the plot: Nausicaa is able to help Odysseus when he arrives on Schería because she has gone to the shore to do the family's laundry; Odysseus' entry into his house in disguise is marked by the response of an old hunting dog lying on a dung pile, who knows his master's smell and dies of joy; when Eurycleia performs the household ritual of washing a guest's feet, she recognizes Odysseus unexpectedly and his careful plans are nearly derailed; the night before the contest of a bow, a serving woman who is staying up late to grind wheat gives voice to her thoughts, and this provides Odysseus with a welcome omen. Throughout the *Odyssey*, there is an appreciative interest in the concrete details of places and things. The architecture of Odysseus' house is fully described, as the plan included in this volume reflects, as is that of Eumaeus' hut. Even the fantasy realm of the adventures is presented in concrete terms—so much so that generations of travelers have imagined they could retrace Odysseus' journey through the Mediterranean, using the *Odyssey* as a kind of guide.

In its attention to Eumaeus and other humble characters, and in Odysseus' adoption of the persona of a luckless beggar, the *Odyssey* stresses the shared conditions of human life and even suggests that aristocratic status may be more a matter of chance than of merit. While in that beggar's role, Odysseus himself, speaking to one of the more sympathetic suitors, describes human beings as united by their unpredictable subjection to fortune.

> So I'll tell you something you should take to heart.
> Of all the things that breathe and move upon it,
> Earth nurtures nothing feebler than man.
> While the gods favor him and his step is quick,
> He thinks he will never have to suffer in life.
> Then when the blessed ones bring evil his way,
> He bears it in sorrow with an enduring heart.
> Our outlook changes with the kind of day
> Zeus our father decides to give us.
> I, too, once got used to prosperity . . .
>
> (18.137–46)

The loyal, upright members of Odysseus' household express a similar sensitivity to the randomness of fortune, which they link to their concerns for Odysseus in his absence, speculating that he must somewhere be in the same tough circumstances as the beggar in their midst. In fact, the poet plays with this awareness in his virtuous characters, making it seem as if they might recognize Odysseus because of it. In Book 19, during Odysseus' conversation with Penelope by the fire, Penelope asks Eurycleia to wash the beggar's feet in terms that sound for a moment as if she knows who he is:

> Eurycleia, rise and wash your master's—that is,
> Wash the feet of this man who is your master's age.
> Odysseus' feet and hands are no doubt like his now,
> For men age quickly when life is hard.
>
> (19.388–91)

A central virtue in the *Odyssey* is the ability to see another person as potentially like oneself, and this ethic of similitude is reflected in its distinctive use of the poetic figure of the simile. Both of the Homeric epics are marked by their use of these extended comparisons, but they employ them very differently. In the *Iliad*, similes tend to juxtapose the world of battle to some quite different realm of experience, such as the activities of wild animals or those of peaceful farmers and herdsmen. The *Odyssey*, on the other hand, is notable for similes that bring together the experiences of different characters in the poem, such as the ones already quoted in which Eumaeus is compared to a father like Odysseus or in which Penelope struggling with the suitors is compared to Odysseus at sea.

And yet, while Eurycleia shows her virtue through the way she connects the beggar's fate with Odysseus', it is through a glimpse of his scar that she actually recognizes him. However plausible as an image of what might be expected, Odysseus' state of worn-out destitution is not his real condition but his disguise, and the story he tells of a loss of fortune and status is a false one designed to maintain that disguise. Through the motif of disguise, the *Odyssey* preserves a distinction between Odysseus and ordinary mortals, making hardship, decline, and even old age into temporary states that he can discard at will and that do not describe his true nature. As Athena's maneuvers throughout the poem indicate, disguise is frequently a divine strategy, and his use of it sets Odysseus apart as just that much closer to the gods than other humans.

Odysseus constantly takes risks—including the risks involved in doing without his illustrious name and status—out of a sense of confidence and control. Similarly, the *Odyssey* itself takes the risk of incorporating challenges to its own dominant viewpoint because it

can keep them under control, subordinating them to a plot that is
dedicated to Odysseus and his claims. Telemachus' ability to replace
his father is deferred to a future beyond the horizon of this poem.
Eumaeus and Philoetius, honored and treasured as they are, are
never really on an equal footing with Odysseus' actual family. After
Odysseus and Penelope celebrate their reunion with a night of love-
making and storytelling, he reasserts the traditionally separate roles
of husband and wife, instructing her to guard the possessions in the
house and remain silently in her room while he goes out to meet his
father and deal with the suitors' relatives. Odysseus' dominance
over his household as over the poem that tells his story is never
really in doubt.

The *Odyssey* is able to tell a story of such assured dominance in
part because of its domestic focus, because it identifies its plot with
the stage in Odysseus' history at which he is recovering his home. It
is only at home that a hero can expect the kind of total acceptance
and steady deference that Odysseus receives from his loyal support-
ers. In the world beyond, he is subject to constant competition with
other men who are his peers and who have their own powerful home
bases. On the battlefield and in the military camp, heroes constantly
challenge one another and jockey for position, never able to stake a
permanent claim to preeminence. Because the *Odyssey* begins long
after the Trojan expedition has dispersed, Odysseus is relatively free
from this need to compete and the groups of men who do challenge
him can be portrayed as acting improperly. The inappropriateness of
such challenges grows in proportion to Odysseus' proximity to
home. The young men of Phaeacia, who try to draw him into an ath-
letic contest, are portrayed as simply rude, but the companions on
his journey, who are his Ithacan subjects as well as his comrades in
arms, are portrayed as wrongly insubordinate, although the poem
also displays some unease about their fate, an awareness that they
are, in a sense, sacrificed to Odysseus' success. The first lines of the
Odyssey involve a nervous insistence on the companions' guilt, and
Odysseus' solitary return is depicted throughout as a hardship,
although it is also the source of his distinction and fame. The poem
also displays some unease about the suitors, but much less, because
they bring the competition of the outside world to his home where it
does not belong. It is because the suitors have transgressed against
his rights to his own home that Odysseus' triumph over them can be
both glorious and clearly just.

Not only, then, does the *Odyssey* portray the most accomplished of heroes, it also shapes his story in such a way as to present him at the height of his accomplishments, ridding his home of rivals in a feat that combines the military mastery of the battlefield with the justice and security that are only found at home. This portrait is completed through a shrewd choice of where to close: the poem concludes before Odysseus has settled into the quiet retirement that represents the reward of his achievements but also the end of his heroic career and, with it, the end of his story as material for heroic poetry. The *Odyssey* signals the homebound quality of its plot through its final episode, the aborted battle with the suitors' relatives. As Odysseus and his supporters move beyond the borders of his estate to take on yet another hostile force, Odysseus seems to be on the brink of one more adventure. But, as Athena's intervention makes clear, pressing on would mean risking key elements of his greatness: the unqualified support of the Olympian gods and a peaceful old age surrounded by a harmonious and flourishing people.

History and the Poetic Tradition

This careful choice of an end point, like the equally careful choice of a starting point, is one of many ways in which the *Odyssey* shows its self-consciousness about storytelling as a sophisticated craft. Odysseus himself is a master storyteller, who is at several points compared to a professional bard and who fully recognizes the effectiveness of an artfully shaped narrative. In addition to his great account of his adventures at Alcinous' banquet—which Alcinous finds so well told that he concludes Odysseus could not possibly be a liar—Odysseus tells many invented stories while on Ithaca, each carefully tailored to its audience and designed with a particular aim in mind. Many other characters tell stories: Nestor and Menelaus tell Telemachus about their own and others' experiences returning from Troy; Helen and Menelaus tell him stories about Odysseus in Troy; both Penelope and one of the suitors tell the story of her trick with the shroud, and after their reunion, Penelope tells Odysseus the story of all she suffered in his absence. There are also two professional singers in the poem, the Ithacan bard Phemius and the Phaeacian bard Demodocus, and the songs of Demodocus are described at some length. The pointed arrangement of these internal narratives within the larger plot is a defining feature of the *Odyssey* and serves as a means by which the poem represents its own relationship to history and to the larger poetic tradition out of which it comes.

We know that the *Odyssey* is the product of a long poetic tradition that developed over several periods of early Greek history, all of which have left their mark on the poem. The Trojan legend, with its tales of disaster and destruction for both the defeated Trojans and the victorious Greeks, is a mythic account of the end of the first stage of ancient Greek history, which is known as the Bronze Age, after the widespread use of bronze (rather than iron, which was not yet in common use), or the Mycenaean period, after the city of Mycenae, one of the main power centers of that era. Mycenaean civilization developed in the centuries after 2000 B.C.E., which is approximately when Greek-speaking people first arrived in the area at the southern end of the Balkan peninsula that we now know as Greece. Those Greek speakers gradually established there a rich civilization dominated by a few powerful cities built around large, highly organized palaces. These palaces were at once fortified military strongholds and centers for international trade, in particular trade with the many islands located in the Aegean Sea, to the east of the Greek mainland. On the largest of those islands, the island of Crete, there was already flourishing, by the time the Mycenaeans arrived in Greece, a rich and sophisticated civilization, known as Minoan civilization, by which the Mycenaeans were heavily influenced and which they came ultimately to dominate.

From the Minoans the Mycenaeans gained, along with many other crafts and institutions, a system of writing: a syllabary, in which each symbol stands for a particular syllable, as opposed to an alphabet, in which each symbol stands for a particular sound. The Mycenaeans adapted for writing Greek the syllabary which the Minoans used to write their own language, a language which, although we have examples of their writing, still has not been identified. This earliest Greek writing system is known to present-day scholars as Linear B, and archaeologists excavating on Crete and at various mainland centers including Mycenae and Pylos have recovered examples of it incised on clay tablets. These tablets contain not—as was hoped when they were found—political treaties, mythological poems, or accounts of religious rituals—but detailed accounts of a highly bureaucratic palace economy: inventories of grain or livestock, lists of palace functionaries assigned to perform such specialized roles as "unguent boiler," "chair-maker," or "bath-pourer."

Mycenaean civilization reached its height at about 1600 B.C.E., and came to an end in a series of natural disasters and political disruptions about 400 years later, around 1200 B.C.E. We do not really know what happened, but all of the main archaeological sites show some evidence of destruction, burning, or hasty abandonment at about that time, and a sharp decline thereafter in the ambition and complexity of their material culture. Among these is the site of Troy itself, which was discovered in the late 19th century by Heinrich Schliemann, who followed the topographical details given in the *Iliad*; through this discovery, Schliemann both vindicated the historical validity of Homer and helped to found the field of archaeology.

Related in some way to the disruptions that ended the Bronze Age was the emergence of a new group of Greek speakers as the dominant people on the mainland. The classical Greeks referred to these people as the Dorians and believed that they had invaded Greece from the north. Modern historians are uncertain whether they were new migrants or people already present in Greece who newly came to power in the upheavals of this period. In any case, many people left the mainland as a consequence and moved east, settling on various islands of the Aegean and along the coast of Asia Minor, in the area that is now western Turkey but which then became, in its coastal region, as much a part of the Greek world as was the mainland itself. Both the Greeks who remained on the mainland and those who migrated to Asia Minor lived in conditions that involved less wealth and less highly organized concentrations of political and military power than were characteristic of the Mycenaean period. Their period is traditionally known as the "Dark Age" because their physical remains suggest a less magnificent level of civilization and because we know relatively little about it, although recent work in archaeology is increasing our knowledge and revealing more evidence of prosperity and artistic achievement than had previously been available. One result of the transition to the Dark Age was that writing, which was probably practiced in the Mycenaean period only by a small class of professional scribes, fell out of use, and the Greeks became once again a culture without writing. On the other hand, they had always relied, and they continued to rely, on oral communication as their central means of recalling, preserving, and transmitting the historical memories, religious beliefs, and shared stories that in our culture would be committed to writing—or now to various forms of electronic media. In particular, the Greeks of Asia Minor, known as the Ionians, developed a tradition of heroic poetry, through which they recalled their own history, looking back and recounting the experiences of that earlier lost era. This poetry centered on certain legendary figures and events, among them the events surrounding the Trojan War, which, as mentioned earlier, appear to reflect the final moments of Mycenaean civilization.

The so-called Dark Age came to an end during a period roughly corresponding to the eighth century—the 700s—B.C.E. The cultural shift that we label the end of the Dark Age and the beginning of the Archaic period involved not a series of upheavals, as with the end of the Bronze Age, but the emergence of new activity in a variety of fields. A growth in population led to a wave of colonization, with established Greek centers sending out colonies to such places as the Black Sea, Sicily, southern Italy, and southern France. There was also greater contact among the various Greek communities, which were politically distinct and remained so for centuries. This led to the development of institutions designed to unite those communities culturally and to reinforce a shared Greek, or panhellenic, heritage, such as the oracle of Apollo at Delphi and the Olympic games (founded in 776 B.C.E.). Around this time, the Greeks began to build large-scale stone temples and to make large-scale statues and a new kind of pottery decorated with elaborate geometric patterns. Many of the features of Greek culture that we associate with the Classical Period—the period that loosely corresponds to the fifth and fourth centuries B.C.E.—had their origins in the eighth century.

In addition to colonization, this was also a time of increased trade and thus of greater contact with other Mediterranean cultures. One consequence of this trade was the renewal of contacts, which had been intensive in the Mycenaean period, with cultures of the Near East. Through their dealings with the Phoenicians, a Semitic people living in present-day Lebanon, the Greeks learned a new system of writing—not a syllabary like Linear B, but an alphabet, the alphabet which is still used to write Greek and which was adapted to become the Roman alphabet, now widely used for many languages, including English. This new way of writing Greek quickly became much more widespread than Linear B had been, and it was put to a greater variety of uses. Among these was the writing down of poetry, and it is generally believed among scholars (although by no means universally agreed) that the *Odyssey* and a number of other surviving poems (including the other Homeric epic, the *Iliad*; two poems by Hesiod, the *Theogony* and the *Works and Days*; and a group of hymns also attributed to Homer) came into being in the written form in which we know them at that time.

While we know these poems in written form, we can see in their style and in their narrative techniques traces of their oral origins, although there is considerable disagreement among scholars over how close to those origins these particular works may be. Specifically, these poems manifest a use of repeated elements—phrases, lines, groups of lines, and types of episodes—that are an essential feature of an oral poet's style. Because a poet who performs orally does not memorize and recite an unchanging artifact but composes his song as he goes at the same rate at which he delivers it, he relies on a supply of stock elements; acquiring that supply is a key aspect of his training. Analysts of Homeric style have discovered that these repeated features form an elaborate system, involving both ready-made whole lines and shorter phrases that allowed the poet easily to generate new lines that fit the meter in which he composed, known as the dactylic hexameter. Among the most striking of these are the phrases used to identify the characters, which link their names with their attributes or their ancestry, and exist in different forms to be used as needed at different places in the line and in different grammatical cases. But the poet's reliance on repetition extends to much larger units as well, including obvious repetition of whole blocks of lines, as when a character reports on an event in the same words in which it was originally narrated, and more subtle uses of repeated sequences of actions to describe such circumstances as a host welcoming a guest or one character visiting another in search of important information.

Because repeated elements such as epithets have such a clear usefulness as aids to oral composition, it is hard to be sure how much further significance they are meant to bear in any particular context, although they certainly are meaningful as general expressions of a character's nature. For example, two of the epithets most frequently applied to Odysseus are *polumêtis* (having much *mêtis*) and *polutlas* (enduring much), which clearly pertain to his most defining characteristics, but that does not mean that he is acting especially cleverly at the points at which he is called *polumêtis* or that he is being particularly patient when he is called *polutlas*. The question of how integral these repeated elements are to the meaning of Homeric poetry is especially pressing for the translator, who has to decide whether to carry this stylistic feature over into a new language and a poetic form that does not have the same strict metrical rules as Homer's hexameters. The modern translator is also involved in a different relationship between the poem and the audience—not a live performance at which all parties were present at once and at which the conventions of Homeric style were familiar and unremarkable, but a less direct form of communication over large stretches of time and space, mediated through the printed page.

Stanley Lombardo has played down the repetitive dimension of the Greek original more than some other translators do for the sake of a swift narrative pace and of making the characters speak in English as real people do. He has also taken advantage of some of Homer's repetitions for a creative solution to one of the most difficult problems of translation, the way in which there is almost never a single word or phrase that captures what is in the original. The fact that the same expressions occur over and over again gives him a chance to try a range of different versions that cumulatively add up to what is in the Greek. For example, one of the most famous lines in Homeric poetry describes the coming of dawn. This is a routine building block of Homeric poetry, which appears twenty times in the *Odyssey* and twice in the *Iliad*, a convenient, efficient way of marking a new phase in the action that comes with a new day. But the announcement of dawn's appearance is made to fill an entire line through the addition of two epithets, which mean "early born" and "rosy-fingered." By offering us several different versions of this line, Lombardo is able to bring out much more fully the many meanings of these wonderfully suggestive adjectives: "Dawn's pale rose fingers brushed across the sky" (2.1); "Dawn came early, touching the sky with rose" (5.228); "Dawn spread her roselight over the sky" (8.1); "Dawn came early, with palmettoes of rose" (9.146); "Light blossomed like roses in the eastern sky" (12.8); "At the first blush of Dawn . . . " (half of 12.324).

The relationship between oral poetry and Homeric style was not fully understood until earlier in this century. A crucial step in this understanding was the comparative work of an American scholar, Milman Parry, who during the 1920s and 1930s studied oral poets who were then still practicing their art in the Balkan region and saw that many of their techniques corresponded to the conventions of Homeric style. For well over a century before Parry's discoveries, scholars had been worrying over the ways in which Homeric poetry is different from later poetry produced through the medium of writing, speculating about how these poems were produced, or what came to be known as "the Homeric question." Much attention was given to inconsistencies between different sections of the narrative or to places in which sections of the narrative seem to be awkwardly joined; for example: the fact that Circe's description to Odysseus of what will happen in the Underworld does not match what actually takes place; the fact that the parallel stories involving Odysseus and Telemachus between the divine council in Book 1 and their reunion in Book 16, while occupying the same span of time, actually involve different numbers of days; the fact that in the Underworld scene in Book 24, a dead suitor claims that Odysseus told Penelope to set the contest of the bow, while in Book 19 she comes up with the idea herself; the way the poem seems to backtrack to start over again with a new divine council when the second part of Athena's plan is put into effect at the beginning of Book 5. These inconsistencies were seen by scholars known as "analysts" as supporting a theory according to which the *Odyssey* was created through the joining together by editors of several shorter traditional poems composed by illiterate bards: perhaps one about Telemachus, one about Odysseus' adventures, and one about Odysseus' revenge. The analysts were countered by "unitarians," scholars who found in the poem an overall unity of theme and conception that outweighs those inconsistencies and points to a single intelligence shaping the entire work. Parry's discoveries have tended to uphold the unitarian position because they reveal that the kinds of small inconsistencies that concerned the analysts are both common and unimportant in the context of oral performance.

Although the answers to the Homeric question proposed during the 18th and 19th centuries are not generally accepted today, the scholars who wrestled with it helped to show how different these works are from modern poetry, and they recognized early on that an important clue to their origins might be provided by the bards actually portrayed in the *Odyssey*, Phemius and Demodocus, who perform songs as entertainment for groups of people gathered in aristocratic households. Phemius and Demodocus are like the modern bards studied by Parry in that they perform songs that are at once new and traditional, original retellings of legendary material that is the common property of the singer and the audience. Also like modern oral poets, they display a high degree of responsiveness to their audiences as they give shape to each particular version of a story.

The fact that Demodocus is blind marks the poet as a figure who relies on inner resources. In Homeric terms, that means that he is divinely inspired, instilled by the Muses with knowledge of past events that he has not himself witnessed. For divine inspiration, we might substitute the inherited skills and familiarity with poetic tradition of an oral poet, but in either case those inner resources can be contrasted with the external aid of writing, which is never alluded to in the *Odyssey*, and only once in the *Iliad*. Interestingly, ancient legends about Homer, the poet to whom both the *Odyssey* and the *Iliad*, along with other poems, were attributed, claim that he was blind, so that he too was seen as both a visionary figure—in myth, prophets are also often blind—and one who did not write. It should be noted, though, that ancient stories about Homer, like most of the biographical information we have about early Greek poets, are largely fictitious, based mainly on the events of the *Odyssey*, so that Homer is portrayed as an itinerant beggar resembling the figure impersonated by Odysseus.

We have no reliable information about Homer that would allow us to decide whether, for example, he really was responsible for both the *Iliad* and the *Odyssey* or just what role he played in the process by which the poems we have came into being. A key step in that process was the point at which the traditions of oral performance intersected with the new practice of writing and the epics took on the written form in which we now know them. One of the main challenges now facing Homeric scholars is that of figuring out to what extent the distinctive qualities of the *Iliad* and the *Odyssey* are due to the use of writing. On the one hand, the poems bear all the marks of oral style, which tend to disappear quickly once a poet learns to write. On the other hand, they are far too long to have ever been performed on a single occasion like the ones depicted in the *Odyssey*, and there is considerable debate about whether the large-scale design and complex structure exhibited by both the *Iliad* and the *Odyssey* could have been produced without the aid of writing. And, while most scholars believe that the poems were written down in the eighth century B.C.E., when writing first became available, others argue that this happened later, possibly in Athens in the sixth century B.C.E., where we know that official versions of both epics were produced.

Whenever they were actually written down and however much they may have been shaped by writing, the Homeric epics were still primarily oral works, in the sense that they were regularly performed and were known to their audiences through performance, well into the Classical Period. The process of transmission by which the *Iliad* and the *Odyssey* became what they are today, poems experienced almost exclusively through reading, whether in Greek or in translation, is a long and complicated one. It starts with that first, still mysterious moment when the epics were first written down and encompasses many stages of editing and copying: by ancient scholars, especially those working in Alexandria in the third century B.C.E., who were responsible, for example, for the division of both poems into twenty-four books; by medieval scribes, who copied out the manuscripts on which our modern editions are based; and by modern scholars who have produced the texts from which translations like this one are made.

Amid such uncertainty, the idea that Phemius and Demodocus might represent singers of the kind who helped to shape the *Odyssey* is not implausible. Many of the customs and institutions represented there reflect the times in which the poem and its tradition took shape rather than the earlier period during which the events depicted supposedly occurred. Historians and archaeologists who have compared the culture described in the Homeric epics to what we know of Greek history have discovered that the epics describe a world that does not correlate to any one period but combines elements of the Bronze Age with elements of the Dark Age: memories of the earlier time in which the Trojan legend is set have been woven together with circumstances borrowed from the period during which the Trojan legend evolved. The depictions of daily life that come in the sections of the *Odyssey* that involve Ithaca or the visit of Telemachus to Sparta and Pylos tend to reflect that later period. The kingdoms depicted there are much smaller and much less highly organized than those of the Mycenaean period, and many details of their material culture and social organization accord more closely to what we know of Dark Age life—a way of life that, we then assume, must have seemed quite familiar to the poem's original audience.

The *Odyssey*'s complicated structure serves as an elegant means of handling this combination of different historical eras. The events of its narrative present are those set in this more mundane world resembling that of the audience, while the events of the Trojan War and its aftermath are treated as part of the past. These past events are placed at a distance as they are conveyed through embedded narratives, such as the songs of Phemius and Demodocus or the reminiscences of figures like Odysseus or like Nestor and Menelaus, who have clearly passed on from that realm of experience to a new life of quiet retirement. The survivors of Troy are like time-travelers, who have spanned several eras. In this way, the *Odyssey* reflects the notion, expressed more explicitly in other versions of the Troy legend, that the Trojan War marked the end of a distinct age of heroes. Odysseus, in particular, is seen in Phaeacia as living into a time in which he himself, as the subject of heroic song, already belongs to cultural memory. Phaeacia serves as a transition for him chronologically as well as geographically, since it combines elements of both the magical world of the adventures and the realistic world of home. Alcinous' magnificent palace may be influenced by memories of the elaborate palaces of the Minoan and Mycenaean periods, but many of the Phaeacians' customs are similar to those found on Ithaca. When Odysseus leaves the Phaeacians, journeying to Ithaca in a deep sleep, their world is frozen and cut off from the rest of humanity as if permanently consigned to the inaccessible past. The Phaeacians no longer perform the service of taking travelers on their way; their ship turns to stone; and their city is—perhaps—walled off behind a mountain.

The *Odyssey*'s structure also allows it to integrate material from a wide range of sources and traditions. If the songs of Demodocus and the tales of Nestor and Menelaus are vehicles for elements of the Trojan legend, Odysseus' adventures bring in material adapted from other legends, especially those concerning the journey of the Argonauts—the first sea adventurers of Greek myth, who followed their leader, Jason, on a quest for the Golden Fleece in the region of the Black Sea—and also from a rich heritage of folklore. A number of Odysseus' adventures, such as the episodes involving the Cyclops and Circe, are reworkings of traditional folktales. The many different settings of the *Odyssey*'s action, both those of its narrative present and those of its embedded stories, allow for a remarkable range of moods and atmospheres and for illuminating comparisons. Deploying the traditional storytelling tool of the typical episode, the poet uses repeated actions to define the different worlds of the poem in relation to each other.

As mentioned already, the visit of Telemachus to Sparta and the visit of Odysseus to Phaeacia are described in similar terms, and father and son both play the role of guest in the conventional rituals of hospitality. Thus each of them has the experience of receiving gifts from his hosts, but each in a different way that reflects the different significance for each of the transaction. Telemachus is offered by Menelaus a set of gifts that involves three horses, but he declines them on the grounds that Ithaca is no good for pasturing horses. This interaction thus becomes for him an opportunity to display tact in a delicate situation and to express a newly realized identity tied up with his rightful possession of his home. Where Odysseus is concerned, what is most striking is simply how many gifts he gets, how much the process is elaborated, with more gifts, for example, being given in response to his wonderful story. This extensive gift-giving makes an appropriate culmination to an episode in which he recovers his threatened status. Through his success in impressing the Phaeacians, Odysseus makes up for the losses of his Trojan loot on his adventures and of his Ithacan possessions through the suitors' depredations, so that he returns to Ithaca with an important element of his previous power and prosperity already restored.

In yet another setting, when Odysseus visits the Cyclops, he has a host to whom the laws of hospitality mean nothing, so he has to ask for a gift. The Cyclops replies with a taunt that mocks those laws: "Noman I will eat last after his friends. / Friends first, him last. That's my gift to you" (9.367–68). Back on Ithaca, Odysseus as the beggar receives similar treatment from one of the suitors, Ctessipus, who hurls a cow's hoof at him proclaiming that it is a guest-gift. This recurrent motif of the travestied guest-gift sets up a revealing parallel between the Cyclops and the suitors, who are like the Cyclops in their brutality and their endless devouring of what they should not. This is characteristic of the way in which the adventures provide a heightened, fantastic, dreamlike preview of the more realistic world of Ithaca, so that, for example, Penelope is prefigured in certain ways by Circe just as the suitors are by the Cyclops.

That this difference between the two realms is one of poetic style, even genre, is signaled by Odysseus' false tales, in which the true adventures he narrates in Phaeacia are reworked in a more realistic, readily believable form—as the *Odyssey* playfully subverts familiar expectations about truth and fiction. The false tales work out possible fates that Odysseus or someone like him might have had were he not so extraordinary, were he not fated to go beyond the limits of normal human experience. Through these tales, the poem acknowledges other stories that might have been told about its hero—including some that did come to be told in later times. A distinctive feature of the *Odyssey's* Odysseus is that, although his story reflects an unmistakable interest in exploration and adventure, that is not part of his character. He is represented by the poet, and presents himself, as burdened by the need to travel and interested only in getting home and staying there. Later poets, most famously Dante and Tennyson, have responded to the stimulus of Odysseus' travels and have turned what is in the *Odyssey* an unwilled, externally imposed fate into the inner motivation of their Odysseus figures, figures who are not happy to stay home and who need to press on to new worlds and experiences. That way of imagining Odysseus' story is already anticipated in the *Odyssey*, but only in the form of one of his fictions. As he gives a false account of his origins to Eumaeus, Odysseus portrays himself as a restless adventurer, a survivor of Troy who could only stand to be home for a month before he was off again on a trip to Egypt.

For the most part, we can only guess at the ways in which the *Odyssey* plays with and comments on the long preexisting tradition of earlier accounts of the same characters and events. That this is not the first telling of Odysseus' story seems clear from the opening of the poem, in which the subject is simply identified as "the cunning hero, / The wanderer, blown off course" (1:1–2), as if the audience knows well who that is; his name is not mentioned until many lines later, in a delay that replicates that hero's defining tactic of withholding his name until the strategic moment. And the very complexity of the narrative suggests that it is the outcome of a history of experimentation.

There can be no doubt that the *Odyssey* is quite self-conscious about its place in a larger tradition, as it takes pains to fit Odysseus' story into the overall picture of the Greeks' experience after Troy. And we can try to assess its relationship to the one other account of the Trojan legend that does survive from the same period, the *Iliad*, the poem that was in antiquity attributed to the same author. An English scholar of the late 19th century, David Munro, compared the two poems and discovered an interesting phenomenon (now known as Munro's law), which is that there is no overlap in their contents: neither poem recounts any events that are told in the other. This discovery lends itself to several conclusions, such as that the two poems were composed in complete ignorance of each other, but the most likely is that they were designed to complement one another. The *Odyssey* seems, in fact, to go out of its way to fill in the rest of the story of the *Iliad*. Not only does it give a comprehensive account of the "Returns" of the Greeks, but it finishes the story of the war itself, recounting events that are implicit but still untold at the end of the *Iliad*: the death and burial of Achilles and the taking of Troy.

The *Odyssey*'s account of the taking of Troy is not simply a way of supplying information that the *Iliad* does not, but one more means by which the poem champions its singular hero. This account comes in the context of Demodocus' performances at the court of Alcinous. The first of Demodocus' songs is a curious one because it seems to be a kind of alternate version of the *Iliad*. While the *Iliad* focuses on a quarrel between the two major Greek heroes, Achilles and Agamemnon, this song focuses on a quarrel between Achilles and Odysseus. From other sources, we know what this quarrel must have been about, for the two heroes were evidently supposed to have disputed whether Troy would ultimately be taken by *biê*, or "force," the quality at which Achilles excelled, or *mêtis*, the quality at which Odysseus excelled. When, as a prelude to identifying himself, Odysseus asks Demodocus for another song and specifies that its subject should be the story of the Trojan Horse, he is implicitly pointing to the resolution of this dispute. Although, as the *Iliad* recounts, Achilles' might is essential to the Trojan defeat, especially through his killing of Hector, the city is only taken in the end through the trick contrived by Odysseus and Athena, the infiltration of the city by a band of men hidden within a huge statue of a horse, one more example of Odysseus' masterful use of disguise. In having Demodocus sing, at Odysseus' request, a kind of alternative *Iliad* concerned with the opposition between Achilles and Odysseus, the *Odyssey* sets up a competition with both the *Iliad* and its hero that Odysseus wins. Achilles is famous for the choice he has to make between *kleos*, glory won at war, and *nostos*, homecoming. Odysseus, the *Odyssey* tells us, is the hero who does not have to make that choice, who manages to have it all—thanks to his remarkable mind, his *mêtis*, as described in a poem that is as clearly focused, as wide-ranging, as varied, and as subtle as he is.

Sheila Murnaghan
University of Pennsylvania

Note on the Text

The translation is based on the Greek text of W. B. Stanford, *The Odyssey*, 2nd edition, London and New York, 1967. Stanford's text itself is based on T. W. Allen's Oxford Classical Text. Line numbers in the margins of the translation and in the appendixes refer to the translation. Line numbers of the Greek text appear in the translation in brackets at the top of the page.

ODYSSEY 1

S<small>PEAK</small>, M<small>EMORY</small>—

     O<small>f</small> the cunning hero,
The wanderer, blown off course time and again
After he plundered Troy's sacred heights.

       S<small>peak</small>
Of all the cities he saw, the minds he grasped,
The suffering deep in his heart at sea   *5*
As he struggled to survive and bring his men home
But could not save them, hard as he tried—
The fools—destroyed by their own recklessness
When they ate the oxen of Hyperion the Sun,
And that god snuffed out their day of return.   *10*

     O<small>f</small> these things,
S<small>peak</small>, I<small>mmortal</small> O<small>ne</small>,
And tell the tale once more in our time.

B<small>y</small> now, all the others who had fought at Troy—
At least those who had survived the war and the sea—
Were safely back home. Only Odysseus   *15*
Still longed to return to his home and his wife.
The nymph Calypso, a powerful goddess—
And beautiful—was clinging to him
In her caverns and yearned to possess him.
The seasons rolled by, and the year came   *20*
In which the gods spun the thread

For Odysseus to return home to Ithaca,
Though not even there did his troubles end,
Even with his dear ones around him.
All the gods pitied him, except Poseidon,   25
Who stormed against the godlike hero
Until he finally reached his own native land.

But Poseidon was away now, among the Ethiopians,
Those burnished people at the ends of the earth—
Some near the sunset, some near the sunrise—   30
To receive a grand sacrifice of rams and bulls.
There he sat, enjoying the feast.
                    The other gods
Were assembled in the halls of Olympian Zeus,
And the Father of Gods and Men was speaking.
He couldn't stop thinking about Aegisthus,   35
Whom Agamemnon's son, Orestes, had killed:

"Mortals! They are always blaming the gods
For their troubles, when their own witlessness
Causes them more than they were destined for!
Take Aegisthus now. He marries Agamemnon's   40
Lawful wife and murders the man on his return
Knowing it meant disaster—because we did warn him,
Sent our messenger, quicksilver Hermes,
To tell him not to kill the man and marry his wife,
Or Agamemnon's son, Orestes, would pay him back   45
When he came of age and wanted his inheritance.
Hermes told him all that, but his good advice
Meant nothing to Aegisthus. Now he's paid in full."

Athena glared at him with her owl-grey eyes:

"Yes, O our Father who art most high—   50
That man got the death he richly deserved,
And so perish all who would do the same.
But it's Odysseus I'm worried about,
That discerning, ill-fated man. He's suffered
So long, separated from his dear ones,   55
On an island that lies in the center of the sea,

A wooded isle that is home to a goddess,
The daughter of Atlas, whose dread mind knows
All the depths of the sea and who supports
The tall pillars that keep earth and heaven apart.   60
His daughter detains the poor man in his grief,
Sweet-talking him constantly, trying to charm him
Into forgetting Ithaca. But Odysseus,
Longing to see even the smoke curling up
From his land, simply wants to die. And yet you   65
Never think of him, Olympian. Didn't Odysseus
Please you with sacrifices beside the Greek ships
At Troy? Why is Odysseus so odious, Zeus?"

Zeus in his thunderhead had an answer for her:

"Quite a little speech you've let slip through your teeth,   70
Daughter. How could I forget godlike Odysseus?
No other mortal has a mind like his, or offers
Sacrifice like him to the deathless gods in heaven.
But Poseidon is stiff and cold with anger
Because Odysseus blinded his son, the Cyclops   75
Polyphemus, the strongest of all the Cyclopes,
Nearly a god. The nymph Thoösa bore him,
Daughter of Phorcys, lord of the barren brine,
After mating with Poseidon in a scalloped sea-cave.
The Earthshaker has been after Odysseus   80
Ever since, not killing him, but keeping him away
From his native land. But come now,
Let's all put our heads together and find a way
To bring Odysseus home. Poseidon will have to
Put aside his anger. He can't hold out alone   85
Against the will of all the immortals."

And Athena, the owl-eyed goddess, replied:

"Father Zeus, whose power is supreme,
If the blessed gods really do want
Odysseus to return to his home,   90
We should send Hermes, our quicksilver herald,
To the island of Ogygia without delay

To tell that nymph of our firm resolve
That long-suffering Odysseus gets to go home.
I myself will go to Ithaca   95
To put some spirit into his son—
Have him call an assembly of the long-haired Greeks
And rebuke the whole lot of his mother's suitors.
They have been butchering his flocks and herds.
I'll escort him to Sparta and the sands of Pylos   100
So he can make inquiries about his father's return
And win for himself a name among men."

Athena spoke, and she bound on her feet
The beautiful sandals, golden, immortal,
That carry her over landscape and seascape   105
On a puff of wind. And she took the spear,
Bronze-tipped and massive, that the Daughter uses
To level battalions of heroes in her wrath.
She shot down from the peaks of Olympus
To Ithaca, where she stood on the threshold   110
Of Odysseus' outer porch. Holding her spear,
She looked like Mentes, the Taphian captain,
And her eyes rested on the arrogant suitors.

They were playing dice in the courtyard,
Enjoying themselves, seated on the hides of oxen   115
They themselves had slaughtered. They were attended
By heralds and servants, some of whom were busy
Blending water and wine in large mixing bowls,
Others wiping down the tables with sponges
And dishing out enormous servings of meat.   120

Telemachus spotted her first.
He was sitting with the suitors, nursing
His heart's sorrow, picturing in his mind
His noble father, imagining he had returned
And scattered the suitors, and that he himself,   125
Telemachus, was respected at last.
Such were his reveries as he sat with the suitors.
And then he saw Athena.
                              He went straight to the porch,

Indignant that a guest had been made to wait so long.
Going up to her he grasped her right hand in his   130
And took her spear, and his words had wings:

"Greetings, stranger. You are welcome here.
After you've had dinner, you can tell us what you need."

Telemachus spoke, and Pallas Athena
Followed him into the high-roofed hall.   135
When they were inside he placed her spear
In a polished rack beside a great column
Where the spears of Odysseus stood in a row.
Then he covered a beautifully wrought chair
With a linen cloth and had her sit on it   140
With a stool under her feet. He drew up
An intricately painted bench for himself
And arranged their seats apart from the suitors
So that his guest would not lose his appetite
In their noisy and uncouth company—   145
And so he could inquire about his absent father.
A maid poured water from a silver pitcher
Into a golden basin for them to wash their hands
And then set up a polished table nearby.
Another serving woman, grave and dignified,   150
Set out bread and generous helpings
From the other dishes she had. A carver set down
Cuts of meat by the platter and golden cups.
Then a herald came by and poured them wine.

Now the suitors swaggered in. They sat down   155
In rows on benches and chairs. Heralds
Poured water over their hands, maidservants
Brought around bread in baskets, and young men
Filled mixing bowls to the brim with wine.
The suitors helped themselves to all this plenty,   160
And when they had their fill of food and drink,
They turned their attention to the other delights,
Dancing and song, that round out a feast.
A herald handed a beautiful zither
To Phemius, who sang for the suitors,   165

Though against his will. Sweeping the strings
He struck up a song. And Telemachus,
Putting his head close to Pallas Athena's
So the others wouldn't hear, said this to her:

"Please don't take offense if I speak my mind.   *170*
It's easy for them to enjoy the harper's song,
Since they are eating another man's stores
Without paying anything—the stores of a man
Whose white bones lie rotting in the rain
On some distant shore, or still churn in the waves.   *175*
If they ever saw him make landing on Ithaca
They would pray for more foot speed
Instead of more gold or fancy clothes.
But he's met a bad end, and it's no comfort to us
When some traveler tells us he's on his way home.   *180*
The day has long passed when he's coming home.
But tell me this, and tell me the truth:
Who are you, and where do you come from?
Who are your parents? What kind of ship
Brought you here? How did your sailors   *185*
Guide you to Ithaca, and how large is your crew?
I don't imagine you came here on foot.
And tell me this, too. I'd like to know,
Is this your first visit here, or are you
An old friend of my father's, one of the many   *190*
Who have come to our house over the years?"

Athena's seagrey eyes glinted as she said:

"I'll tell you nothing but the unvarnished truth.
I am Mentes, son of Anchialus, and proud of it.
I am also captain of the seafaring Taphians.   *195*
I just pulled in with my ship and my crew,
Sailing the deep purple to foreign ports.
We're on our way to Cyprus with a cargo of iron
To trade for copper. My ship is standing
Offshore of wild country away from the city,   *200*
In Rheithron harbor under Neion's woods.
You and I have ties of hospitality,

Just as our fathers did, from a long way back.
Go and ask old Laertes. They say he never
Comes to town any more, lives out in the country,   *205*
A hard life with just an old woman to help him.
She gets him his food and drink when he comes in
From the fields, all worn out from trudging across
The ridge of his vineyard plot.
                  I have come
Because they say your father has returned,   *210*
But now I see the gods have knocked him off course.
He's not dead, though, not godlike Odysseus,
No way in the world. No, he's alive all right.
It's the sea keeps him back, detained on some island
In the middle of the sea, held captive by savages.   *215*
And now I will prophesy for you, as the gods
Put it in my heart and as I think it will be,
Though I am no soothsayer or reader of birds.
Odysseus will not be gone much longer
From his native land, not even if iron chains   *220*
Hold him. He knows every trick there is
And will think of some way to come home.
But now tell me this, and I want the truth:
Tall as you are, are you Odysseus' son?
You bear a striking resemblance to him,   *225*
Especially in the head and those beautiful eyes.
We used to spend quite a bit of time together
Before he sailed for Troy with the Argive fleet.
Since then, we haven't seen each other at all."

Telemachus took a deep breath and said: *230*

"You want the truth, and I will give it to you.
My mother says that Odysseus is my father.
I don't know this myself. No one witnesses
His own begetting. If I had my way, I'd be the son
Of a man fortunate enough to grow old at home.   *235*
But it's the man with the most dismal fate of all
They say I was born from—since you want to know."

Athena's seagrey eyes glinted as she said:

"Well, the gods have made sure your family's name
Will go on, since Penelope has borne a son like you.   *240*
But there is one other thing I want you to tell me.
What kind of a party is this? What's the occasion?
Some kind of banquet? A wedding feast?
It's no neighborly potluck, that's for sure,
The way this rowdy crowd is carrying on   *245*
All through the house. Any decent man
Would be outraged if he saw this behavior."

Telemachus breathed in the salt air and said:

"Since you ask me these questions as my guest—
This, no doubt, was once a perfect house,   *250*
Wealthy and fine, when its master was still home.
But the gods frowned and changed all that
When they whisked him off the face of the earth.
I wouldn't grieve for him so much if he were dead,
Gone down with his comrades in the town of Troy,   *255*
Or died in his friends' arms after winding up the war.
The entire Greek army would have buried him then,
And great honor would have passed on to his son.
But now the whirlwinds have snatched him away
Without a trace. He's vanished, gone, and left me   *260*
Pain and sorrow. And he's not the only cause
I have to grieve. The gods have given me other trials.
All of the nobles who rule the islands—
Doulichium, Samê, wooded Zacynthus—
And all those with power on rocky Ithaca   *265*
Are courting my mother and ruining our house.
She refuses to make a marriage she hates
But can't stop it either. They are eating us
Out of house and home, and will kill me someday."

And Pallas Athena, with a flash of anger: *270*

"Damn them! You really do need Odysseus back.
Just let him lay his hands on these mangy dogs!
If only he would come through that door now
With a helmet and shield and a pair of spears,

Just as he was when I saw him first,   275
Drinking and enjoying himself in our house
On his way back from Ephyre. Odysseus
Had sailed there to ask Mermerus' son, Ilus,
For some deadly poison for his arrowheads.
Ilus, out of fear of the gods' anger,   280
Would not give him any, but my father
Gave him some, because he loved him dearly.
That's the Odysseus I want the suitors to meet.
They wouldn't live long enough to get married!
But it's on the knees of the gods now   285
Whether he comes home and pays them back
Right here in his halls, or doesn't.

                          So it's up to you
To find a way to drive them out of your house.
Now pay attention and listen to what I'm saying.
Tomorrow you call an assembly and make a speech   290
To these heroes, with the gods as witnesses.
The suitors you order to scatter, each to his own.
Your mother—if in her heart she wants to marry—
Goes back to her powerful father's house.
Her kinfolk and he can arrange the marriage,   295
And the large dowry that should go with his daughter.
And my advice for you, if you will take it,
Is to launch your best ship, with twenty oarsmen,
And go make inquiries about your long-absent father.
Someone may tell you something, or you may hear ·   300
A rumor from Zeus, which is how news travels best.
Sail to Pylos first and ask godly Nestor,
Then go over to Sparta and red-haired Menelaus.
He was the last home of all the bronzeclad Greeks.
If you hear your father's alive and on his way home,   305
You can grit your teeth and hold out one more year.
If you hear he's dead, among the living no more,
Then come home yourself to your ancestral land,
Build him a barrow and celebrate the funeral
Your father deserves. Then marry off your mother.   310
After you've done all that, think up some way
To kill the suitors in your house either openly
Or by setting a trap. You've got to stop

Acting like a child. You've outgrown that now.
Haven't you heard how Orestes won glory   *315*
Throughout the world when he killed Aegisthus,
The shrewd traitor who murdered his father?
You have to be aggressive, strong—look at how big
And well-built you are—so you will leave a good name.
Well, I'm off to my ship and my men,   *320*
Who are no doubt wondering what's taking me so long.
You've got a job to do. Remember what I said."

And Telemachus, in his clear-headed way:

"My dear guest, you speak to me as kindly
As a father to his son. I will not forget your words.   *325*
I know you're anxious to leave, but please stay
So you can bathe and relax before returning
To your ship, taking with you a costly gift,
Something quite fine, a keepsake from me,
The sort of thing a host gives to his guest."   *330*

And Athena, her eyes grey as saltwater:

"No, I really do want to get on with my journey.
Whatever gift you feel moved to make,
Give it to me on my way back home,
Yes, something quite fine. It will get you as good."   *335*

With these words the Grey-eyed One was gone,
Flown up and away like a seabird. And as she went
She put courage in Telemachus' heart
And made him think of his father even more than before.
Telemachus' mind soared. He knew it had been a god,   *340*
And like a god himself he rejoined the suitors.

They were sitting hushed in silence, listening
To the great harper as he sang the tale
Of the hard journeys home that Pallas Athena
Ordained for the Greeks on their way back from Troy.   *345*

His song drifted upstairs, and Penelope,

Wise daughter of Icarius, took it all in.
She came down the steep stairs of her house—
Not alone, two maids trailed behind—
And when she had come among the suitors   350
She stood shawled in light by a column
That supported the roof of the great house,
Hiding her cheeks behind her silky veils,
Grave handmaidens standing on either side.
And she wept as she addressed the brilliant harper: 355

"Phemius, you know many other songs
To soothe human sorrows, songs of the exploits
Of gods and men. Sing one of those
To your enraptured audience as they sit
Sipping their wine. But stop singing this one,   360
This painful song that always tears at my heart.
I am already sorrowful, constantly grieving
For my husband, remembering him, a man
Renowned in Argos and throughout all Hellas."

And Telemachus said to her coolly: 365

"Mother, why begrudge our singer
Entertaining us as he thinks best?
Singers are not responsible; Zeus is,
Who gives what he wants to every man on earth.
No one can blame Phemius for singing the doom   370
Of the Danaans: it's always the newest song
An audience praises most. For yourself,
You'll just have to endure it and listen.
Odysseus was not the only man at Troy
Who didn't come home. Many others perished.   375
You should go back upstairs and take care of your work,
Spinning and weaving, and have the maids do theirs.
Speaking is for men, for all men, but for me
Especially, since I am the master of this house."

Penelope was stunned and turned to go,   380
Her son's masterful words pressed to her heart.
She went up the stairs to her room with her women

And wept for Odysseus, her beloved husband,
Until grey-eyed Athena cast sleep on her eyelids.

All through the shadowy halls the suitors   385
Broke into an uproar, each of them praying
To lie in bed with her. Telemachus cut them short:

"Suitors of my mother—you arrogant pigs—
For now, we're at a feast. No shouting, please!
There's nothing finer than hearing   390
A singer like this, with a voice like a god's.
But in the morning we will sit in the meeting ground,
So that I can tell all of you in broad daylight
To get out of my house. Fix yourselves feasts
In each others' houses, use up your own stockpiles.   395
But if it seems better and more profitable
For one man to be eaten out of house and home
Without compensation—then eat away!
For my part, I will pray to the gods eternal
That Zeus grant me requital: Death for you   400
Here in my house. With no compensation."

Thus Telemachus. And they all bit their lips
And marveled at how boldly he had spoken to them.
Then Antinous, son of Eupeithes, replied:

"Well, Telemachus, it seems the gods, no less,   405
Are teaching you how to be a bold public speaker.
May the son of Cronus never make you king
Here on Ithaca, even if it is your birthright."

And Telemachus, taking in a breath:

"It may make you angry, Antinous,   410
But I'll tell you something. I wouldn't mind a bit
If Zeus granted me this—if he made me king.
You think this is the worst fate a man can have?
It's not so bad to be king. Your house grows rich,
And you're held in great honor yourself. But,   415
There are many other lords on seawashed Ithaca,

Young and old, and any one of them
Could get to be king, now that Odysseus is dead.
But I will be master of my own house
And of the servants that Odysseus left me."   420

Then Eurymachus, Polybus' son, responded:

"It's on the knees of the gods, Telemachus,
Which man of Greece will rule this island.
But you keep your property and rule your house,
And may no man ever come to wrest them away   425
From you by force, not while men live in Ithaca.
But I want to ask you, sir, about your visitor.
Where did he come from, what port
Does he call home, where are his ancestral fields?
Did he bring news of your father's coming   430
Or was he here on business of his own?
He sure up and left in a hurry, wouldn't stay
To be known. Yet by his looks he was no tramp."

And Telemachus, with a sharp response:

"Eurymachus, my father is not coming home.   435
I no longer trust any news that may come,
Or any prophecy my mother may have gotten
From a seer she has summoned up to the house.
My guest was a friend of my father's from Taphos.
He says he is Mentes, son of Anchialus   440
And captain of the seafaring Taphians."

Thus Telemachus. But in his heart he knew
It was an immortal goddess.

                         And now
The young men plunged into their entertainment,
Singing and dancing until the twilight hour.   445
They were still at it when the evening grew dark,
Then one by one went to their own houses to rest.

Telemachus' room was off the beautiful courtyard,

Built high and with a surrounding view.
There he went to his bed, his mind teeming,   *450*
And with him, bearing blazing torches,
Went true-hearted Eurycleia, daughter of Ops
And Peisenor's grandaughter. Long ago,
Laertes had bought her for a small fortune
When she was still a girl. He paid twenty oxen   *455*
And honored her in his house as he honored
His wedded wife, but he never slept with her
Because he would rather avoid his wife's wrath.
Of all the women, she loved Telemachus the most
And had nursed him as a baby. Now she bore   *460*
The blazing torches as Telemachus opened
The doors to his room and sat on his bed.
He pulled off his soft tunic and laid it
In the hands of the wise old woman, and she
Folded it and smoothed it and hung it on a peg   *465*
Beside the corded bed. Then she left the room,
Pulled the door shut by its silver handle,
And drew the bolt home with the strap.

                                        There Telemachus
Lay wrapped in a fleece all the night through,
Pondering the journey Athena had shown him.   *470*

ODYSSEY 2

Dawn's pale rose fingers brushed across the sky,
And Odysseus' son got out of bed and dressed.
He slung his sharp sword around his shoulder,
Then tied oiled leather sandals onto his feet,
And walked out of the bedroom like a god.   5
Wasting no time, he ordered the heralds
To call an assembly. The heralds' cries
Rang out through the town, and the men
Gathered quickly, their long hair streaming.
Telemachus strode along carrying a spear   10
And accompanied by two lean hounds.
Athena shed a silver grace upon him,
And everyone marveled at him as he entered.
The elders made way as he took his father's seat.

First to speak was the hero Aegyptius,   15
A man bowed with age and wise beyond telling.
His son, Antiphus, had gone off to Troy
In the ships with Odysseus (and was killed
In the cave of the Cyclops, who made of him
His last savage meal). Of three remaining sons,   20
One, Eurynomus, ran with the suitors,
And the other two kept their father's farm.
But Aegyptius couldn't stop mourning the one that was lost
And was weeping for him as he spoke out now:

"Hear me now, men of Ithaca.   25
We have never once held assembly or sat
In council since Odysseus left.

Who has called us together today?
Which of the young men, or of the elders,
Has such urgent business as this?   30
Has he had news of the army's return,
Some early report he wants to tell us about?
Or is there some other public matter
He wants to address? He's a fine man
In my eyes, and may Zeus bless him."   35

Telemachus was glad to hear these words,
And he rose from his seat, eager to speak.
There he stood, in the midst of the assembly,
And the herald Peisenor, a wise counselor,
Placed the staff in the hands of Odysseus' son.   40
In his speech he addressed old Aegyptius first:

"You won't have to look very far to find out
Who called this assembly. I called it myself.
No, I have not had news of the army's return,
Any early report I could tell you about.   45
Nor is there any other public matter
I want to address. It's a private matter,
My own need. Trouble has come to my house
In two forms. First, I have lost my noble father.
He was your king once, and like a father   50
To all of you, gentle and kind. And now,
There is even greater trouble, far greater,
Which will destroy my house and home.
Suitors have latched on to my mother,
Against her will, and they are the sons   55
Of the noblest men here. They shrink
From going to her father Icarius' house
So that he could arrange his daughter's dowry
And give her away to the man he likes best.
Instead, they gather at our house day after day,   60
Slaughtering our oxen and sheep and fat goats,
Living high and drinking wine recklessly.
We've lost almost everything, because
We don't have Odysseus to protect our house.
We can't defend ourselves. If it came to a fight   65

We would only show how pathetic we are.
Not that I wouldn't defend myself
If I had the power. Things have gone too far.
The ruin of my house has become a public disgrace.
You should all be indignant, and feel shame   70
Before your neighbors, and fear the wrath
Of the gods, who may yet turn against you.
I beg you by Olympian Zeus and by Themis,
Who calls and dismisses assemblies of men,
Stop this, my friends, and let me be alone   75
In my grief—unless my father, Odysseus,
Was your enemy and did you some harm
And now you are paying me back in malice
By urging these suitors on. Better for me
If you yourselves, Ithacans all,   80
Were to eat up my treasures and flocks.
Then I might get restitution someday.
I'd go through the town and bend people's ears
And ask for our goods until they were all given back.
But there is nothing I can do now. There's no cure   85
For what you are making me suffer now."

He spoke in anger, bursting into tears
As he threw the scepter onto the ground.
The crowd was motionless with pity. No one
Had the heart to respond to him harshly,   90
Except Antinous, who now said:

"Well, the big speaker, the mighty orator.
You've got some nerve, Telemachus,
Laying the blame on us. It's not the suitors
Who are at fault, but your own mother,   95
Who knows more tricks than any woman alive.
It's been three years now, almost four,
Since she's been toying with our affections.
She encourages each man, leading us on,
Sending messages. But her mind is set elsewhere.   100
Here's just one of the tricks she devised:
She set up a great loom in the main hall
And started weaving a sizeable fabric

With a very fine thread, and she said to us:

'Young men—my suitors, since Odysseus is dead—   *105*
Eager as you are to marry me, you must wait
Until I finish this robe—it would be a shame
To waste my spinning—a shroud for the hero
Laertes, when death's doom lays him low.
I fear the Achaean women would reproach me   *110*
If he should lie in death shroudless for all his wealth.'

"We were persuaded by this appeal to our honor.
Every day she would weave at the great loom,
And every night she would unweave by torchlight.
She fooled us for three years with her craft.   *115*
But in the fourth year, as the seasons rolled by,
And the moons waned, and the days dragged on,
One of her women who knew all about it
Told us, and we caught her unweaving
The gloried shroud. Then we forced her to finish it.   *120*
Now here is the suitors' answer to you,
And let every Achaean hear it as well:
Send your mother away with orders to marry
Whichever man her father likes best.
But if she goes on like this much longer,   *125*
Torturing us with all she knows and has,
All the gifts Athena has given her,
Her talent for handiwork, her good sense,
Her cleverness—all of which go far beyond
That of any of the heroines of old,   *130*
Tyro or Alcmene or garlanded Mycene,
Not one of whom had a mind like Penelope's,
Even though now she is not thinking straight—
We will continue to eat you out of house and home
For as long as she holds to this way of thinking   *135*
Which the immortal gods have put in her breast.
She is building quite a reputation for herself,
But at your expense. As for us, we're staying put
Until she chooses one of the Achaeans to marry."

Telemachus, drawing a deep breath, responded: *140*

"Antinous, I cannot throw out of my house
The mother who bore me and raised me.
As for my father, he may be alive or dead
But he is not here. It would not be fair
If I had to pay a great price to Icarius,   *145*
As I would if I sent my mother back to him
On my own initiative. And the spirits would send me
Other evils, for my mother would curse me
As she left the house, and call on the Furies.
And men all over would hold me at fault.   *150*
So I will never tell my mother to leave.
As for you, if you don't like it,
If this offends your sense of fairness,
Get out of my house! Fix yourselves feasts
In each others' houses, use up your own stockpiles.   *155*
But if it seems better and more profitable
For one man to be eaten out of house and home
Without compensation—then eat away!
But I will pray to the gods eternal
That Zeus grant me requital: Death for you   *160*
Here in my house. With no compensation."

Telemachus spoke, and Zeus in answer
Sent forth two eagles from a mountain peak.
They drifted lazily for a while on the wind,
Side by side, with wings outstretched.   *165*
But when they were directly above the assembly
With its hub-bub of voices, they wheeled about
And beat their wings hard, looking down
On the heads of all with death in their eyes.
Then they savaged each others' craws   *170*
With their talons and veered off to the east
Across the city and over the houses
Of the men below. Everyone was amazed,
And they all wondered what these birds portended.
Then the old hero Halitherses stepped forth,   *175*
Mastor's son, the best man of his time
In reading bird flight and uttering oracles.
He was full of good will in the speech that he made.

"Hear me men of Ithaca, and I mean
The suitors especially, since a great tide of woe   *180*
Is rising to engulf them. Odysseus
Shall not be away from his home much longer.
Even now he is near, sowing death for the suitors, ·
One and all, grim for them and grim for many others
Who dwell on Ithaca. But let us take thought now   *185*
Of how to make an end of this. Or better,
Let the suitors themselves make an end.
I am no inexperienced prophet,
But one who knows well, and I declare
That everything is coming true for that man,   *190*
Just as I told him when he left for Troy:
That after bitter pain and loss of all comrades
He would finally reach home after twenty years
Unknown to anyone. Now it is all coming true."

Eurymachus, Polybus' son, answered him: *195*

"Get out of here, old man. Go home and prophesy
For your own children—you don't want them to get hurt.
I'm a better prophet than you when it comes to this.
There are lots of birds under the sun, flying
All over the place, and not all of them are omens.   *200*
As for Odysseus, he died a long way from here,
And you should have died with him.
Then you wouldn't spout so many prophecies,
Or be egging Telemachus on in his anger,
Hoping he'll give you a gift to take home.   *205*
I'll tell you this, and I guarantee it'll be done:
If you, with all your experience and lore,
Talk a younger man into getting angry,
First, we'll go harder on him, and second,
We'll slap you with a fine so big   *210*
It'll make you choke when you have to pay it.
And this is my advice to Telemachus:
Send your mother back to her father's house
And have them prepare a wedding feast
And all the gifts that go with a beloved daughter.   *215*
Until then, the sons of the Achaeans will not stop

Their bitter courtship. One thing's for sure,
We fear no man, no, not even Telemachus
With all his big talk. We don't give a damn
For your prophecies, old man, and when they don't   220
Come true, you'll be more despised than ever.
And you, Telemachus, your inheritance
Is going down the drain and will never be restored
As long as your mother puts off this marriage.
After all, we wait here patiently day after day   225
Competing for her, and do not go after
Other women who might make us good wives."

And Telemachus, keeping his wits about him:

"I'm done pleading with you, Eurymachus,
And all the rest of you suitors. I've had my say.   230
Now the gods know all this, and so do the Achaeans.
All I want now is a fast ship and twenty men
Who will crew for me as I sail here and there.
I'm going to Sparta and to sandy Pylos
For news of my father, who has been long gone.   235
Someone may tell me something, or I may hear
A rumor from Zeus, which is how news travels best.
If I hear my father's alive and on his way home,
I can grit my teeth and hold out one more year.
If I hear he's dead, among the living no more,   240
I'll come home myself to my ancestral land,
Build him a barrow and celebrate the funeral
My father deserves. Then I'll marry off my mother."

He spoke and sat down. Then up rose Mentor,
An old friend of Odysseus. It was him,   245
Old Mentor, that Odysseus had put in charge
Of all his house when he left with the ships.
He spoke out now with good will to all:

"Hear me now, men of Ithaca.
Kings might as well no longer be gentle and kind   250
Or understand the correct order of things.
They might as well be tyrannical butchers

For all that any of Odysseus' people
Remember him, a godly king as kind as a father.
I have no quarrel with the suitors. True,   255
They are violent and malicious men,
But at least they are risking their own lives
In devouring the house of Odysseus,
Who, they say, will never return.
It is the rest of the people I am angry with.   260
You all sit here in silence and say nothing,
Not a word of rebuke to make the suitors quit,
Although you easily outnumber them."

Leocritus, Evenor's son, answered him:

"What kind of thing is that to say, Mentor,   265
You stubborn old fool, telling us to stop?
And do you think that even with superior numbers
People are going to fight us over a dinner?
Even if Odysseus, your Ithacan hero himself
Showed up, all hot to throw the suitors   270
Out of his house—well, let's just say
His wife wouldn't be too happy to see him,
No matter how much she missed him, that's how ugly
His death would be. No, you're way off the mark.
Now let's everybody scatter and go home.   275
Mentor and Halitherses can outfit Telemachus.
They're old friends of his father. But I think
He'll be getting his news sitting here in Ithaca
For a long time to come. He's not going anywhere."

With those words the brief assembly was over.   280
Everyone returned to their homes, but the suitors
Went off to the house of godlike Odysseus.

Telemachus, though, went down to the shore,
Washed his hands in the surf, and prayed to Athena:

"Hear me, god of yesterday. You came to our house   285
And commanded me to sail the misty sea
In search of news of my long-absent father.

Now the townspeople are blocking all that,
Especially the suitors, those arrogant bastards."

He prayed, and Athena was with him,   290
Looking just like Mentor and with Mentor's voice.
Her words flew to Telemachus on wings:

"You won't turn out to be a fool or a coward,
Telemachus, not if any of Odysseus' spirit
Has been instilled in you. Now there was a man   295
Who made sure of his words and deeds! Don't worry,
You'll make this journey, and it won't be in vain.
If you're really Odysseus' and Penelope's son,
You'll finish whatever you set your mind to.
You know, few sons turn out to be like their fathers;   300
Most turn out worse, a few better.
No, you don't have it in you to be a fool or a coward,
And you've got something of Odysseus' brains,
So there's reason to think you'll finish this job.
Never mind, then, about the suitors' schemes.   305
They're mad, not an ounce of sense or justice in them,
And they have no idea of the dark death
Closing in on them, doomed all to die on a single day.
As for you, the journey you have your heart set on
Won't be delayed. I myself, your father's old comrade,   310
Will equip a fast ship and sail along with you.
You get the provisions and stow them aboard,
Wine in jars and barley meal in tight skins,
Food that will stick to men's ribs. I'll go through town
And round up a volunteer crew. There are plenty of ships   315
In Ithaca, old and new. I'll scout out the best one,
Get her rigged, and launch her onto the open sea."

Thus Athena, daughter of Zeus.

And Telemachus, the voice of the goddess
Ringing in his ears, went on to his house   320
With a troubled heart. There he found
The haughty suitors, flaying goats
And singeing swine in the courtyard.

Antinous came up to him with a laugh
And clasped his hand and said to him: *325*

"Ah, Telemachus, the dauntless orator,
That's the spirit! No hard feelings now!
Let's just eat and drink as we always have.
The townspeople will provide you with everything—
A ship, a crew—to speed you on to sacred Pylos   *330*
In your search for news of your noble father."

And Telemachus, drawing in his breath:

"Antinous, there is no way I can relax
Or enjoy myself with you arrogant bastards.
Isn't it bad enough that you have eaten through   *335*
Much of my wealth while I was still a child?
Now that I'm grown, and hear things from others,
And get angrier and angrier at what I see and hear,
I'm going to do my best to nail you to the wall,
Either by going to Pylos or staying here in this land.   *340*
But I am going, and I'll make the journey count,
Even though I have to sail in another man's ship
And can't captain my own, which I'm sure suits you fine."

And he withdrew his hand from Antinous'.
The suitors, busy with preparing the feast,   *345*
Jeered at him as they swaggered through the hall:

"Hey, everybody! Telemachus is planning to murder us!
He'll bring reinforcements from sandy Pylos,
Or even from Sparta. He's really serious.
Or he'll go to Ephyre and get deadly poisons   *350*
To put in our wine-bowl and kill us all."

And another would sneer:

                    "Who knows?
If he goes off wandering in a hollow ship,
He may die as Odysseus did, far from his friends.
That would mean more work for us, dividing   *355*

All his possessions and giving his house
Over to his mother—and the man she marries."

That's how their talk went. But Telemachus
Went down to his father's treasure chamber,
A large room where there lay gold and bronze   *360*
Piled to the ceiling. And there were clothes in chests,
Fragrant olive oil, and great jars of wine,
Old and sweet, an undiluted, heavenly drink,
Ranged in rows along the wall, ready for Odysseus
Should he ever return after all his suffering.   *365*
The close-fitting, double doors were locked,
And the room was watched day and night
By a wise old stewardess, Eurycleia,
Daughter of Ops, son of Peisenor. Telemachus
Had summoned her and now spoke to her there: *370*

"Nurse, siphon me off some wine in jars,
The sweetest, mellowest wine we have
After what you are holding in reserve
For Odysseus, that unlucky man,
Should he ever return from the jaws of death.   *375*
Fill twelve jars and fit them with lids,
And pour some barley meal into well-sewn skins.
I'll need twenty quarts of ground barley meal.
But don't let anyone know. Just have all this
Ready to go. I'll pick it up this evening   *380*
After my mother has gone to bed upstairs.
I'm off to Sparta and to sandy Pylos
To see if I can get some news of my father."

He spoke, and Eurycleia gave a shrill cry.
She sobbed as her words went out to him: *385*

"Ah, where did you get this idea, child?
Why would you want to travel abroad, you,
A beloved only son? Zeus-born Odysseus
Perished far from home, in a strange land.
These men, as soon as you are gone, will plot   *390*
To have you killed by treachery, and then divide

All these things among themselves. No, stay here
With what is yours. There is no need for you
To wander and suffer on the barren sea."

And Telemachus, in his cool-headed way: *395*

"Don't worry, nurse. There is a god
Behind all this. But swear you won't say
Anything to my mother for a dozen days or so,
Or until she misses me herself or has heard
That I am gone. I don't want her crying."   *400*

And the old woman swore to the gods
That she would say nothing. That done,
She drew the wine for him in jars
And poured the barley meal into skins,
While Telemachus went back to join the suitors.   *405*

Owl-eyed Athena saw what to do next.
Assuming the form of Telemachus,
She went through the town recruiting sailors,
Telling them to gather by the ship at dusk.
Then she asked Noemon, Phronius' son,   *410*
For a fast ship, and he cheerfully agreed.

When the sun set and shadows hung everywhere,
She drew the swift ship down to the sea,
Put in all the gear a benched sailing ship needs,
And then moored it at the harbor's mouth. The crew   *415*
Gathered around, and the goddess encouraged each man.

Then she moved on, making her way
To the house of godlike Odysseus. There
She shed sweet sleep on the suitors
And made their minds wander in their wine   *420*
And knocked the cups from their hands. Eyelids heavy,
They stumbled to their feet and one by one
Staggered through the city home and to bed.

Athena's eyes flashed in the dark.

She looked like Mentor now, and in his voice   425
She called Telemachus out from the hall:

"Telemachus, your crew is ready with the oars
And waiting for you. It's time to set forth."

Pallas Athena led the way quickly,
And the man followed in the deity's footsteps.   430
They came down to the ship and the sea
And found the crew standing on the beach,
Their hair blowing in the offshore breeze.
And Telemachus, feeling his father's blood:

"This way, men! We have provisions to haul.   435
Everything's ready at my house. My mother
Knows nothing of all this, nor do any
Of the women, except for one I told."

He led the way, and they brought the provisions
Down to the ship and stowed them below.   440
Athena went aboard, followed by Telemachus,
And they sat side by side on the stern of the ship
As the men untied the cables and then came aboard
To sit at their benches. The Grey-eyed One
Put the wind at their backs, a strong gust from the West   445
That came in chanting over the wine-dark water.
Telemachus called to the crew to rig the sail.
Falling to, they raised the fir mast,
Set it in its socket, braced it with forestays
And hauled up the white sail. The wind   450
Bellied the canvas, and an indigo wave
Hissed off the bow as the ship sped on.
When they had made all the tackle secure
In their swift black ship, they set out bowls
Brimming with wine, and poured libations   455
To the immortal gods, most of all
To the daughter of Zeus with seagrey eyes.

The ship bore through the night and into the dawn.

ODYSSEY 3

The sun rose from the still, beautiful water
Into the bronze sky, to shine upon the gods
And upon men who die on the life-giving earth.

The ship came to Pylos, Nestor's great city.
Onshore, black bulls were being sacrificed   5
To the blue-maned Lord of the Sea.
Nine companies of five hundred men
Were each assigned nine bulls for sacrifice.
They had just tasted the innards and were burning
The thigh pieces for the god when the ship   10
Pulled in to shore. The crew furled the sail,
Moored the vessel and disembarked.
Telemachus stepped off the ship behind Athena,
And the goddess, eyes glinting, said to him:

"There's no need to feel embarrassed, Telemachus,   15
Not at all. This is why you have sailed the sea—
To get news of your father, to find out his fate
And where the earth conceals him. Come on, now,
Go straight up to Nestor. Let's see what he knows.
Ask him yourself, so he'll tell you the truth.   20
Not that he would lie. He's very wise."

And Telemachus, taking in a breath:

"How should I go up to him, Mentor,
And what should I say? I'm not used
To making clever speeches. And besides,   25

28

A young man just doesn't question an elder."

Athena's eyes glinted in the morning light:

"You'll come up with some things yourself, Telemachus,
And a god will suggest others. I do not think
You were born and bred without the gods' good will."   *30*

Thus Pallas Athena. She led the way quickly,
And the man followed in the deity's footsteps.
They came to the great company of Pylians
And there found Nestor sitting with his sons.
All around him were men preparing for the feast,   *35*
Skewering meat on spits and roasting it.
But when they saw the new arrivals, they all
Crowded around, clasping their hands in welcome
And inviting them to sit down. Nestor's son
Peisistratus was first, taking them both by the hand   *40*
And having them sit down at the feast
On soft fleeces spread on the sandy beach
Beside his father and Thrasymedes his brother.
Then he gave them servings of the inner organs
And poured wine into a golden cup. Passing it on   *45*
To Pallas Athena, he spoke directly to her,
The daughter of Zeus, who wields the aegis:

"Pray now, stranger, to Lord Poseidon,
For it is his feast you have happened upon.
When you have poured libations and have said   *50*
The ritual prayers, pass the cup of sweet wine
On to your friend, so that he too may pour,
Since I have no doubt he also prays to the gods.
All men have need of the immortal gods.
But he is younger than you, about my age,   *55*
So to you I will give the golden cup first."

He spoke, and handed her the cup of sweet wine,
And Athena rejoiced at his respect for custom
In handing her the golden cup first.
Without hesitation she prayed to Poseidon: *60*

"Hear me, Poseidon who laps all the earth,
And do not refuse to fulfill my prayer.
Bring renown to Nestor first, and his sons,
And grant your grace to all the men of Pylos
In return for this glorious sacrifice.   65
And grant also to Telemachus and to me
A safe return home, having accomplished
All that we came for in our swift black ship."

Thus Athena's prayer, which she herself granted.
Then she gave Telemachus the beautiful cup,   70
And Odysseus' true son prayed the same way.

The meat was roasted now. They drew it
Off the spits and served it up for the feast.
When they had eaten and drunk all that they wanted,
Nestor, the Gerenian horseman, spoke: 75

"It is seemlier to ask our guests who they are
Now that they have enjoyed some food with us.
Who are you, strangers? Where do you sail from?
Are you on some business, or are you adventurers
Wandering the seas, risking your own lives   80
And bringing trouble to men in foreign lands?"

Telemachus felt a sudden surge of courage,
Implanted in his heart by Athena herself
So that he would inquire about his absent father
And win for himself a name among men: 85

"Nestor, son of Neleus, glory of the Achaeans,
You ask where we are from, and I will tell you.
We have come from Ithaca, under Mount Neion,
But my business is my own, not the Ithacans'.
I come for news of my father, any news at all   90
About noble Odysseus, who once, they say,
Fought beside you and sacked the city of Troy.
We have heard where each of the other heroes
Who fought the Trojans met his bitter end.
But Zeus has placed Odysseus' death   95

Beyond hope of knowing. No one can say
Exactly where Odysseus died,
Whether it was on land, overcome by enemies,
Or on the deep sea in Amphtrite's waves.
And so I am at your knees, to see if you   100
Can tell me how my father met his end,
Whether you saw it with your own eyes,
Or heard about it from someone else,
Some wanderer. He was born to sorrow,
More than any man on earth. And do not,   105
Out of pity, spare me the truth, but tell me
Whatever you have seen, whatever you know.
I beseech you, if my father, noble Odysseus,
Ever fulfilled a promise he made to you
In the land of Troy, where the Achaeans suffered,   110
Remember it now, and tell me the truth."

And Nestor, the Gerenian horseman, answered:

"Ah, my friend, you bring to my mind
The sorrow we bravely endured in that land,
Heroes all and the sons of heroes—   115
Everything we suffered on the misty sea,
Looting and plundering wherever Achilles led,
And all of our battles around Priam's great city,
Where our best were killed. There lies
Ajax, dear to Ares, there great Achilles,   120
There Patroclus, like a god in council,
There my own dear son, Antilochus,
Strong and swift, a peerless warrior.
And there were many more losses we suffered.
No mortal man could recount them all.   125
Even if you stayed for five or six years
And wanted to hear the whole tale of woe,
You would return home weary before the end.
For nine years we devised all sorts of strategies
To bring Troy down—which the son of Cronus   130
Scarcely brought to pass. In that effort
No man could match Odysseus for cunning.
Your father was the master of all strategies—

If indeed you are his son. I am amazed
As I look upon you. The way you speak   135
Is very much like him. One would not think
A younger man could speak so appropriately.
Now all that time Odysseus and I
Never disagreed in assembly or council.
We had one heart, and with our wisdom   140
We advised the Argives on the best course to take.
But when we had sacked Priam's tall town,
Zeus planned in his heart a bitter journey home
For the Greeks—who were not all prudent or just,
Which is why the wrath of the Grey-eyed One   (Athena)   145
Brought many of them to an evil end.
She caused a quarrel between Atreus' two sons,
Agamemnon and Menelaus. It happened this way:
These two called an assembly of the entire army
In a reckless manner, toward sunset   150
And all out of order. We had all been drinking.
They made their speeches, and announced their purpose
In assembling the troops. Menelaus wanted
The entire army to set their sights homeward,
To begin shipping out on the open sea,   "pacify"   155
But this was not at all to Agamemnon's liking.
He wanted to delay their departure
And offer formal sacrifice to appease
The wrath of Athena—the fool,
He had no idea she would never relent.   160
The minds of the eternal ones are not quickly turned.
So these two stood there exchanging insults,
And the soldiers rose up with one huge roar
And took sides. We spent that night
Nursing our resentment against each other,   165
For Zeus was bringing on our doom.
At dawn some of us hauled our ships
To the bright water and loaded on board
Our goods and our softly belted women.
Half of the army held back, remaining   170
With King Agamemnon, son of Atreus,
But half of us embarked and launched our ships,
Which pulled away swiftly, for some god

Had made the teeming water smooth as glass.
We pulled in to Tenedos and offered sacrifice,   *175*
Eager to reach home, but Zeus held firm
Against our immediate return and stirred up
Still more dissension. Some now turned back
Their curved ships, following Odysseus,
A wise leader with a flexible mind,   *180*
Out of respect for Lord Agamemnon.
But I fled on with all my ships,
For I knew that Zeus had evil in mind.
Diomedes also got his men out then,
And Menelaus brought up the rear.   *185*
He caught up with us in Lesbos
As we were debating the long journey ahead,
Whether we should sail above rugged Chios
And on to Psyria, keeping Chios on our left,
Or go below Chios past windy Mimas.   *190*
We asked the god to give us a sign
And he showed us one, telling us
To cut through the sea straight to Euboea,
The sooner to get ourselves out of danger.
A shrill wind rose up and started to blow,   *195*
And the ships flew over the teeming brine.
We put in at Geraestus that night,
And, with all that water behind us,
We sacrificed many bulls to Poseidon.
On the fourth day Diomedes made Argos,   *200*
But I held on toward Pylos, and the wind
Did not die down once since it began to blow.

"And so I came home, dear child, knowing nothing
Of who survived and who was lost.
But what I have heard sitting here in my halls   *205*
You too shall hear, as is only right.
The Myrmidons, they say, made it safely home,
Led by the son of great-souled Achilles;
Philoctetes too; and Idomeneus
Brought back to Crete all of his men   *210*
Who survived the war; he lost none at sea.
Of Agamemnon you have already heard,

Far off though you be, how he came home
And how Aegisthus plotted his grisly death
And then paid for it in a horrible way.   *215*
How good it is for a son to be left
When a man dies! Agamemnon's son
Avenged his death, killing his murderer,
The treacherous Aegisthus. You too, my friend—
For I see that you are handsome and tall—   *220*
Should be brave and strong, and win a name for yourself."

And Telemachus, in his clear-headed way:

"Nestor, son of Neleus, glory of the Achaeans,
Truly, Orestes was a son who took vengeance,
And the Achaeans will spread his fame   *225*
To future generations. I wish the gods
Would clothe me in such strength, that I
Might take vengeance on the suitors
For their transgressions against me.
They are violent and malicious men.   *230*
But the gods have spun into the web of my life
No such happiness for me or my father,
And so I will simply have to endure."

Nestor, the Gerenian horseman, answered:

"Now that you've mentioned it, I recall hearing   *235*
That a crowd of suitors for your mother's hand,
Uninvited by you, are causing you trouble.
Why do you put up with this? Has some god
Turned the townspeople against you?
Who knows but that Odysseus may come some day,   *240*
Alone or with an army, and make them pay in blood.
Ah, if only grey-eyed Athena chose to love you
The way she did glorious Odysseus
In the land of Troy! I have never seen
A god show love so openly   *245*
As Athena did to him. You could see her
Standing at his side! If she would choose
To love you like that and take care of you,

Some of those suitors might forget about marriage!"

And Telemachus answered him: *250*

"I do not think, sir, this will ever happen.
The very thought amazes me. It is too much
To hope for, even if the gods willed it."

Then Athena, eyes flashing, put in:

"Telemachus, what a thing to say!   *255*
It is easy for a god to bring a man safely home,
Even from far away. And speaking for myself,
I would rather suffer on my homeward journey
Than be killed at my hearth, as Agamemnon was—
By the treachery of Aegisthus and of his own wife.   *260*
But even the gods cannot ward off death,
The great leveler, from a man they love,
Not when destiny comes to lay him low."

And Telemachus answered him:

"Mentor, let us speak of this no longer,   *265*
For all our grief. He cannot return.
The gods have already devised his death.
But now I have another question for Nestor,
Steeped as he is in knowledge and wisdom.
He has been king for three generations   *270*
And has the look of an immortal god.
Nestor, son of Neleus, tell me this:
How was Agamemnon, son of Atreus, slain?
Where was Menelaus? How could Aegisthus
Dare to plot the murder of a king, a man   *275*
Far more powerful than he himself was?
Was Menelaus not in Argos, and did his absence
Encourage Aegisthus to commit the murder?"

And Nestor, the Gerenian horseman:

"Well then, my child, I will tell you all.   *280*

You yourself have guessed what would have happened
If Atreus' son, red-haired Menelaus,
Had come back from Troy and found Aegisthus
Still alive in his halls. His dead body
Would never have been buried in earth;   285
Dogs and birds would have ripped it apart
As it lay on the plain far from the city,
Nor would any Greek woman have wept for him,
So monstrous was the crime he planned and committed.
While we toiled and sweated over there in Troy,   290
He relaxed in a corner of bluegrass Argos
Sweet-talking the wife of Agamemnon,
Noble Clytemnestra. At first she refused
The whole sordid affair. She had good sense,
And with her was a singer whom Agamemnon,   295
When he left for Troy, had strictly ordered
To guard his wife. But when the gods doomed her
To be undone, Aegisthus took the singer of tales
To a desert island and left him there
For the dogs and birds. And he led her off,   300
Just as willing as he was, to his own house.
Many an ox's thigh he burned on the altars,
Many an offering he made of tapestries and gold
When he accomplished the great deed
He had never hoped in his heart to achieve.   305
　　　　　Menelaus and I were sailing then
On our way back from Troy, the best of friends.
But when we came to holy Sunium,
The cape of Athens, Phoebus Apollo
Shot Menelaus' pilot with his arrows,   310
Killing him softly as he held the tiller
Of the speeding ship—Phrontis his name,
The best rough-weather pilot in all the world.
So Menelaus stopped, eager though he was
To press on, and gave his comrade a funeral.   315
When he got his ships on the deep purple again
He made good time to Malea's steep height,
But then Zeus put trouble in his way, shearing
Blasts of shrill winds down from the sky,
And the waves swelled to the size of mountains.   320

Then he split the fleet into two, bringing some
To the part of Crete where the Cydonians live,
Near the Iardanus river. There is a smooth cliff
Sheer to the misty sea on the border of Gortyn,
Where the Southwest Wind drives huge waves   325
Against the headland on the left, toward Phaestus.
The only breakwater is a small rock offshore.
So, some of the fleet came there. The men
Barely escaped with their lives, but the ships
Were broken to pieces against the reef.   330
Five other black ships, though, were blown
All the way to Egypt, and Menelaus
Wandered up and down that coast with his ships,
A stranger in a strange land, amassing
A fortune in gold and goods. Aegisthus,   335
Meanwhile, was working his evil at home.
Having killed the son of Atreus
And subdued the people, he reigned
For seven years in gold-crusted Mycenae.
In the eighth year, though, he met his doom   340
In the person of Orestes, come back from Athens.
Orestes killed his father's murderer,
The treacherous Aegisthus, and, having killed him,
Invited all the Argives to a funeral feast
For his hateful mother and her craven lover.   345
On that very day Menelaus arrived,
Bearing all the treasure his ships could hold.
          So don't you wander long from home, my friend,
Leaving your wealth behind, and in your house
Insolent men who might divide up your goods   350
While you are gone on a useless journey.
Still, I think you should visit Menelaus,
For he has just lately returned from abroad,
From a country no one would hope to return to
Once a storm has driven him off course   355
Into a sea so wide that not even migrating birds
Make the trip more than once a year,
So great is that sea and so terrible.
                              So then,
Go off now with your ship and your crew.

Or if you would rather travel by land,   *360*
We have chariots and horses at your disposal.
My sons are at your service, ready to guide you
To gleaming Lacedaemon, where Menelaus lives.
Beseech him yourself, so he'll tell you the truth.
Not that he would lie. He's very wise."   *365*

The sun set on his words, and darkness came on.
Athena's eyes flashed grey as she said:

"You have told the tale well, old man.
But come, cut the tongues and mix the wine
So we can pour libations to Poseidon   *370*
And the other gods, and then think of sleep.
It is late. Twilight has faded to dark,
And it is not right to linger at feasts of the gods."

Thus Zeus' daughter, and they did as she said.
Heralds poured water over their hands   *375*
And youths filled bowls to the brim with drink
And served it to all, first pouring into each cup
A few drops for libation. They cut the tongues,
Threw them on the fire, and standing up in turn
Poured libations upon them. Having done so,   *380*
And having drunk to their heart's content,
Athena and godlike Telemachus
Both started to head for their hollow ship,
But Nestor prevailed upon them to stay:

"God forbid you should go to your ship—   *385*
As if I were poor and didn't have enough
Cloaks and blankets for myself and my guests
To sleep softly upon! I have plenty of cloaks and blankets,
And Odysseus' son shall never lie down
On the deck of a ship while I am alive,   *390*
Or any child of mine is left in the halls
To entertain strangers who come to my house."

And Athena, her eyes flecked with dark gold:

"Well spoken, old friend, and Telemachus
Would do well to accept your invitation.   395
It is better that way. So he will go with you
To sleep in your house, but I will go back
To the black ship and have a word with the crew
To raise their spirits. I am the only
Older man among them. They are all youngsters,   400
Telemachus' age, and sail with us as friends.
I will spend this night down there by the ship,
But at dawn I am off to the Cauconians
To collect an old debt, and not a small one at that.
But send this young man on his way   405
In a chariot, and send your son with him,
And the fastest, strongest horses you have."

Thus Athena, her eyes flashing in the dark,
And as she left they saw only a vulture
Beating its long, dusky wings.
                     Their jaws dropped   410
And the old man could scarcely believe his eyes.
He grabbed Telemachus' hand and said to him:

"If you have gods as escorts when you are so young,
I do not think you will turn out badly at all!
This was no other of the Olympian gods   415
But the daughter of Zeus, Tritogeneia,
Most glorious Athena, who also honored
Your noble father among the Argive forces.
Be gracious, Lady, and grant me renown—
Me, my sons, and my venerable wife.   420
And in return I will sacrifice to you
A yearling heifer, broad of brow and unbroken,
Which no man has ever led beneath the yoke.
And I will plate her horns with gold for sacrifice."

Thus Nestor, and Pallas Athena heard his prayer.   425
Then the old Gerenian horseman led his sons
And daughters' husbands to his beautiful palace,
Where they sat down in rows on benches and chairs.
The housekeeper opened a jar of wine

Eleven years old. The old man mixed a bowl   *430*
Of this sweet wine, and as he poured libations
He prayed over and over to Pallas Athena,
Daughter of Zeus who holds the aegis.

When they had all poured libations
And drunk wine to their hearts' content,   *435*
They went home to their houses to take their rest.
But Nestor told Telemachus to sleep
Under the echoing portico on a corded bed
Next to Peisistratus, a good man with a spear
And the only of Nestor's sons still unmarried.   *440*
Nestor himself slept in an inner room
With his wife, the lady of the house, beside him.

As soon as Dawn appeared in the sky
Nestor, the Gerenian horseman, rose
And went to sit on the polished stones   *445*
Outside his high doors, the white stones,
Glistening with oil, upon which of old
Neleus would sit, like a god in counsel.
Neleus had met his fate long ago
And gone down to Hades' undergloom,   *450*
And now upon these stones in his turn
Sat Nestor of Gerenia, holding a scepter.
His sons came out and gathered about him,
Echephron and Stratius and Perseus,
Aretus and godlike Thrasymedes,   *455*
And as the sixth, the hero Peisistratus.
And they brought godlike Telemachus
And had him sit beside Gerenian Nestor,
Who then spoke:

                    "Quickly now, my sons,
That I may propitiate Athena,   *460*
Who came to me at the feast of the god
As clear as day. One of you go to the plain
For a heifer, and have the cowherd
Drive her here speedily. Let another go
To the black ship of great-hearted Telemachus   *465*

And bring his crew, leaving only two behind.
And someone go fetch the goldsmith Laerces
To plate the horns of the heifer with gold.
The rest of you stay here, and have the serving women
Prepare a feast throughout our glorious halls,   *470*
And bring seats, plenty of logs, and fresh water."

Thus Nestor, and they all set to work. The heifer
Came from the plain, and from the sailing ship
Came Telemachus' crew. The smith came
With the tools of his trade, a bronze hammer,   *475*
An anvil, and a pair of well-made tongs
With which he wrought gold. And Athena came
To accept the sacrifice.
                              Nestor, the old charioteer,
Gave the smith gold, and the smith worked it
And leafed it around the heifer's horns   *480*
To make the goddess rejoice at the offering.
Stratius and Echephron led the heifer up
By the horns, and Aretus came from the chamber
Carrying water for their hands in a basin
Embossed with flowers. In his other hand he held   *485*
A basket of barley. Thrasymedes stood by
With a sharp axe to strike down the heifer,
And Perseus held the blood-bowl. Nestor began
The washing of hands and sprinkling of barley,
Praying hard to Athena as he cut the first hairs   *490*
From the victim's head and threw them on the fire.
These rites done, high-hearted Thrasymedes
Came up and struck. When the axe severed
The sinews of the neck, and the heifer collapsed,
The women raised the ritual cry, Nestor's daughters,   *495*
The wives of his sons, and his august wife,
Eurydice, eldest of Clymenus' daughters.
Then the men raised the heifer's head from the ground
And held it for Peisistratus to cut the throat.
When the black blood had flowed out, and the life   *500*
Left the bones, they butchered the heifer,
Jointing the thigh pieces in ritual order
And covering them with a double layer of fat

And with bits cut raw from the rest of the carcass.
These the old man burned on split logs   *505*
And poured bright wine over them. At his side
Were young men holding five-tined forks.
When the thigh pieces were burned and the innards tasted,
They carved up the rest, skewered the pieces,
And roasted them holding the spits in their hands.   *510*

Meanwhile, Telemachus was being bathed
By Polycaste, Nestor's youngest daughter.
When this lovely girl had bathed him, rubbed him with oil,
And thrown on his shoulders a tunic and cloak,
Telemachus came forth like an immortal god   *515*
And took his seat beside Nestor, shepherd of the people.

When they had roasted the meat and drawn it
Off the spits, they sat down and feasted,
Waited upon by worthy men who poured their wine
Into golden cups. When they had enough   *520*
To eat and drink, Gerenian Nestor spoke:

"My sons, yoke the combed horses to the chariot
So that Telemachus may begin his journey."

He spoke, and they did as he said,
Quickly yoking the horses. The housekeeper   *525*
Placed in the chariot bread and wine
And the sort of fare kings and lords eat.
Telemachus mounted the beautiful chariot,
And Peisistratus, Nestor's son,
Stepped in beside him and took the reins.   *530*
He flicked the lash and the horses took off,
Eating up the plain and leaving behind them
The high rock of Pylos. All day long
They jostled the yoke that held them together.

As the sun set and the world grew dark   *535*
They came to Pherae and pulled up at the house
Of Diocles, son of Ortilochus,
Himself a son of the river Alpheus.

There they spent the night, and Diocles
Gave them the hospitality due to guests.   *540*

When Dawn brushed the pale sky with rose,
They yoked the horses, stepped up into
The inlaid chariot and drove out through the gate
And echoing portico. Peisistratus
Flicked the lash and the horses took off.   *545*
When they reached the level, wheat-bearing plains
They kept pushing on—so strong were their horses—
Until the sun set and the world grew dark.

ODYSSEY 4

They came to the hollows of Lacedaemon
And drove to Menelaus' palace,
Which they found filled with guests. Menelaus
Was hosting a double wedding party
For his son and his daughter. He was sending her   5
To wed the son of Achilles, as he had promised
Long ago in Troy, and now the gods
Were bringing the marriage to pass.
He was sending her off with horses and chariots
For her journey to the city of the Myrmidons,   10
Over whom her husband-to-be was lord.
For his son he was bringing a bride
From Sparta, the daughter of Alector.
This son, Megapenthes, was born from a slave woman,
For the gods had made Helen barren   15
After the birth of her daughter Hermione,
Who had the beauty of golden Aphrodite.
So Menelaus' kinsfolk and neighbors
Were feasting in the great hall. A bard
Was singing and playing the lyre,   20
And two tumblers whirled among the guests
And led them in the dancing.
                            Telemachus
And Nestor's son halted their horses
At the gate, and Eteoneus,
Menelaus' right-hand man, came out and saw them   25
And went through the hall to bring the news
To the shepherd of the people. He stood
At Menelaus' shoulder and his words flew fast:

"Two strangers have arrived, Lord Menelaus,
Two men in the line of Zeus by their looks.   *30*
Should we unyoke their horses, or should we
Send them elsewhere for hospitality?"

And red-haired Menelaus, greatly displeased:

"It's not like you to talk nonsense like this,
Eteoneus. How many times have you and I   *35*
Enjoyed the hospitality of others,
Hoping that Zeus would someday put an end
To our hard traveling? Unyoke their horses
And bring our new guests in to the feast."

He spoke, and Eteoneus hurried through the halls,   *40*
Calling other attendants to come along with him.
They unyoked the sweating horses and tied them
At the stalls, where they threw before them
A mixture of spelt and white barley. They leaned
The chariot against the gleaming entrance walls   *45*
And led the men into the palace. Their eyes
Went wide as they looked around the mansion
Of this sky-bred king, for a light as of the sun
Or the moon played over the high-roofed home
Of glorious Menelaus. When they had taken it all in,   *50*
They went into the polished tubs. When the maids
Had bathed them and rubbed them down with oil,
And clothed them in tunics and fleecy cloaks,
They sat down on chairs beside Menelaus.
A maid poured water from a golden pitcher   *55*
Into a silver basin for them to wash their hands
And then set up a polished table nearby.
Another serving woman, grave and dignified,
Set out bread and served generous helpings
From the other dishes she had; a carver set down   *60*
Cuts of meat by the platter and golden cups;
And a herald came by and poured them wine.
Then red-haired Menelaus said in greeting:

"Enjoy yourselves and eat. After supper

We will ask who you are—your bloodlines   *65*
Have not been lost in you. You belong
To the race of men who are sceptered kings,
Bred from Zeus. You're not just anybody."

And he set before them the prime cut of roast beef
That had been served to him as a mark of honor.   *70*
They helped themselves to the feast before them,
And when they had enough of food and drink,
Telemachus spoke to Nestor's son, holding
His head close so the others wouldn't hear:

"Do you see all this, Peisistratus, my friend,   *75*
These echoing halls flashing with bronze,
With gold, amber, silver, and ivory?
This must be what the court of Olympian Zeus
Looks like. This is unimaginable wealth!"

Menelaus, the red-haired king, overheard him,   *80*
And, speaking to both of them, had this to say:

"No mortal man could challenge Zeus, my boys.
His halls and possessions are everlasting.
My wealth may be matched by another man's
Or maybe not. For it is true I brought home   *85*
Shiploads after wandering for eight hard years.
Cyprus, Phoenicia, Egypt—I went all over,
Came to the Ethiopians, the Sidonians,
The Erembi, even to Libya,
Where the lambs have horns soon after they're born.   *90*
The ewes give birth three times a year there,
And neither shepherd nor lord ever runs short
Of cheese, meat or milk; the flocks are milked year round.
While I wandered through those lands amassing wealth
My brother was murdered, caught off guard   *95*
By treachery and the guile of his accursed wife.
So I do not enjoy being lord of this wealth.
You may have heard of all this from your fathers,
Whoever they may be, for I suffered greatly
And saw my house ruined, with all its treasures.   *100*

I would gladly live with a third of my wealth
And have those men back who perished in Troy
Far from the bluegrass pastures of Argos. And yet,
Though I weep for them often in my halls,
Easing my heart, I do not grieve constantly—   *105*
A man can get too much of chill grief.
I miss them all, but there is one man I miss
More than all the others. When I think of him
I don't want to sleep or eat, for no one
In the entire Greek army worked as hard   *110*
As Odysseus, and all he ever got for it
Was pain and sorrow, and I cannot forget
My sorrow for him. He has been gone so long,
And we do not know whether he is alive or dead.
Old Laertes must mourn for him, Penelope too,   *115*
And Telemachus, who was an infant when he left."

His words roused in Telemachus the desire
To weep for his father. Hot tears
Fell from his eyes when he heard his father's name,
And he pulled his purple cloak over his face.   *120*
Seeing this, Menelaus wondered
Whether he should allow Telemachus
To bring up his father himself, or whether
He should draw him out with pointed questions.

While Menelaus pondered this,   *125*
Helen came from her fragrant bedroom
Like gold-spindled Artemis. Adraste,
Her attendant, drew up a beautiful chair for her,
And Alcippe brought her a soft wool rug.
Another maid, Phylo, brought a silver basket—   *130*
A gift from Alcandre, wife of Polybus,
Who lived in Thebes, the city in Egypt
That has the wealthiest houses in the world.
Polybus had given Menelaus two silver baths,
Two tripods, and ten bars of gold.   *135*
And his wife, Alcandre, gave to Helen
Beautiful gifts of her own—a golden spindle
And a silver basket with gold-rimmed wheels.

This basket Phylo now placed beside her,
Filled with fine-spun yarn, and across it   *140*
Was laid the spindle, twirled with violet wool.
Helen sat upon the chair, a footstool
Under her feet, and questioned her husband:

"Do we know, Menelaus, who our guests
Claim to be? Shall I speak my mind or not?   *145*
My heart urges me to speak. I have never seen
Such a resemblance between any two people,
Man or woman, as between this man
And Odysseus' son—as I imagine him now—
Telemachus, who was a newborn baby   *150*
When for my sake, shameless thing that I was,
The Greeks came to Troy with war in their hearts."

And Menelaus, the red-haired king:

"Now that you mention it, I see
The resemblance myself—the feet, the hands,   *155*
The way he looks at you, that head of hair.
And just now when I was talking about Odysseus,
Saying how much he went through for my sake,
Tears welled up in his eyes, bitter tears,
And he covered his face with his purple cloak."   *160*

At this Nestor's son Peisistratus spoke up:

"Menelaus, son of Atreus, Zeus-bred king,
This is indeed, as you say, Odysseus' son.
But he is prudent and would not think it proper,
When he just got here, to make a big speech   *165*
Before you—whose voice delights us as a god's.
Nestor of Gerenia sent me with him as a guide,
For he was eager to see you, hoping that
You could suggest something he could do or say.
A son has many problems to face at home   *170*
When his father is gone and there is no one else
To help him. So it is now with Telemachus,
Whose father is gone, and there is no one else

Among the people to keep him from harm."

And Menelaus, the red-haired king: *175*

"What's this? Here in my house, the son
Of my dear friend who did so much for me!
I used to think that if he came back
I would give him a welcome no other Greek
Could ever hope to have—if Olympian Zeus   *180*
Had brought us both home from over the sea
In our swift ships. I would have given him
A city of his own in Argos, built him a house,
Brought him over from Ithaca with his goods,
His son and all of his people—a whole city   *185*
Cleared out just for him! We would have been together,
Enjoying each other's company, and nothing
Would have parted us until death's black cloud
Finally enfolded us. But I suppose Zeus himself
Begrudged us this, for Odysseus alone,   *190*
That unlucky man, was never brought home."

His words aroused in all of them
A longing for lamentation. Argive Helen,
A child of Zeus, wept; Telemachus wept;
And Menelaus wept, the son of Atreus.   *195*
Nor could Nestor's son keep his eyes dry,
For he remembered Antilochus,
His flawless brother, who had been killed
By Memnon, Dawn's resplendent son,
And this memory gave wings to his words: *200*

"Son of Atreus, old Nestor used to say,
Whenever we talked about things like this,
That no one could match your understanding.
So please understand me when I say
That I do not enjoy weeping after supper—   *205*
And it will be dawn before we know it.
Not that I think it's wrong to lament the dead.
This is all we can do—cut our hair
And shed some tears. I lost someone myself

At Troy, my brother, not the least hero there.   210
You probably knew him. I am too young
Ever to have seen him, but men say Antilochus
Could run and fight as well as any man alive."

And Menelaus, the red-haired king:

"No one could have put that better, my friend,   215
Not even someone much older. Your speech,
Wise and clear, shows the sort of father you have.
It's easy to spot a man for whom Zeus
Has spun out happiness in marriage and children,
As he has done for Nestor throughout his life.   220
And now he has reached a sleek old age in his halls,
And his sons are wise and fight with the best.
So we will stop this weeping, and once more
Think of supper. Let the servants pour water
Over our hands. Telemachus and I will have   225
Much to say to each other come morning."

So he spoke, and Asphalion,
Menelaus' attendant, poured water
Over their hands, and they reached out
For all the good cheer spread out before them.   230

But Helen, child of Zeus, had other ideas.
She threw a drug into the wine bowl
They were drinking from, a drug
That stilled all pain, quieted all anger
And brought forgetfulness of every ill.   235
Whoever drank wine laced with this drug
Would not be sad or shed a tear that day,
Not even if his own father and mother
Should lie there dead, or if someone killed
His brother, or son, before his eyes.   240
Helen had gotten this potent, cunning drug
From Polydamna, the wife of Thon,
A woman in Egypt, where the land
Proliferates with all sorts of drugs,
Many beneficial, many poisonous.   245

Men there know more about medicines
Than any other people on earth,
For they are of the race of Paeeon, the Healer.
When she had slipped the drug into the wine,
Helen ordered another round to be poured,   250
And then she turned to the company and said:

"Menelaus, son of Atreus in the line of Zeus,
And you sons of noble fathers, it is true
That Zeus gives easy lives to some of us
And hard lives to others—he can do anything, after all—   255
But you should sit now in the hall and feast
And entertain yourselves by telling stories.
I'll start you off. I couldn't begin to tell you
All that Odysseus endured and accomplished,
But listen to what that hero did once   260
In the land of Troy, where the Achaeans suffered.
First, he beat himself up—gave himself some nasty bruises—
Then put on a cheap cloak so he looked like a slave,
And in this disguise he entered the wide streets
Of the enemy city. He looked like a beggar,   265
Far from what he was back in the Greek camp,
And fooled everyone when he entered Troy.
I alone recognized him in his disguise
And questioned him, but he cleverly put me off.
It was only after I had bathed him   270
And rubbed him down with oil and clothed him
And had sworn a great oath not to tell the Trojans
Who he really was until he got back to the ships,
That he told me, at last, what the Achaeans planned.
He killed many Trojans before he left   275
And arrived back at camp with much to report.
The other women in Troy wailed aloud,
But I was glad inside, for my heart had turned
Homeward, and I rued the infatuation
Aphrodite gave me when she led me away   280
From my native land, leaving my dear child,
My bridal chamber, and my husband,
A man who lacked nothing in wisdom or looks."

And Menelaus, the red-haired king:

"A very good story, my wife, and well told.   *285*
By now I have come to know the minds
Of many heroes, and have traveled far and wide,
But I have never laid eyes on anyone
Who had an enduring heart like Odysseus.
Listen to what he did in the wooden horse,   *290*
Where all we Argive chiefs sat waiting
To bring slaughter and death to the Trojans.
You came there then, with godlike Deiphobus.
Some god who favored the Trojans
Must have lured you on. Three times you circled   *295*
Our hollow hiding place, feeling it
With your hands, and you called out the names
Of all Argive leaders, making your voice
Sound like each of our wives' in turn.
Diomedes and I, sitting in the middle   *300*
With Odysseus, heard you calling
And couldn't take it. We were frantic
To come out, or answer you from inside,
But Odysseus held us back and stopped us.
Then everyone else stayed quiet also,   *305*
Except for Anticlus, who wanted to answer you,
But Odysseus saved us all by clamping
His strong hands over Anticlus' mouth
And holding them there until Athena led you off."

Then Telemachus said in his clear-headed way: *310*

"Menelaus, son of Atreus in the line of Zeus,
It is all the more unbearable then, isn't it?
My father may have had a heart of iron,
But it didn't do him any good in the end.
Please send us to bed now. It is time   *315*
We rested and enjoyed some sweet sleep."

He spoke, and Helen of Argos told her maids
To place beds on the porch and spread upon them
Beautiful purple blankets and fleecy cloaks.

The maids went out of the hall with torches   320
And made up the beds, and a herald
Led the guests out to them. So they slept there
On the palace porch, the hero Telemachus
And Nestor's glorious son. But Menelaus slept
In the innermost chamber of that high house   325
Next to Helen, Zeus' brightness upon her.

Dawn brushed her pale rose fingers across the sky,
And Menelaus got out of bed and dressed.
He slung his sharp sword around his shoulder,
Tied oiled leather sandals onto his feet,   330
And walked out of the bedroom like a god.
Then he sat down next to Telemachus and said:

"Tell me, Telemachus, what has brought you here
To gleaming Sparta over the sea's broad back?
Public business or private? Tell me the truth."   335

Telemachus took a deep breath and said:

"Menelaus, son of Atreus in the line of Zeus,
I came to see if you could tell me anything
About my father. My land is in ruin.
I'm being eaten out of house and home   340
By hostile men who constantly throng my halls
Slaughtering my sheep and horned cattle
In their arrogant courtship of my mother.
And so I am at your knees. Tell me
How my father, Odysseus, met his end,   345
Whether you saw it with your own eyes,
Or heard about it from someone else,
Some wanderer. He was born to sorrow,
More than any man on earth. And do not,
Out of pity, spare me the truth, but tell me   350
Whatever you have seen, whatever you know.
I beseech you, if my father, noble Odysseus,
Ever fulfilled a promise he made to you
In the land of Troy, where the Achaeans suffered,
Remember it now, and tell me the truth."   355

And Menelaus, deeply troubled by this:

"Those dogs! Those puny weaklings,
Wanting to sleep in the bed of a hero!
A doe might as well bed her suckling fawns
In the lair of a lion, leaving them there   360
In the bush and then going off over the hills
Looking for grassy fields. When the lion
Comes back, the fawns die an ugly death.
That's the kind of death these men will die
When Odysseus comes back. O Father Zeus,   365
And Athena and Apollo, bring Odysseus back
With the strength he showed in Lesbos once
When he wrestled a match with Philomeleides
And threw him hard, making all of us cheer—
That's the Odysseus I want the suitors to meet!   370
They'd get married all right—to bitter death.
But, as to what you ask me about,
I will not stray from the point or deceive you.
No, I will tell you all that the infallible
Old Man of the Sea told me, and hide nothing.   375
          I was in Egypt, held up by the gods
Because I failed to offer them sacrifice.
The gods never allow us to forget them.
There is an island in the whitecapped sea
Just north of Egypt. Men call it Pharos,   380
And it lies one hard day's sailing offshore.
There is a good harbor there where ships
Take on fresh water before heading out to sea.
The gods kept me stuck in that harbor
For twenty days. A good sailing breeze   385
Never rose up, and all my supplies
Would have been exhausted, and my crew spent,
Had not one of the gods taken pity on me
And saved me. This was Eidothea,
Daughter of Proteus, the Old Man of the Sea.   390
Somehow I had moved her heart. She met me
As I wandered alone, apart from my crew,
Who roamed the island continually, fishing
With bent hooks, their bellies cramped with hunger.

She came close to me and spoke: *395*

'Are you completely out of your mind, stranger,
Or do you actually like suffering like this?
You've been marooned on this island a long time
With no end in sight, and your crew's fading fast.'

"She spoke like this, and I answered her: *400*

'I tell you, goddess—whichever goddess you are—
That I am not stranded here of my own free will.
I must have offended one of the immortals.
But you tell me—for gods know everything—
Which of the immortals is pinning me down here   *405*
And won't let me go. And tell me how
I can sail back home over the teeming sea.'

"And the shining goddess answered me:

'Well, all right, stranger, since you ask.
This is the haunt of an unerring immortal,   *410*
Egyptian Proteus, the Old Man of the Sea,
Who serves Poseidon and knows all the deeps.
They say he's my father. If you can
Somehow catch him in ambush here,
He will tell you the route, and the distance too,   *415*
Of your journey home over the teeming sea.
And he will tell you, prince, if you so wish,
What has been done in your house for better or worse
While you have been gone on your long campaign.'

"So she spoke, and I answered her: *420*

'Show me yourself how to ambush
The old god, or he may give me the slip.
It's hard for a mortal to master a god.'

"And the shining goddess answered me:

'I'll tell you exactly what you need to know.   *425*

When the sun is at high noon, the unerring
Old Man of the Sea comes from the salt water,
Hidden in dark ripples the West Wind stirs up,
And then lies down to sleep in the scalloped caves.
All around him seals, the brine-spirit's brood,   430
Sleep in a herd. They come out of the grey water
With breath as fetid as the depths of the sea.
I will lead you there at break of day
And lay you in a row, you and three comrades
Chosen by you as the best on your ship.   435
Now I'll tell you all the old man's wiles.
First, he will go over the seals and count them,
And when he has counted them off by fives,
He will lie down like a shepherd among them.
As soon as you see him lying down to rest,   440
Screw up your courage to the sticking point
And pin him down, no matter how he struggles
And tries to escape. He will try everything,
And turn into everything that moves on the earth,
And into water also, and a burning flame.   445
Just hang on and grip him all the more tightly.
When he finally speaks to you of his own free will
In the shape you saw him in when he lay down to rest,
Then ease off, hero, and let the old man go,
And ask him which of the gods is angry with you,   450
And how you can sail home over the teeming sea.'

"And with that she slipped into the surging sea.
I headed for my ships where they stood on the sand
And brooded on many things as I went.
When I had come down to the ships and the sea,   455
We made supper, and when night came on,
We lay down to take our rest on the beach.
When dawn came, a palmetto of rose,
I went along the shore of the open sea
Praying over and over to the immortal gods,   460
Taking with me the three of my crew
I trusted the most for any adventure.

"The goddess, meanwhile, dove underwater

And now came back with the skins of four seals,
All newly flayed. She was out to trick her father.   *465*
She scooped out hiding places for us in the sand
And sat waiting as we cautiously drew near.
Then she had us lie down in a row, and threw
A seal skin over each of us. It would have been
A gruesome ambush—the stench of the seals   *470*
Was unbearable—but the goddess saved us
By putting ambrosia under each man's nose,
Drowning out the stench with its immortal fragrance.
So we waited patiently all morning long,
And then the seals came from the water in throngs.   *475*
They lay down in rows along the seashore,
And at noon the Old One came from the sea.
He found the fat seals and went over the herd,
Counting them up. He counted us first,
Never suspecting any kind of trick,   *480*
And then he lay down. We rushed him
With a shout and got our hands on him,
And the Old One didn't forget his wiles,
Turning first into a bearded lion,
Then a serpent, a leopard, and a huge boar.   *485*
He even turned into flowing water,
And into a high, leafy tree. But we
Held on, gritting our teeth, and at last
The wily Old One grew weary, and said to me:

'Which god have you plotted with, son of Atreus,   *490*
To catch me off-guard? What do you want?'

"He spoke, and I answered him:

'You know, old man—don't try to put me off—
How long I have been stuck on this island
With no end in sight. I'm losing heart.   *495*
Just tell me this—you gods know everything—
Which of the immortals has marooned me here?
How can I sail home over the teeming sea?'

"When I said this, he answered:

'You should have offered noble sacrifice to Zeus   *500*
And the other gods before embarking
If you wanted a speedy journey home
Over the deep purple sea. It is not your fate
To come home to your friends and native land
Until you go once more to the waters of the Aegyptus,   *505*
The sky-fed river, and offer holy hecatombs
To the immortal gods who hold high heaven.
Only then will they grant the journey you desire.'

"When he said this my spirit was crushed.
It was a long, hard pull over the misty deep   *510*
Back to the Aegyptus. Still, I answered:

'I will do all these things, just as you say.
But tell me this, and tell me the truth:
Did all the Achaeans make it home in their ships,
All those whom Nestor and I left at Troy?   *515*
Or did any die on shipboard, or in their friends' arms,
After winding up the war?'

            "To which Proteus said:

'Why, son of Atreus, ask me about this?
You don't need to know. Nor do I think
You will be free from tears once you have heard it.   *520*
Many were killed in the war. You were there
And know who they were. Many, too, survived.
On the homeward journey two heroes died.
Another still lives, perhaps, held back by the sea.

'Ajax went down among his long-oared ships.   *525*
Poseidon had driven him onto Gyrae's rocks
But saved him from the sea. He would have escaped,
Despite Athena's hatred, but he lost his wits
And boasted loudly that he had survived the deep
In spite of the gods. Poseidon heard this boast,   *530*
And with his trident he struck Gyrae's rock
And broke it asunder. One part held firm,
But the other part, upon which Ajax sat

In his blind arrogance, fell into the gulf
And took Ajax with it. And so he perished,   *535*
His lungs full of salt water.
                        Your brother, though,
Outran the fates in his hollow ships,
With the help of Hera. But when he was nearing
Malea's heights, a stormwind caught him
And carried him groaning over the teeming sea   *540*
To the frontier of the land where Thyestes once lived
And after him Thyestes' son, Aegisthus.
Then the gods gave him a following wind
And safe passage homeward. Agamemnon
Rejoiced to set foot on his ancestral land.   *545*
He fell to the ground and kissed the good earth
And hot tears of joy streamed from his eyes,
So glad was he to see his homeland again.
But from a high lookout a watchman saw him.
Aegisthus had treacherously posted him there   *550*
And promised a reward of two bars of gold.
He had been keeping watch for a year by then
So that Agamemnon would not slip by unseen
And unleash his might, and now he reported
His news to Aegisthus, who acted quickly   *555*
And set a trap. He chose his twenty best men
And had them wait in ambush. Opposite them,
On the hall's farther side, he had a feast prepared,
And then he drove off in his chariot,
Brooding darkly, to invite Agamemnon.   *560*
So he brought Agamemnon up to the palace
Unaware of his doom and slaughtered him
The way an ox is slaughtered at the stall.
None of Agamemnon's men was left alive,
Nor any of Aegisthus'. All were slain in the hall.'   *565*

"Proteus spoke, and my heart was shattered.
I wept and wept as I sat on the sand, losing
All desire to live and see the light of the sun.
When I could not weep or flail about any more,
The unerring Old Man of the Sea addressed me: *570*

'Weep no more, son of Atreus. We gain nothing
By such prolonged bouts of grief. Instead,
Go as quickly as you can to your native land.
Either Aegisthus will still be alive, or
Orestes may have beat you to it and killed him,   575
And you may happen to arrive during his funeral.'

"These words warmed my heart, although
I was still in shock. Then I asked him:

'I know now what became of these two,
But who is the third man, the one who's alive,   580
But held back by the sea, or perhaps is dead.
I want to hear about him, despite my grief.'

"Proteus answered me without hesitation:

'It is Laertes' son, whose home is in Ithaca.
I saw him on an island, shedding salt tears,   585
In the halls of Calypso, who keeps him there
Against his will. He has no way to get home
To his native land. He has no ships left,
No crew to row him over the sea's broad back.
As for you, Menelaus, Zeus' cherished king,   590
You are not destined to die and to meet your fate
In bluegrass Argos. The immortals will take you
To the ends of the earth and the Elysian Fields,
Where Rhadamanthus lives and life is easiest.
No snow, nor storm, nor heavy rain comes there,   595
But a sighing wind from the West always blows
Off the Ocean, a cooling breeze for men.
For Helen is your wife, and in the gods' eyes
You are the son-in-law of great Zeus himself.'

"And with that he dove into the surging sea.   600
I went back to the ships with my godlike companions
And brooded on many things as I went.
When we had come down to the ships and the sea,
And had made supper, immortal night came on,
And we lay down to take our rest on the beach.   605

When dawn came with palmettoes of rose,
We hauled our ships down to the shining water,
And set up the masts and sails in the hulls.
The crews came aboard, and sitting in rows
They beat the sea white with their churning oars.   610
And so I sailed back to the rain-fed Aegyptus,
Moored my ships, and offered perfect sacrifice.
When I had appeased the everlasting gods
I heaped up a barrow for Agamemnon
So that his memory would not fade. Only then   615
Did I set sail for home, and the gods gave me
A following wind that brought me back swiftly.
          Well, now, I want you to stay in my halls
Until eleven or twelve days have passed,
And then I will give you a royal send-off   620
And these splendid gifts: three horses
And a polished chariot, and a beautiful cup,
So that you can pour libations to the deathless gods
And remember me all the days of your life."

Telemachus answered in his clear-headed way: 625

"Son of Atreus, do not keep me here long.
I could spend a year in your house
And never miss my home or my parents.
That's how much I enjoy listening to you
And hearing your tales. But even now   630
My crew is getting restless back in Pylos
And you are keeping me long here.
                              As for gifts,
Give me whatever treasure you will,
But I will not take horses to Ithaca.
They are better off here for you to enjoy,   635
For you rule a wide plain, with lotus
Everywhere, and galingale, and wheat and spelt,
And heavy ears of white barley. But Ithaca
Has no broad horse-runs or meadowlands at all.
Its pasture is for goats, and more lovely   640
Than horse pasture. None of the islands
That slope to the sea has rich meadows, or is good

For driving horses, and Ithaca least of all."

And Menelaus, who could make his voice
Carry in battle, said to Telemachus: 645

"You are of good blood, my boy, to talk like that!
All right, I will change my gifts, as I easily can.
Of all the gifts that lie stored in my house
I will give you the most beautiful—
And the most valuable—a well-wrought bowl,   650
Solid silver, with the lip finished in gold,
The work of Hephaestus. The hero Phaedimus,
King of the Sidonians, gave it to me
When I stayed at his house on my way home.
Now I want you to take it home with you."   655

And while they talked to each other,
The banqueters came to their lord's palace,
Driving sheep with them and bringing wine,
And bread that their veiled wives had sent with them.
And so they were busy with the feast in Menelaus' halls.   660

Meanwhile, back in Ithaca,
The suitors were entertaining themselves
In front of Odysseus' palace again,
Throwing the javelin and discus
On the level terrace, arrogant as ever.   665
Antinous and Eurymachus, who were
Their natural leaders, were sitting there,
And Noemon, son of Phronius,
Came up to them and asked Antinous:

"Antinous, do we have any idea   670
When Telemachus will return from Pylos?
He's gone off with a ship of mine,
And I need her to cross over to Elis,
Where I have twelve brood mares
And ten mules still at the teat. I would like   675
To drive one of them off and break him in."

When he said this, Antinous and Eurymachus
Just looked at each other. They had no idea
Telemachus had gone to Neleian Pylos.
They thought he was somewhere out in the field   680
With the sheep flocks, or off with the swineherd.
Antinous questioned Noemon closely:

"Tell me exactly when Telemachus left
And who went with him, a hand-picked crew
From the island, or his own fieldhands and slaves?   685
He could have done it either way. And tell me this,
So I'll have it right. Did he force you to give him
The ship, or were you just doing him a favor?"

And Noemon answered him:

"I gave it freely. What else could I do,   690
When a man like that, with all his troubles,
Asks me? It would be hard to refuse him.
Those who went with him are the best in town,
After ourselves, and when they boarded
I noticed Mentor going on board, too,   695
As their leader, either Mentor or a god
Who looked just like him. I wonder about this,
Because I saw Mentor here yesterday morning,
After he had set sail for sandy Pylos."

With that, Noemon left for his father's house.   700
Antinous and Eurymachus were furious.
They made the suitors stop their games
And had them sit down. Antinous
Addressed them. His black heart was seething
With anger, and his eyes burned like fire: 705

"Unbelievable! Telemachus has some nerve,
Pulling off this voyage. We never thought
We'd see it happen, and the boy is up and gone,
Just like that, with all of us against it,
Launching a ship and picking the best crew around.   710
He's going to start giving us trouble soon.

May Zeus cripple him before he reaches manhood!
All right, now, give me a ship and twenty men
So I can lie in ambush and watch for him
As he comes through the strait between Ithaca   715
And rocky Samos. He'll be sorry
He ever made this voyage in search of his father."

They all praised his speech and urged him on.
Then they stood up and went to Odysseus' palace.

It did not take Penelope long to find out   720
The suitors' dark intentions. The herald,
Medon, was the one who brought her word.
He had overheard the suitors talking
As he stood outside the courtyard
Where they were weaving their plots, and now   725
He went through the hall to tell Penelope.
As he crossed the threshold, she asked him:

"Medon, why have the suitors sent you here?
To tell the handmaids of divine Odysseus
To drop everything and prepare a feast for them?   730
May this be their last courtship, their last party,
Oh, may this latest feast be their last of all!
Do you hear me, you thronging leeches
Who are eating away Telemachus' property?
You surely weren't listening to your fathers   735
When you were children, or you would have heard
What kind of man Odysseus was to them,
How he never wronged anyone in word or deed,
How he was fair to everyone, unlike
Most sceptered kings, who all have their favorites.   740
He never lost his temper with any man at all.
But your vile deeds and hearts are plain to see,
And there is no gratitude for kindness past."

Then Medon, the tactful herald:

"If only this were the greatest evil, Lady,   745
But there is a greater and more grievous.

The suitors are planning—and may Zeus
Never bring their plans to pass—to kill Telemachus
On his way back home. He went to sandy Pylos
And gleaming Lacedaemon for news of his father."   750

When Medon said these things, Penelope felt
That her heart had been unstrung. Her eyes
Filled with tears, and she was unable to speak
For a long time. Finally she said to the herald:

"Medon, why is my son gone? There was no need   755
For him to board any sea-going ships,
Which men use to cross the wide water
As they use horses on land. Why did he go?
So that not even his name would be left among men?"

And Medon, the tactful herald: 760

"I do not know whether a god urged him on,
Or his own heart moved him to go to Pylos
To learn either of his father's return
Or of the manner in which he met his fate."

So saying, Medon went into Odysseus' house.   765
Pain washed over Penelope and seeped
Into her bones. She could not bring herself
To sit down in one of the many chairs
That were there in the house, but sat curled
On the worn threshold of her bedroom   770
And wept. Around her the women of the house
Moaned softly, the old and the young,
And Penelope spoke to them through her tears:

"Hear me, my friends, for the god on Olympus
Has given me pain beyond all other women   775
Of my generation. I have lost a fine husband
With a heart like a lion, the glory of the Danaans,
The pride of all Hellas, a man of many virtues.
And now the winds have ripped my beloved son
From my house. I never even heard him leave.   780

You were cruel, each of you, not to think
Of getting me from bed, for you must have known
He was going aboard that hollow black ship.
If I had known he was setting out on this journey,
He would have stayed here, despite his willfulness,　　　785
Or else he would have left me dead in our halls.
Quick now, someone go get old Dolios,
The servant whom my father gave me
Before I left home and who now tends my orchards.
He should sit with Laertes and tell him all this.　　　790
Laertes may be able to weave some plan
And complain to the people about these men
Who want to destroy his and Odysseus' line."

And her beloved nurse, Eurycleia, said:

"Child, you can spare me or stab me　　　795
With a sword, but I will not hide what I know.
I was in on all this. I got his provisions,
Bread and sweet wine. He made me swear
Not to tell you until twelve days had passed
Or until you missed him yourself or heard　　　800
He had gone. He didn't want you crying.
Now take a bath and put on some clean clothes.
Then go upstairs with the serving women
And pray to Athena, daughter of Zeus.
No matter what, she can save your son from death.　　　805
But do not trouble the old man. He has
Troubles enough. Yet I do not think
The line of Laertes, son of Arcesius,
Is entirely hated by the blessed gods.
There may still be someone in that line to own　　　810
This high hall and all the rich fields around."

So the old nurse soothed Penelope's grief
And kept her eyes dry. Penelope bathed
And put on clean clothes. Then she went upstairs
With the serving women, put barley for strewing　　　815
In a basket, and prayed to Athena:

"Hear me, Mystic Daughter of Zeus.
If ever in these halls my cunning Odysseus
Burned fat thighbones of bulls or sheep for you,
Remember it now and save my beloved son.   820
Protect him from the arrogant suitors' violence."

Penelope voiced this prayer, and Athena heard it,
While down in the shadowy halls below
These same suitors were talking noisily,
Making crude comments such as these: 825

"So while the lady upstairs gets ready to marry
One of her suitors, she has no idea
That her suitors are arranging to murder her son!"

But they had no idea of what was being arranged.
Antinous had some words for all of them: 830

"Are you crazy? Stow that kind of talk,
Or someone may report it to those inside.
We're going to do what we said we would
Under cover of silence. We're all in this together."

And he picked out the twenty best men there.   835
They went down to the shore of the sea
And hauled a fast ship out onto the water.
They set up mast and sail in that black ship
And fit the oars into the leather thole-straps,
All in due order. Then they unfurled the white sails. 840
Their attendants brought all their gear aboard,
And they moored the ship where she would catch
The evening breeze. Then they disembarked,
Ate their dinner, and waited for twilight.

Penelope lay in her room upstairs.   845
She would not touch any food or drink
But only lay there worrying about her son,
Wondering whether he would escape from death
Or be killed by the insolent suitors.

> *Surrounded by men, a lion broods and then panics*   *850*
> *When they begin to tighten their crafty ring.*

So too Penelope, until sleep drifted over her,
And she sank back with all her body relaxed.

Athena's eyes were flashing in the dark.
She made a phantom in the form of a woman,   *855*
Iphthime, daughter of great Icarius,
Now wed to Eumelus, whose home was in Pherae.
She sent the phantom into Odysseus' house
To stop Penelope's weeping and sobbing.
It drifted into her room through the keyhole   *860*
And stood above her head, and spoke to her:

"Asleep, Penelope, and broken-hearted?
The blessed gods are unwilling that you
Should weep and be sad, for your son will return.
He has not offended the gods at all."   *865*

And Penelope, slumbering sweetly
At the gate of dreams, answered her:

"Why have you come here, sister? You live
Far away and have seldom come before.
You tell me to stop grieving, tell me to rest   *870*
From the sorrows that plague my mind and heart.
Long ago now I lost my fine husband,
A lion-hearted man, the glory of the Danaans,
The pride of Hellas, a man of many virtues.
And now my beloved son has gone away   *875*
In a hollow ship, a mere child, who knows nothing
Of the world of men. I grieve for him even more
Than for my husband. I am trembling with fear
That he will get hurt, either among the people
He has gone off to visit, or on the open sea.   *880*
For his many enemies are plotting against him
And mean to kill him before he gets home."

The glimmering phantom answered her:

"Take heart, and don't be so afraid. The guide
Who goes with him is one many men pray for   *885*
To stand at their side, a powerful ally—
Pallas Athena. And she pities you in your grief,
For it is she who sent me to tell you this."

And Penelope, in her circumspect way:

"If you are truly a god and have heard a god's voice,   *890*
Tell me also of that man of many sorrows,
Whether he still lives and sees the light of the sun,
Or whether he is dead and in Hades' dark world."

The glimmering phantom answered her:

"No, I will not speak of him, whether he be   *895*
Alive or dead. Empty words are ill spoken."

And the phantom slipped through the keyhole
And became a sigh in the air. Penelope
Started up from sleep, and her heart was warmed
By the clear dream that had come in the soft black night.   *900*

By now the suitors had embarked and set sail,
Their hearts set on murdering Telemachus.
There is a rockly island out in the sea,
Midway between Ithaca and rugged Samos.
Asteris is its name, not very big,   *905*
But it has a harbor with outlets on either side
Where a ship can lie. There the suitors waited.

ODYSSEY 5

Dawn reluctantly
Left Tithonus in her rose-shadowed bed,
Then shook the morning into flakes of fire.

Light flooded the halls of Olympus
Where Zeus, high Lord of Thunder,   5
Sat with the other gods, listening to Athena
Reel off the tale of Odysseus' woes.
It galled her that he was still in Calypso's cave:

"Zeus, my father—and all you blessed immortals—
Kings might as well no longer be gentle and kind   10
Or understand the correct order of things.
They might as well be tryannical butchers
For all that any of Odysseus' people
Remember him, a godly king as kind as a father.
No, he's still languishing on that island, detained   15
Against his will by that nymph Calypso,
No way in the world for him to get back to his land.
His ships are all lost, he has no crew left
To row him across the sea's crawling back.
And now the islanders are plotting to kill his son   20
As he heads back home. He went for news of his father
To sandy Pylos and white-bricked Sparta."

Storm Cloud Zeus had an answer for her:

"Quite a little speech you've let slip through your teeth,
Daughter. But wasn't this exactly your plan   25

So that Odysseus would make them pay for it later?
You know how to get Telemachus
Back to Ithaca and out of harm's way
With his mother's suitors sailing in a step behind."

Zeus turned then to his son Hermes and said: 30

"Hermes, you've been our messenger before.
Go tell that ringleted nymph it is my will
To let that patient man Odysseus go home.
Not with an escort, mind you, human or divine,
But on a rickety raft—tribulation at sea—   35
Until on the twentieth day he comes to Schería
In the land of the Phaeacians, our distant relatives,
Who will treat Odysseus as if he were a god
And take him on a ship to his own native land
With gifts of bronze and clothing and gold,   40
More than he ever would have taken back from Troy
Had he come home safely with his share of the loot.
That's how he's destined to see his dear ones again
And return to his high-gabled Ithacan home."

Thus Zeus, and the quicksilver messenger   45
Laced on his feet the beautiful sandals,
Golden, immortal, that carry him over
Landscape and seascape on a puff of wind.
And he picked up the wand he uses to charm
Mortal eyes to sleep and make sleepers awake.   50

Holding this wand the tough quicksilver god
Took off, bounded onto Pieria
And dove through the ether down to the sea,

> *Skimming the waves like a cormorant,*
> *The bird that patrols the saltwater billows*   55
> *Hunting for fish, seaspume on its plumage,*

Hermes flying low and planing the whitecaps.

When he finally arrived at the distant island

He stepped from the violet-tinctured sea
On to dry land and proceeded to the cavern   *60*
Where Calypso lived. She was at home.
A fire blazed on the hearth, and the smell
Of split cedar and arbor vitae burning
Spread like incense across the whole island.
She was seated inside, singing in a lovely voice   *65*
As she wove at her loom with a golden shuttle.
Around her cave the woodland was in bloom,
Alder and poplar and fragrant cypress.
Long-winged birds nested in the leaves,
Horned owls and larks and slender-throated shorebirds   *70*
That screech like crows over the bright saltwater.
Tendrils of ivy curled around the cave's mouth,
The glossy green vine clustered with berries.
Four separate springs flowed with clear water, criss-
Crossing channels as they meandered through meadows   *75*
Lush with parsley and blossoming violets.
It was enough to make even a visiting god
Enraptured at the sight. Quicksilver Hermes
Took it all in, then turned and entered
The vast cave.
        Calypso knew him at sight.   *80*
The immortals have ways of recognizing each other,
Even those whose homes are in outlying districts.
But Hermes didn't find the great hero inside.
Odysseus was sitting on the shore,
As ever those days, honing his heart's sorrow,   *85*
Staring out to sea with hollow, salt-rimmed eyes.

Calypso, sleek and haloed, questioned Hermes
Politely, as she seated him on a lacquered chair:

"My dear Hermes, to what do I owe
The honor of this unexpected visit? Tell me   *90*
What you want, and I'll oblige you if I can."

The goddess spoke, and then set a table
With ambrosia and mixed a bowl of rosy nectar.
The quicksilver messenger ate and drank his fill,

Then settled back from dinner with heart content   *95*
And made the speech she was waiting for:

"You ask me, goddess to god, why I have come.
Well, I'll tell you exactly why. Remember, you asked.
Zeus ordered me to come here; I didn't want to.
Who would want to cross this endless stretch   *100*
Of deserted sea? Not a single city in sight
Where you can get a decent sacrifice from men.
But you know how it is: Zeus has the aegis,
And none of us gods can oppose his will.
He says you have here the most woebegone hero   *105*
Of the whole lot who fought around Priam's city
For nine years, sacked it in the tenth, and started home.
But on the way back they offended Athena,
And she swamped them with hurricane winds and waves.
His entire crew was wiped out, and he   *110*
Drifted along until he was washed up here.
Anyway, Zeus wants you to send him back home. Now.
The man's not fated to rot here far from his friends.
It's his destiny to see his dear ones again
And return to his high-gabled Ithacan home."   *115*

He finished, and the nymph's aura stiffened.
Words flew from her mouth like screaming hawks:

"You gods are the most jealous bastards in the universe—
Persecuting any goddess who ever openly takes
A mortal lover to her bed and sleeps with him.   *120*
When Dawn caressed Orion with her rosy fingers,
You celestial layabouts gave her nothing but trouble
Until Artemis finally shot him on Ortygia—
Gold-throned, holy, gentle-shafted assault goddess!
When Demeter followed her heart and unbound   *125*
Her hair for Iasion and made love to him
In a late-summer field, Zeus was there taking notes
And executed the man with a cobalt lightning blast.
And now you gods are after me for having a man.
Well, I was the one who saved his life, unprying him   *130*
From the spar he came floating here on, sole survivor

Of the wreck Zeus made of his streamlined ship,
Slivering it with lightning on the wine-dark sea.
I loved him, I took care of him, I even told him
I'd make him immortal and ageless all of his days. 135
But you said it, Hermes: Zeus has the aegis
And none of us gods can oppose his will.
So all right, he can go, if it's an order from above,
Off on the sterile sea. How I don't know.
I don't have any oared ships or crewmen 140
To row him across the sea's broad back.
But I'll help him. I'll do everything I can
To get him back safely to his own native land."

The quicksilver messenger had one last thing to say:

"Well send him off now and watch out for Zeus' temper. 145
Cross him and he'll really be rough on you later."

With that the tough quicksilver god made his exit.

Calypso composed herself and went to Odysseus,
Zeus' message still ringing in her ears.
She found him sitting where the breakers rolled in. 150
His eyes were perpetually wet with tears now,
His life draining away in homesickness.
The nymph had long since ceased to please.
He still slept with her at night in her cavern,
An unwilling lover mated to her eager embrace. 155
Days he spent sitting on the rocks by the breakers,
Staring out to sea with hollow, salt-rimmed eyes.
She stood close to him and started to speak:

"You poor man. You can stop grieving now
And pining away. I'm sending you home. 160
Look, here's a bronze axe. Cut some long timbers
And make yourself a raft fitted with topdecks,
Something that will get you across the sea's misty spaces.
I'll stock it with fresh water, food and red wine—
Hearty provisions that will stave off hunger—and 165
I'll clothe you well and send you a following wind

To bring you home safely to your own native land,
If such is the will of the gods of high heaven,
Whose minds and powers are stronger than mine."

Odysseus' eyes shone with weariness. He stiffened,   170
And shot back at her words fletched like arrows:

"I don't know what kind of send-off you have in mind,
Goddess, telling me to cross all that open sea on a raft,
Painful, hard sailing. Some well-rigged vessels
Never make it across with a stiff wind from Zeus.   175
You're not going to catch me setting foot on any raft
Unless you agree to swear a solemn oath
That you're not planning some new trouble for me."

Calypso's smile was like a shower of light.
She touched him gently, and teased him a little: 180

"Blasphemous, that's what you are—but nobody's fool!
How do you manage to say things like that?
All right. I swear by Earth and Heaven above
And the subterranean water of Styx—the greatest
Oath and the most awesome a god can swear—   185
That I'm not planning more trouble for you, Odysseus.
I'll put my mind to work for you as hard as I would
For myself, if ever I were in such a fix.
My heart is in the right place, Odysseus,
Nor is it a cold lump of iron in my breast."   190

With that the haloed goddess walked briskly away
And the man followed in the deity's footsteps.
The two forms, human and divine, came to the cave
And he sat down in the chair which moments before
Hermes had vacated, and the nymph set out for him   195
Food and drink such as mortal men eat.
She took a seat opposite godlike Odysseus
And her maids served her ambrosia and nectar.
They helped themselves to as much as they wanted,
And when they had their fill of food and drink   200
Calypso spoke, an immortal radiance upon her:

"Son of Laertes in the line of Zeus, my wily Odysseus,
Do you really want to go home to your beloved country
Right away? Now? Well, you still have my blessings.
But if you had any idea of all the pain   205
You're destined to suffer before getting home,
You'd stay here with me, deathless—
Think of it, Odysseus!—no matter how much
You missed your wife and wanted to see her again.
You spend all your daylight hours yearning for her.   210
I don't mind saying she's not my equal
In beauty, no matter how you measure it.
Mortal beauty cannot compare with immortal."

Odysseus, always thinking, answered her this way:

"Goddess and mistress, don't be angry with me.   215
I know very well that Penelope,
For all her virtues, would pale beside you.
She's only human, and you are a goddess,
Eternally young. Still, I want to go back.
My heart aches for the day I return to my home.   220
If some god hits me hard as I sail the deep purple,
I'll weather it like the sea-bitten veteran I am.
God knows I've suffered and had my share of sorrows
In war and at sea. I can take more if I have to."

The sun set on his words, and the shadows darkened.   225
They went to a room deep in the cave, where they made
Sweet love and lay side by side through the night.

Dawn came early, touching the sky with rose.

Odysseus put on a shirt and cloak,
And the nymph slipped on a long silver robe   230
Shimmering in the light, cinched it at the waist
With a golden belt and put a veil on her head.
What to do about sending Odysseus off?
She handed him an axe, bronze, both edges honed.
The olive-wood haft felt good in his palms.   235

She gave him a sharp adze, too, then led the way
To the island's far side where the trees grew tall,
Alder and poplar and silver fir, sky-topping trees
Long-seasoned and dry that would keep him afloat.
Calypso showed him where the trees grew tall   240
Then went back home, a glimmer in the woods,
While Odysseus cut timber.
                              Working fast,
He felled twenty trees, cut them to length,
Smoothed them skillfully and trued them to the line.
The glimmer returned—Calypso with an auger—   245
And he drilled the beams through, fit them up close
And hammered them together with joiners and pegs.
About the size of a deck a master shipwright
Chisels into shape for a broad-bowed freighter
Was the size Odysseus made his wide raft.   250
He fit upright ribs close-set in the decking
And finished them with long facing planks.
He built a mast and fit in a yardarm,
And he made a rudder to steer her by.
Then he wove a wicker-work barrier   255
To keep off the waves, plaiting it thick.
Calypso brought him a large piece of cloth
To make into a sail, and he fashioned that, too.
He rigged up braces and halyards and lines,
Then levered his craft down to the glittering sea.   260

Day four, and the job was finished.
Day five, and Calypso saw him off her island,
After she had bathed him and dressed him
In fragrant clothes. She filled up a skin
With wine that ran black, another large one   265
With water, and tucked into a duffel
A generous supply of hearty provisions.
And she put a breeze at his back, gentle and warm.

Odysseus' heart sang as he spread sail to the wind,
And he steered with the rudder, a master mariner   270
Aboard his craft. Sleep never fell on his eyelids
As he watched the Pleiades and slow-setting Boötes

And the Bear (also known as the Wagon)
That pivots in place and chases Orion
And alone is aloof from the wash of Ocean.   *275*
Calypso, the glimmering goddess, had told him
To sail with the stars of the Bear on his left.
Seventeen days he sailed the deep water,
And on the eighteenth day the shadowy mountains
Of the Phaeacians' land loomed on the horizon,   *280*
To his eyes like a shield on the misty sea.

And Poseidon saw him.
                         From the far Solymi Mountains
The Lord of Earthquake, returning from Aethiopia,
Saw him, an image in his mind bobbing on the sea.
Angrier than ever, he shook his head   *285*
And cursed to himself:

                    "Damn it all, the gods
Must have changed their minds about Odysseus
While I was away with the Aethiopians.
He's close to Phaeacia, where he's destined to escape
The great ring of sorrow that has closed around him.   *290*
But I'll bet I can still blow some trouble his way."

He gathered the clouds, and gripping his trident
He stirred the sea. And he raised all the blasts
Of every wind in the world and covered with clouds
Land and sea together. Night rose in the sky.   *295*
The winds blew hard from every direction,
And lightning-charged Boreas rolled in a big wave.
Odysseus felt his knees and heart weaken.
Hunched over, he spoke to his own great soul:

"Now I'm in for it.   *300*
I'm afraid that Calypso was right on target
When she said I would have my fill of sorrow
On the open sea before I ever got home.
It's all coming true. Look at these clouds
Zeus is piling like flowers around the sky's rim,   *305*
And he's roughened the sea, and every wind

In the world is howling around me.
Three times, four times luckier than I
Were the Greeks who died on Troy's wide plain!
If only I had gone down on that day   310
When the air was whistling with Trojan spears
In the desperate fight for Achilles' dead body.
I would have had burial then, honored by the army.
As it is I am doomed to a wretched death at sea."

His words weren't out before a huge cresting wave   315
Crashed on his raft and shivered its timbers.
He was pitched clear of the deck. The rudder flew
From his hands, the mast cracked in two
Under the force of the hurricane winds,
And the yardarm and sail hove into the sea.   320
He was under a long time, unable to surface
From the heaving swell of the monstrous wave,
Weighed down by the clothes Calypso had given him.
At last he came up, spitting out saltwater,
Seabrine gurgling from his nostrils and mouth.   325
For all his distress, though, he remembered his raft,
Lunged through the waves, caught hold of it
And huddled down in its center shrinking from death.

An enormous wave rode the raft into cross-currents.

> *The North Wind in autumn sweeps through a field*   330
> *Rippling with thistles and swirls them around.*

So the winds swirled the raft all over the sea,
South Wind colliding at times with the North,
East Wind shearing away from the West.

And the White Goddess saw him, Cadmus' daughter   335
Ino, once a human girl with slim, beautiful ankles
Who had won divine honors in the saltwater gulfs.
She pitied Odysseus his wandering, his pain,
And rose from the water like a flashing gull,
Perched on his raft, and said this to him: 340

"Poor man. Why are you so odious to Poseidon,
Odysseus, that he sows all this grief for you?
But he'll not destroy you, for all of his fury.
Now do as I say—you're in no way to refuse:
Take off those clothes and abandon your raft   *345*
To the winds' will. Swim for your life
To the Phaeacians' land, your destined safe harbor.
Here, wrap this veil tightly around your chest.
It's immortally charmed: Fear no harm or death.
But when with your hands you touch solid land   *350*
Untie it and throw it into the deep blue sea
Clear of the shore so it can come back to me."

With these words the goddess gave him the veil
And slipped back into the heavy seas
Like a silver gull. The black water swallowed her.   *355*
Godlike Odysseus brooded on his trials
And spoke these words to his own great soul:

"Not this. Not another treacherous god
Scheming against me, ordering me to abandon my raft.
I will not obey. I've seen with my own eyes   *360*
How far that land is where she says I'll be saved.
I'll play it the way that seems best to me.
As long as the timbers are still holding together
I'll hang on and gut it out right here where I am.
When and if a wave shatters my raft to pieces,   *365*
Then I'll swim for it. What else can I do?"

As he churned these thoughts in the pit of his stomach
Poseidon Earthshaker raised up a great wave—
An arching, cavernous, cresting tsunami—
And brought it crashing down on him.   *370*

    As storm winds blast into a pile of dry chaff
    And scatter the stuff all over the place,

So the long beams of Odysseus' raft were scattered.
He went with one beam and rode it like a stallion,
Stripping off the clothes Calypso had given him   *375*

And wrapping the White Goddess' veil round his chest.
Then he dove into the sea and started to swim
A furious breaststroke. The Lord of Earthquake saw him
And said to himself with a slow toss of his head:

"That's right. Thrash around in misery on the open sea   *380*
Until you come to human society again.
I hope that not even then will you escape from evil."

With these words he whipped his sleek-coated horses
And headed for his fabulous palace on Aegae.

But Zeus' daughter Athena had other ideas.   *385*
She barricaded all the winds but one
And ordered them to rest and fall asleep.
Boreas, though, she sent cracking through the waves,
A tailwind for Odysseus until he was safe on Phaeacia,
And had beaten off the dark birds of death.   *390*

Two nights and two days the solid, mitered waves
Swept him on, annihilation all his heart could foresee.
But when Dawn combed her hair in the third day's light,
The wind died down and there fell
A breathless calm. Riding a swell   *395*
He peered out and saw land nearby.

You know how precious a father's life is
To children who have seen him through a long disease,
Gripped by a malevolent spirit and melting away,
But then released from suffering in a spasm of joy.   *400*

The land and woods were that welcome a sight
To Odysseus. He kicked hard for the shoreline,
But when he was as close as a shout would carry
He heard the thud of waves on the rocks,
Thundering surf that pounded the headland   *405*
And bellowed eerily. The sea churned with foam.
There were no harbors for ships, no inlets or bays,
Only jutting cliffs and rocks and barnacled crags.
Odysseus' heart sank and his knees grew weak.

With a heavy sigh he spoke to his own great soul: 410

"Ah, Zeus has let me see land I never hoped to see
And I've cut my way to the end of this gulf,
But there's no way to get out of the grey saltwater.
Only sharp rocks ahead, laced by the breakers,
And beyond them slick stone rising up sheer   415
Right out of deep water, no place for a foothold,
No way to stand up and wade out of trouble.
If I try to get out here a wave might smash me
Against the stone cliff. Some mooring that would be!
If I swim around farther and try to find   420
A shelving shore or an inlet from the sea,
I'm afraid that a squall will take me back out
Groaning deeply on the teeming dark water,
Or some monster will attack me out of the deep
From the swarming brood of great Amphitrítê.   425
I know how odious I am to the Earthshaker."

As these thoughts welled up from the pit of his stomach
A breaker bore him onto the rugged coast.
He would have been cut to ribbons and his bones crushed
But grey-eyed Athena inspired him.   430
Slammed onto a rock he grabbed it with both hands
And held on groaning until the breaker rolled by.
He had no sooner ducked it when the backwash hit him
And towed him far out into open water again.

   It was just like an octopus pulled out of its hole   435
   With pebbles stuck to its tentacles,

Odysseus' strong hands clinging to the rocks
Until the skin was ripped off. The wave
Pulled him under, and he would have died
Then and there. But Athena was with him.   440
He surfaced again: the wave spat him up landwards,
And he swam along parallel to the coast, scanning it
For a shelving beach, an inlet from the sea,
And when he swam into the current of a river delta
He knew he had come to the perfect spot,   445

Lined with smooth rocks and sheltered from the wind.
He felt the flowing of the rivergod, and he prayed:

"Hear me, Riverlord, whoever you are
And however men pray to you:
I am a fugitive from the sea   450
And Poseidon's persecution,
A wandering mortal, pitiful
To the gods, I come to you,
To your water and your knees.
I have suffered much, O Lord,   455
Lord, hear my prayer."

At these words the god stopped his current,
Made his waters calm and harbored the man
In his river's shallows. Odysseus crawled out
On hands and knees. The sea had broken his spirit.   460
His whole body was swollen, and saltwater trickled
From his nose and mouth. Breath gone, voice gone,
He lay scarcely alive, drained and exhausted.
When he could breathe again and his spirit returned
He unbound the goddess' veil from his body   465
And threw it into the sea-melding river
Where it rode the crest of a wave down the current
And into Ino's own hands. He turned away from the river,
Sank into a bed of rushes, and kissed the good earth.
Huddled over he spoke to his own great soul: 470

"What am I in for now? How will this end?
If I keep watch all night here by the river
I'm afraid a hard frost—or even a gentle dew—
Will do me in, as weak as I am.
The wind blows cold from a river toward dawn.   475
But if I climb the bank to the dark woods up there
And fall asleep in a thicket, even if I survive
Fatigue and cold and get some sweet sleep,
I'm afraid I'll fall prey to some prowling beast."

He thought it over and decided it was better   480
To go to the woods. They were near the water

On an open rise. He found two olive trees there,
One wild, one planted, their growth intertwined,
Proof against blasts of the wild, wet wind,
The sun unable to needle light through,   *485*
Impervious to rain, so thickly they grew
Into one tangle of shadows. Odysseus burrowed
Under their branches and scraped out a bed.
He found a mass of leaves there, enough to keep warm
Two or three men on the worst winter day.   *490*
The sight of these leaves was a joy to Odysseus,
And the godlike survivor lay down in their midst
And covered himself up.

> *A solitary man*
> *Who lives on the edge of the wilderness*
> *And has no neighbors, will hide a charred log*   *495*
> *Deep in the black embers and so keep alive*
> *The fire's seed and not have to rekindle it*
> *From who knows where.*

                              So Odysseus buried
Himself in the leaves. And Athena sprinkled
His eyes with sleep for quickest release   *500*
From pain and fatigue.
                              And she closed his eyelids.

ODYSSEY 6

So Odysseus slept, the godlike survivor
Overwhelmed with fatigue.
                          But the goddess Athena
Went off to the land of the Phaeacians,
A people who had once lived in Hypereia,
Near to the Cyclopes, a race of savages   5
Who marauded their land constantly. One day
Great Nausithous led his people
Off to Schería, a remote island,
Where he walled off a city, built houses
And shrines, and parceled out fields.   10
After he died and went to the world below,
Alcinous ruled, wise in the gods' ways.
Owl-eyed Athena now came to his house
To devise a passage home for Odysseus.
She entered a richly decorated bedroom   15
Where a girl as lovely as a goddess was sleeping,
Nausicaa, daughter of noble Alcinous.
Two maids, blessed with the beauty of Graces,
Slept on either side of the closed, polished doors.
Athena rushed in like a breath of wind,   20
Stood over Nausicaa's head, and spoke to her
In the guise of her friend, the daughter
Of the famed mariner Dymas. Assuming
This girl's form, the owl-eyed goddess spoke:

"Nausicaa, how could your mother have raised   25
Such a careless child? Your silky clothes
Are lying here soiled, and your wedding is near!

You'll have to dress yourself and your party well,
If you want the people to speak highly of you
And make your mother and father glad.   30
We'll wash these clothes at the break of dawn.
I'll go with you and help so you'll get it done quickly.
You're not going to be a virgin for long, you know!
All the best young men in Phaeacia are eager
To marry you—as well they should be.   35
Wake up now, and at dawn's first blush
Ask your father if he will hitch up the mulecart
To carry all these sashes and robes and things.
It'll be much more pleasant than going on foot.
The laundry pools are a long way from town."   40

The grey-eyed goddess spoke and was gone,
Off to Olympus, which they say is forever
The unmoving abode of the gods, unshaken
By winds, never soaked by rain, and where the snow
Never drifts, but the brilliant sky stretches   45
Cloudless away, and brightness streams through the air.
There, where the gods are happy all the world's days,
Went the Grey-eyed One after speaking to the girl.

Dawn came throned in light, and woke Nausicaa,
Who wondered at the dream as it faded away.   50
She went through the house to tell her parents,
Her dear father and mother. She found them within,
Her mother sitting by the hearth with her women,
Spinning sea-blue yarn. Her father she met
As he headed for the door accompanied by elders   55
On his way to a council the nobles had called.
She stood very close to her father and said:

"Daddy, would you please hitch up a wagon for me—
A high one that rolls well—so I can go to the river
And wash our good clothes that are all dirty now.   60
You yourself should wear clean clothes
When you sit among the first men in council.
And you have five sons who live in the palace,
Two married and three still bachelors.

They always want freshly washed clothes   *65*
To wear to the dances. This has been on my mind."

She was too embarrassed to mention marriage
To her father, but he understood and said:

"Of course you can have the mules, child,
And anything else. Go on. The servants will rig up   *70*
A high, smooth-rolling wagon fitted with a trunk."

He called the servants, and they got busy
Rolling out a wagon and hitching up mules.
Nausicaa brought out a pile of laundry
And loaded it into the polished cart,   *75*
While her mother packed a picnic basket
With all sorts of food and filled a goatskin with wine.
The girl put these up on the cart, along with
A golden flask of oil her mother gave her
For herself and her maids to rub on their skin.   *80*
She took the lash and the glossy reins
And had the mules giddyup. They jangled along
At a steady pace, pulling the clothes and the girl,
While the other girls, her maids, ran alongside.

They came to the beautiful, running river   *85*
And the laundry pools, where the clear water
Flowed through strongly enough to clean
Even the dirtiest clothes. They unhitched the mules
And shooed them out along the swirling river's edge
To munch the sweet clover. Then they unloaded   *90*
The clothes, brought them down to the water,
And trod them in the trenches, working fast
And making a game of it. When the clothes were washed
They spread them out neatly on the shore of the sea
Where the waves scoured the pebbled beach clean.   *95*
Then they bathed themselves and rubbed rich olive oil
Onto their skin, and had a picnic on the river's banks
While they waited for the sun to dry the clothes.
When the princess and her maids had enough to eat
They began to play with a ball, their hair streaming free. *100*

Artemis sometimes roams the mountains—
Immense Taygetus, or Erymanthus—
Showering arrows upon boars or fleet antelope,
And with her play the daughters of Zeus
Who range the wild woods—and Leto is glad   *105*
That her daughter towers above them all
With her shining brow, though they are beautiful all—

So the unwed princess among her attendants.

But when she was about to fold the clothes,
Yoke the mules, and head back home,   *110*
The Grey-eyed One sprung her plan:
Odysseus would wake up, see the lovely girl,
And she would lead him to the Phaeacians' city.
The princess threw the ball to one of the girls,
But it sailed wide into deep, swirling water.   *115*
The girls screamed, and Odysseus awoke.
Sitting up, he tried to puzzle it out:

"What kind of land have I come to now?
Are the natives wild and lawless savages,
Or godfearing men who welcome strangers?   *120*
That sounded like girls screaming, or the cry
Of the spirit women who hold the high peaks,
The river wells, and the grassy meadows.
Can it be I am close to human voices?
I'll go have a look and see for myself."   *125*

With that Odysseus emerged from the bushes.
He broke off a leafy branch from the undergrowth
And held it before him to cover himself.

A weathered mountain lion steps into a clearing,
Confident in his strength, eyes glowing.   *130*
The wind and rain have let up, and he's hunting
Cattle, sheep, or wild deer, but is hungry enough
To jump the stone walls of the animal pens.

So Odysseus advanced upon these ringleted girls,

Naked as he was. What choice did he have?   *135*
He was a frightening sight, disfigured with brine,
And the girls fluttered off to the jutting beaches.
Only Alcinous' daughter stayed. Athena
Put courage in her heart and stopped her trembling.
She held her ground, and Odysseus wondered   *140*
How to approach this beautiful girl. Should he
Fall at her knees, or keep his distance
And ask her with honeyed words to show him
The way to the city and give him some clothes?
He thought it over and decided it was better   *145*
To keep his distance and not take the chance
Of offending the girl by touching her knees.
So he started this soft and winning speech:

"I implore you, Lady: Are you a goddess
Or mortal? If you are one of heaven's divinities   *150*
I think you are most like great Zeus' daughter
Artemis. You have her looks, her stature, her form.
If you are a mortal and live on this earth,
Thrice blest is your father, your queenly mother,
Thrice blest your brothers! Their hearts must always   *155*
Be warm with happiness when they look at you,
Just blossoming as you enter the dance.
And happiest of all will be the lucky man
Who takes you home with a cartload of gifts.
I've never seen anyone like you,   *160*
Man or woman. I look upon you with awe.
Once, on Delos, I saw something to compare—
A palm shoot springing up near Apollo's altar.
I had stopped there with the troops under my command
On what would prove to be a perilous campaign.   *165*
I marveled long and hard when I saw that tree,
For nothing like it had ever grown from the earth.
And I marvel now, Lady, and I am afraid
To touch your knees. Yet my pain is great.
Yesterday, after twenty days, I pulled myself out   *170*
Of the wine-dark sea. All that time, wind and wave
Bore me away from Ogygia Island,
And now some spirit has cast me up here

To suffer something new. I do not think
My trials will end soon. The gods have much more   175
In store for me before that ever happens.
Pity me, mistress. After all my hardships
It is to you I have come first. I don't know
A soul who lives here, not a single one.
Show me the way to town, and give me   180
A rag to throw over myself, some piece of cloth
You may have brought along to bundle the clothes.
And for yourself, may the gods grant you
Your heart's desire, a husband and a home,
And the blessing of a harmonious life.   185
For nothing is greater or finer than this,
When a man and woman live together
With one heart and mind, bringing joy
To their friends and grief to their foes."

And white-armed Nausicaa answered him: 190

"Stranger, you do not seem to be a bad man
Or a fool. Zeus himself, the Olympian god,
Sends happiness to good men and bad men both,
To each as he wills. To you he has given these troubles,
Which you have no choice but to bear. But now,   195
Since you have come to our country,
You shall not lack clothing, nor anything needed
By a sore-tried suppliant who presents himself.
I will show you where the city is and tell you
That the people here are called Phaeacians.   200
This is their country, and I am the daughter
Of great-hearted Alcinous, the Phaeacians' lord."

Then the princess called to the ringleted girls:

"Stop this now. Running away at the sight of a man!
Do you think he is part of an enemy invasion?   205
There is no man on earth, nor will there ever be,
Slippery enough to invade Phaeacia,
For we are very dear to the immortal gods,
And we live far out in the surging sea,

At the world's frontier, out of all human contact.   *210*
This poor man comes here as a wanderer,
And we must take care of him now. All strangers,
All beggars, are under the protection of Zeus,
And even small gifts are welcome. So let's feed
This stranger, give him something to drink,   *215*
And bathe him in the river, out of the wind."

The girls stopped, turned, and urged each other on.
They took Odysseus to a sheltered spot,
As Nausicaa, Alcinous' daughter, had ordered.
They set down a mantle and a tunic,   *220*
Gave him a golden flask of olive oil,
And told him to wash in the river.
Then sunlit Odysseus said to them:

"Stay off a ways there, girls, and let me
Wash the brine off my shoulders myself   *225*
And rub myself down. It's been a long time
Since my skin has felt oil. But I don't want
To wash in front of you. I'd be ashamed
To come out naked in front of young girls."

The girls went off and talked with Nausicaa,   *230*
And Odysseus rinsed off with river water
All the brine that caked his shoulders and back,
And he scrubbed the salty scurf from his scalp.
He finished his bath, rubbed himself down with oil,
And put on the clothes the maiden had given him.   *235*
Then Athena, born from Zeus, made him look
Taller and more muscled, and made his hair
Tumble down his head like hyacinth flowers.

> *Imagine a craftsman overlaying silver*
> *With pure gold. He has learned his art*   *240*
> *From Pallas Athena and Lord Hephaestus,*
> *And creates works of breathtaking beauty.*

So Athena herself made Odysseus' head and shoulders
Shimmer with grace. He walked down the beach

And sat on the sand. The princess was dazzled,   *245*
And she said to her white-armed serving girls:

"Listen, this man hasn't come to Phaeacia
Against the will of the Olympian gods.
Before, he was a terrible sight, but now,
He's like one of the gods who live in the sky.   *250*
If only such a man would be called my husband,
Living here, and content to stay here.
Well, go on, give him something to eat and drink."

They were only too glad to do what she said.
They served Odysseus food and drink,   *255*
And the long-suffering man ate and drank
Ravenously. It had been a long fast.

Nausicaa had other things on her mind.
She folded the clothes and loaded the wagon,
Hitched up the mules and climbed aboard.   *260*
Then she called to Odysseus and said:

"Get ready now, stranger, to go to the city,
So I can show you the way to my father's house,
Where I promise you will meet the best of the Phaeacians.
Now this is what you must do—and I think you understand: *265*
As long as we're going through countryside and farms,
Keep up with my handmaidens behind the wagon.
Just jog along with them. I'll lead the way,
And we'll soon come to the city. It has a high wall
Around it, and a harbor on each side.   *270*
The isthmus gets narrow, and the upswept hulls
Are drawn up to the road. Every citizen
Has his own private slip. The market's there, too,
Surrounding Poseidon's beautiful temple
And bounded by stones set deep in the earth.   *275*
There men are always busy with their ships' tackle,
With cables and sails, and with planing their oars.
Phaeacians don't care for quivers and bows
But for oars and masts and streamlined ships
In which they love to cross the grey, salt sea.   *280*

It's their rude remarks I would rather avoid.
There are some insolent louts in this town,
And I can just hear one of them saying:
'Well, who's this tall, handsome stranger trailing along
Behind Nausicaa? Where'd she pick him up?   *285*
She'll probably marry him, some shipwreck she's taken in
From parts unknown. He's sure not local.
Maybe a god has come to answer her prayers,
Dropped out of the sky for her to have and to hold.
It's just as well she's found herself a husband   *290*
From somewhere else, since she turns her nose up
At the many fine Phaeacians who woo her.'
That's what they'll say, and it will count against me.
I myself would blame anyone who acted like this,
A girl who, with her father and mother to tell her better,   *295*
Kept the company of men before her wedding day.
No, stranger, be quick to understand me,
So that you can win from my father an escort home,
And soon at that.
                    Close by the road you will find
A grove of Athena, beautiful poplars   *300*
Surrounded by a meadow. A spring flows through it.
Right there is my father's estate and vineyard,
About as far from the city as a shout would carry.
Sit down there and wait for a while, until
We reach the city and arrive at my house.   *305*
When you think we've had enough time to get there,
Go into the city and ask any Phaeacian
For the house of my father, Lord Alcinous.
It's very easy to spot, and any child
Can lead you there. There's no other house   *310*
In all Phaeacia built like the house
Of the hero Alcinous. Once you're safely within
The courtyard, go quickly though the hall
Until you come to my mother. She'll be sitting
By the hearth in the firelight, spinning   *315*
Sea-blue yarn—a sight worth seeing—
As she leans against a column, her maids behind her.
Right beside her my father sits on his throne,
Sipping his wine like an immortal god.

Pass him by and throw your arms   320
Around my mother's knees, if you want to see
Your homeland soon, however far it may be.
If she smiles upon you, there is hope that you will
Return to your home and see your loved ones again."

And she smacked the mules with the shining lash.   325
They trotted on smartly, leaving the river behind.
She drove so that Odysseus and the girls
Could keep up, and used the lash with care.
The sun had set when they reached the grove
Sacred to Athena. Odysseus sat down there   330
And said this prayer to great Zeus' daughter:

"Hear me, mystic child of the Storm God,
O hear me now, as you heard me not
When I was shattered by the Earthshaker's blows.
Grant that I come to Phaeacia pitied and loved."   335

Thus his prayer, and Pallas Athena heard it
But did not appear to him face to face, not yet,
Out of respect for her uncle, who would rage against
Godlike Odysseus until he reached home.

ODYSSEY 7

While Odysseus was praying in the grove,
The strong mules bore Nausicaa to the city.
She pulled up at the gate of her father's palace,
And her brothers, men like gods, crowded around,
Unhitched the mules, and took the clothes inside.   5
Nausicaa went to her bedroom, where Eurymedusa,
Her waiting-woman, kindled a fire for her.
Eurymedusa had come from Apeire
In the curved ships, long ago, and had been chosen
From the spoils of war for Alcinous,   10
Who ruled the Phaeacians as if he were a god.
It was this old woman who had reared
White-armed Nausicaa in the palace
And who now prepared her supper on the fire.

As Odysseus started out for the city,   15
Athena enveloped him in magic mist,
So that none of the Phaeacians he might meet
Along the way would challenge him
And ask him who he was.
                            He was about to enter
The lovely city when the Grey-eyed One   20
Came up to him. She looked like a young girl
Carrying a pitcher, standing there before him,
And godlike Odysseus questioned her:

"My child, I wonder if you could guide me
To the house of Alcinous, the man   25
Who is lord of this people? I am a traveler

From a far land, a stranger in need,
And I know no one in this city."

Athena's eyes flashed in the blue sealight:

"Well of course, grandad, I'll show you   30
Where Alcinous lives. His house is close to ours.
Come on, I'll lead the way. But you'll have to be quiet.
Don't look at anyone or ask any questions.
The people here aren't very tolerant of strangers
Or very welcoming. All they trust are their ships,   35
In which they cross the great ocean, because
Poseidon lets them. Their ships are very fast,
Fast as a flying bird, or even a thought."

Thus Pallas Athena, and she led the way
Quickly, while Odysseus followed   40
In the goddess' footsteps. None of the Phaeacians
Noticed him as he moved through their city,
For the dread goddess, her hair done up in braids,
Would not allow them, shedding around him
A magical mist that made him invisible.   45
She had a soft spot in her heart for the hero.

Odysseus marveled at the harbors
And the shapely ships, at the meeting grounds
And the long walls capped with palisades.
When they came to the king's palace,   50
The Grey-eyed One was the first to speak:

"Here you are, grandad, the house you asked for.
You will find the lords feasting at a banquet.
Go inside and don't be afraid of anything.
Things turn out better for a man who is bold,   55
Especially if he's a stranger from a distant land.
The first person you'll meet is the queen. Arete
Is her name, and she's from the same line
As King Alcinous. It goes like this:
First Nausithous was born from Poseidon   60
And Periboea, a most beautiful woman,

The youngest daughter of Eurymedon,
Who once was king of the arrogant Giants.
He brought destruction down on his reckless people
And on himself. Well, anyway, Poseidon   65
Lay with Periboea and she bore a son,
Nausithous, who ruled the Phaeacians.
Nausithous fathered Rhexenor and Alcinous.
Rhexenor had just got married when Apollo
Shot him with his silver bow in his hall.   70
He didn't leave a son, but did leave a daughter,
Only one, Arete. Alcinous married her
And honored her as no other woman on earth
Is honored, of all the women who keep house
For their husbands—that's how she is honored,   75
From the heart, and always has been,
Both by her children and by Alcinous himself
As by the people, who look to her as a goddess
And greet her as one when she goes through the city.
She understands everything, and has sound judgment   80
And settles quarrels with a generous heart.
If she likes you, there is a very good chance
You will get to see your dear ones again
And the high-roofed hall in your own native land."

Thus the goddess with the seagrey eyes,   · 85
And then she was off over the desolate water,
Leaving lovely Schería. She came to Marathon
And the wide streets of Athens, and she disappeared
Into the great house of Erechtheus.

                          But Odysseus
Went to the glorious palace of Alcinous.   90
There he stood, heart pounding as he took it all in
Before crossing the bronze threshold. Gleams
As of the sun or the moon played over the high roof
Of Alcinous' house. The bronze walls, surmounted
With a blue enamel frieze, stretched from the threshold   95
To the inner hall. The outer doors were golden,
And silver doorposts were set in the bronze threshold.
The lintel was silver and the door handle gold.

Flanking the door were two gold and silver dogs
Made by Hephaestus with all his art   *100*
To guard the palace, and they were immortal
And ageless. Inside, seats were built flush to the walls
On either side, stretching from the threshold
To the inner hall, and upon them were flung
Robes of a fine, soft weave, the craft of women.   *105*
The Phaeacian leaders would sit on these seats
Eating and drinking, and they lacked for nothing.
Golden statues of young men stood on pedestals
Holding torches to light the night for banqueters.
There were fifty slave women scattered through the house,   *110*
Some grinding yellow grain on the millstone,
Others weaving cloth or twirling yarn on spindles
As they sat, fluttering like so many leaves on a poplar,
And the finely woven fabric glistened with oil.
For just as the Phaeacian men outstrip all others   *115*
In sailing ships on the sea, so too are the women
Skilled above all others in working the loom.
Athena has given them a deep understanding
Of beautiful handiwork.
                         Outside the courtyard,
Just beyond the doors, are four acres of orchard   *120*
Surrounded by a hedge. The trees there grow tall,
Blossoming pear trees and pomegranates,
Apple trees with bright, shiny fruit, sweet figs
And luxuriant olives. The fruit of these trees
Never perishes nor fails, summer or winter—   *125*
It lasts year round, and the West Wind's breath
Continually ripens apple after apple, pear upon pear,
Fig after fig, and one bunch of grapes after another.
The fruitful vineyard is planted there, too.
One warm, level spot is for drying grapes   *130*
In the sun; elsewhere, some grapes are being gathered
And others trod upon. In front, the unripe clusters
Are losing their bloom, and others are turning purple.
By the last row of vines are trim garden plots
With rich blooms of all sorts throughout the year.   *135*
Two separate springs flow through the orchard,
One of them meandering throughout the garden,

While the other flows under the courtyard threshold,
And from this spring the townspeople draw their water.

Odysseus stood and gazed at all of the blessings   140
The gods had lavished on the house of Alcinous.
When he had taken it all in, he passed quickly
Over the threshold and entered the house.
There he found the Phaeacian nobles
Tipping their cups in honor of Hermes,   145
To whom they poured libations last of all
When they thought it was time to take their rest.
Odysseus, the godlike survivor, went through the hall
In the heavy mist Athena had wrapped him in,
Until he came to Arete and Lord Alcinous.   150
There he threw his arms around Arete's knees,
And the magical mist melted away at that moment.
They were all hushed to silence, marveling
At the sight of Odysseus, who now made his prayer:

"Arete, daughter of godlike Rhexenor,   155
To your husband and to your knees I come
In great distress, and to these banqueters also—
May the gods grant prosperity to them
In this life, and may each of them hand down
Their wealth and honor to their children after them.   160
Grant me but this: a speedy passage home,
For I have suffered long, far from my people."

And with that he sat down in the ashes
By the fireside. The hall fell silent.
Finally Echeneus, a Phaeacian elder,   165
Wise in the old ways and the ways of words,
Spoke out with good will among them:

"Alcinous, this will not do at all. It is not proper
That a guest sit in the ashes on the hearth.
We are all holding back, waiting on your word.   170
Come, help the stranger up and have him sit
Upon a silver-studded chair. And bid the heralds
Mix wine, so we may pour libations also to Zeus,

Lord of Thunder, who walks beside suppliants.
And let the housekeeper bring out food for our guest."   *175*

When the sacred King Alcinous heard this,
He took the hand of Odysseus, the cunning hero,
And raised him from the fireside and had him sit
On a polished chair from which he asked his son
Laodamas to rise, for he was Alcinous'   *180*
Best beloved son, and sat at his right hand.
A maid poured water from a golden pitcher
Into a silver basin for him to wash his hands
And then set up a polished table nearby.
Another serving woman, grave and dignified,   *185*
Set out bread and generous helpings
From the other dishes she had. So Odysseus,
Who had endured much, ate and drank.
And the sacred King Alcinous spoke to the herald:

"Pontonous, mix the bowl and serve wine   *190*
To all, so we may pour libations also to Zeus,
Lord of Thunder, who walks beside suppliants."

Pontonous mixed the mellow wine
And served it to all, pouring out first
Drops for libation, which they all tipped out.   *195*
When they had drunk to their heart's content,
Alcinous addressed them and said:

"Hear me, Phaeacian lords and counselors,
So I may speak to you what is in my heart.
Now that you have feasted, go home to your rest.   *200*
In the morning we will invite more of the elders
And entertain the stranger in our halls
And offer fine sacrifices to the gods.
Then we will think of how to convey our guest
To his own native land, so he may come home   *205*
Speedily and with joy, be it ever so far.
Nor shall he suffer any harm or misfortune
Before he sets foot upon his own land. Thereafter,
He shall suffer whatever fate

The Spinners spun for him when he was born.   210
But if he is one of the immortals
Come down from heaven, then the gods
Have changed their ways. Always before this,
Whenever we offered sacrifice to them,
They appeared to us in their own bright forms,   215
And they sat with us and shared the feast.
Even when one of us meets them on the road
They do not conceal themselves, for we are kin,
Just like the Cyclopes and savage Giants."

Odysseus, always thinking, answered him: 220

"Don't worry about that, Alcinous. I am not like
The immortals, either in build or looks.
I am completely human. Better to liken me
To the most woebegone man you ever knew.
That's who I'd compare myself to.   225
I could tell you much more, a long tale
Of the suffering I've had by the will of the gods,
But all I want now is to be allowed to eat,
Despite my grief. There is nothing more shameless
Than this belly of ours, which forces a man   230
To pay attention to it, no matter how many
Troubles he has, how much pain in his heart.
I have pain in my heart, but my belly always
Makes me eat and drink and forget my troubles,
Pestering me to keep it filled. So then,   235
Please do move quickly at break of day
To set me ashore on my own native land,
Even though it be after all my suffering.
I'd die gladly once I've seen my home again,
My household servants and my high-roofed hall."   240

They praised him, and urged that the stranger
Be sped on his way. He had said all the right things.
Then, when they had poured libations and drunk
To their heart's content, they went home to rest.
Odysseus was left behind in the hall   245
Sitting beside Arete and godlike Alcinous.

The serving women cleared away the dishes,
And then white-armed Arete broke the silence.
She had recognized the mantle and tunic
As soon as she saw them, for she had made   *250*
These beautiful clothes herself, with her handmaids,
And when she spoke her words flew on wings:

"Stranger, I myself will ask you this first.
Who are you, and where do you come from?
And who gave you these clothes? Did you not say   *255*
That you came here wandering over the sea?"

And Odysseus, never at a loss for words:

"It would be hard, my lady, to tell the tale
Of all my troubles, since the heavenly gods
Have given me many. But I will tell you what   *260*
You ask me about.
                              There is an island,
Ogygia, that lies far off in the sea.
Atlas' daughter lives there, guileful Calypso,
Her hair rich as sea-foam, a dread goddess.
No one, mortal or divine, ever visits her.   *265*
It was my bad luck to be led to her hearth
By some mysterious force, all alone,
Washed up there after Zeus shattered my ship,
Slivering it with lightning on the wine-dark sea.
My whole crew went down in that wreck,   *270*
But I hung on to the curved keel of my ship,
Adrift for nine days. The tenth black night
Brought me to the island of Ogygia
And the awesome goddess. She took me in,
Gave me food, and said she would make me   *275*
Immortal and ageless for all of my days.
But she never touched my heart. I spent
Seven years with Calypso. The immortal clothes
She gave me were always wet with my tears.
Then, when the eighth year came around, she told me   *280*
I could go, either because of some message from Zeus,
Or because she herself had changed her mind.

She sent me off on a sturdy raft, well stocked
With bread and wine, and she clothed me well,
And put a breeze at my back, gentle and warm.   *285*
Seventeen days I sailed the deep water,
And on the eighteenth day the shadowy mountains
Of your land appeared, and my heart was glad.
But my luck turned sour, and I was soon engulfed
In suffering sent by the Earthshaker Poseidon.   *290*
He stirred up the winds, blocking my course,
And roused up huge seas that left me groaning
And unable to stay with my raft, which was
Shattered to pieces by the hurricane winds.
I swam my way through all that saltwater   *295*
Until wind and wave brought me here to your coast.
But if I had tried to come ashore, the pounding surf
Would have smashed me to bits on the beetling crags.
I swam back out and then along the coast
Until I came to a river, the perfect spot,   *300*
Lined with smooth stones and sheltered from the wind.
I staggered out, exhausted. Night was coming on.
I climbed the river bank and lay down to sleep
In the bushes, covering myself with dry leaves.
Some god shed upon me boundless slumber,   *305*
And I slept in the leaves, my heart troubled—
Slept through the night, through dawn and high noon,
And did not wake until the sun was going down.
When I awoke I saw your daughter's handmaids
Playing on the shore, and saw your daughter   *310*
Like a goddess among them. It was she
I supplicated, and she understood
Everything perfectly. You would not expect
Anyone so young to act with such grace,
For the young are thoughtless. She gave me bread   *315*
And bright red wine, bathed me in the river
And gave me these clothes.
                          As much as it pains me
To recall it, all I have told you is true."

And Alcinous responded:

                    "Stranger,
My daughter was out of line in not bringing you   *320*
Here to our house along with her handmaids,
Since you went to her first as a suppliant."

And Odysseus, with his usual presence of mind:

"Do not rebuke your blameless daughter for this,
My lord. She did tell me to follow along   *325*
With the girls, but I refused out of fear and shame,
Thinking your heart might cloud over with anger.
People everywhere, I have found, have tempers."

Alcinous answered him:

                    "Stranger,
My heart is not like that, to grow angry   *330*
Without cause. Better to give all things their due.
I would wish, by Zeus, by Athena and Apollo,
That you, being the kind of man you are—
My kind of man—would marry my daughter
And stay here and be called my son. I would   *335*
Give you a house filled with possessions
If you chose to remain, but no Phaeacian
Will ever keep you here against your will—
And may such a thing never please Father Zeus.
As for your send-off, so you can be sure of it,   *340*
It will be tomorrow. You will lie down and sleep
While they row you over the calm water
Until you come to your home, or wherever you will,
Even if it is much farther away than Euboea,
Which our sailors say is the farthest of lands.   *345*
They went there once when they took Rhadamanthus
To visit Tityus, the son of Earth.
They made the round trip in a single day
Without even trying. But you will see for yourself
How good our ships and rowers are."   *350*

Odysseus, the godlike survivor, was glad,
And he spoke in prayer:

"Father Zeus,
Let Alcinous accomplish all that he says.
May his fame never fade over all the earth,
And may I reach at last my own native land."   *355*

So they spoke, and white-armed Arete told her maids
To place a bed on the porch and spread upon it
Beautiful purple blankets and fleecy cloaks.
The maids went out of the hall with torches
And made up the bed. Then they called to Odysseus: *360*

"You may lie down, stranger. Your bed is made."

These were welcome words, and Odysseus,
Who had suffered much, fell asleep on the bed
Under the echoing portico. But Alcinous lay down
In the innermost chamber of that lofty house,   *365*
And his lady shared his bed and slept beside him.

ODYSSEY 8

Dawn spread her roselight over the sky,
And Alcinous awoke in all his sacred might,
As did Zeus-born Odysseus, sacker of cities.
Alcinous led the way to the Phaeacian assembly,
Which was built near the harbor. The Phaeacians   5
Filed in and sat on the polished stones
Close by each other, and Pallas Athena,
Disguised as Alcinous' herald, went through the city
To lay the groundwork for Odysseus' trip home,
Going up to each man and saying to him: 10

"Gather round, Phaeacian leaders and counselors,
And go to the assembly to learn of the stranger
Who has just arrived at Alcinous' palace,
Driven over the sea, a man like a god."

This got their attention, and the seats   15
In the assembly filled up quickly with men
Who marveled at the sight of Laertes' son,
For Athena poured on his shoulders and head
A shimmering grace and made him taller
And more heavily muscled, so that he would be   20
Welcomed by the Phaeacians as a man to respect,
And so he would be able to accomplish the feats
The Phaeacians would use to test his mettle.
When the men were all gathered, Alcinous spoke:

"Hear me, Phaeacian lords and counselors,   25
So I may speak what is in my heart.

This stranger has come to my house
In his wanderings. I don't know who he is,
Or if he has come from the east or the west.
He asks for passage home, and asks us to set   30
A firm time for departure. Let us speed him
On his way, as we have always done.
No one has ever come to my house
And languished here long for lack of transport.
Haul a black ship, then, onto the bright saltwater   35
For her maiden voyage. And pick two and fifty
Of the best young sailors in all the land.
When you have lashed the oars well at the benches,
Disembark and hurry to my house. We have a feast
To prepare, and I will provide well for all!   40
Those are my orders for the younger men.
But you others, all the sceptered kings,
Come to my palace and help me entertain
The stranger in the hall. Let no one refuse.
And summon the godlike singer of tales,   45
Demodocus. For the god has given him,
Beyond all others, song that delights
However his heart urges him to sing."

So saying, he led the way, followed
By the sceptered kings. A herald went   50
For the godlike singer, and two and fifty
Chosen young sailors went, as he ordered,
Down to the shore of the barren sea.
There they hauled a ship out onto the water.
They set up mast and sail in that swift, black ship,   55
Fit the oars into the leather thole-straps,
All in due order, and then unfurled the white sails.
They moored the ship where her sails would catch
The evening breeze, and then went their way
To the great palace of wise Alcinous.   60
The porticoes, courtyards, and rooms were filled
With crowds of men both young and old.
Alcinous sacrificed for them a dozen sheep,
Eight white-tusked boars, and two shambling oxen,
Which they flayed and dressed for the feast.   65

Then the herald came up leading Demodocus.
The Muse loved this man, but gave him
Good and evil both, snuffing out the light
Of his eyes as she opened his heart to sweet song.
Pontonous, the herald, had the bard sit   70
Among the banqueters on a silver-studded chair
Propped against a column, and he hung the clear-toned lyre
On a peg above Demodocus' head
And showed him how to reach it with his hands.
He set up a table and basket beside the bard   75
And a cup of wine ready at hand.
They all reached out to the feast before them,
And when they had satisfied their appetites,
The Muse moved the bard to sing of heroes.
The piece that he sang was already famed   80
Throughout the world—the quarrel
Odysseus once had with Achilles,
Going head to head at a feast of the gods
With violent words, and Agamemnon,
The warlord, rejoiced that these two,   85
The best of the Greeks, were at each other's throats.
For long ago, when he crossed the stone threshold
In sacred Pytho to consult the oracle,
Apollo had prophesied that this would happen.
That was in the days when the great tide of woe   90
Was rolling in upon Trojans and Greeks alike
Through the will of great Zeus.
                                        This was the song
The renowned bard sang. But Odysseus
Pulled his great purple cloak over his head
And hid his handsome face. He was ashamed   95
To let the Phaeacians see his tears falling down.
Whenever the singer paused, Odysseus
Would wipe away his tears, pick up his great cup
And pour libations to the gods. But when the singer
Started again, urged on by the Phaeacian lords,   100
Who delighted in his words, Odysseus
Would cover his head again and moan.
He managed to conceal his tears from everyone
Except Alcinous, who sat at his elbow

And could not help but hear his heavy sighs.   *105*
Alcinous acted quickly and said to his guests:

"Hear me, Phaeacian nobles and lords.
We have had enough of feasting now,
And of the lyre that complements a feast.
We should go outdoors for some contests now,   *110*
All the athletic events, so that this stranger
Can tell his friends back home how good we are
In boxing, wrestling, jumping, and footraces."

And with that he led them outdoors. The herald
Hung the clear-toned lyre on its peg   *115*
And led Demodocus by the hand
Out of the hall and along the road
The nobles had gone down to see the games.
They made their way to the assembly grounds,
And huge crowds trailed along, thousands   *120*
Past counting.
                    Then up rose the young heroes.
Up rose Acroneus and Ocyalus and Elatreus;
Nauteus, Prymneus, Anchialus, and Eretmeus;
Ponteus, Proreus, Thoön, and Anabesineus;
Amphialus, Polyneus' son and Tecton's grandson;   *125*
And Euryalus, a match for the War God
And son of Naubolus. He was the handsomest
Of the Phaeacians, after peerless Laodamas.
And up rose the three sons of Alcinous,
Laodamas, Halius, and godlike Clytoneus.   *130*

The first contest was a footrace. The course
Stretched out before them from the starting post,
And they were off, raising dust from the plain
As they sped along. No one could keep up
With Clytoneus, who extended his lead   *135*
To the length of a furrow a mule-team plows.
That's how far ahead he was when he reached the crowd,
Leaving the rest of the field far behind.
Wrestling was next, and in this painful sport
Euryalus outdid the other young princes.   *140*

The best jumper proved to be Amphialus;
Elatreus took the discus throw; and Laodamas,
Alcinous' son, outboxed all comers.
Everyone had enjoyed the games, and then
Alcinous' son Laodamas said to his friends: *145*

"Come on, now. We should ask the stranger
Whether he is skilled in any sport. His build
Is impressive enough, his thighs and calves,
His arms and stout neck. This man is strong!
He's still got what it takes, but he has been broken   *150*
By many hardships. Nothing's worse than the sea
To get a man out of shape, no matter how strong he is."

And Euryalus answered him:

"Well spoken, Laodamas. Go ahead
And challenge him yourself, in public."   *155*

When Laodamas heard this, he strode out
Front and center and spoke to Odysseus:

"You should come forward, too, as our guest,
And try your hand at one of the sports,
If you are skilled in any. I'm sure you are,   *160*
For there is no greater glory a man can win in life
Than the glory he wins with his hands and feet.
So shrug off your cares and give it a try.
It won't delay your journey. Your ship
Is already launched and the crew is ready."   *165*

Odysseus, always thinking, answered him this way:

"Laodamas, why do you provoke me like this?
I have more serious things on my mind
Than track and field. I've had my share of suffering,
And paid my dues. Now I sit in the middle   *170*
Of your assembly, longing to return home,
A suppliant before your king and all the people."

Then Euryalus taunted him to his face:

"You know, stranger, I've seen a lot of sportsmen,
And you don't look like one to me at all.   *175*
You look more like the captain of a merchant ship,
Plying the seas with a crew of hired hands
And keeping a sharp eye on his cargo,
Greedy for profit. No, you're no athlete."

Odysseus stared the man down and said: *180*

"That's an ugly thing to say, stranger,
And it makes you look like a reckless fool.
The sad truth is that the gods don't give anyone
All their gifts, whether it's looks, intelligence,
Or eloquence. One man might not have good looks,   *185*
But the gods crown his words with beauty,
And men look at him with delight. He speaks
With unfaltering grace and sweet modesty,
And stands out in any crowd. When he walks
Through town, men look upon him as a god.   *190*
Another man might look like an immortal,
But his words are not crowned with beauty.
That's how it is with you. Your looks
Are outstanding. Not even a god
Could improve them. But your mind is crippled.   *195*
And now you've got my blood pumping
With your rude remarks. I'm no novice in sports,
As you suggest. No, I was one of the best,
When I could trust my youth and my hands.
Now I'm slowed down by my aches and pains   *200*
And the suffering I've had in war and at sea.
Even so, even with all I've been through,
I'll give your games a try. Your words
Cut deep, and now you've got me going."

He jumped up, cloak still on, and grabbed a discus   *205*
Larger than the others, thicker and much heavier
Than the one the Phaeacians used for competition.
Winding up, he let it fly, and the stone,

Launched with incredible force from his hand,
Hummed as it flew. The Phaeacians ducked   *210*
As the discus zoomed overhead and finally landed
Far beyond the other marks. Pallas Athena,
Who looked like a man now, marked the spot
Where it came down, and she called out to him:

"Even a blind man could find your mark, stranger,   *215*
For it's not all mixed up with the others
But way out front. You can be confident
No Phaeacian will come close to this throw."

Odysseus cheered up at this, glad to see
A loyal supporter out on the field.   *220*
In a lighter mood now, he spoke to the Phaeacians:

"Match that if you can, boys. In a minute
I'll get another one out just as far or farther.
And if anyone else has the urge to try me,
Step right up—I'm angry now—   *225*
I don't care if it's boxing, wrestling,
Or even running. Come one, come all—
Except Laodamas, who is my host.
Only a fool would challenge the man
Who gives him hospitality in a distant land.   *230*
He would only wind up hurting himself.
But I wouldn't turn down anyone else,
Or take any of you lightly. I only want
To see what you're made of, and to test myself.
I'm not weak in any athletic event,   *235*
And I really know how to handle a bow.
I'm always the first to hit my man
In the enemy lines, no matter how many archers
Are standing with me and getting off shots.
Only Philoctetes, of all the Greeks,   *240*
Outshot me at Troy. No one else came close,
Nor could any man now alive on this earth.
I do not compare myself to the men of old,
To Heracles, or Oechalian Eurytus,
Who tried to outshoot the immortal gods.   *245*

Eurytus died young, killed by Apollo,
Who was angry that he had challenged him
To a contest with the bow.
                              As for the spear,
I can throw it farther than you can shoot an arrow.
It's only in running that I fear some Phaeacian   250
May beat me to the line. I've taken a pounding
Out in the waves, and didn't come here aboard
A well-stocked ship, so my legs are still shaky."

He spoke, and they were all stunned to silence.
Only Alcinous was able to answer: 255

"Your words, stranger, are not ungracious.
You want only to demonstrate your prowess,
Angry that this man stood up at the games
And taunted you in a way no one ever would
Who knew in his heart how to speak fitly.   260
But now listen to my words, so that one day,
As you sit feasting with your wife and children,
You may tell another hero what you remember
Of the Phaeacians' skill in the feats that Zeus
Established as ours in our forefathers' days.   265
For we are not flawless boxers or wrestlers,
But we are swift of foot, and the best sailors,
And we love feasts and the lyre and dancing,
Fresh clothes, warm baths, and soft beds.
Up now, let the best dancers in Phaeacia dance,   270
So that the stranger can tell his friends back home
How superior we are in seamanship,
In fleetness of foot, in dancing, and in song.
Someone go get Demodocus his lyre,
Which is lying somewhere in the palace halls."   275

Thus godlike Alcinous, and the herald left
To get the hollow lyre from the king's palace.
Then up rose the officials, nine in all,
Who were in charge of the games. They marked out
A wide dancing ring and made the ground level.   280
The herald returned with the lyre, and Demodocus

Moved to the middle of the dancing ring,
Surrounded by boys in the bloom of youth,
Accomplished dancers all. Their feet struck the floor
Of the sacred ring, and as Odysseus watched   285
He marveled at how their feet flashed in the air.

Then Demodocus swept the strings of his lyre
And began his song. He sang of the passion
Between Ares and gold-crowned Aphrodite,
How they first made love in Hephaestus' house,   290
Sneaking around, and how the War God Ares
Showered her with gifts and shamed the bed
Of her husband, Hephaestus. But it wasn't long
Before Hephaestus found out. Helios told him
That he had seen them lying together in love.   295
When Hephaestus heard this heart-wrenching news
He went to his forge, brooding on his wrongs,
And set the great anvil up on its block
And hammered out a set of unbreakable bonds,
Bonds that couldn't loosen, bonds meant to stay put.   300
When he had wrought this snare, furious with Ares,
He went to his bedroom and spread the bonds
All around the bedposts, and hung many also
From the high roofbeams, as fine as cobwebs,
So fine not even the gods could see them.   305
When he had spread this cunning snare
All around the bed, he pretended to leave
On a trip to Lemnos, his favorite city.
Ares wasn't blind, and when he saw Hephaestus
On his way out, he headed for the house   310
Of the glorious smith, itching to make love
To the Cytherean goddess. She had been visiting
Her father, Zeus, and was just sitting down
When Ares came in, took her hand, and said:

"Let's go to bed, my love, and lie down together.   315
Hephaestus has left town, off to Lemnos no doubt
To visit the barbarous Sintians."

This suggestion appealed to the goddess,

And they climbed into bed. They were settling in
When the chains Hephaestus had cunningly wrought　　　　320
Fell all around them. They couldn't move an inch,
Couldn't lift a finger, and by the time it sank in
That there was no escape, there was Hephaestus,
Gimpy-legged and glorious, coming in the door.
He had turned back on his way to Lemnos　　　　　　325
As soon as Helios, his spy, gave him the word.
He stood in the doorway, seething with anger,
And with an ear-splitting yell called to the gods:

"Father Zeus and all you blessed gods eternal,
Come see something that is as ridiculous　　　　　　330
As it is unendurable, how Aphrodite,
Daughter of Zeus, scorns me for being lame
And loves that marauder Ares instead
Because he is handsome and well-knit, whereas I
Was born misshapen, which is no one's fault　　　　335
But my parents', who should have never begotten me!
Come take a look at how these two
Have climbed into my bed to make love and lie
In each other's arms. It kills me to see it!
But I don't think they will want to lie like this　　　340
Much longer, no matter how loving they are.
No, they won't want to sleep together for long,
But they're staying put in my little snare
Until her father returns all of the gifts
I gave him to marry this bitch-faced girl,　　　　　345
His beautiful, yes, but faithless daughter."

Thus Hephaestus, and the gods gathered
At his bronze threshold.
　　　　　　　　Poseidon came,
The God of Earthquake, and Hermes the Guide,
And the Archer Apollo. The goddesses　　　　　　350
All stayed home, out of modesty; but the gods
Stood in the doorway and laughed uncontrollably
When they saw Hephaestus' cunning and craft.
One of them would look at another and snigger:

"Crime doesn't pay."
                              "The slow catches the swift.   *355*
Slow as he is, old Gimpy caught Ares,
The fastest god on Olympus."
"Ares has to pay the fine for adultery."

That was the general drift of their jibes.
And then Apollo turned to Hermes and said: *360*

"Tell me, Hermes, would you be willing
To be pinched in chains if it meant you could lie
Side by side with golden Aphrodite?"

And the quicksilver messenger shot back:

"I tell you what, Apollo. Tie me up   *365*
With three times as many unbreakable chains,
And get all the gods and goddesses, too,
To come here and look, if it means I can sleep
Side by side with golden Aphrodite."

The gods roared with laughter, except Poseidon   *370*
Who did not think it was funny. He kept
Pleading that Ares should be released,
And his words winged their way to Hephaestus:

"Let him go, and I will ensure he will pay you
Fair compensation before all the gods."   *375*

And the renowned god, lame in both legs:

"Do not ask me to do this, Poseidon.
Worthless is the surety assured for the worthless.
How could I ever hold you to your promise
If Ares slipped out of the bonds and the debt?"   *380*

Poseidon the Earthshaker did not back off:

"Hephaestus, if Ares gets free and disappears
Without paying the debt, I will pay it myself."

And the renowned god, lame in both legs:

"I cannot refuse you. It wouldn't be right."   385

And with that the strong smith undid the bonds,
And the two of them, free at last from their crimp,
Shot out of there, Ares to Thrace,
And Aphrodite, who loves laughter and smiles,
To Paphos on Cyprus, and her precinct there   390
With its smoking altar. There the Graces
Bathed her and rubbed her with the ambrosial oil
That glistens on the skin of the immortal gods.
And then they dressed her in beautiful clothes,
A wonder to see.

           This was the song   395
The renowned bard sang, and Odysseus
Was glad as he listened, as were the Phaeacians,
Men who are famed for their long-oared ships.

Then Alcinous had Halius and Laodamas
Dance alone, for no one could match them.   400
They picked up a beautiful iridescent ball,
The work of Polybus. One of them
Would lean backward and toss it high
Toward the shadowy clouds, and the other
Would leap and catch it and shoot it back up   405
Before his feet ever touched ground again.
When they had tried their skill with upward throws
They started to dance on the bounteous earth,
Tossing the ball constantly back and forth.
The others beat time as they stood on the field,   410
And thunderous applause rose from the crowd.

Then Odysseus said to Alcinous:

"Lord Alcinous, you said that your dancers
Are the best in the world, and your words
Have proved true. I am in awe before them."   415

So he spoke, and the sacred king was glad.
He turned to his sea-loving people and said:

"Hear me Phaeacian lords and counselors.
Our guest seems in my eyes to be a man
Of the highest discernment. Come, then,   *420*
Let us give him a gift that befits a guest.
Twelve honored kings are lords in Phaeacia,
And I myself am the thirteenth king.
Let each of you twelve bring here now
A fresh cloak and tunic and a bar of fine gold.   *425*
Let us get these all together at once,
So that our guest may have these gifts in hand
And be glad at heart when he goes to supper.
And let Euryalus apologize and give him a gift,
For what he said to our guest was in no way proper."   *430*

The lords all approved of what Alcinous said,
And each sent a herald to fetch the gifts.
Then Euryalus in turn answered Alcinous:

"Lord Alcinous, renowned above all men,
I will indeed apologize to our guest, as you bid.   *435*
And I will give him this sword, all bronze
And with a silver hilt. It comes with a scabbard
Of newly sawn ivory, and will be worth much to him."

And he put the silver-studded sword
Into Odysseus' hands and said to him: *440*

"Revered stranger and guest, if any word
Has been harshly spoken, may the winds
Snatch it away. And may the gods grant
That you see your wife and come to your homeland,
For you have suffered long apart from your people."   *445*

And Odysseus, whose thoughts were many:

"And you, my friend, be well, and may the gods
Grant you happiness. And may you never miss

This sword you have given me to make amends."

He spoke, and slung the silver-studded sword   450
Around one shoulder.
                        The sun went down,
And the gifts were ready to be presented.
The heralds brought them into the palace
And Alcinous' sons set them down
Before their mother. They were beautiful gifts.   455
Alcinous, the sacred king, led the way
And the lords entered and sat on their thrones.
Then Alcinous in his might addressed Arete:

"Bring out the finest chest you have, my wife,
And place in it a newly washed cloak and tunic.   460
And heat water for our guest in a bronze cauldron,
So that when he has bathed and seen the gifts
The Phaeacians have brought all neatly stowed,
He will enjoy the feast and the words of the song.
And I will give him this beautiful cup,   465
Pure gold, to remember me by all of his days
As he pours wine to Zeus and to the other gods."

He spoke, and Arete signaled her women
To set a cauldron on the fire instantly.
They filled the cauldron with water for a bath,   470
Set kindling beneath it and lit the fire.
The flames licked the belly of the cauldron
And the water grew warm.
                        Arete meanwhile
Brought out a handsome chest for the stranger
And placed within it the beautiful gifts,   475
The clothes and the gold which the nobles gave.
And she herself placed in it a cloak
And beautiful tunic. And she said to Odysseus:

"There is the lid. Tie it down with a knot
As a precaution against someone robbing you   480
On your way back, when you are lying asleep

On your journey home in the swift, black ship."

When Odysseus, who had borne much, heard this,
He tied the lid down quickly with a cunning knot
He had learned from Circe. Then the housekeeper came   *485*
To tell him it was time to go and bathe. The warm bath
Was a welcome sight to Odysseus. He had not been
Cared for like this since leaving Calypso,
Who had treated him as if he were a god.

When the women had bathed him, rubbed him with oil,   *490*
And clothed him in a beautiful tunic and cloak,
Odysseus strode from the bath and was on his way
To join the men drinking wine.
                              Nausicaa,
Beautiful as only the gods could make her,
Stood by the doorpost of the great hall.   *495*
Her eyes went wide when she saw Odysseus,
And her words beat their way to him on wings:

"Farewell, stranger, and remember me
In your own native land. I saved your life."

And Odysseus, whose thoughts ran deep: *500*

"Nausicaa, daughter of great Alcinous,
So may Zeus, Hera's thundering lord,
Grant that I see my homeland again.
There I will pray to you, as to a god,
All of my days. I owe you my life."   *505*

And he took his seat next to Lord Alcinous.
They were serving food and mixing the wine
When the herald came up leading the bard,
Honored Demodocus, and seated him on a chair
Propped against a tall pillar in the middle of the hall.   *510*
Odysseus, with his great presence of mind,
Cut off part of a huge chine of roast pork
Glistening with fat, and said to the herald:

"Herald, take this cut of meat to Demodocus
For him to eat. And I will greet him   515
Despite my grief. Bards are revered
By all men upon earth, for the Muse
Loves them well and has taught them the songways."

The herald brought the cut of meat to Demodocus
And placed it in his hands, much to the bard's delight.   520
Then everyone reached out to the feast before them,
And when they had eaten and drunk to their hearts' content,
Odysseus spoke to Demodocus:

"I don't know whether it was the Muse
Who taught you, or Apollo himself,   525
But I praise you to the skies, Demodocus.
When you sing about the fate of the Greeks
Who fought at Troy, you have it right,
All that they did and suffered, all they endured.
It's as if you had been there yourself,   530
Or heard a first-hand account. But now,
Switch to the building of the wooden horse
Which Epeius made with Athena's help,
The horse which Odysseus led up to Troy
As a trap, filled with men who would   535
Destroy great Ilium. If you tell me this story
Just as it happened, I will tell the whole world
That some god must have opened his heart
And given to you the divine gift of song."

So he spoke, and the bard, moved by the god,   540
Began to sing. He made them see it happen,
How the Greeks set fire to their huts on the beach
And were sailing away, while Odysseus
And the picked men with him sat in the horse,
Which the Trojans had dragged into their city.   545
There the horse stood, and the Trojans sat around it
And could not decide what they should do.
There were three ways of thinking:
Hack open the timbers with pitiless bronze,
Or throw it from the heights to the rocks below,   550

Or let it stand as an offering to appease the gods.
The last was what would happen, for it was fated
That the city would perish once it enclosed
The great wooden horse, in which now sat
The Greek heroes who would spill Troy's blood.   555
The song went on. The Greeks poured out
Of their hollow ambush and sacked the city.
He sang how one hero here and another there
Ravaged tall Troy, but how Odysseus went,
Like the War God himself, with Menelaus   560
To the house of Deiphobus, and there, he said,
Odysseus fought his most daring battle
And won with the help of Pallas Athena.

This was his song. And Odysseus wept. Tears
Welled up in his eyes and flowed down his cheeks.   565

> *A woman wails as she throws herself upon*
> *Her husband's body. He has fallen in battle*
> *Before the town walls, fighting to the last*
> *To defend his city and protect his children.*
> *As she sees him dying and gasping for breath*   570
> *She clings to him and shrieks, while behind her*
> *Soldiers prod their spears into her shoulders and back,*
> *And as they lead her away into slavery*
> *Her tear-drenched face is a mask of pain.*

So too Odysseus, pitiful in his grief.   575
He managed to conceal his tears from everyone
Except Alcinous, who sat at his elbow
And could not help but hear his heavy sighs.
Alcinous acted quickly and said to his guests:

"Hear me, Phaeacian counselors and lords—   580
Demodocus should stop playing his lyre.
His song is not pleasing to everyone here.
Ever since dinner began and the divine bard
Rose up to sing, our guest has not ceased
From lamentation. He is overcome with grief.   585
Let the lyre stop. It is better if we all,

Host and guest alike, can enjoy the feast.
All that we are doing we are doing on behalf
Of the revered stranger, providing him
With passage home and gifts of friendship.   590
A stranger and suppliant is as dear as a brother
To anyone with even an ounce of good sense.
So there is no need, stranger, for you to withhold
What I am about to ask for, no need to be crafty
Or think of gain. Better to speak the plain truth.   595
Tell me your name, the one you were known by
To your mother and father and your people back home.
No one is nameless, rich man or poor.
Parents give names to all of their children
When they are born. And tell me your country,   600
Your city, and your land, so that our ships
May take you there, finding their way by their wits.
For Phaeacian ships do not have pilots,
Nor steering oars, as other ships have.
They know on their own their passengers' thoughts,   605
And know all the cities and rich fields in the world,
And they cross the great gulfs with the greatest speed,
Hidden in mist and fog, with never a fear
Of damage or shipwreck.
                            But I remember hearing
My father, Nausithous, say how Poseidon   610
Was angry with us because we always give
Safe passage to men. He said that one day
Poseidon would smite a Phaeacian ship
As it sailed back home over the misty sea,
And would encircle our city within a mountain.   615
The old man used to say that, and either the god
Will bring it to pass or not, as suits his pleasure.
But tell me this, and tell me the truth.
Where have you wandered, to what lands?
Tell me about the people and cities you saw,   620
Which ones are cruel and without right and wrong,
And which are godfearing and kind to strangers.
And tell me why you weep and grieve at heart
When you hear the fate of the Greeks and Trojans.
This was the gods' doing. They spun that fate   625

So that in later times it would turn into song.
Did some kinsman of yours die at Troy,
A good, loyal man, your daughter's husband
Or your wife's father, someone near and dear,
Or perhaps even a relative by blood?   *630*
Or was it a comrade, tried and true?
A friend like that is no less than a brother."

ODYSSEY 9

And Odysseus, his great mind teeming:

"My Lord Alcinous, what could be finer
Than listening to a singer of tales
Such as Demodocus, with a voice like a god's?
Nothing we do is sweeter than this—   5
A cheerful gathering of all the people
Sitting side by side throughout the halls,
Feasting and listening to a singer of tales,
The tables filled with food and drink,
The server drawing wine from the bowl   10
And bringing it around to fill our cups.
For me, this is the finest thing in the world.
But you have a mind to draw out of me
My pain and sorrow, and make me feel it again.
Where should I begin, where end my story?   15
Heaven has sent me many tribulations.
I will tell you my name first, so that you, too,
Will know who I am, and when I escape
The day of my doom, I will always be
Your friend and host, though my home is far.   20
I am Odysseus, great Laertes' son,
Known for my cunning throughout the world,
And my fame reaches even to heaven.
My native land is Ithaca, a sunlit island
With a forested peak called Neriton,   25
Visible for miles. Many other islands
Lie close around her—Doulichion, Samê,
And wooded Zacynthos—off toward the sunrise,

But Ithaca lies low on the evening horizon,
A rugged place, a good nurse of men.   *30*
No sight is sweeter to me than Ithaca. Yes,
Calypso, the beautiful goddess, kept me
In her caverns, yearning to possess me;
And Circe, the witch of Aeaea, held me
In her halls and yearned to possess me;   *35*
But they could not persuade me or touch my heart.
Nothing is sweeter than your own country
And your own parents, not even living in a rich house—
Not if it's far from family and home.
But let me tell you of the hard journey homeward   *40*
Zeus sent me on when I sailed from Troy.

From Ilion the wind took me to the Cicones
In Ismaros. I pillaged the town and killed the men.
The women and treasure that we took out
I divided as fairly as I could among all hands   *45*
And then gave the command to pull out fast.
That was my order, but the fools wouldn't listen.
They drank a lot of wine and slaughtered
A lot of sheep and cattle on the shore.
Some of the town's survivors got away inland   *50*
And called their kinsmen. There were more of them,
And they were braver, too, men who knew how to fight
From chariots and on foot. They came on as thick
As leaves and flowers in spring, attacking
At dawn. We were out of luck, cursed by Zeus   *55*
To suffer heavy losses. The battle-lines formed
Along our beached ships, and bronze spears
Sliced through the air. As long as the day's heat
Climbed toward noon, we held our ground
Against superior numbers. But when the sun   *60*
Dipped down, the Cicones beat us down, too.
We lost six fighting men from each of our ships.
The rest of us cheated destiny and death.

We sailed on in shock, glad to get out alive
But grieving for our lost comrades.   *65*
I wouldn't let the ships get under way

Until someone had called out three times
For each mate who had fallen on the battlefield.
And then Zeus hit us with a norther,
A freak hurricane. The clouds blotted out   70
Land and sea, and night climbed up the sky.
The ships pitched ahead. When their sails
Began to shred in the gale-force winds,
We lowered them and stowed them aboard,
Fearing the worst, and rowed hard for the mainland.   75
We lay offshore two miserable days and nights.
When Dawn combed her hair in the third day's light,
We set up the masts, hoisted the white sails,
And took our seats. The wind and the helmsmen
Steered the ships, and I would have made it home   80
Unscathed, but as I was rounding Cape Malea
The waves, the current, and wind from the North
Drove me off course past Cythera Island.

Nine days of bad winds blew us across
The teeming seas. On the tenth day we came   85
To the land of the Lotus-Eaters.
                                  We went ashore,
And the crews lost no time in drawing water
And preparing a meal beside their ships.
After they had filled up on food and drink,
I sent out a team—two picked men and a herald—   90
To reconnoiter and sound out the locals.
They headed out and made contact with the Lotus-Eaters,
Who meant no harm but did give my men
Some lotus to eat. Whoever ate that sweet fruit
Lost the will to report back, preferring instead   95
To stay there, munching lotus, oblivious of home.
I hauled them back wailing to the ships,
Bound them under the benches, then ordered
All hands to board their ships on the double
Before anyone else tasted the lotus.   100
They were aboard in no time and at their benches,
Churning the sea white with their oars.

We sailed on, our morale sinking,

And we came to the land of the Cyclopes,
Lawless savages who leave everything   *105*
Up to the gods. These people neither plow nor plant,
But everything grows for them unsown:
Wheat, barley, and vines that bear
Clusters of grapes, watered by rain from Zeus.
They have no assemblies or laws but live   *110*
In high mountain caves, ruling their own
Children and wives and ignoring each other.

A fertile island slants across the harbor's mouth,
Neither very close nor far from the Cyclopes' shore.
It's well-wooded and populated with innumerable   *115*
Wild goats, uninhibited by human traffic.
Not even hunters go there, tramping through the woods
And roughing it on the mountainsides.
It pastures no flocks, has no tilled fields—
Unplowed, unsown, virgin forever, bereft   *120*
Of men, all it does is support those bleating goats.
The Cyclopes do not sail and have no craftsmen
To build them benched, red-prowed ships
That could supply all their wants, crossing the sea
To other cities, visiting each other as other men do.   *125*
These same craftsmen would have made this island
Into a good settlement. It's not a bad place at all
And would bear everything in season. Meadows
Lie by the seashore, lush and soft,
Where vines would thrive. It has level plowland   *130*
With deep, rich soil that would produce bumper crops
Season after season. The harbor's good, too,
No need for moorings, anchor-stones, or tying up.
Just beach your ship until the wind is right
And you're ready to sail. At the harbor's head   *135*
A spring flows clear and bright from a cave
Surrounded by poplars.
                         There we sailed in,
Some god guiding us through the murky night.
We couldn't see a thing. A thick fog
Enveloped the ships, and the moon   *140*
Wasn't shining in the cloud-covered sky.

None of us could see the island, or the long waves
Rolling toward the shore, until we ran our ships
Onto the sandy beach. Then we lowered sail,
Disembarked, and fell asleep on the sand.   *145*

Dawn came early, with palmettoes of rose,
And we explored the island, marveling at it.
The spirit-women, daughters of Zeus,
Roused the mountain goats so that my men
Could have a meal. We ran to the ships,   *150*
Got our javelins and bows, formed three groups
And started to shoot. The god let us bag our game,
Nine goats for each of the twelve ships,
Except for my ship, which got ten.

So all day long until the sun went down   *155*
We feasted on meat and sweet wine.
The ships had not yet run out of the dark red
Each crew had taken aboard in large jars
When we ransacked the Cicones' sacred city.
And we looked across at the Cyclopes' land.   *160*
We could see the smoke from their fires
And hear their voices, and their sheep and goats.
When the sun set, and darkness came on
We went to sleep on the shore of the sea.
As soon as dawn brightened in the rosy sky,   *165*
I assembled all the crews and spoke to them:

'The rest of you will stay here while I go
With my ship and crew on reconnaissance.
I want to find out what those men are like,
Wild savages with no sense of right or wrong   *170*
Or hospitable folk who fear the gods.'

With that, I boarded ship and ordered my crew
To get on deck and cast off. They took their places
And were soon whitening the sea with their oars.
As we pulled in over the short stretch of water,   *175*
There on the shoreline we saw a high cave
Overhung with laurels. It was a place

Where many sheep and goats were penned at night.
Around it was a yard fenced in by stones
Set deep in the earth, and by tall pines and crowned oaks.   *180*
This was the lair of a huge creature, a man
Who pastured his flocks off by himself,
And lived apart from others and knew no law.
He was a freak of nature, not like men who eat bread,
But like a lone wooded crag high in the mountains.   *185*

I ordered part of my crew to stay with the ship
And counted off the twelve best to go with me.
I took along a goatskin filled with red wine,
A sweet vintage I had gotten from Maron,
Apollo's priest on Ismaros, when I spared both him   *190*
And his wife and child out of respect for the god.
He lived in a grove of Phoebus Apollo
And gave me splendid gifts: seven bars of gold,
A solid-silver bowl, and twelve jars of wine,
Sweet and pure, a drink for the gods.   *195*
Hardly anyone in his house, none of the servants,
Knew about this wine—just Maron, his wife,
And a single housekeeper. Whenever he drank
This sweet dark red wine, he would fill one goblet
And pour it into twenty parts of water,   *200*
And the bouquet that spread from the mixing bowl
Was so fragrant no one could hold back from drinking.
I had a large skin of this wine, a sack
Of provisions—and a strong premonition
We had a rendezvous with a man of great might,   *205*
A savage with no notion of right and wrong.

We got to the cave quickly. He was out,
Tending his flocks in the rich pastureland.
We went inside and had a good look around.
There were crates stuffed with cheese, and pens   *210*
Crammed with lambs and kids—firstlings,
Middlings, and newborns in separate sections.
The vessels he used for milking—pails and bowls
Of good workmanship—were brimming with whey.
My men thought we should make off with some cheese   *215*

And then come back for the lambs and kids,
Load them on board, and sail away on the sea.
But I wouldn't listen. It would have been far better
If I had! But I wanted to see him, and see
If he would give me a gift of hospitality.   220
When he did come he was not a welcome sight.

We lit a fire and offered sacrifice
And helped ourselves to some of the cheese.
Then we sat and waited in the cave
Until he came back, herding his flocks.   225
He carried a huge load of dry wood
To make a fire for his supper and heaved it down
With a crash inside the cave. We were terrified
And scurried back into a corner.
He drove his fat flocks into the wide cavern,   230
At least those that he milked, leaving the males—
The rams and the goats—outside in the yard.
Then he lifted up a great doorstone,
A huge slab of rock, and set it in place.
Two sturdy wagons—twenty sturdy wagons—   235
Couldn't pry it from the ground—that's how big
The stone was he set in the doorway. Then,
He sat down and milked the ewes and bleating goats,
All in good order, and put the sucklings
Beneath their mothers. Half of the white milk   240
He curdled and scooped into wicker baskets,
The other half he let stand in the pails
So he could drink it later for his supper.
He worked quickly to finish his chores,
And as he was lighting the fire he saw us and said: 245

'Who are you strangers? Sailing the seas, huh?
Where from, and what for? Pirates, probably,
Roaming around causing people trouble.'

He spoke, and it hit us like a punch in the gut—
His booming voice and the sheer size of the monster—   250
But even so I found the words to answer him:

'We are Greeks, blown off course by every wind
In the world on our way home from Troy, traveling
Sea routes we never meant to, by Zeus' will no doubt.
We are proud to be the men of Agamemnon,   255
Son of Atreus, the greatest name under heaven,
Conquerer of Troy, destroyer of armies.
Now we are here, suppliants at your knees,
Hoping you will be generous to us
And give us the gifts that are due to strangers.   260
Respect the gods, sir. We are your suppliants,
And Zeus avenges strangers and suppliants,
Zeus, god of strangers, who walks at their side.'

He answered me from his pitiless heart:

'You're dumb, stranger, or from far away,   265
If you ask me to fear the gods. Cyclopes
Don't care about Zeus or his aegis
Or the blessed gods, since we are much stronger.
I wouldn't spare you or your men
Out of fear of Zeus. I would spare them only   270
If I myself wanted to. But tell me,
Where did you leave your ship? Far
Down the coast, or close? I'd like to know.'

Nice try, but I knew all the tricks and said:

'My ship? Poseidon smashed it to pieces   275
Against the rocks at the border of your land.
He pushed her in close and the wind did the rest.
These men and I escaped by the skin of our teeth.'

This brought no response from his pitiless heart
But a sudden assault upon my men. His hands   280
Reached out, seized two of them, and smashed them
To the ground like puppies. Their brains spattered out
And oozed into the dirt. He tore them limb from limb
To make his supper, gulping them down
Like a mountain lion, leaving nothing behind—   285
Guts, flesh, or marrowy bones.

Crying out, we lifted our hands to Zeus
At this outrage, bewildered and helpless.
When the Cyclops had filled his huge belly
With human flesh, he washed it down with milk,   290
Then stretched out in his cave among his flocks.
I crept up close and was thinking about
Drawing my sharp sword and driving it home
Into his chest where the lungs hide the liver.
I was feeling for the spot when another thought   295
Checked my hand: we would die to a man in that cave,
Unable to budge the enormous stone
He had set in place to block the entrance. And so,
Groaning through the night, we waited for dawn.

As soon as dawn came, streaking the sky red,   300
He rekindled the fire and milked his flocks,
All in good order, and placing the sucklings
Beneath their mothers. His chores done,
He seized two of my men and made his meal.
After he had fed he drove his flocks out,   305
Easily lifting the great stone, which he then set
Back in place as lightly as if he were setting
A lid upon a quiver. And then, with loud whistling,
The Cyclops turned his fat flocks toward the mountain,
And I was left there, brooding on how   310
I might make him pay and win glory from Athena.

This was the best plan I could come up with:
Beside one of the sheep pens lay a huge pole
Of green olive which the Cyclops had cut
To use as a walking stick when dry. Looking at it   315
We guessed it was about as large as the mast
Of a black ship, a twenty-oared, broad-beamed
Freighter that crosses the wide gulfs.
That's how long and thick it looked. I cut off
About a fathom's length from this pole   320
And handed it over to my men. They scraped it
And made it smooth, and I sharpened the tip
And took it over to the fire and hardened it.
Then I hid it, setting it carefully in the dung

That lay in piles all around the cave.   *325*
And I told my men to draw straws to decide
Which of them would have to share the risk with me—
Lift that stake and grind it in his eye
While he was asleep. They drew straws and came up with
The very men I myself would have chosen.   *330*
There were four of them, and I made five.

At evening he came, herding his fleecy sheep.
He drove them straight into the cave, drove in
All his flocks in fact. Maybe he had some
Foreboding, or maybe some god told him to.   *335*
Then he lifted the doorstone and set it in place,
And sat down to milk the goats and bleating ewes,
All in good order, and setting the sucklings
Beneath their mothers. His chores done,
Again he seized two of my men and made his meal.   *340*
Then I went up to the Cyclops and spoke to him,
Holding an ivy-wood bowl filled with dark wine.

'Cyclops, have some wine, now that you have eaten
Your human flesh, so you can see what kind of drink
Was in our ship's hold. I was bringing it to you   *345*
As an offering, hoping you would pity me
And help me get home. But you are a raving
Maniac! How do you expect any other man
Ever to visit you after acting like this?'

He took the bowl and drank it off, relishing   *350*
Every last, sweet drop. And he asked me for more:

'Be a pal and give me another drink. And tell me
Your name, so I can give you a gift you'll like.
Wine grapes grow in the Cyclopes' land, too.
Rain from the sky makes them grow from the earth.   *355*
But this—this is straight ambrosia and nectar.'

So I gave him some more of the ruby-red wine.
Three times the fool drained the bowl dry,
And when the wine had begun to work on his mind,

I spoke these sweet words to him:

                 'Cyclops,   *360*
You ask me my name, my glorious name,
And I will tell it to you. Remember now,
To give me the gift just as you promised.
Noman is my name. They call me Noman—
My mother, my father, and all my friends, too.'   *365*

He answered me from his pitiless heart:

'Noman I will eat last after his friends.
Friends first, him last. That's my gift to you.'

He listed as he spoke and then fell flat on his back,
His thick neck bent sideways. He was sound asleep,   *370*
Belching out wine and bits of human flesh
In his drunken stupor. I swung into action,
Thrusting the stake deep in the embers,
Heating it up, and all the while talking to my men
To keep up their morale. When the olivewood stake   *375*
Was about to catch fire, green though it was,
And was really glowing, I took it out
And brought it right up to him. My men
Stood around me, and some god inspired us.
My men lifted up the olivewood stake   *380*
And drove the sharp point right into his eye,
While I, putting my weight behind it, spun it around
The way a man bores a ship's beam with a drill,
Leaning down on it while other men beneath him
Keep it spinning and spinning with a leather strap.   *385*
That's how we twirled the fiery-pointed stake
In the Cyclops' eye. The blood formed a whirlpool
Around its searing tip. His lids and brow
Were all singed by the heat from the burning eyeball
And its roots crackled in the fire and hissed   *390*
Like an axe-head or adze a smith dips into water
When he wants to temper the iron—that's how his eye
Sizzled and hissed around the olivewood stake.
He screamed, and the rock walls rang with his voice.

We shrank back in terror while he wrenched   *395*
The blood-grimed stake from his eye and flung it
Away from him, blundering about and shouting
To the other Cyclopes, who lived around him
In caverns among the windswept crags.
They heard his cry and gathered from all sides   *400*
Around his cave and asked him what ailed him:

'Polyphemus, why are you hollering so much
And keeping us up the whole blessed night ?
Is some man stealing your flocks from you,
Or killing you, maybe, by some kind of trick?'   *405*

And Polyphemus shouted out to them:

'Noman is killing me by some kind of trick!'

They sent their words winging back to him:

'If no man is hurting you, then your sickness
Comes from Zeus and can't be helped.   *410*
You should pray to your father, Lord Poseidon.'

They left then, and I laughed in my heart
At how my phony name had fooled them so well.
Cyclops meanwhile was groaning in agony.
Groping around, he removed the doorstone   *415*
And sat in the entrance with his hands spread out
To catch anyone who went out with the sheep—
As if I could be so stupid. I thought it over,
Trying to come up with the best plan I could
To get us all out from the jaws of death.   *420*
I wove all sorts of wiles, as a man will
When his life is on the line. My best idea
Had to do with the sheep that were there, big,
Thick-fleeced beauties with wool dark as violets.
Working silently, I bound them together   *425*
With willow branches the Cyclops slept on.
I bound them in threes. Each middle sheep
Carried a man underneath, protected by

The two on either side: three sheep to a man.
As for me, there was a ram, the best in the flock. 430
I grabbed his back and curled up beneath
His shaggy belly. There I lay, hands twined
Into the marvelous wool, hanging on for dear life.
And so, muffling our groans, we waited for dawn.

When the first streaks of red appeared in the sky, 435
The rams started to bolt toward the pasture.
The umilked females were bleating in the pens,
Their udders bursting. Their master,
Worn out with pain, felt along the backs
Of all of the sheep as they walked by, the fool, 440
Unaware of the men under their fleecy chests.
The great ram headed for the entrance last,
Heavy with wool—and with me thinking hard.
Running his hands over the ram, Polyphemus said:

'My poor ram, why are you leaving the cave 445
Last of all? You've never lagged behind before.
You were always the first to reach the soft grass
With your big steps, first to reach the river,
First to want to go back to the yard
At evening. Now you're last of all. Are you sad 450
About your master's eye? A bad man blinded me,
Him and his nasty friends, getting me drunk,
Noman—but he's not out of trouble yet!
If only you understood and could talk,
You could tell me where he's hiding. I would 455
Smash him to bits and spatter his brains
All over the cave. Then I would find some relief
From the pain this no-good Noman has caused me.'

He spoke, and sent the ram off through the door.
When we had gone a little way from the cave, 460
I first untangled myself from the ram
And then untied my men. Then, moving quickly,
We drove those fat, long-shanked sheep
Down to the ship, keeping an eye on our rear.
We were a welcome sight to the rest of the crew, 465

But when they started to mourn the men we had lost
I forbade it with an upward nod of my head,
Signaling each man like that and ordering them
To get those fleecy sheep aboard instead,
On the double, and get the ship out to sea.   470
Before you knew it they were on their benches
Beating the sea to white froth with their oars.
When we were offshore but still within earshot,
I called out to the Cyclops, just to rub it in:

'So, Cyclops, it turns out it wasn't a coward   475
Whose men you murdered and ate in your cave,
You savage! But you got yours in the end,
Didn't you? You had the gall to eat the guests
In your own house, and Zeus made you pay for it.'

He was even angrier when he heard this.   480
Breaking off the peak of a huge crag
He threw it toward our ship, and it carried
To just in front of our dark prow. The sea
Billowed up where the rock came down,
And the backwash pushed us to the mainland again,   485
Like a flood tide setting us down at the shore.
I grabbed a long pole and shoved us off,
Nodding to the crew to fall on the oars
And get us out of there. They leaned into it,
And when we were twice as far out to sea as before   490
I called to the Cyclops again, with my men
Hanging all over me and begging me not to:

'Don't do it, man! The rock that hit the water
Pushed us in and we thought we were done for.
If he hears any sound from us, he'll heave   495
Half a cliff at us and crush the ship and our skulls
With one throw. You know he has the range.'

They tried, but didn't persuade my hero's heart—
I was really angry—and I called back to him:

'Cyclops, if anyone, any mortal man,   500

Asks you how you got your eye put out,
Tell him that Odysseus the marauder did it,
Son of Laertes, whose home is on Ithaca.'

He groaned, and had this to say in response:

'Oh no! Now it's coming to me, the old prophecy.   505
There was a seer here once, a tall handsome man,
Telemos Eurymides. He prophesied well
All his life to the Cyclopes. He told me
That all this would happen some day,
That I would lose my sight at Odysseus' hands.   510
I always expected a great hero
Would come here, strong as can be.
Now this puny, little, good-for-nothing runt
Has put my eye out—because he got me drunk.
But come here, Odysseus, so I can give you a gift,   515
And ask Poseidon to help you on your way.
I'm his son, you know. He claims he's my father.
He will heal me, if he wants. But none
Of the other gods will, and no mortal man will.'

He had his say and then prayed to Poseidon,   520
Stretching his arms out to starry heaven:

'Hear me, Poseidon, blue-maned Earth-Holder,
If you are the father you claim to be.
Grant that Odysseus, son of Laertes,
May never reach his home on Ithaca.   525
But if he is fated to see his family again,
And return to his home and own native land,
May he come late, having lost all companions,
In another's ship, and find trouble at home.'

He prayed, and the blue-maned sea-god heard him.   530
Then he broke off an even larger chunk of rock,
Pivoted, and threw it with incredible force.
It came down just behind our dark-hulled ship,
Barely missing the end of the rudder. The sea
Billowed up where the rock hit the water,   535

And the wave pushed us forward all the way
To the island where our other ships waited
Clustered on the shore, ringed by our comrades
Sitting on the sand, anxious for our return.
We beached the ship and unloaded the Cyclops' sheep,   540
Which I divided up as fairly as I could
Among all hands. The veterans gave me the great ram,
And I sacrificed it on the shore of the sea
To Zeus in the dark clouds, who rules over all.
I burnt the thigh pieces, but the god did not accept   545
My sacrifice, brooding over how to destroy
All my benched ships and my trusty crews.

So all the long day until the sun went down
We sat feasting on meat and drinking sweet wine.
When the sun set and darkness came on   550
We lay down and slept on the shore of the sea.
Early in the morning, when the sky was streaked red,
I roused my men and ordered the crews
To get on deck and cast off. They took their places
And were soon whitening the sea with their oars.   555

We sailed on in shock, glad to get away alive
But grieving for the comrades we had lost."

Odyssey 10

"We came next to the island of Aeolia,
Home of Aeolus, son of Hippotas,
Dear to the immortals. Aeolia
Is a floating island surrounded by a wall
Of indestructible bronze set on sheer stone. 5
Aeolus' twelve children live there with him,
Six daughters and six manly sons.
He married his daughters off to his boys,
And they all sit with their father and mother
Continually feasting on abundant good cheer 10
Spread out before them. Every day
The house is filled with steamy savor
And the courtyard resounds. Every night
The men sleep next to their high-born wives
On blankets strewn on their corded beds. 15
We came to their city and their fine palace,
And for a full month he entertained me.
He questioned me in great detail about Troy,
The Greek fleet, and the Greeks' return home.
I told him everything, from beginning to end. 20
And when I, in turn, asked if I might leave
And requested him to send me on my way,
He did not refuse, and this was his send-off:
He gave me a bag made of the hide of an ox
Nine years old, which he had skinned himself, 25
And in this bag he bound the wild winds' ways,
For Zeus had made him keeper of the winds,
To still or to rouse whichever he will.
He tied this bag down in the hold of my ship

With a bright silver cord, so that not a puff   30
Could escape. But he let the West Wind out
To blow my ships along and carry us home.
It was not to be. Our own folly undid us.

For nine days and nights we sailed on.
On the tenth day we raised land, our own   35
Native fields, and got so close we saw men
Tending their fires. Then sleep crept up on me,
Exhausted from minding the sail the whole time
By myself. I wouldn't let any of my crew
Spell me, because I wanted to make good time.   40
As soon as I fell asleep, the men started to talk,
Saying I was bringing home for myself
Silver and gold as gifts from great Aeolus.
You can imagine the sort of things they said:

'This guy gets everything wherever he goes.   45
First, he's freighting home his loot from Troy,
Beautiful stuff, while we, who made the same trip,
Are coming home empty-handed. And now
Aeolus has lavished these gifts upon him.
Let's have a quick look, and see what's here,   50
How much gold and silver is stuffed in this bag.'

All malicious nonsense, but it won out in the end,
And they opened the bag. The winds rushed out
And bore them far out to sea, weeping
As their native land faded on the horizon.   55
When I woke up and saw what had happened
I thought long and hard about whether I should
Just go over the side and end it all in the sea
Or endure in silence and remain among the living.
In the end I decided to bear it and live.   60
I wrapped my head in my cloak and lay down on the deck
While an evil wind carried the ships
Back to Aeolia. My comrades groaned.

We went ashore and drew water
And the men took a meal beside the swift ships.   65

When we had tasted food and drink
I took a herald and one man
And went to Aeolus' glorious palace.
I found him feasting with his wife and children,
And when we came in and sat on the threshold   70
They were amazed and questioned me:

'What happened, Odysseus? What evil spirit
Abused you? Surely we sent you off
With all you needed to get back home
Or anywhere else your heart desired.'   75

I answered them from the depths of my sorrow:

'My evil crew ruined me, that and stubborn sleep.
But make it right, friends, for you have the power.'

I made my voice soft and tried to persuade them,
But they were silent. And then their father said: 80

'Begone from this island instantly!
You are the most cursed of all living things.
It would go against all that is right
For me to help or send on his way
A man so despised by the blessed gods.   85
Begone! You are cursed by heaven!'

And with that he sent me from his house,
Groaning heavily. We sailed on from there
With grief in our hearts. Because of our folly
There was no breeze to push us along,   90
And our morale sank because the rowing was hard.
We sailed on for six solid days and nights,
And on the seventh we came to Lamus,
The lofty city of Telepylus
In the land of the Laestrygonians,   95
Where a herdsman driving in his flocks at dusk
Calls to another driving his out at dawn.
A man could earn a double wage there
If he never slept, one by herding cattle

And another by pasturing white sheep,   *100*
For night and day make one twilight there.
The harbor we came to is a glorious place,
Surrounded by sheer cliffs. Headlands
Jut out on either side to form a narrow mouth,
And there all the others steered in their ships   *105*
And moored them close together in the bay.
No wave, large or small, ever rocks a boat
In that silvery calm. I alone moored my black ship
Outside the harbor, tying her up
On the rocks that lie on the border of the land.   *110*
Then I climbed to a rugged lookout point
And surveyed the scene. There was no sign
Of plowed fields, only smoke rising up from the land.

I sent out a team—two picked men and a herald—
To reconnoiter and find out who lived there.   *115*
They went ashore and followed a smooth road
Used by wagons to bring wood from the mountains
Down to the city. In front of the city
They met a girl drawing water. Her father
Was named Antiphates, and she had come down   *120*
To the flowing spring Artacia,
From which they carried water to the town.
When my men came up to her and asked her
Who the people there were and who was their king,
She showed them her father's high-roofed house.   *125*
They entered the house and found his wife inside,
A woman, to their horror, as huge as a mountain top.
At once she called her husband, Antiphates,
Who meant business when he came. He seized
One of my men and made him into dinner.   *130*
The other two got out of there and back to the ships,
But Antiphates had raised a cry throughout the city,
And when they heard it, the Laestrygonians
Came up on all sides, thousands of them,
Not like men but like the Sons of the Earth,   *135*
The Giants. They pelted us from the cliffs
With rocks too large for a man to lift.
The sounds that came from the ships were sickening,

Sounds of men dying and boats being crushed.
The Laestrygonians speared the bodies like fish,   *140*
And carried them back for their ghastly meal.
While this was happening I drew my sword
And cut the cables of my dark-prowed ship,
Barking out orders for the crew to start rowing
And get us out of there. They rowed for their lives,   *145*
Ripping the sea, and my ship sped joyfully
Out and away from the beetling rocks,
But all of the others were destroyed as they lay.

We sailed on in shock, glad to get out alive
But grieving for the comrades we'd lost.   *150*
And we came to Aeaea, the island that is home
To Circe, a dread goddess with richly coiled hair
And a human voice. She is the sister
Of dark-hearted Aeetes, and they are both sprung
From Helios and Perse, daughter of Ocean.   *155*
Some god guided us into a harbor
And we put in to shore without a sound.
We disembarked and lay there for two days and nights,
Eating our hearts out with weariness and grief.
But when Dawn combed her hair in the third day's light,   *160*
I took my sword and spear and went up
From the ship to open ground, hoping to see
Plowed fields, and to hear human voices.
So I climbed to a rugged lookout point
And surveyed the scene. What I saw was smoke   *165*
Rising up from Circe's house. It curled up high
Through the thick brush and woods, and I wondered
Whether I should go and have a closer look.
I decided it was better to go back to the ship
And give my crew their meal, and then   *170*
Send out a party to reconnoiter.
I was on my way back and close to the ship
When some god took pity on me,
Walking there alone, and sent a great antlered stag
Right into my path. He was on his way   *175*
Down to the river from his pasture in the woods,
Thirsty and hot from the sun beating down,

And as he came out I got him right on the spine
In the middle of his back. The bronze spear bored
All the way through, and he fell in the dust   *180*
With a groan, and his spirit flew away.
Planting my foot on him, I drew the bronze spear
Out of the wound and laid it down on the ground.
Then I pulled up a bunch of willow shoots
And twisted them together to make a rope   *185*
About a fathom long. I used this to tie
The stag's feet together so I could carry him
Across my back, leaning on my spear
As I went back to the ship. There was no way
An animal that large could be held on one shoulder.   *190*
I flung him down by the ship and roused my men,
Going up to each in turn and saying to them:

'We're not going down to Hades, my friends,
Before our time. As long as there is still
Food and drink in our ship, at least   *195*
We don't have to starve to death.'

When they heard this, they drew their cloaks
From their faces, and marveled at the size
Of the stag lying on the barren seashore.
When they had seen enough, they washed their hands   *200*
And prepared a glorious feast. So all day long
Until the sun went down we sat there feasting
On all that meat, washing it down with wine.
When the sun set and darkness came on,
We lay down to sleep on the shore of the sea.   *205*

When Dawn brushed the eastern sky with rose,
I called my men together and spoke to them:

'Listen to me, men. It's been hard going.
We don't know east from west right now,
But we have to see if we have any good ideas left.   *210*
We may not. I climbed up to a lookout point.
We're on an island, ringed by the endless sea.
The land lies low, and I was able to see

Smoke rising up through the brushy woods.'

This was too much for them. They remembered   215
What Antiphates, the Laestrygonian, had done,
And how the Cyclops had eaten their comrades.
They wailed and cried, but it did them no good.
I counted off the crew into two companies
And appointed a leader for each. Eurylochus   220
Headed up one group and I took the other,
And then we shook lots in a bronze helmet.
Out jumped the lot of Eurylochus, brave heart,
And so off he went, with twenty-two men,
All in tears, leaving us behind in no better mood.   225

They went through the woods and found Circe's house
In an upland clearing. It was built of polished stone
And surrounded by mountain lions and wolves,
Creatures Circe had drugged and bewitched.
These beasts did not attack my men, but stood   230
On their hind legs and wagged their long tails,
Like dogs fawning on their master who always brings
Treats for them when he comes home from a feast.
So these clawed beasts were fawning around my men,
Who were terrified all the same by the huge animals.   235
While they stood like this in the gateway
They could hear Circe inside, singing in a lovely voice
As she moved about weaving a great tapestry,
The unfading handiwork of an immortal goddess,
Finely woven, shimmering with grace and light.   240
Polites, a natural leader, and of all the crew
The one I loved and trusted most, spoke up then:

'Someone inside is weaving a great web,
And singing so beautifully the floor thrums with the sound.
Whether it's a goddess or a woman, let's call her out now.'   245

And so they called to her, and she came out
And flung open the bright doors and invited them in.
They all filed in naively behind her,
Except Eurylochus, who suspected a trap.

When she had led them in and seated them   250
She brewed up a potion of Pramnian wine
With cheese, barley, and pale honey stirred in,
And she laced this potion with insidious drugs
That would make them forget their own native land.
When they had eaten and drunk, she struck them   255
With her wand and herded them into the sties outside.
Grunting, their bodies covered with bristles,
They looked just like pigs, but their minds were intact.
Once in the pens, they squealed with dismay,
And Circe threw them acorns and berries—   260
The usual fare for wallowing swine.

Eurylochus at once came back to the ship
To tell us of our comrades' unseemly fate,
But, hard as he tried, he could not speak a word.
The man was in shock. His eyes welled with tears,   265
And his mind was filled with images of horror.
Finally, under our impatient questioning,
He told us how his men had been undone:

'We went through the woods, as you told us to,
Glorious Odysseus, and found a beautiful house   270
In an upland clearing, built of polished stone.
Someone inside was working a great loom
And singing in a high, clear voice, some goddess
Or a woman, and they called out to her,
And she came out and opened the bright doors   275
And invited them in, and they naively
Filed in behind her. But I stayed outside,
Suspecting a trap. And they all disappeared,
Not one came back. I sat and watched
For a long, long time, and not one came back.'   280

He spoke, and I threw my silver-studded sword
Around my shoulders, slung on my bow,
And ordered Eurylochus to retrace his steps
And lead me back there. But he grabbed me by the knees
And pleaded with me, wailing miserably: 285

'Don't force me to go back there. Leave me here,
Because I know that you will never come back yourself
Or bring back the others. Let's just get out of here
With those that are left. We might still make it.'

Those were his words, and I answered him: 290

'All right, Eurylochus, you stay here by the ship.
Get yourself something to eat and drink.
I'm going, though. We're in a really tight spot.'

And so I went up from the ship and the sea
Into the sacred woods. I was closing in   295
On Circe's house, with all its bewitchment,
When I was met by Hermes. He had a golden wand
And looked like a young man, a hint of a moustache
Above his lip—youth at its most charming.
He clasped my hand and said to me: 300

'Where are you off to now, unlucky man,
Alone, and in rough, uncharted terrain?
Those men of yours are up in Circe's house,
Penned like pigs into crowded little sties.
And you've come to free them? I don't think so.   305
You'll never return; you'll have to stay there, too.
Oh well, I will keep you out of harm's way.
Take this herb with you when you go to Circe,
And it will protect you from her deadly tricks.
She'll mix a potion and spike it with drugs,   310
But she won't be able to cast her spell
Because you'll have a charm that works just as well—
The one I'll give you—and you'll be forewarned.
When Circe strikes you with her magic wand,
Draw your sharp sword from beside your thigh   315
And rush at her with murder in your eye.
She'll be afraid and invite you to bed.
Don't turn her down—that's how you'll get
Your comrades freed and yourself well loved.
But first make her swear by the gods above   320
She will not unsex you when you are nude,

Or drain you of your manly fortitude.'

So saying, Hermes gave me the herb,
Pulling it out of the ground, and showed it to me.
It was black at the root, with a milk-white flower.   *325*
Moly, the gods call it, hard for mortal men to dig up,
But the gods can do anything. Hermes rose
Through the wooded island and up to Olympus,
And I went on to Circe's house, brooding darkly
On many things. I stood at the gates   *330*
Of the beautiful goddess' house and gave a shout.
She heard me call and came out at once,
Opening the bright doors and inviting me in.
I followed her inside, my heart pounding.
She seated me on a beautiful chair   *335*
Of finely wrought silver, and prepared me a drink
In a golden cup, and with evil in her heart
She laced it with drugs. She gave me the cup
And I drank it off, but it did not bewitch me.
So she struck me with her wand and said: *340*

'Off to the sty, with the rest of your friends.'

At this, I drew the sharp sword that hung by my thigh
And lunged at Circe as if I meant to kill her.
The goddess shrieked and, running beneath my blade,
Grabbed my knees and said to me wailing: *345*

'Who are you, and where do you come from?
What is your city and who are your parents?
I am amazed that you drank this potion
And are not bewitched. No other man
Has ever resisted this drug once it's past his lips.   *350*
But you have a mind that cannot be beguiled.
You must be Odysseus, the man of many wiles,
Who Quicksilver Hermes always said would come here
In his swift black ship on his way home from Troy.
Well then, sheath your sword and let's   *355*
Climb into my bed and tangle in love there,
So we may come to trust each other.'

She spoke, and I answered her:

'Circe, how can you ask me to be gentle to you
After you turned my men into swine?   *360*
And now you have me here and want to trick me
Into going to bed with you, so that you can
Unman me when I am naked. No, Goddess,
I'm not getting into any bed with you
Unless you agree first to swear a solemn oath   *365*
That you're not planning some new trouble for me.'

Those were my words, and she swore an oath at once
Not to do me any harm, and when she finished
I climbed into Circe's beautiful bed.

Meanwhile, her serving women were busy,   *370*
Four maidens who did all the housework,
Spirit women born of the springs and groves
And of the sacred rivers that flow to the sea.
One of them brought rugs with a purple sheen
And strewed them over chairs lined with fresh linen.   *375*
Another drew silver tables up to the chairs
And set golden baskets upon them. The third
Mixed honey-hearted wine in a silver bowl
And set out golden cups. The fourth
Filled a cauldron with water and lit a great fire   *380*
Beneath it, and when the water was boiling
In the glowing bronze, she set me in a tub
And bathed me, mixing in water from the cauldron
Until it was just how I liked it, and pouring it over
My head and shoulders until she washed from my limbs   *385*
The weariness that had consumed my soul.
When she had bathed me and rubbed me
With rich olive oil, and had thrown about me
A beautiful cloak and tunic, she led me to the hall
And had me sit on a silver-studded chair,   *390*
Richly wrought and with a matching footstool.
A maid poured water from a silver pitcher
Over a golden basin for me to wash my hands
And then set up a polished table nearby.

And the housekeeper, grave and dignified,   395
Set out bread and generous helpings
From all the dishes she had. She told me to eat,
But nothing appealed. I sat there with other thoughts
Occupying my mind, and my mood was dark.
When Circe noticed I was just sitting there,   400
Depressed, and not reaching out for food,
She came up to me and spoke winged words:

'Why are you just sitting there, Odysseus,
Eating your heart out and not touching your food?
Are you afraid of some other trick? You need not be.   405
I have already sworn I will do you no harm.'

So she spoke, and I answered her:

'Circe, how could anyone bring himself—
Any decent man—to taste food and drink
Before seeing his comrades free?   410
If you really want me to eat and drink,
Set my men free and let me see them.'

So I spoke, and Circe went outside
Holding her wand and opened the sty
And drove them out. They looked like swine   415
Nine or ten years old. They stood there before her
And she went through them and smeared each one
With another drug. The bristles they had grown
After Circe had given them the poisonous drug
All fell away, and they became men again,   420
Younger than before, taller and far handsomer.
They knew me, and they clung to my hands,
And the house rang with their passionate sobbing.
The goddess herself was moved to pity.

Then she came to my side and said: 425

'Son of Laertes in the line of Zeus,
My wily Odysseus, go to your ship now
Down by the sea and haul it ashore.

Then stow all the tackle and gear in caves
And come back here with the rest of your crew.'   430

So she spoke, and persuaded my heart.
I went to the shore and found my crew there
Wailing and crying beside our sailing ship.
When they saw me they were like farmyard calves
Around a herd of cows returning to the yard.   435
The calves bolt from their pens and run friskily
Around their mothers, lowing and mooing.
That's how my men thronged around me
When they saw me coming. It was as if
They had come home to their rugged Ithaca,   440
And wailing miserably they said so to me:

'With you back, Zeus-born, it is just as if
We had returned to our native Ithaca.
But tell us what happened to the rest of the crew.'

So they spoke, and I answered them gently: 445

'First let's haul our ship onto dry land
And then stow all the tackle and gear in caves.
Then I want all of you to come along with me
So you can see your shipmates in Circe's house,
Eating and drinking all they could ever want.'   450

They heard what I said and quickly agreed.
Eurylochus, though, tried to hold them back,
Speaking to them these winged words:

'Why do you want to do this to yourselves,
Go down to Circe's house? She will turn all of you   455
Into pigs, wolves, lions, and make you guard her house.
Remember what the Cyclops did when our shipmates
Went into his lair? It was this reckless Odysseus
Who led them there. It was his fault they died.'

When Eurylochus said that, I considered   460
Drawing my long sword from where it hung

By my thigh and lopping off his head,
Close kinsman though he was by marriage.
But my crew talked me out of it, saying things like:

'By your leave, let's station this man here   *465*
To guard the ship. As for the rest of us,
Lead us on to the sacred house of Circe.'

And so the whole crew went up from the sea,
And Eurylochus did not stay behind with the ship
But went with us, in mortal fear of my temper.   *470*

Meanwhile, back in Circe's house, the goddess
Had my men bathed, rubbed down with oil,
And clothed in tunics and fleecy cloaks.
We found them feasting well in her halls.
When they recognized each other, they wept openly   *475*
And their cries echoed throughout Circe's house.
Then the shining goddess stood near me and said:

'Lament no more. I myself know
All that you have suffered on the teeming sea
And the losses on land at your enemies' hands.   *480*
Now you must eat, drink wine, and restore the spirit
You had when you left your own native land,
Your rugged Ithaca. You are skin and bones now
And hollow inside. All you can think of
Is your hard wandering, no joy in your heart,   *485*
For you have, indeed, suffered many woes.'

She spoke, and I took her words to heart.
So we sat there day after day for a year,
Feasting on abundant meat and sweet wine.
But when a year had passed, and the seasons turned,   *490*
And the moons waned and the long days were done,
My trusty crew called me out and said:

'Good god, man, at long last remember your home,
If it is heaven's will for you to be saved
And return to your house and your own native land.'   *495*

They spoke, and I saw what they meant.
So all that long day until the sun went down
We sat feasting on meat and sweet red wine.
When the sun set and darkness came on,
My men lay down to sleep in the shadowy hall,   500
But I went up to Circe's beautiful bed
And touching her knees I beseeched the goddess:

'Circe, fulfill now the promise you made
To send me home. I am eager to be gone
And so are my men, who are wearing me out   505
Sitting around whining and complaining
Whenever you happen not to be present.'

So I spoke, and the shining goddess answered:

'Son of Laertes in the line of Zeus,
My wily Odysseus—you need not stay   510
Here in my house any longer than you wish.
But there is another journey you must make first—
To the house of Hades and dread Persephone,
To consult the ghost of Theban Tiresias,
The blind prophet, whose mind is still strong.   515
To him alone Persephone has granted
Intelligence even after his death.
The rest of the dead are flitting shadows.'

This broke my spirit. I sat on the bed
And wept. I had no will to live, nor did I care   520
If I ever saw the sunlight again.
But when I had my fill of weeping and writhing,
I looked at the goddess and said:

'And who will guide me on this journey, Circe?
No man has ever sailed his black ship to Hades.'   525

And the goddess, shining, answered at once:

'Son of Laertes in the line of Zeus,
My wily Odysseus—do not worry about

A pilot to guide your ship. Just set up the mast,
Spread the white sail, and sit yourself down.   530
The North Wind's breath will bear her onwards.
But when your ship crosses the stream of Ocean
You will see a shelving shore and Persephone's groves,
Tall poplars and willows that drop their fruit.
Beach your ship there by Ocean's deep eddies,   535
And go yourself to the dank house of Hades.
There into Acheron flow Pyriphlegethon
And Cocytus, a branch of the water of Styx.
And there is a rock where the two roaring rivers
Flow into one. At that spot, hero, gather yourself   540
And do as I say.
                         Dig an ell-square pit,
And around it pour libation to all the dead,
First with milk and honey, then with sweet wine,
And a third time with water. Then sprinkle barley
And pray to the looming, feeble death-heads,   545
Vowing sacrifice on Ithaca, a barren heifer,
The herd's finest, and rich gifts on the altar,
And to Tiresias alone a great black ram.
After these supplications to the spirits,
Slaughter a ram and a black ewe, turning their heads   550
Toward Erebus, yourself turning backward
And leaning toward the streams of the river.
Then many ghosts of the dead will come forth.
Call to your men to flay the slaughtered sheep
And burn them as a sacrifice to the gods below,   555
To mighty Hades and dread Persephone.
You yourself draw your sharp sword and sit there,
Keeping the feeble death-heads from the blood
Until you have questioned Tiresias.
Then, and quickly, the great seer will come.   560
He will tell you the route and how long it will take
For you to reach home over the teeming deep.'

Dawn rose in gold as she finished speaking.
Circe gave me a cloak and tunic to wear
And the nymph slipped on a long silver robe   565
Shimmering in the light, cinched it at the waist

With a golden belt and put a veil on her head.
I went through the halls and roused my men,
Going up to each with words soft and sweet:

'Time to get up! No more sleeping late.   570
We're on our way. Lady Circe has told me all.'

So I spoke, and persuaded their heroes' hearts.
But not even from Circe's house could I lead my men
Unscathed. One of the crew, Elpenor, the youngest,
Not much of a warrior nor all that smart,   575
Had gone off to sleep apart from his shipmates,
Seeking the cool air on Circe's roof
Because he was heavy with wine.
He heard the noise of his shipmates moving around
And sprang up suddenly, forgetting to go   580
To the long ladder that led down from the roof.
He fell headfirst, his neck snapped at the spine,
And his soul went down to the house of Hades.

As my men were heading out I spoke to them:

'You think, no doubt, that you are going home,   585
But Circe has plotted another course for us,
To the house of Hades and dread Persephone,
To consult the ghost of Theban Tiresias.'

This broke their hearts. They sat down
Right where they were and wept and tore their hair,   590
But no good came of their lamentation.

While we were on our way to our swift ship
On the shore of the sea, weeping and crying,
Circe had gone ahead and tethered a ram and a black ewe
By our tarred ship. She had passed us by   595
Without our ever noticing. Who could see
A god on the move against the god's will?"

ODYSSEY 11

"When we reached our black ship
We hauled her onto the bright saltwater,
Set up the mast and sail, loaded on
The sheep, and boarded her ourselves,
Heartsick and weeping openly by now.   5
The dark prow cut through the waves
And a following wind bellied the canvas,
A good sailing breeze sent by Circe,
The dread goddess with a human voice.
We lashed everything down and sat tight,   10
Leaving the ship to the wind and helmsman.
All day long she surged on with taut sail;
Then the sun set, and the sea grew dark.

The ship took us to the deep, outermost Ocean
And the land of the Cimmerians, a people   15
Shrouded in mist. The sun never shines there,
Never climbs the starry sky to beam down at them,
Nor bathes them in the glow of its last golden rays;
Their wretched sky is always racked with night's gloom.
We beached our ship there, unloaded the sheep,   20
And went along the stream of Ocean
Until we came to the place spoken of by Circe.

There Perimedes and Eurylochus held the victims
While I dug an ell-square pit with my sword,
And poured libation to all the dead,   25
First with milk and honey, then with sweet wine,
And a third time with water. Then I sprinkled

White barley and prayed to the looming dead,
Vowing sacrifice on Ithaca—a barren heifer,
The herd's finest, and rich gifts on the altar,   30
And to Tiresias alone a great black ram.
After these supplications to the spirits,
I cut the sheeps' throats over the pit,
And the dark blood pooled there.
                            Then out of Erebus
The souls of the dead gathered, the ghosts   35
Of brides and youths and worn-out old men
And soft young girls with hearts new to sorrow,
And many men wounded with bronze spears,
Killed in battle, bearing blood-stained arms.
They drifted up to the pit from all sides   40
With an eerie cry, and pale fear seized me.
I called to my men to flay the slaughtered sheep
And burn them as a sacrifice to the gods,
To mighty Hades and dread Persephone.
Myself, I drew my sharp sword and sat,   45
Keeping the feeble death-heads from the blood
Until I had questioned Tiresias.

First to come was the ghost of Elpenor,
Whose body still lay in Circe's hall,
Unmourned, unburied, since we'd been hard pressed.   50
I wept when I saw him, and with pity in my heart
Spoke to him these feathered words:

'Elpenor, how did you get to the undergloom
Before me, on foot, outstripping our black ship?'

I spoke, and he moaned in answer: 55

'Bad luck and too much wine undid me.
I fell asleep on Circe's roof. Coming down
I missed my step on the long ladder
And fell headfirst. My neck snapped
At the spine and my ghost went down to Hades.   60
Now I beg you—by those we left behind,
By your wife and the father who reared you,

And by Telemachus, your only son,
Whom you left alone in your halls—
When you put the gloom of Hades behind you   *65*
And beach your ship on the Isle of Aeaea,
As I know you will, remember me, my lord.
Do not leave me unburied, unmourned,
When you sail for home, or I might become
A cause of the gods' anger against you.   *70*
Burn me with my armor, such as I have,
Heap me a barrow on the grey sea's shore,
In memory of a man whose luck ran out.
Do this for me, and fix in the mound the oar
I rowed with my shipmates while I was alive.'   *75*

Thus Elpenor, and I answered him:

'Pitiful spirit, I will do this for you.'

Such were the sad words we exchanged
Sitting by the pit, I on one side holding my sword
Over the blood, my comrade's ghost on the other.   *80*

Then came the ghost of my dead mother,
Anticleia, daughter of the hero Autolycus.
She was alive when I left for sacred Ilion.
I wept when I saw her, and pitied her,
But even in my grief I would not allow her   *85*
To come near the blood until I had questioned Tiresias.

And then he came, the ghost of Theban Tiresias,
Bearing a golden staff. He knew me and said:

'Odysseus, son of Laertes, master of wiles,
Why have you come, leaving the sunlight   *90*
To see the dead and this joyless place?
Move off from the pit and take away your sword,
So I may drink the blood and speak truth to you.'

I drew back and slid my silver-studded sword
Into its sheath. After he had drunk the dark blood   *95*

The flawless seer rose and said to me:

'You seek a homecoming sweet as honey,
Shining Odysseus, but a god will make it bitter,
For I do not think you will elude the Earthshaker,
Who has laid up wrath in his heart against you,   100
Furious because you blinded his son. Still,
You just might get home, though not without pain,
You and your men, if you curb your own spirit,
And theirs, too, when you beach your ship
On Thrinacia. You will be marooned on that island   105
In the violet sea, and find there the cattle
Of Helios the Sun, and his sheep, too, grazing.
Leave these unharmed, keep your mind on your homecoming,
And you may still reach Ithaca, though not without pain.
But if you harm them, I foretell doom for you,   110
Your ship, and your crew. And even if you
Yourself escape, you will come home late
And badly, having lost all companions
And in another's ship. And you shall find
Trouble in your house, arrogant men   115
Devouring your wealth and courting your wife.
Yet vengeance will be yours, and when you have slain
The suitors in your hall, by ruse or by sword,
Then you must go off again, carrying a broad-bladed oar,
Until you come to men who know nothing of the sea,   120
Who eat their food unsalted, and have never seen
Red-prowed ships or oars that wing them along.
And I will tell you a sure sign that you have found them,
One you cannot miss. When you meet another traveler
Who thinks you are carrying a winnowing fan,   125
Then you must fix your oar in the earth
And offer sacrifice to Lord Poseidon,
A ram, a bull, and a boar in its prime.
Then return to your home and offer
Perfect sacrifice to the immortal gods   130
Who hold high heaven, to each in turn.
And death will come to you off the sea,
A death so gentle, and carry you off
When you are worn out in sleek old age,

Your people prosperous all around you.   *135*
All this will come true for you as I have told.'

Thus Tiresias. And I answered him:

'All that, Tiresias, is as the gods have spun it.
But tell me this: I see here the ghost
Of my dead mother, sitting in silence   *140*
Beside the blood, and she cannot bring herself
To look her son in the eye or speak to him.
How can she recognize me for who I am?'

And Tiresias, the Theban prophet:

'This is easy to tell you. Whoever of the dead   *145*
You let come to the blood will speak truly to you.
Whoever you deny will go back again.'

With that, the ghost of Lord Tiresias
Went back into Hades, his soothsaying done.
But I stayed where I was until my mother   *150*
Came up and drank the dark blood. At once
She knew me, and her words reached me on wings:

'My child, how did you come to the undergloom
While you are still alive? It is hard for the living
To reach these shores. There are many rivers to cross,   *155*
Great bodies of water, nightmarish streams,
And Ocean itself, which cannot be crossed on foot
But only in a well-built ship. Are you still wandering
On your way back from Troy, a long time at sea
With your ship and your men? Have you not yet come   *160*
To Ithaca, or seen your wife in your halls?'

So she spoke, and I answered her:

'Mother, I came here because I had to,
To consult the ghost of the prophet Tiresias.
I have not yet come to the coast of Achaea   *165*
Or set foot on my own land. I have had nothing

But hard travels from the day I set sail
With Lord Agamemnon to go to Ilion,
Famed for its horses, to fight the Trojans.
But tell me truly, how did you die?   *170*
Was it a long illness, or did Artemis
Shoot you suddenly with her gentle arrows?
And tell me about my father and my son,
Whom I left behind. Does the honor I had
Still remain with them, or has it passed   *175*
To some other man, and do they all say
I will never return? And what about my wife?
What has she decided, what does she think?
Is she still with my son, keeping things safe?
Or has someone already married her,   *180*
Whoever is now the best of the Achaeans?'

So I spoke, and my mother answered at once:

'Oh, yes indeed, she remains in your halls,
Her heart enduring the bitter days and nights.
But the honor that was yours has not passed   *185*
To any man. Telemachus holds your lands
Unchallenged, and shares in the feasts
To which all men invite him as the island's lawgiver.
Your father, though, stays out in the fields
And does not come to the city. He has no bed   *190*
Piled with bright rugs and soft coverlets
But sleeps in the house where the slaves sleep,
In the ashes by the fire, and wears poor clothes.
In summer and autumn his vineyard's slope
Is strewn with beds of leaves on the ground,   *195*
Where he lies in his sorrow, nursing his grief,
Longing for your return. His old age is hard.
I died from the same grief. The keen-eyed goddess
Did not shoot me at home with her gentle shafts,
Nor did any long illness waste my body away.   *200*
No, it was longing for you, my glorious Odysseus,
For your gentle heart and your gentle ways,
That robbed me of my honey-sweet life.'

So she spoke, and my heart yearned
To embrace the ghost of my dead mother.   *205*
Three times I rushed forward to hug her,
And three times she drifted out of my arms
Like a shadow or a dream. The pain
That pierced my heart grew ever sharper,
And my words rose to my mother on wings: *210*

'Mother, why do you slip away when I try
To embrace you? Even though we are in Hades,
Why can't we throw our arms around each other
And console ourselves with chill lamentation?
Are you a phantom sent by Persephone   *215*
To make me groan even more in my grief?'

And my mother answered me at once:

'O my child, most ill-fated of men,
It is not that Persephone is deceiving you.
This is the way it is with mortals.   *220*
When we die, the sinews no longer hold
Flesh and bones together. The fire destroys these
As soon as the spirit leaves the white bones,
And the ghost flutters off and is gone like a dream.
Hurry now to the light, and remember these things,   *225*
So that later you may tell them all to your wife.'

That was the drift of our talk.

                          Then the women came,
Sent by Persephone, all those who had been
The wives and daughters of the heroes of old.
They flocked together around the dark blood,   *230*
But I wanted to question them one at a time.
The best way I could think of to question them
Was to draw the sharp sword from beside my thigh,
And keep them from drinking the blood all at once.
They came up in procession then, and one by one   *235*
They declared their birth, and I questioned them all.

The first one I saw was highborn Tyro,
Who said she was born of flawless Salmoneus
And was wed to Cretheus, a son of Aeolus.
She fell in love with a river, divine Enipeus,   240
The most beautiful of all the rivers on earth,
And she used to play in his lovely streams.
But the Earthshaker took Enipeus' form
And lay with her in the swirling eddies
Near the river's mouth. And an indigo wave,   245
Towering like a mountain, arched over them
And hid the god and the mortal woman from view.
He unbound the sash that had kept her virgin
And shed sleep upon her. And when the god
Had finished his lovemaking, he took her hand   250
And called her name softly and said to her:

'Be happy in this love, woman. As the year turns
You will bear glorious children, for a god's embrace
Is never barren. Raise them and care for them.
Now go to your house and say nothing of this,   255
But I am Poseidon, who makes the earth tremble.'

With that he plunged into the surging sea.
And Tyro conceived and bore Pelias and Neleus,
Who served great Zeus as strong heroes both,
Pelias with his flocks in Iolcus' grasslands,   260
And Neleus down in sandy Pylos.
She bore other children to Cretheus: Aeson,
Pheres, and the charioteer Amythaon.

Then I saw Antiope, daughter of Asopus,
Who boasted she had slept in the arms of Zeus   265
And bore two sons, Amphion and Zethus,
Who founded seven-gated Thebes and built its walls,
Since they could not live in the wide land of Thebes
Without walls and towers, mighty though they were.

Next I saw Alcmene, Amphitryon's wife,   270
Who bore Heracles, the lionhearted battler,
After lying in Zeus' almighty embrace.

And I saw Megara, too, wife of Heracles,
The hero whose strength never wore out.

I saw Oedipus' mother, beautiful Epicaste,   *275*
Who unwittingly did a monstrous deed,
Marrying her son, who had killed his father.
The gods soon brought these things to light;
Yet, for all his misery, Oedipus still ruled
In lovely Thebes, by the gods' dark designs.   *280*
But Epicaste, overcome by her grief,
Hung a deadly noose from the ceiling rafters
And went down to implacable Hades' realm,
Leaving behind for her son all of the sorrows
A mother's avenging spirits can cause.   *285*

And then I saw Chloris, the great beauty
Whom Neleus wedded after courting her
With myriad gifts. She was the youngest daughter
Of Amphion, king of Minyan Orchomenus.
As queen of Pylos, she bore glorious children,   *290*
Nestor, Chromius, and lordly Periclymenus,
And magnificent Pero, a wonder to men.
Everyone wanted to marry her, but Neleus
Would only give her to the man who could drive
The cattle of mighty Iphicles to Pylos,   *295*
Spiral-horned, broad-browed, stubborn cattle,
Difficult to drive. Only Melampus,
The flawless seer, rose to the challenge,
But he was shackled by Fate. Country herdsmen
Put him in chains, and months went by   *300*
And the seasons passed and the year turned
Before he was freed by mighty Iphicles,
After he had told him all of his oracles,
And so the will of Zeus was fulfilled.

I saw Leda also, wife of Tyndareus,   *305*
Who bore to him two stout-hearted sons,
Castor the horseman and the boxer Polydeuces.
They are under the teeming earth though alive,
And have honor from Zeus in the world below,

Living and dying on alternate days.   310
Such is the honor they have won from the gods.

After her I saw Iphimedeia,
Aloeus' wife. She made love to Poseidon
And bore two sons, who did not live long,
Godlike Otus and famed Ephialtes,   315
The tallest men ever reared upon earth
And the handsomest after gloried Orion.
At nine years old they measured nine cubits
Across the chest, and were nine fathoms tall.
They threatened to wage a furious war   320
Against the immortal Olympian gods,
And were bent on piling Ossa on Olympus,
And forested Pelion on top of Ossa
And so reach the sky. And they would have done it,
But the son of Zeus and fair-haired Leto   325
Destroyed them both before the down blossomed
Upon their cheeks and their beards had come in.

And I saw Phaedra and Procnis
And lovely Ariadne, whom Theseus once
Tried to bring from Crete to sacred Athens   330
But had no joy of her. Artemis first
Shot her on Dia, the seagirt island,
After Dionysus told her he saw her there.

And I saw Maera and Clymene
And hateful Eriphyle, who valued gold   335
More than her husband's life.
                              But I could not tell you
All the wives and daughters of heroes I saw.
It would take all night. And it is time
To sleep now, either aboard ship with the crew
Or here in this house. My journey home   340
Is up to you, and to the immortal gods."

He paused, and they sat hushed in silence,
Spellbound throughout the shadowy hall.
And then white-armed Arete began to speak:

"Well, Phaeacians, does this man impress you   345
With his looks, stature, and well-balanced mind?
He is my guest, moreover, though each of you
Shares in that honor. Do not send him off, then,
Too hastily, and do not stint your gifts
To one in such need. You have many treasures   350
Stored in your halls by grace of the gods."

Then the old hero Echeneus spoke up:

"Friends, the words of our wise queen
Are not wide of the mark. Give them heed.
But upon Alcinous depend both word and deed."   355

And Alcinous answered:

"Arete's word will stand, as long as I live
And rule the Phaeacians who love the oar.
But let our guest, though he longs to go home,
Endure until tomorrow, until I have time   360
To make our gift complete. We all have a stake
In getting him home, but mine is greatest,
For mine is the power throughout the land."

And Odysseus, who missed nothing:

"Lord Alcinous, most renowned of men,   365
You could ask me to stay for even a year
While you arranged a send-off with glorious gifts,
And I would assent. Better far to return
With a fuller hand to my own native land.
I would be more respected and loved by all   370
Who saw me come back to Ithaca."

Alcinous answered him:

"Odysseus, we do not take you
For the sort of liar and cheat the dark earth breeds
Among men everywhere, telling tall tales   375
No man could ever test for himself.

Your words have outward grace and wisdom within,
And you have told your tale with the skill of a bard—
All that the Greeks and you yourself have suffered.
But tell me this, as accurately as you can: *380*
Did you see any of your godlike comrades
Who went with you to Troy and met their fate there?
The night is young—and magical. It is not yet time
To sleep in the hall. Tell me these wonders.
Sit in our hall and tell us of your woes   *385*
For as long as you can bear. I could listen until dawn."

And Odysseus, his mind teeming:

"Lord Alcinous, most glorious of men,
There is a time for words and a time for sleep.
But if you still yearn to listen, I will not refuse   *390*
To tell you of other things more pitiable still,
The woes of my comrades who died after the war,
Who escaped the Trojans and their battle-cry
But died on their return through a woman's evil.

When holy Persephone had scattered   *395*
The women's ghosts, there came the ghost
Of Agamemnon, son of Atreus,
Distraught with grief. Around him were gathered
Those who died with him in Aegisthus' house.
He knew me as soon as he drank the dark blood.   *400*
He cried out shrilly, tears welling in his eyes,
And he stretched out his hands, trying to touch me,
But he no longer had anything left of the strength
He had in the old days in those muscled limbs.
I wept when I saw him, and with pity in my heart   *405*
I spoke to him these winged words:

'Son of Atreus, king of men, most glorious
Agamemnon—what death laid you low?
Did Poseidon sink your fleet at sea,
After hitting you hard with hurricane winds?   *410*
Or were you killed by enemy forces on land,
As you raided their cattle and flocks of sheep

Or fought to capture their city and women?'

And Agamemnon answered at once:

'Son of Laertes in the line of Zeus,   *415*
My crafty Odysseus—No,
Poseidon did not sink my fleet at sea
After hitting us hard with hurricane winds,
Nor was I killed by enemy forces on land.
Aegisthus was the cause of my death.   *420*
He killed me with the help of my cursed wife
After inviting me to a feast in his house,
Slaughtered me like a bull at a manger.
So I died a most pitiable death,
And all around me my men were killed   *425*
Relentlessly, like white-tusked swine
For a wedding banquet or dinner party
In the house of a rich and powerful man.
You have seen many men cut down, both
In single combat and in the crush of battle,   *430*
But your heart would have grieved
As never before at the sight of us lying
Around the wine-bowl and the laden tables
In that great hall. The floor steamed with blood.
But the most piteous cry I ever heard   *435*
Came from Cassandra, Priam's daughter.
She had her arms around me down on the floor
When Clytemnestra ran her through from behind.
I lifted my hands and beat the ground
As I lay dying with a sword in my chest,   *440*
But that bitch, my wife, turned her back on me
And would not shut my eyes or close my lips
As I was going down to Death. Nothing
Is more grim or more shameless than a woman
Who sets her mind on such an unspeakable act   *445*
As killing her own husband. I was sure
I would be welcomed home by my children
And all my household, but she, with her mind set
On stark horror, has shamed not only herself
But all women to come, even the rare good one.'   *450*

Thus Agamemnon, and I responded:

'Ah, how broad-browed Zeus has persecuted
The house of Atreus from the beginning,
Through the will of women. Many of us died
For Helen's sake, and Clytemnestra   455
Set a snare for you while you were far away.'

And Agamemnon answered me at once:

'So don't go easy on your own wife either,
Or tell her everything you know.
Tell her some things, but keep some hidden.   460
But your wife will not bring about your death,
Odysseus. Icarius' daughter,
Your wise Penelope, is far too prudent.
She was newly wed when we went to war.
We left her with a baby boy still at the breast,   465
Who must by now be counted as a man,
And prosperous. His father will see him
When he comes, and he will embrace his father,
As is only right. But my wife did not let me
Even fill my eyes with the sight of my son.   470
She killed me before I could do even that.
But let me tell you something, Odysseus:
Beach your ship secretly when you come home.
Women just can't be trusted any more.
And one more thing. Tell me truthfully   475
If you've heard anything about my son
And where he is living, perhaps in Orchomenus,
Or in sandy Pylos, or with Menelaus in Sparta.
For Orestes has not yet perished from the earth.'

So he spoke, and I answered him: 480

'Son of Atreus, why ask me this?
I have no idea whether he is alive or dead,
And it is not good to speak words empty as wind.'

Such were the sad words we had for each other

As we stood there weeping, heavy with grief.   *485*

Then came the ghost of Achilles, son of Peleus,
And those of Patroclus and peerless Antilochus
And Ajax, who surpassed all the Danaans,
Except Achilles, in looks and build.
Aeacus' incomparable grandson, Achilles, knew me,   *490*
And when he spoke his words had wings:

'Son of Laertes in the line of Zeus,
Odysseus, you hard rover, not even you
Can ever top this, this bold foray
Into Hades, home of the witless dead   *495*
And the dim phantoms of men outworn.'

So he spoke, and I answered him:

'Achilles, by far the mightiest of the Achaeans,
I have come here to consult Tiresias,
To see if he has any advice for me   *500*
On how I might get back to rugged Ithaca.
I've had nothing but trouble, and have not yet set foot
On my native land. But no man, Achilles,
Has ever been as blessed as you, or ever will be.
While you were alive the army honored you   *505*
Like a god, and now that you are here
You rule the dead with might. You should not
Lament your death at all, Achilles.'

I spoke, and he answered me at once:

'Don't try to sell me on death, Odysseus.   *510*
I'd rather be a hired hand back up on earth,
Slaving away for some poor dirt farmer,
Than lord it over all these withered dead.
But tell me about that boy of mine.
Did he come to the war and take his place   *515*
As one of the best? Or did he stay away?
And what about Peleus? What have you heard?
Is he still respected among the Myrmidons,

Or do they dishonor him in Phthia and Hellas,
Crippled by old age in hand and foot?   *520*
And I'm not there for him up in the sunlight
With the strength I had in wide Troy once
When I killed Ilion's best and saved the army.
Just let me come with that kind of strength
To my father's house, even for an hour,   *525*
And wrap my hands around his enemies' throats.
They would learn what it means to face my temper.'

Thus Achilles, and I answered him:

'I have heard nothing of flawless Peleus,
But as for your son, Neoptolemus,   *530*
I'll tell you all I know, just as you ask.
I brought him over from Scyros myself,
In a fine vessel, to join the Greek army
At Troy, and every time we held council there,
He was always the first to speak, and his words   *535*
Were never off the mark. Godlike Nestor and I
Alone surpassed him. And every time we fought
On Troy's plain, he never held back in the ranks
But charged ahead to the front, yielding
To no one, and he killed many in combat.   *540*
I could not begin to name them all,
All the men he killed when he fought for us,
But what a hero he dismantled in Telephus' son,
Eurypylus, dispatching him and a crowd
Of his Ceteian compatriots. Eurypylus   *545*
Came to Troy because Priam bribed his mother.
After Memnon, I've never seen a handsomer man.
And then, too, when all our best climbed
Into the wooden horse Epeius made,
And I was in command and controlled the trapdoor,   *550*
All the other Danaan leaders and counselors
Were wiping away tears from their eyes
And their legs shook beneath them, but I never saw
Neoptolemus blanch or wipe away a tear.
No, he just sat there handling his sword hilt   *555*
And heavy bronze spear, and all he wanted

Was to get out of there and give the Trojans hell.
And after we had sacked Priam's steep city,
He boarded his ship with his share of the loot
And more for valor. And not a scratch on him.   *560*
He never took a hit from a spear or sword
In close combat, where wounds are common.
When Ares rages anyone can be hit.'

So I spoke, and the ghost of swift-footed Achilles
Went off with huge strides through the fields of asphodel,   *565*
Filled with joy at his son's preeminence.

The other ghosts crowded around in sorrow,
And each asked about those who were dear to him.
Only the ghost of Telamonian Ajax
Stood apart, still furious with me   *570*
Because I had defeated him in the contest at Troy
To decide who would get Achilles' armor.
His goddess mother had put it up as a prize,
And the judges were the sons of the Trojans
And Pallas Athena. I wish I had never won.   *575*
That contest buried Ajax, that brave heart,
The best of the Danaans in looks and deeds,
After the incomparable son of Peleus.
I tried to win him over with words like these:

'Ajax, son of flawless Telamon,   *580*
Are you to be angry with me even in death
Over that accursed armor? The gods
Must have meant it to be the ruin of the Greeks.
We lost a tower of strength to that armor.
We mourn your loss as we mourn the loss   *585*
Of Achilles himself. Zeus alone
Is to blame. He persecuted the Greeks
Terribly, and he brought you to your doom.
No, come back, Lord Ajax, and listen!
Control your wrath and rein in your proud spirit.'   *590*

I spoke, but he said nothing. He went his way
To Erebus, to join the other souls of the dead.

He might yet have spoken to me there, or I
Might yet have spoken to him, but my heart
Yearned to see the other ghosts of the dead.   595

There I saw Minos, Zeus' glorious son,
Scepter in hand, judging the dead
As he sat in the wide-gated house of Hades;
And the dead sat, too, and asked him for judgments.

And then Orion loomed up before me,   600
Driving over the fields of asphodel
The beasts he had slain in the lonely hills,
In his hands a bronze club, forever unbroken.

And I saw Tityos, a son of glorious Earth,
Lying on the ground, stretched over nine acres,   605
And two vultures sat on either side of him
And tore at his liver, plunging their beaks
Deep into his guts, and he could not beat them off.
For Tityos had raped Leto, a consort of Zeus,
As she went to Pytho through lovely Panopeus.   610

And I saw Tantalus there in his agony,
Standing in a pool with water up to his chin.
He was mad with thirst, but unable to drink,
For every time the old man bent over
The water would drain away and vanish,   615
Dried up by some god, and only black mud
Would be left at his feet. Above him dangled
Treetop fruits, pears and pomegranates,
Shiny apples, sweet figs, and luscious olives.
But whenever Tantalus reached up for them,   620
The wind tossed them high to the shadowy clouds.

And I saw Sisyphus there in his agony,
Pushing a monstrous stone with his hands.
Digging in hard, he would manage to shove it
To the crest of a hill, but just as he was about   625
To heave it over the top, the shameless stone
Would teeter back and bound down to the plain.

Then he would strain every muscle to push it back up,
Sweat pouring from his limbs and dusty head.

And then mighty Heracles loomed up before me—   630
His phantom that is, for Heracles himself
Feasts with the gods and has as his wife
Beautiful Hebe, daughter of great Zeus
And gold-sandaled Hera. As he moved
A clamor arose from the dead around him,   635
As if they were birds flying off in terror.
He looked like midnight itself. He held his bow
With an arrow on the string, and he glared around him
As if he were always about to shoot. His belt,
A baldric of gold crossing his chest,   640
Was stark horror, a phantasmagoria
Of Bears, and wild Boars, and green-eyed Lions,
Of Battles, and Bloodshed, Murder and Mayhem.
May this be its maker's only masterpiece,
And may there never again be another like it.   645
Heracles recognized me at once,
And his words beat down on me like dark wings:

'Son of Laertes in the line of Zeus,
Crafty Odysseus—poor man, do you too
Drag out a wretched destiny   650
Such as I once bore under the rays of the sun?
I was a son of Zeus and grandson of Cronus,
But I had immeasurable suffering,
Enslaved to a man who was far less than I
And who laid upon me difficult labors.   655
Once he even sent me here, to fetch
The Hound of Hell, for he could devise
No harder task for me than this. That hound
I carried out of the house of Hades,
With Hermes and grey-eyed Athena as guides.'   660

And Heracles went back into the house of Hades.
But I stayed where I was, in case any more
Of the heroes of yesteryear might yet come forth.
And I would have seen some of them—

Heroes I longed to meet, Theseus and Peirithous,   665
Glorious sons of the gods—but before I could,
The nations of the dead came thronging up
With an eerie cry, and I turned pale with fear
That Persephone would send from Hades' depths
The pale head of that monster, the Gorgon.   670

I went to the ship at once and called to my men
To get aboard and untie the stern cables.
They boarded quickly and sat at their benches.
The current bore the ship down the River Ocean.
We rowed at first, and then caught a good tailwind."   675

ODYSSEY 12

"Our ship left the River Ocean
And came to the swell of the open sea
And the Island of Aeaea,
Where Dawn has her dancing grounds
And the Sun his risings. We beached our ship   5
On the sand, disembarked, and fell asleep
On the shore, waiting for daybreak.

Light blossomed like roses in the eastern sky,
And I sent some men to the house of Circe
To bring back the body of Elpenor.   10
We cut wood quickly, and on the headland's point
We held a funeral, shedding warm tears.
When the body was burned, and the armor with it,
We heaped up a mound, dragged a stone onto it,
And on the tomb's very top we planted his oar.   15

While we were busy with these things,
Circe, aware that we had come back
From the Underworld, put on her finest clothes
And came to see us. Her serving women
Brought meat, bread, and bright red wine,   20
And the goddess shone with light as she spoke:

'So you went down alive to Hades' house.
Most men die only once, but you twice.
Come, though, eat and drink wine
The whole day through. You sail at dawn.   25
I will tell you everything on your route,

So that you will not come to grief
In some web of evil on land or sea.'

She spoke, and our proud hearts consented.
All day long until the sun went down   30
We sat feasting on meat and good red wine.
When the sun set and darkness came on
My men went to sleep beside the ship's stern-cables.
But Circe took me by the hand and had me sit
Away from my men. And she lay down beside me   35
And asked me about everything. I told her all
Just as it happened, and then the goddess spoke:

'So all that is done. But now listen
To what I will tell you. One day a god
Will remind you of it. First, you will come   40
To the Sirens, who bewitch all men
Who come near. Anyone who approaches
Unaware and hears their voice will never again
Be welcomed home by wife and children
Dancing with joy at his return—   45
Not after the Sirens bewitch him with song.
They loll in a meadow, and around them are piled
The bones of shriveled and moldering bodies.
Row past them, first kneading sweet wax
And smearing it into the ears of your crew   50
So they cannot hear. But if you yourself
Have a mind to listen, have them bind you
Hand and foot upright in the mast-step
And tie the ends of the rope to the mast.
Then you can enjoy the song of the Sirens.   55
If you command your crew and plead with them
To release you, they should tie you up tighter.
After your men have rowed past the Sirens,
I will not prescribe which of two ways to go.
You yourself must decide. I will tell you both.   60

'One route takes you past beetling crags
Pounded by blue-eyed Amphitrítê's seas.
The blessed gods call these the Wandering Rocks.

Not even birds can wing their way through.
Even the doves that bring ambrosia to Zeus   *65*
Crash and perish on that slick stone,
And the Father has to replenish their numbers.
Ships never get through. Whenever one tries,
The sea is awash with timbers and bodies
Blasted by the waves and the fiery winds.   *70*
Only one ship has ever passed through,
The famous Argo as she sailed from Aeetes,
And even she would have been hurled onto those crags
Had not Hera loved Jason and sent his ship through.

'On the other route there are two rocks.   *75*
One stabs its peak into the sky
And is ringed by a dark blue cloud. This cloud
Never melts, and the air is never clear
During summer or autumn. No mortal man
Could ever scale this rock, not even if he had   *80*
Twenty hands and feet. The stone is as smooth
As if it were polished. Halfway up the cliff
Is a misty cave facing the western gloom.
It is there you will sail your hollow ship
If you listen to me, glorious Odysseus.   *85*
The strongest archer could not shoot an arrow
Up from his ship all the way to the cave,
Which is the lair of Scylla. She barks and yelps
Like a young puppy, but she is a monster,
An evil monster that not even a god   *90*
Would be glad to see. She has—listen to this—
Twelve gangly legs and six very long necks,
And on each neck is perched a bloodcurdling head,
Each with three rows of close-set teeth
Full of black death. Up to her middle   *95*
She is concealed in the cave, but her heads dangle
Into the abyss, and she fishes by the rock
For dolphins and seals or other large creatures
That the moaning sea breeds in multitudes.
No crew can boast to have sailed past Scylla   *100*
Unscathed. With each head she carries off a man,
Snatching him out of his dark-prowed vessel.

'The other rock, as you will see, Odysseus,
Lies lower—the two are close enough
That you could shoot an arrow across—   *105*
And on this rock is a large, leafy fig tree.
Beneath this tree the divine Charybdis
Sucks down the black water. Three times a day
She belches it out and three times a day
She sucks it down horribly. Don't be there   *110*
When she sucks it down. No one could save you,
Not even Poseidon, who makes the earth tremble.
No, stay close to Scylla's rock, and push hard.
Better to mourn six than the whole crew at once.'

Thus Circe. And I, in a panic: *115*

'I beg you, goddess, tell me, is there
Any way I can escape from Charybdis
And still protect my men from the other?'

And the goddess, in a nimbus of light:

'There you go again, always the hero.   *120*
Won't you yield even to the immortals?
She's not mortal, she's an immortal evil,
Dread, dire, ferocious, unfightable.
There is no defense. It's flight, not fight.
If you pause so much as to put on a helmet   *125*
She'll attack again with just as many heads
And kill just as many men as before.
Just row past as hard as you can. And call upon
Crataïs, the mother who bore her as a plague to men.
She will stop her from attacking a second time.   *130*

'Then you will come to Thrinacia,
An island that pastures the cattle of the Sun,
Seven herds of cattle and seven flocks of sheep,
Fifty in each. They are immortal.
They bear no young and they never die off,   *135*
And their shepherds are goddesses,
Nymphs with gorgeous hair, Phaethusa

And Lampetiê, whom gleaming Neaera
Bore to Helios, Hyperion the Sun.
When she had borne them and reared them   *140*
She sent them to Thrinacia, to live far away
And keep their father's spiral-horned cattle.
If you leave these unharmed and keep your mind
On your journey, you might yet struggle home
To Ithaca. But if you harm them, I foretell   *145*
Disaster for your ship and crew, and even if you
Escape yourself, you shall come home late
And badly, having lost all your companions.'

Dawn rose in gold as she finished speaking,
And light played about her as she disappeared   *150*
Up the island.
                    I went to the ship
And got my men going. They loosened
The stern cables and were soon in their benches,
Beating the water white with their oars.
A following wind rose in the wake   *155*
Of our dark-prowed ship, a sailor's breeze
Sent by Circe, that dread, beautiful goddess.
We tied down the tackling and sat tight,
Letting the wind and the helmsman take over.

Then I made a heavy-hearted speech to my men: *160*

'Friends, it is not right that one or two alone
Should know what the goddess Circe foretold.
Better we should all know, live or die.
We may still beat death and get out of this alive.
First, she told us to avoid the eerie voices   *165*
Of the Sirens and sail past their soft meadows.
She ordered me alone to listen. Bind me
Hand and foot upright in the mast-step
And tie the ends of the rope to the mast.
If I command you and plead with you   *170*
To release me, just tie me up tighter.'

Those were my instructions to the crew.

Meanwhile, our good ship was closing fast
On the Sirens' island, when the breeze we'd had
Tailed off, and we were becalmed—not a breath   *175*
Of wind left—some spirit lulled the waves.
My men got up and furled the sails,
Stowed them in the ship's hold, then sat down
At their oars and whitened the water with pine.
Myself, I got out a wheel of wax, cut it up   *180*
With my sharp knife, and kneaded the pieces
Until they were soft and warm, a quick job
With Lord Helios glaring down from above.
Then I went down the rows and smeared the wax
Into all my men's ears. They in turn bound me   *185*
Hand and foot upright to the mast,
Tied the ends of the rope to the mast, and then
Sat down and beat the sea white with their oars.
We were about as far away as a shout would carry,
Surging ahead, when the Sirens saw our ship   *190*
Looming closer, and their song pierced the air:

'Come hither, Odysseus,
   glory of the Achaeans,
Stop your ship
   so you can hear our voices.
No one has ever sailed
   his black ship past here
Without listening to the honeyed
   sound from our lips.   *195*
He journeys on delighted
   and knows more than before.
For we know everything
   that the Greeks and Trojans
Suffered in wide Troy
   by the will of the gods.
We know all that happens
   on the teeming earth.'

They made their beautiful voices carry,   *200*
And my heart yearned to listen. I ordered my men
To untie me, signaling with my brows,

But they just leaned on their oars and rowed on.
Perimedes and Eurylochus jumped up,
Looped more rope around me, and pulled tight.   *205*
When we had rowed past, and the Sirens' song
Had faded on the waves, only then did my crew
Take the wax from their ears and untie me.

We had no sooner left the island when I saw
The spray from an enormous wave   *210*
And heard its booming. The oars flew
From my men's frightened hands
And shirred in the waves, stopping the ship
Dead in the water. I went down the rows
And tried to boost the crew's morale: *215*

'Come on, men, this isn't the first time
We've run into trouble. This can't be worse
Than when the Cyclops with his brute strength
Had us penned in his cave. We got out
By my courage and fast thinking. One day   *220*
We'll look back on this. Now let's do as I say,
Every man of you! Stay on your benches
And beat the deep surf with your oars!
Zeus may yet deliver us from death.
Helmsman, here's my command to you,   *225*
And make sure you remember it, since
You're steering this vessel: Keep the ship
Away from this heavy surf. Hug the cliff,
Or before you know it she'll swerve
To starboard and you'll send us all down.'   *230*

I spoke, they obeyed. But I didn't mention
Scylla. There was nothing we could do about that,
And I didn't want the crew to freeze up,
Stop rowing, and huddle together in the hold.
Then I forgot Circe's stern warning   *235*
Not to arm myself no matter what happened.
I strapped on my bronze, grabbed two long spears
And went to the foredeck, where I thought
Scylla would first show herself from the cliff.

But I couldn't see her anywhere, and my eyes   *240*
Grew weary scanning the misty rock face.

We sailed on up the narrow channel, wailing,
Scylla on one side, Charybdis on the other
Sucking down saltwater. When she belched it up
She seethed and bubbled like a boiling cauldron   *245*
And the spray would reach the tops of the cliffs.
When she sucked it down you could see her
Churning within, and the rock bellowed
And roared, and you could see the sea floor
Black with sand. My men were pale with fear.   *250*
While we looked at her, staring death in the eyes,
Scylla seized six of my men from our ship,
The six strongest hands aboard. Turning my eyes
To the deck and my crew, I saw above me
Their hands and feet as they were raised aloft.   *255*
They cried down to me, calling me by name
That one last time in their agony.
                              You know
How a fisherman on a jutting rock
Casts his bait with his long pole. The horned hook
Sinks into the sea, and when he catches a fish   *260*
He pulls it writhing and squirming out of the water.
Writhing like that my men were drawn up the cliff.
And Scylla devoured them at her door, as they shrieked
And stretched their hands down to me
In their awful struggle. Of all the things   *265*
That I have borne while I scoured the seas,
I have seen nothing more pitiable.

When we had fled Charybdis, the rocks,
And Scylla, we came to the perfect island
Of Hyperion the Sun, where his herds ranged   *270*
And his flocks browsed. While our black ship
Was still out at sea I could hear the bleating
Of the sheep and the lowing of the cattle
As they were being penned, and I remembered
The words of the blind seer, Theban Tiresias,   *275*
And of Circe, who gave me strict warnings

To shun the island of the warmth-giving Sun.
And so I spoke to my crew with heavy heart:

'Hear my words, men, for all your pain.
So I can tell you Tiresias' prophecies   280
And Circe's, too, who gave me strict warnings
To shun the island of the warmth-giving Sun,
For there she said was our gravest peril.
No, row our black ship clear of this island.'

This broke their spirits, and at once   285
Eurylochus answered me spitefully:

'You're a hard man, Odysseus, stronger
Than other men, and you never wear out,
A real iron-man, who won't allow his crew,
Dead tired from rowing and lack of sleep,   290
To set foot on shore, where we might make
A meal we could enjoy. No, you just order us
To wander on through the swift darkness
Over the misty deep, and be driven away
From the island. It is at night that winds rise   295
That wreck ships. How could we survive
If we were hit by a South Wind or a West,
Which sink ships no matter what the great gods want?
No, let's give in to black night now
And make our supper. We'll stay by the ship,   300
Board her in the morning, and put out to sea.'

Thus Eurylochus, and the others agreed.
I knew then that some god had it in for us,
And my words had wings:

                    'Eurylochus,
It's all of you against me alone. All right,   305
But swear me a great oath, every last man:
If we find any cattle or sheep on this island,
No man will kill a single cow or sheep
In his recklessness, but will be content
To eat the food immortal Circe gave us.'   310

They swore they would do just as I said,
And when they had finished the words of the oath,
We moored our ship in a hollow harbor
Near a sweet-water spring. The crew disembarked
And skillfully prepared their supper.   315
When they had their fill of food and drink,
They fell to weeping, remembering how Scylla
Had snatched their shipmates and devoured them.
Sweet sleep came upon them as they wept.
Past midnight, when the stars had wheeled around,   320
Zeus gathered the clouds and roused a great wind
Against us, an ungodly tempest that shrouded
Land and sea and blotted out the night sky.
At the first blush of Dawn we hauled our ship up
And made her fast in a cave where you could see   325
The nymphs' beautiful seats and dancing places.
Then I called my men together and spoke to them:

'Friends, there is food and drink in the ship.
Let's play it safe and keep our hands
Off those cattle, which belong to Helios,   330
A dread god who hears and sees all.'

So I spoke, and their proud hearts consented.

Then for a full month the South Wind blew,
And no other wind but the East and the South.
As long as my men had grain and red wine   335
They didn't touch the cattle—life was still worth living.
But when all the rations from the ship were gone,
They had to roam around in search of game—
Hunting for birds and whatever they could catch
With fishing hooks. Hunger gnawed at their bellies.   340

I went off by myself up the island
To pray to the gods to show me the way.
When I had put some distance between myself
And the crew, and found a spot
Sheltered from the wind, I washed my hands   345
And prayed to the gods, but all they did

Was close my eyelids in sleep.

                         Meanwhile,
Eurylochus was giving bad advice to the crew:

'Listen to me, shipmates, despite your distress.
All forms of death are hateful, but to die   350
Of hunger is the most wretched way to go.
What are we waiting for? Let's drive off
The prime beef in that herd and offer sacrifice
To the gods of broad heaven. If we ever
Return to Ithaca, we will build a rich temple   355
To Hyperion the Sun, and deposit there
Many fine treasures. If he becomes angry
Over his cattle and gets the other gods' consent
To destroy our ship, well, I would rather
Gulp down saltwater and die once and for all   360
Than waste away slowly on a desert island.'

Thus Eurylochus, and the others agreed.
In no time they had driven off the best
Of Helios' cattle, pretty, spiral-horned cows
That were grazing close to our dark-prowed ship.   365
They surrounded these cows and offered prayers
To the gods, plucking off tender leaves
From a high-crowned oak in lieu of white barley,
Of which there was none aboard our benched ship.
They said their prayers, cut the cows' throats,   370
Flayed the animals and carved out the thigh joints,
Wrapped these in a double layer of fat
And laid all the raw bits upon them.
They had no wine to pour over the sacrifice
And so used water as they roasted the entrails.   375
When the thighs were burned and the innards tasted,
They carved up the rest and skewered it on spits.

That's when I awoke, bolting upright.
I started down to the shore, and as I got near the ship
The aroma of sizzling fat drifted up to me.   380
I groaned and cried out to the undying gods:

'Father Zeus, and you other immortals,
You lulled me to sleep—and to my ruin—
While my men committed this monstrous crime!'

Lampetiê rushed in her long robes to Helios   385
And told him that we had killed his cattle.
Furious, the Sun God addressed the immortals:

'Father Zeus, and you other gods eternal,
Punish Odysseus' companions, who have insolently
Killed the cattle I took delight in seeing   390
Whenever I ascended the starry heaven
And whenever turned back from heaven to earth.
If they don't pay just atonement for the cows
I will sink into Hades and shine on the dead.'

And Zeus, who masses the clouds, said: 395

'Helios, you go on shining among the gods
And for mortal men on the grain-giving earth.
I will soon strike their ship with sterling lightning
And shatter it to bits on the wine-purple sea.'

All this I heard from rich-haired Calypso,   400
Who said she heard it from Hermes the Guide.

When I reached the ship I chewed out my men,
Giving each one an earful. But there was nothing
We could do. The cattle were already dead.
Then the gods showed some portents   405
Directed at my men. The hides crawled,
And the meat, both roasted and raw,
Mooed on the spits, like cattle lowing.

Each day for six days my men slaughtered oxen
From Helios' herd and gorged on the meat.   410
But when Zeus brought the seventh day,
The wind tailed off from gale force.
We boarded ship at once and put out to sea
As soon as we had rigged the mast and sail.

When we left the island behind, there was   415
No other land in sight, only sea and sky.
Then Zeus put a black cloud over our ship
And the sea grew dark beneath it. She ran on
A little while, and then the howling West Wind
Blew in with hurricane force. It snapped   420
Both forestays, and the mast fell backward
Into the bilge with all of its tackle.
On its way down the mast struck the helmsman
And crushed his skull. He fell from the stern
Like a diver, and his proud soul left his bones.   425
In the same instant, Zeus thundered
And struck the ship with a lightning bolt.
She shivered from stem to stern and was filled
With sulfurous smoke. My men went overboard,
Bobbing in the waves like sea crows   430
Around the black ship, their day of return
Snuffed out by the Sun God.
I kept pacing the deck until the sea surge
Tore the sides from the keel. The waves
Drove the bare keel on and snapped the mast   435
From its socket; the leather backstay
Was still attached, and I used this to lash
The keel to the mast. Perched on these timbers
I was swept along by deathly winds.

Then the West Wind died down,   440
And, to my horror, the South Wind rose.
All that way, back to the whirlpool,
I was swept along the whole night through
And at dawn reached Scylla's cliff
And dread Charybdis. She was sucking down   445
Seawater, and I leapt up
To the tall fig tree, grabbed hold of it
And hung on like a bat. I could not
Plant my feet or get myself set on the tree
Because its roots spread far below   450
And its branches were high overhead,
Long, thick limbs that shaded Charybdis.
I just grit my teeth and hung on

Until she spat out the mast and keel again.
It seemed like forever. Finally,   455
About the hour a man who has spent the day
Judging quarrels that young men bring to him
Rises from the marketplace and goes to dinner,
My ship's timbers surfaced again from Charybdis.
I let go with my hands and feet   460
And hit the water hard beyond the spars.
Once aboard, I rowed away with my hands.
As for Scylla, Zeus never let her see me,
Or I would have been wiped out completely.

I floated on for nine days. On the tenth night   465
The gods brought me to Ogygia
And to Calypso, the dread, beautiful goddess,
Who loved me and took care of me.
But I have told that tale only yesterday,
Here in your hall, to yourself and your wife,   470
And I wouldn't bore you by telling it again."

ODYSSEY 13

Odysseus finished his story,
And they were all spellbound, hushed
To silence throughout the shadowy hall,
Until Alcinous found his voice and said:

"Odysseus, now that you have come to my house,   5
High-roofed and founded on bronze, I do not think
You will be blown off course again
Before reaching home.
                            Hear now my command,
All who drink the glowing wine of Elders
Daily in my halls and hear the harper sing: 10
Clothes for our guest lie in a polished sea-chest,
Along with richly wrought gold and all the other gifts
The Phaeacian lords have brought to the palace.
But now each man of us gives him a cauldron, too.
We will recoup ourselves later with a general tax.   15
It is hard to make such generous gifts alone."

They were all pleased with what Alcinous said.
Each man went to his own house to sleep,
And when Dawn's rosy fingers appeared in the sky
They hurried to the ship with their gifts of bronze.   20
Alcinous, the sacred king himself, went on board
And stowed them away beneath the benches
Where they would not hinder the rowers' efforts.
Then they all went back to feast in the palace.

In their honor Alcinous sacrificed an ox   25

To Zeus, the Dark Cloud, who rules over all.
They roasted the haunches and feasted gloriously
While the godlike harper, honored Demodocus,
Sang in their midst.
                    But Odysseus
Kept turning his head toward the shining sun,   *30*
Urging it down the sky. He longed to set forth.

> *A man who has been in the fields all day*
> *With his wooden plow and wine-faced oxen*
> *Longs for supper and welcomes the sunset*
> *That sends him homeward with weary knees,*   *35*

So welcome to Odysseus was the evening sun.
As soon as it set he addressed the Phaeacians,
Alcinous especially, and his words had wings:

"Lord Alcinous, I bid you and your people
To pour libation and send me safely on my way.   *40*
And I bid you farewell. All is now here
That my heart has desired—passage home
And cherished gifts that the gods in heaven
Have blessed me with. When I reach home
May I find my wife and loved ones unharmed.   *45*
May you enjoy your wife and children here,
May the gods send you everything good,
And may harm never come to your island people."

They all cheered this speech, and demanded
That the stranger and guest be given passage home.   *50*
Alcinous then nodded to his herald:

"Pontonous, mix a bowl of wine and serve
Cups to all, that we may pray to Lord Zeus
And send our guest to his own native land."

Thus the King, and Pontonous mixed   *55*
The mellow-hearted wine and served it to all.
Still seated, they tipped their cups to the gods
Who possess wide heaven. Then Odysseus

Stood up and placed a two-handled cup
In Arete's hands, and his words rose on wings: 60

"Be well, my queen, all of your days, until age
And death come to you, as they come to all.
I am leaving now. But you, Lady—enjoy this house,
Your children, your people, and Lord Alcinous."

And godlike Odysseus stepped over the threshold. 65
Alcinous sent a herald along
To guide him to the shore and the swift ship there,
And Arete sent serving women with him,
One carrying a cloak and laundered shirt,
And another to bring the strong sea-chest. 70
A third brought along bread and red wine.
They came down to the sea, and the ship's crew
Stowed all these things away in the hold,
The food and drink, too. Then they spread out
A rug and a linen sheet on the stern deck 75
For Odysseus to sleep upon undisturbed.
He climbed on board and lay down in silence
While they took their places upon the benches
And untied the cable from the anchor stone.
As soon as they dipped their oars in the sea, 80
A deep sleep fell on his eyelids, a sleep
Sound, and sweet, and very much like death.

   And as four yoked stallions spring all together
   Beneath the lash, leaping high,
   And then eat up the dusty road on the plain, 85

So lifted the keel of that ship, and in her wake
An indigo wave hissed and roiled
As she ran straight ahead. Not even a falcon,
Lord of the skies, could have matched her pace,
So light her course as she cut through the waves, 90
Bearing a man with a mind like the gods',
A man who had suffered deep in his heart,
Enduring men's wars and the bitter sea—
But now he slept, his sorrows forgotten.

The sea turned silver   95
Under the star that precedes the dawn,
And the great ship pulled up to Ithaca.

Phorcys, the Old Man of the Sea,
Has a harbor there. Two fingers of rock
Curl out from the island, steep to seaward   100
But sloping down to the bay they protect
From hurricane winds and high waves outside.
Inside, ships can ride without anchor
In the still water offshore.
At the harbor's head a slender-leaved olive   105
Stands near a cave glimmering through the mist
And sacred to the nymphs called Naiades.
Inside are bowls and jars of stone
Where bees store honey, and long stone looms
Where the nymphs weave shrouds as dark as the sea.   110
Waters flow there forever, and there are two doors,
One toward the North Wind, by which humans
Go down, the other toward the South Wind,
A door for the gods. No men enter there:
It is the Way of Immortals.

                    The Phaeacians   115
Had been here before. In they rowed,
And with such force that their ship was propelled
Half of its length onto the shelving shore.
The crew disembarked, lifting Odysseus
Out of the ship—sheet, carpet, and all—   120
And laying him down, sound asleep, on the sand.
Then they hauled from the ship all of the goods
The Phaeacian lords had given him
As he was going home—all thanks to Athena.
They piled these together near the bole of the olive,   125
Away from the path, fearing that someone
Might come along before Odysseus awoke
And rob him blind.

                    Then the Phaeacians went home.
But the Earthshaker did not forget the threats

He had leveled against Odysseus,   *130*
And he asked Zeus what he intended to do:

"I lose face among the gods, Zeus,
When I'm not respected by mortal men—
The Phaeacians yet, my own flesh and blood!
I swore that Odysseus would have to suffer   *135*
Before getting home—I didn't say
He would never get home, because you had already
Agreed that he would—and now they've brought him
Over the sea while he napped on their ship,
And set him down in Ithaca, and given him   *140*
Gifts of bronze and clothing and gold,
More than he ever would have taken out of Troy
Had he come home safely with his share of the loot."

And Zeus, clouds scudding around him:

"What a thing for you to say—you, the Temblor!   *145*
Dishonored by the gods? It would be hard for us
To sling insults at our eldest and best.
And if some over-confident hero fails
To pay you respect, you can always pay him back.
Do as you please, and as your heart desires."   *150*

And Poseidon, the Lord of Earthquake:

"I would do just that, Dark Cloud,
But I like to keep an eye on your temper.
I want to smash that beautiful Phaeacian ship
As it sails for home over the misty sea,   *155*
Smash it, so that they will stop this nonsense
Once and for all, giving men safe passage!
And I'll hem their city in with a mountain."

And Zeus, from out of his nimbus of cloud:

"Well, now, this is what I would do: *160*
Wait until all of the people in the city see her
Pulling in to port, and then turn her to stone,

Stone shaped like a ship, a marvel for all men.
And then hem their city in with a mountain."

When he heard this, the Lord of Earthquake   *165*
Went to Schería, where the Phaeacians live,
And waited. The great seafaring ship
Was closing in fast when Poseidon slapped it
With the flat of his hand and turned it to stone
Rooted in the seafloor. Then the god was gone.   *170*

The Phaeacians, men who understood the sea,
Kept turning to each other, saying things like:

"Who did that?"
                    "Stopped her dead in the water
When she was at top speed, pulling in home."

"She was in plain view, from stem to stern!"

                              Winged words,   *175*
But they had no idea what had happened.

Then Alcinous spoke to his people:

"Alas for the prophecy of old that I heard
From my father. He said that Poseidon
Would be angry with us for giving safe passage   *180*
And that one day he would wreck a beautiful ship
As it sailed for home over the misty sea.
And he would hem our city in with a mountain.
What the old man said is all coming true.
Now hear what I have to say. Let us all agree   *185*
Never again to provide safe escort
To any man who comes to our city.
And we will sacrifice twelve chosen bulls
To Lord Poseidon, so may he pity us
And not enclose our town with a mountain."   *190*

Trembling with fear they prepared the bulls,
And soon all the Phaeacian leaders and lords

Were standing around Poseidon's altar
Saying their prayers.

Odysseus, meanwhile,
Awoke from sleep in his ancestral land—   195
And did not recognize it. He had been gone so long,
And Pallas Athena had spread haze all around.
The goddess wanted to explain things to him,
And to disguise him, so that his wife and dear ones
Would not know who he was until he had made   200
The arrogant suitors pay for their outrage.
So everything on Ithaca now looked different
To its lord—the winding trails, the harbors,
The towering rocks and the trees. Odysseus
Sprang to his feet and gazed at his homeland.   205
He groaned, smacked his thighs with his hands,
And in a voice choked with tears, said:

"What land have I come to now? Who knows
What kind of people live here—lawless savages,
Or godfearing men who take kindly to strangers?   210
Where am I going to take all these things? Where
Am I going to go myself? I should have stayed
With the Phaeacians until I could go on from there
To some other powerful king who would have
Entertained me and sent me off homeward bound.   215
Now I don't even know where to put this stuff.
I can't leave it here as easy pickings for a thief.
Those Phaeacian lords were not as wise
As they seemed, nor as just, bringing me here
To this strange land. They said they would bring me   220
To Ithaca's shore, but that's not what they've done.
May Zeus pay them back, Zeus, god of suppliants,
Who spots transgressors and punishes them.
Well, I'd better count my goods and go over them.
Those sailors may have made off with some in their ship."   225

And he set about counting the hammered tripods,
The cauldrons, the gold, the finely woven clothes.
Nothing was missing. It was his homeland he missed

As he paced along the whispering surf-line,
Utterly forlorn.
              And then Athena was beside him   230
In the form of a young man out herding sheep.
She had the delicate features of a prince,
A fine-spun mantle folded over her shoulders,
Sandals on her glistening feet, a spear in her hand.
Odysseus' spirits soared when he saw her,   235
And he turned to her with these words on his lips:

"Friend—you are the first person I've met here—
I wish you well. Now don't turn on me.
Help me keep these things safe, and keep me safe,
I beg you at your knees as if you were a god.   240
And tell me this, so I will know:
What land is this, who are the people here?
Is this an island, or a rocky arm
Of the mainland shore stretching out to sea?"

Athena's eyes glinted with azure light: 245

"Where in the world do you come from, stranger,
That you have to ask what land this is?
It's not exactly nameless! Men from all over
Know this land, sailing in from the sunrise
And from far beyond the evening horizon.   250
It's got rough terrain, not for driving horses,
But it's not at all poor even without wide open spaces.
There's abundant grain here, and wine-grapes,
Good rainfalls, and rich, heavy dews.
Good pasture, too, for goats and for cattle,   255
And all sorts of timber, and year-round springs.
That's why Ithaca is a name heard even in Troy,
Which they say is far from any Greek land."

And Odysseus, who had borne much,
Felt joy at hearing his homeland described   260
By Pallas Athena, Zeus' own daughter.
His words flew out as if on wings—
But he did not speak the truth. He checked that impulse,

And, jockeying for an advantage, made up this story:

"I've heard of Ithaca, of course—even in Crete,   *265*
Far over the sea, and now I've just come ashore
With my belongings here. I left as much
To my sons back home. I've been on the run
Since killing a man, Orsilochus,
Idomeneus' son, the great sprinter.   *270*
No one in all Crete could match his speed.
He wanted to rob me of all of the loot
I took out of Troy—stuff I had sweated for
In hand-to-hand combat in the war overseas—
Because I wouldn't serve under his father at Troy   *275*
But led my own unit instead. I ambushed him
With one of my men, got him with a spear
As he came back from the fields. It was night,
Pitch-black. No one saw us, and I got away
With a clean kill with sharp bronze. Then,   *280*
I found a ship, Phoenician, and made it
Worth the crew's while to take me to Pylos,
Or Elis maybe, where the Epeans are in power.
Well, the wind pushed us back from those shores—
It wasn't their fault, they didn't want to cheat me—   *285*
And we were driven here in the middle of the night
And rowed like hell into the harbor. Didn't even
Think of chow, though we sure could have used some,
Just got off the boat and lay down, all of us.
I slept like a baby, dead to the world,   *290*
And they unloaded my stuff from the ship's hold
And set it down next to me where I lay on the sand.
Then off they went to Sidonia, the big city,
And I was left here, stranded, just aching inside."

Athena smiled at him, her eyes blue as the sea,   *295*
And her hand brushed his cheek. She was now
A tall, beautiful woman, with an exquisite touch
For handiwork, and her words had wings:

"Only a master thief, a real con artist,
Could match your tricks—even a god   *300*

Might come up short. You wily bastard,
You cunning, elusive, habitual liar!
Even in your own land you weren't about
To give up the stories and sly deceits
That are so much a part of you.   305
Never mind about that though. Here we are,
The two shrewdest minds in the universe,
You far and away the best man on earth
In plotting strategies, and I famed among gods
For my clever schemes. Not even you   310
Recognized Pallas Athena, Zeus' daughter,
I who stand by you in all your troubles
And who made you dear to all the Phaeacians.
And now I've come here, ready to weave
A plan with you, and to hide the goods   315
The Phaeacians gave you—which was my idea—
And to tell you what you still have to endure
In your own house. And you do have to endure,
And not tell anyone, man or woman,
That you have come home from your wanderings.   320
No, you must suffer in silence, and take a beating."

And Odysseus, his mind teeming:

"It would be hard for the most discerning man alive
To see through all your disguises, Goddess.
I know this, though: you were always kind to me   325
When the army fought at Troy.
But after we plundered Priam's steep city,
And boarded our ships, and a god scattered us,
I didn't see you then, didn't sense your presence
Aboard my ship or feel you there to help me.   330
No, and I suffered in my wanderings
Until the gods released me from my troubles.
It wasn't until I was on Phaeacia
That you comforted me—and led me to the city.
Now I beg you, by your Father—I don't believe   335
I've come to sunlit Ithaca, but to some other land.
I think you're just giving me a hard time,
And trying to put one over on me. Tell me

If I've really come to my own native land."

And Athena, her eyes glinting blue: *340*

"Ah, that mind of yours! That's why
I can't leave you when you're down and out:
Because you're so intelligent and self-possessed.
Any other man come home from hard travels
Would rush to his house to see his children and wife.   *345*
But you don't even want to hear how they are
Until you test your wife, who,
As a matter of fact, just sits in the house,
Weeping away the lonely days and nights.
I never lost faith, though. I always knew in my heart   *350*
You'd make it home, all your companions lost,
But I couldn't bring myself to fight my uncle,
Poseidon, who had it in for you,
Angry because you blinded his son.
And now, so you will believe, I will show you   *355*
Ithaca from the ground up: There is the harbor
Of Phorcys, the Old Man of the Sea, and here,
At its head, is the slender-leaved olive tree
Standing near a cave that glimmers in the mist
And is sacred to the nymphs called Naiades.   *360*
Under that cavern's arched roof you sacrificed
Many a perfect victim to the nymphs.
And there stands Mount Neriton, mantled in forest."

As she spoke, the goddess dispelled the mist.
The ground appeared, and Odysseus,   *365*
The godlike survivor, felt his mind soar
At the sight of his land. He kissed the good earth,
And with his palms to the sun, Odysseus prayed:

"Nymphs, Naiades, daughters of Zeus!
I never thought I would see you again.   *370*
Take pleasure in my whispered prayers
And we will give you gifts as before,
If Zeus' great daughter Athena
Allows me to live and my son to reach manhood."

And Athena, her eyes glinting blue: *375*

"You don't have to worry about that.
Right now, let's stow these things in a nook
Of the enchanted cave, where they'll be safe for you.
Then we can talk about a happy ending."

With that, the goddess entered the shadowy cave   *380*
And searched out its recesses while Odysseus
Brought everything closer—the gold, the bronze,
The well-made clothes the Phaeacians had given him.
And Zeus' own daughter stored them away
And blocked the entrance to the cave with a stone.   *385*
Then, sitting at the base of the sacred olive,
The two plotted death for the insolent suitors.
Athena began their discussion this way:

"Son of Laertes in the line of Zeus,
Odysseus, the master tactician—consider how   *390*
You're going to get your hands on the shameless suitors,
Who for three years now have taken over your house,
Proposing to your wife and giving her gifts.
She pines constantly for your return,
But she strings them along, makes little promises,   *395*
Sends messages—while her intentions are otherwise."

And Odysseus, his mind teeming:

"Ah, I'd be heading for the same pitiful death
That Agamemnon met in his house
If you hadn't told me all this, Goddess.   *400*
Weave a plan so I can pay them back!
And stand by me yourself, give me the spirit I had
When we ripped down Troy's shining towers!
With you at my side, your eyes glinting
And your mind fixed on battle—I would take on   *405*
Three hundred men if your power were with me."

And Athena, eyes reflecting the blue sea-light:

"Oh, I'll be there all right, and I'll keep my eye on you
When we get down to business. And I think
More than one of these suitors destroying your home   410
Will spatter the ground with their blood and brains.
Now let's see about disguising you. First,
I'll shrivel the skin on your gnarly limbs,
And wither that tawny hair. A piece of sail-cloth
Will make a nice, ugly cloak. Then   415
We'll make those beautiful eyes bleary and dim.
You'll look disgusting to all the suitors, as well as to
The wife and child you left behind in your halls.
But you should go first to your swineherd.
He may only tend your pigs, but he's devoted to you,   420
And he loves your son and Penelope.
You'll find him with the swine. They are feeding
By Raven's Rock and Arethusa's spring,
Gorging on acorns and drinking black water,
Which fattens swine up nicely. Stay with him,   425
Sit with him a while and ask him about everything,
While I go to Lacedaemon, land of lovely women,
To summon Telemachus. Your son, Odysseus,
Went to Menelaus' house in Sparta
Hoping for news that you are still alive."   430

And Odysseus, his mind teeming:

"You knew. Why didn't you tell him?
So he could suffer too, roving barren seas
While my wife's suitors eat him out of house and home?"

Athena answered, her eyes glinting blue: 435

"You needn't worry too much about him.
I accompanied him in person. I wanted him
To make a name for himself by traveling there.
He's not exactly laboring as he takes his ease
In Menelaus' luxurious palace.   440
Sure, these young louts have laid an ambush for him
In a ship out at sea, meaning to kill him
Before he reaches home. But I don't think they will.

These suitors who have been destroying your home
Will be six feet under before that'll ever happen."   *445*

So saying, Athena touched him with a wand.
She shriveled the flesh on his gnarled limbs,
And withered his tawny hair. She wrinkled the skin
All over his body so he looked like an old man,
And she made his beautiful eyes bleary and dim.   *450*
Then she turned his clothes into tattered rags,
Dirty and smoke-grimed, and cast about him
A great deerskin cloak with the fur worn off.
And she gave him a staff and a ratty pouch
All full of holes, slung by a twisted cord.   *455*

Having laid their plans, they went their own ways,
The goddess off to Sparta to fetch Telemachus.

ODYSSEY 14

Odysseus went up from the harbor
Along a rough path until he reached a high,
Wooded area where Athena had told him
He would find the noble swineherd. This man
Cared for his master's property   5
Better than any other slave Odysseus had.

He found him sitting in front of his house,
Which had a high-fenced yard with a view all around.
It was a fine, spacious yard, built by the herdsman
For his absent master's swine. Neither Penelope   10
Nor old Laertes knew anything of it.
He had built it with huge stones coped with thorns
And wedged on the outside with close-set stakes
Of split, black heart-oak. Inside the yard
He had made twelve sties, one next to the other,   15
As beds for the swine, and in each were penned
Fifty wallowing swine—breeding females.
The boars slept outside, and were far scarcer,
Their numbers depleted by the godlike suitors
Who feasted on them. The swineherd was always   20
Sending the best of all the fatted hogs.
There were three hundred and sixty in all.

                                                  Close by,
The dogs slept, four of them, wild as beasts,
Reared by the swineherd, who was a man
Who could have commanded a platoon in war.   25
At the moment, he was fitting sandals to his feet,

Cutting the tanned leather to size.
The other herdsman had gone off with the swine,
One here, one there, one to drive a boar to town
So that the insolent suitors could sacrifice it   30
And satisfy their hunger for meat.

                                                    Suddenly,
The baying hounds caught sight of Odysseus
And rushed at him barking and snarling.
Odysseus, remembering his tricks, sat down
And let the staff fall from his hand. Even so,   35
He would have been mauled on his own farmstead,
But the swineherd was hot on the dogs' heels,
Dropping the leather as he ran through the gate
And calling aloud to the dogs. He scattered them
With a shower of stones, and then addressed   40
The man who was his master, saying:

"Another moment, old man, and the dogs
Would have ripped you open, and it's me
You would have blamed for it, as if the gods
Haven't given me enough grief already.   45
It's for my master, a man like a god, I grieve
As I stay out here raising fat hogs
For other men to eat, while he wanders hungry
In some foreign land, if he's still alive, that is,
And still sees the sunlight. But come with me.   50
Let's go to my hut, old man, so that you,
When you have had your fill of food and wine,
Can tell me your story—where you are from,
And all the suffering you have endured."

So the godlike swineherd led him into his hut.   55
Once inside, he had him sit down on a pile
Of thick brushwood over which he spread
The skin of a shaggy wild goat, a large, thick hide
On which he usually slept. Odysseus was glad
That he welcomed him like this, and said so: 60

"May Zeus and all the gods bless you, stranger,

For welcoming me with such an open heart."

And you answered him, Eumaeus, my swineherd:

"It would not be right for me to show less respect
Even to someone less worthy than you.   65
All strangers and beggars come from Zeus,
And our gifts to them are welcome though small,
Since this is how it is with slaves, always fearful
Of the masters over them, especially
Young masters. Yes, and the gods have blocked   70
The return of the master who would have treated me
With kindness, given me possessions of my own,
A house, some land, and a wife courted by many,
The things a kind master gives to his servant
Whose long, hard work a god has made prosper,   75
As the work I have done has come to prosper.
My master would have rewarded me richly for this,
Had he grown old here. But he's gone, perished—
As I wish Helen and all her clan had perished,
Since she has unstrung the knees of many heroes.   80
Yes, he too went to Ilion, land of fine horses,
To fight the Trojans on Agamemnon's account."

So saying, he tucked his tunic up in his belt
And went to the sties where the swine were penned.
He picked out two and slaughtered them both,   85
Singed them, butchered them, and put them on spits.
When he had roasted everything, he brought it out
Hot on the spits and served it to Odysseus,
Sprinkling the pork with white barley meal.
Then he mixed sweet wine in an ivy-wood bowl,   90
Sat down across from Odysseus, and said:

"Eat now, stranger, such food as slaves eat,
Young porkers. The fatted hogs the suitors eat,
Men who have no fear of the gods, and feel no pity.
The blessed ones do not love wickedness   95
But honor justice and repay righteousness!
Even men who wage war in a foreign land

And sail for home with their ships filled with loot—
Even men like that fear the wrath of the gods.
But these men here must know something,   *100*
Must have heard from a god that my master is dead,
Since they are so unwilling to conduct their courtship
In a way that is just, or to return to their homes.
They just lounge about squandering our goods,
Sparing nothing in their insolence.   *105*
Every day and night they slaughter our animals—
Not just one or two, either—and waste our wine.
At least my master's holdings are huge. No hero,
Either on the dark mainland or Ithaca itself,
Has nearly as much. Twenty men together   *110*
Could not match his wealth. Let me count it for you.
Twelve herds of cattle over on the mainland,
And as many flocks of sheep, droves of swine,
And spreading herds of goats—all of them pastured
By his own herdsmen or hired foreigners.   *115*
And more herds of goats, eleven in all,
Range our island's coasts. Good men watch them,
And every day each of these men drives up
The best fatted goat in all of his flock
For the suitors to eat. Myself, I keep these swine,   *120*
And always pick out the best to send to them."

As he spoke, Odysseus was silently
Eating his pork and drinking wine—
And chewing on how to punish the suitors.
When he had satisfied his appetite for food,   *125*
The swineherd filled for him the drinking bowl
He ordinarily used himself and gave it to him
Brimming with wine. Odysseus gladly took it,
And his words flew on wings to the swineherd:

"Well, who was it, my friend, who bought you?   *130*
Who is this rich and powerful man?
You said he died fighting on Agamemnon's account.
Tell me his name. I might recognize it.
Zeus only knows who I might have met
And have some news of. I've wandered far."   *135*

And the swineherd, a leader of men:

"Old man, no wanderer who came with news of him
Could ever convince his wife and son. Besides,
All a needy vagabond ever does is tell lies.
He has no interest at all in telling the truth.   *140*
Whenever a wanderer comes to Ithaca,
He goes to my mistress with a cock and bull story.
She receives him kindly and questions him closely,
And tears fall from her eyes and she weeps and cries
The way a woman will whose husband dies abroad.   *145*
And you'd make up a story, too, old man,
In an instant, if you thought you could get
A cloak and tunic out of it.
                        But by now,
Dogs and birds have torn the flesh from his bones,
And his soul has crawled off. Or deep in the sea   *150*
Fish have picked his bones clean, and they now lie
On a shore somewhere, wrapped in deep sand.
No, he's dead and gone, and there is nothing left
For his dear ones but grief, and for me especially,
For never again will I find a master so mild,   *155*
However far I go, even if I go home again
To my mother and father, where I was born
And where they reared me. Yet,
As much as I miss them and miss my homeland,
I miss Odysseus more. There, I said his name.   *160*
I would rather not say his name when he is not here,
For he loved me greatly and cared for me. Instead,
I call him my brother, though he is not here."

Odysseus, who had borne much, replied:

"Well, my friend, since you refuse to believe,   *165*
And since you insist he will never come home,
I'll not just say it, but will solemnly swear
That Odysseus will come back. As for a reward
For bringing this news, give it to me
When he does return—a tunic and cloak—   *170*
And not a moment before. Until that man

Is actually here, I will accept nothing,
However great my need. I hate like hell
A man who caves in to his poverty
And tells a batch of lies.
                              I swear by Zeus,   *175*
Above all gods, and by this hospitable table,
And the hearth of flawless Odysseus himself—
That everything will happen just as I say:
Before this month is out Odysseus will come,
In the dark of the moon, before the new crescent.   *180*
He shall return, and take vengeance upon
All those who dishonor his wife and his son."

And you answered him, Eumaeus, my swineherd:

"I'll never be paying you any reward,
Nor will Odysseus ever come home.   *185*
Now let's just drink quietly and think about
Other things. Don't remind me of all this.
I feel such pain and grief in my heart
Whenever anyone mentions my master.
We'll just let your oath be. May Odysseus   *190*
Come back, as I desire, and as Penelope does,
And the old man Laertes, and godlike Telemachus,
Odysseus' son. And now he weighs on my mind,
Telemachus. The gods made him grow
Like a sapling, and I thought he would be a match   *195*
For his father, a splendid man to look at.
Then one of the immortals, or maybe a man,
Knocked the sense out of him, and he left
For sacred Pylos, trying to track down his father.
And now the suitors are ambushing him   *200*
As he sails for home, so that the line
Of godlike Arceisius may come to an end
On Ithaca, and leave no name behind.
But there's nothing we can do, whether he's caught
Or escapes with a helping hand from Zeus.   *205*
But tell me, old man, about your own troubles,
And tell me this, so that I can be sure of it.
Who are you, and where do you come from?

Where is your city, and where are your parents?
On what kind of ship did you come, and how   *210*
Did sailors bring you to Ithaca? Who were they?
I don't suppose you walked all the way here."

And Odysseus, his mind teeming:

"I will tell you all of this, down to the last detail.
If you and I could only have food and sweet wine   *215*
For the duration, feasting on and on quietly
Here in your hut, leaving the work to others—
It would easily take me a full year, and even then
I would not finish my heart's tale of sorrows,
All that I have endured by the will of the gods.   *220*
          I was born in Crete, son of a wealthy man
Who had many other sons born to his lawful wife.
My own mother was a concubine,
But my father, Castor, son of Hylax,
Treated me like one of his true-born sons.   *225*
He was honored as a god by the Cretans
For his wealth, prosperity, and glorious sons.
But death carried him away to Hades,
And his sons parceled out his estate
Among themselves, leaving me just a small share,   *230*
And a house to live in. But I was able to marry
A wife from a propertied family
Because of my real worth. I was no weakling,
And I held my own in battle. All that's gone now,
But I think you can judge the grain from the stubble.   *235*
I'm overwhelmed now with aches and pains,
But back then Athena and Ares
Gave me the power to crush men in war.
When I set an ambush, lying in wait
With hand-picked men to give the enemy hell,   *240*
I never got nervous, never saw death looming.
I was the first to jump out and kill whoever
Gave way before me and started to run.
I was good in war. But fieldwork
Was not to my taste, nor caring for a household   *245*
Where children are reared. Oared ships are what I liked,

And war, polished spears, and arrows,
All the grim things that make most people shudder.
I suppose I liked what a god put in my heart—
One man's meat is another man's poison.   250
Before the Greeks ever set foot in Troy,
I had already led nine expeditions,
Amphibious assaults against foreign cities.
I made a lot in those wars. I would cull
The loot I liked best and get even more   255
When the rest was divided later by lot.
So my house grew rich, and I became
One of the most feared and respected men in Crete.
          But when thundering Zeus opened the war
That unstrung the knees of many heroes,   260
I was urged to go with glorious Idomeneus
And lead our ships to Troy. I could not refuse.
The people's voice had to be heard. Nine years
We Greeks waged war, and in the tenth
We sacked Priam's city and sailed for home   265
In our ships, and a god scattered the fleet.
But Zeus had more trouble in store for me.
I stayed home for only a month, enjoying
My children, my wife, and all my possessions.
Then I felt an urge to voyage to Egypt   270
With my godlike companions. I fitted out
Nine ships with care. It didn't take long
For my men to gather, and when they had,
I feasted them for six days, giving them
All the animals they needed for sacrifice—   275
Enough for the gods and for their own banquets.
On the seventh day we set sail from Crete
Under a fresh North Wind and ran on as easily
As if we were in a current. My ships sailed
Without any mishap, free of disease,   280
Guided by the wind and the pilot's hand.
          On the fifth day I moored my ships
In the river Nile, and you can be sure I ordered
My trusty mates to stand by and guard them
While I sent out scouts to look around.   285
But the crews got restless and cocky

And started pillaging the Egyptian countryside,
Carrying off the women and children
And killing the men. The cry came to the city,
And at daybreak troops answered the call.   *290*
The whole plain was filled with infantry,
War chariots, and the glint of bronze.
Thundering Zeus threw my men into a panic,
And not one had the courage to stand and fight
Against odds like that. It was bad.   *295*
They killed many of us outright with bronze
And led the rest to their city to work as slaves.
But Zeus put an idea into my mind.
I'm sorry I took it. It would have been better
If I had died in Egypt, met my fate there—   *300*
So much more suffering was waiting for me.
I took off my helmet, dropped my shield,
Let the spear fall from my hands, and walked straight
To the king's chariot. I clasped his knees
And kissed them. It worked. He pitied me,   *305*
Took me in his chariot, and drove me weeping
To his own home, warding off all the spears
That were aimed at me by the angry mob,
For he respected Zeus, god of strangers,
Indignant and wrathful above all other gods.   *310*
        Seven years I stayed there, amassing wealth,
For all the Egyptians gave me gifts.
When the eighth year rolled around, there came
A man from Phoenicia, avaracious and sly,
And a general scoundrel. He persuaded me   *315*
To go off with him to his house in Phoenicia,
And I stayed with him there for one full year,
After which he took me in a seafaring ship
Bound for Libya, pretending we were taking
A cargo there, when his real intent   *320*
Was to sell me there for an enormous price.
I suspected treachery but had to go aboard.
The ship ran on under a fresh North Wind,
Staying above Crete in a mid-sea course.
Then Zeus devised the crew's utter destruction.   *325*
        When we left Crete behind, there was

No other land in sight, only sea and sky.
Then Zeus put a black cloud over our ship.
The sea grew dark beneath it, and Zeus thundered
And struck the ship with a lightning bolt.   330
She shivered from stem to stern and was filled
With sulfurous smoke. The men went overboard,
Bobbing in the waves like sea crows
Around the black ship, their day of return
Snuffed out by the god. As for me,   335
Zeus himself, in the midst of my distress,
Put into my hands the surging mast
Of the dark-prowed ship. That saved my life.
I clung to the mast as the terrible winds
Bore me along. I was out there nine days,   340
And on the tenth black night a great wave
Rolled me ashore in the Thesprotians' land.
The Thesprotian king, the hero Pheidon,
Took me in. There was no talk of ransom,
For his son had found me, overcome   345
With cold and fatigue, and raised me up
By the hand, and led me to his father's palace,
Where he gave me a tunic and cloak to wear.
          It was there I learned of Odysseus.
The king said he had been his guest there   350
On his way back to his native land. He showed me
All the treasure Odysseus had amassed,
Bronze, gold, and wrought iron, enough to feed
His children's children for ten generations,
All stored there for him in the halls of the king.   355
Odysseus, he said, had gone to Dodona
To consult the oak-tree oracle of Zeus
And ask how he should return to Ithaca—
Openly or in secret—after being gone so long.
And he swore to me, as he poured libations   360
There in his house, that a ship was launched,
And a crew standing by, to take him home.
But he sent me off first, since a Thesprotian ship
Happened to be leaving for Dulichium,
Where I wanted to go. He told that crew   365
To escort me to King Acastus there.

Somehow the crew turned against me,
And I was destined for even more pain.
When the ship left land, it wasn't long before
They hatched a plot to sell me as a slave.   370
They stripped off my clothes, the tunic and cloak,
And made me wear the rags you see on me now.
At evening they reached the coast of Ithaca.
They tied me up in the ship and went ashore
And got busy with their supper there on the beach.   375
The gods themselves must have untied my bonds,
They came off so easily, and wrapping my head
In the rags I wore, I slid down the smooth plank
Into the sea. I started to swim a breast stroke
And was soon out of the water and away from them.   380
I went upland a ways and found a leafy thicket
And huddled up in it. They looked all over,
Moaning and groaning, but couldn't see any profit
In continuing their search, and so they went back aboard
Their hollow ship. The gods kept me under cover—   385
Easy for them—and guided me to the farmstead
Of a wise man. It seems I'm still destined to live."

And you answered him, Eumaeus, my swineherd:

"You poor, wandering wretch. You've wrung my heart
With all the particulars of your suffering.   390
But the part of your story about Odysseus
Just isn't right, and I'm not buying it.
Why should a man in such a fix as you are
Want to lie like that? I know all about
The return of my master—how the gods spited him   395
In not letting him die among the Trojans
Or in his friends' arms after he had wound up the war.
The entire Greek army would have buried him then,
And great honor would have passed on to his son.
As it is, the whirlwinds have snatched him away.   400
Myself, I live out here with the swine. I never go
Into the city, unless Penelope asks me to
When news comes to her from somewhere.
Then everyone sits around the visitor

And questions him, both those who miss   *405*
Their absent lord, and those who enjoy
Devouring his goods without recompense.
But I don't ask anything, not since the time
An Aetolian fooled me with his phony story.
He had killed a man and was wandering the earth.   *410*
He came to my house, and I welcomed him.
He said he had seen Odysseus in Crete
At Idomeneus' house, repairing some of his ships
That storms had battered. And he said he would be back
By summer or harvest, bringing with him   *415*
Piles of treasure and his godlike companions.
And now, you woeful old man, since some god
Has steered you my way, don't you try
To charm me or win me over with lies.
It's not for that I'll show you respect or kindness,   *420*
But for fear of Zeus, and out of pity for you."

And Odysseus, his mind teeming:

"You have a heart that just won't believe.
Not even my oath was enough to convince you.
Let's make a bet, with the gods on Olympus   *425*
As witnesses. If your master comes back,
You give me a cloak and tunic to wear
And get me to Dulichium, where I want to be.
But if he doesn't come back as I say he will,
Have your slaves jump me and throw me off a cliff,   *430*
So that the next beggar will think twice before lying."

And the noble, godlike swineherd answered:

"And that would earn me a fine reputation,
Now and forever, wouldn't it, stranger?
First I welcome you into my hut, and then   *435*
I take you outside and end your sweet life.
And afterwards I'll pray to Zeus, son of Cronus,
With a clear conscience!
                 It's time for supper.
I hope my men come back soon

So we can make a tasty meal here in the hut."   *440*

As they were speaking, the herders came up
Driving the swine. They put the sows in the sties
Where they always slept, and an amazing racket
Rose from the animals as they were being penned.
The swineherd called to the workers and said: *445*

"Bring the best boar we have so I can slaughter him
For the stranger here, and for us, too.
We have worked long and hard with these tuskers
While others eat up our labor free of charge."

With that, he started to split wood with an axe   *450*
While they brought in a five-year-old fatted boar
And set him down by the hearth. The swineherd
Did not forget the immortals—he had a good mind for this—
Casting into the fire as a first offering
Bristles from the head of the white-tusked boar   *455*
And praying that Odysseus would return to his home.
Then he came down hard with a piece of split oak
And the boar's spirit left him. They cut his throat,
Singed him, and then butchered him quickly.
The swineherd cut off, as more first offerings,   *460*
Bits of raw flesh from each part of the animal,
Then wrapped them in fat, sprinkled them with barley,
And then threw them into the fire. The rest
They cut up and roasted with care on spits.
When it was done, they pulled the roast pork from the spits   *465*
And piled it on platters. The swineherd carved,
For he had a good sense of fairness,
And he divided the meat into seven portions.
He set aside one for the Nymphs and for Hermes,
Saying a prayer, and served the rest to the men,   *470*
Honoring Odysseus with the long chine
Of the white-tusked boar, and so pleasing his master.
And Odysseus, always thinking, said:

"Eumaeus, may you be as dear to Father Zeus
As you are to me, for so honoring a man like me."   *475*

And you answered him, Eumaeus, my swineherd:

"Eat, my strange guest, and enjoy what we have.
God gives us one thing and holds another back,
Just as he pleases, for he can do all things."

He spoke, and sacrificed the first offerings   480
To the eternal gods, and poured libations
Of sparkling wine. Then he handed the cup
To Odysseus, sacker of cities, and took his seat.
The bread was served by Mesaulius,
Whom the swineherd had bought all on his own   485
While his master was gone, without the help of his mistress
Or of old Laertes, buying him
From the Taphians with his own resources.
They reached for the good cheer spread before them,
And when they had enough of food and drink,   490
Mesaulius took away the leftovers, and they all
Longed for rest, their stomachs full of bread and meat.

The evening sky was foreboding and moonless,
And a damp West Wind was starting to blow.
It began to rain, and it would rain all night.   495
Odysseus spoke, testing the swineherd,
Seeing if he would take off his own cloak
And give it to him, or tell one of his men
To do so, since he cared for him deeply:

"Hear me now, Eumaeus, and the rest of you men,   500
While I boast a little. It must be the wine
Befuddling me, which gets even sensible men
Singing and laughing and up to dance,
And sometimes to say things better left unsaid.
But I've cut loose now and won't hide anything.   505
Oh, to be young again and with the strength I had
When we went out on ambush under Troy's wall.
Our leaders were Odysseus and Menelaus,
And I was third in command, at their request.
When we had come up close to the steep city wall,   510
We took our places on the perimeter

Down in the brush and reeds of the swampland,
Lying there crouched beneath our shields.
The North Wind swooped down, and night came on
Foul and bitter cold. Snow drifted down   *515*
And covered us like frost, and ice rimmed our shields.
Everyone else had on cloaks and tunics
And slept peacefully, their shields on their shoulders.
But I had stupidly left my cloak behind at camp,
Because I didn't think it would be cold that night,   *520*
And had come out with only my shield and belt.
During the third watch, when the stars had turned
In their wheeling course, I nudged Odysseus,
Who was lying next to me, and he heard me say,
'Son of Laertes in the line of Zeus,   *525*
Wily Odysseus—listen, I'm about dead over here;
This cold is killing me. I don't have a cloak.
Some god talked me into coming out here
With only a tunic, and now there's no going back.'
He put his mind to work and came up with a plan.   *530*
That's how he was; he could think up things
As well as he could fight. He whispered to me,
'Be quiet now, or one of our men will hear you.'
Then he propped his head up on an elbow and said,
'Listen, men. I had a dream from the gods.   *535*
We've come too far from the ships. We need someone
To request Agamemnon, commander-in-chief,
To send out more troops from our beach-head camp.'
He had no sooner spoken than Thoas
Was on his feet. He flung aside his purple cloak   *540*
And sprinted off to the ships, and wrapped in that cloak
I lay down gladly until Dawn shone with gold.
Oh, to be young again and still have my strength!
Then one of the swineherds would give me a cloak,
Both out of kindness and out of respect for a man.   *545*
But now they scorn me because I am dressed in rags."

And you answered him, Eumaeus, my swineherd:

"There's nothing wrong with your story, old man,
And nothing you've said is out of line

Or unprofitable. So you won't go without.   *550*
You'll have clothing, yes, and everything else
A·suppliant in need ought to receive—
At least for tonight. But in the morning
You'll have to shake out those old rags of yours.
We don't have extra tunics or cloaks   *555*
Around here. Each man has only one.
But when Odysseus' son comes, he himself
Will give you a cloak and tunic to wear,
And will send you wherever your heart desires."

So saying, the swineherd sprang to his feet   *560*
And started to make up a bed for Odysseus
Near the fire, spreading it with goatskins and fleeces.
There Odysseus lay down, and Eumaeus
Threw over him a large, heavy cloak
That he kept as a spare for stormy weather.   *565*

So there Odysseus slept, with the young men
All around him. But not the swineherd.
He would not settle for a bed inside,
Away from the boars. He got himself ready
To go sleep outdoors, and Odysseus was glad   *570*
That he took such good care of the property
Of his absent master. First, Eumaeus
Slung his sharp sword over his sturdy shoulders
And put on a thick cloak to keep out the wind.
Then picking up the fleece of a large, fatted goat,   *575*
And grabbing a javelin to ward off dogs and men,
He went out to sleep with the white-tusked boars
Under a hollow rock, out of the cold North Wind.

ODYSSEY 15

Pallas Athena now went to wide Lacedaemon
To tell Odysseus' son it was time to return.
She found Telemachus and Nestor's noble son
On the porch of Menelaus' palace.
Nestor's son was sleeping, but Telemachus   5
Had been lying awake all through the night
Thinking about his father. Athena,
Her eyes flashing in the dark, said to him:

"Telemachus, you've been away too long.
Think of the wealth you left behind at home   ·   10
And all those insolent men ready to devour it.
Your journey will have been for nothing.
Hurry, now, and rouse Menelaus
To send you on your way, so you can find
Your blameless mother still at home.   15
Her father and brothers are pressuring her
To marry Eurymachus, because of all the suitors
He gives the best presents, and now has
Stepped up his wooing. You have to watch out
She doesn't carry off all your treasure.   20
You know what a woman's heart is like.
She wants to enrich the house of the one who weds her,
Never mind about her former children
And the husband she once loved. Once he's dead,
She doesn't give any of them a thought.   25
No, you go, and put all your possessions
In the keeping of the best maidservant in the house,
Until the gods show you your honored bride.

And one more thing for you to keep in mind.
The suitors' ringleaders have set up an ambush   30
In the strait between Ithaca and rocky Samos.
They mean to kill you before you make it home.
I don't think they will. Those mooching suitors
Will be in their graves before they can get at you.
But keep your ship out away from the islands,   35
And sail by night as well. One of the gods
Who watches over you will put a wind at your back.
When you make landfall on Ithaca,
Send your crew with the ship on to the city,
But you go first to the swineherd's hut;   40
He has a soft spot in his heart for you.
Spend the night there and tell him to go
Into the city and bring word to Penelope
That you are safe and have come back from Pylos."

And with that she was off to high Olympus.   45

Telemachus awoke and woke up Peisistratus
With a nudge of his heel, saying to him:

"Wake up, Peisistratus. Get your horses
And yoke them up so we can get on the road."
Nestor's son Peisistraus answered: 50

"Telemachus, there's no way we can drive
In the dark, no matter how eager we are
To get on the road. Besides, it'll be light soon,
And we should wait until Menelaus comes out
And sets gifts on the chariot and sends us off   55
With a farewell speech. A guest remembers
A host's hospitality for as long as he lives."

He spoke, and Dawn rose up splashed with gold.
Menelaus, who had just gotten out of bed
With Helen, was coming toward them,   60
And when Telemachus saw him
The young hero quickly threw on his silky tunic,
Flung a cloak on his shoulders, and went out,

The true son of godlike Odysseus.
When he reached Menelaus he said to him: *65*

"Menelaus, son of Atreus in the line of Zeus,
Send me back home to my own native land,
For my heart is now eager to return to my home."

And Menelaus, famed for his war cry:

"Telemachus, far be it from me to detain you here   *70*
When you yearn to go home. I no more approve
Of a host who is too welcoming than of one
Who is too cold. Due measure in all things.
It is just as wrong to rush a guest's departure
When he doesn't want to go, as it is   *75*
To hold him back when he is ready to leave.
Make a guest welcome for as long as he stays
And send him off whenever he wants to go.
But do stay until I can bring some gifts out
And load them onto your chariot, fine gifts,   *80*
As you will see. And I will order the women
To prepare you a meal from our well-stocked larder.
It's a double honor, and sensible, too,
For the traveler to eat before setting forth
Over the boundless earth. And if you wish to go   *85*
All through Hellas and into the heart of Argos,
I myself will go with you. I'll yoke up horses
And give you a tour of the cities of men,
And no one will send us away empty-handed.
Everyone will give us at least one thing,   *90*
A fine bronze tripod or perhaps a cauldron,
A team of mules or a golden cup."

And Telemachus, in his cool-headed way:

"Menelaus, son of Atreus in the line of Zeus,
I would rather go straight home. I did not leave   *95*
Anyone behind to watch my possessions.
I'm afraid that in my search for my godlike father
I may perish myself, or that some precious thing

May be lost from my house while I am away."

When he heard this, Menelaus at once   *100*
Ordered his wife and her serving women
To prepare a meal from their well-stocked larder.
Then Eteoneus, just risen from bed,
Came up—his house was nearby—and Menelaus
Had him kindle a fire and roast some of the meat.   *105*
While he was doing this, Menelaus himself
Went down to his scented treasure chamber
Accompanied by Helen and Megapenthes.
When they came to where the treasure was stored
The son of Atreus took a two-handled cup   *110*
And had his son Megapenthes bring a mixing bowl
Of solid silver. But Helen went to the chests
That held her robes, the richly embroidered robes
She herself had made. And this beautiful woman,
Helen of Argos, lifted out the robe   *115*
That had the finest embroideries, an ample robe
That shone like starlight beneath all the rest.
Then they went back through the house and came
To Telemachus, to whom Menelaus said:

"Telemachus, may Zeus, Hera's thundering lord,   *120*
Bring you to your home, just as you desire.
Of all the gifts that lie stored in my house
I will give you the most beautiful—
And the most valuable—a well-wrought bowl,
Solid silver, with the lip finished in gold,   *125*
Made by Hephaestus. The hero Phaedimus,
King of the Sidonians, gave it to me
When I stayed at his house on my way home.
Now I want you to take it home with you."

And the son of Atreus placed the double-handled goblet *130*
In Telemachus' hands. Then strong Megapenthes
Brought the gleaming silver mixing bowl over
And set it before him. And Helen, lovely in her bones,
Came up with the robe and said to him:

"I, too, give you a gift, dear child, this robe,   *135*
A memento from the hands of Helen,
For your bride to wear on your wedding day.
Until then let it lie in your mother's keeping.
And my wish for you is that you come with joy
To your native land and your ancestral home."   *140*

She put the robe in his hands, and he received it
With gratitude. Then Peisistratus put all of the gifts
Into the chariot's trunk and looked at them a while
With wonder in his heart.
                         Menelaus now
Led them into the house, and the two sat down.   *145*
A maid poured water from a silver pitcher
Over a golden basin for them to wash their hands
And then set up a polished table nearby.
Another serving woman, grave and dignified,
Set out bread and generous helpings   *150*
From the other dishes she had. Boethus' son
Carved the meat nearby and divided it up,
And the son of Menelaus poured the wine.
They reached out to all the good cheer before them,
And when they had their fill of food and drink,   *155*
Telemachus and glorious Nestor's son
Yoked the horses, mounted the inlaid chariot,
And drove through the gate and echoing portico.
And the son of Atreus, red-haired Menelaus,
Went after them, holding in his right hand   *160*
A golden cup filled with honey-hearted wine
So they could pour libations before setting out.
He stood before the horses, lifted the cup, and said:

"Farewell, young men, and bring my greetings
To Nestor, the old commander. He was to me   *165*
Kind as a father when we Greeks fought at Troy."

And Telemachus, in his clear-headed way:

"We will tell him all these things, just as you say,
Zeus-born, when we come to his land,

As surely as I wish I would find Odysseus home,   *170*
So I could tell him how good you have been to me
During my visit with you, and tell him how
I come home myself with many a treasure."

As he spoke, a bird flew by on his right,
An eagle, clutching in his talons a silvery goose,   *175*
A large, tame fowl from the yard. Men and women
Ran after it shouting. The eagle got closer,
Then veered off to the right in front of the horses.
This lifted everyone's spirits. Nestor's son
Peisistratus was the first one to speak: *180*

"Zeus-born Menelaus, what does this mean?
Is it a sign for us two, or for yourself?"

Menelaus, the warlord, was thinking this over,
Looking for the right way to interpret the sign,
When long-robed Helen took the words from his mouth: *185*

"I will prophesy as the immortals prompt me
And as I see it myself. Just as this eagle
Came from the mountain, where he was born and bred,
And snatched up the goose bred in the house,
So shall Odysseus, after long, hard travels,   *190*
Return to his home, and take vengeance.
Or he is already at home and is even now
Sowing the seeds of the suitors' destruction."

And Telemachus, in his spirited way:

"May Hera's thundering lord grant it,   *195*
And I will pray to you as to a god."

He flicked the lash and the horses took off
Through the city and out to the plain. All day long
They jostled the yoke that held them together.

As the sun set and the world grew dark,   *200*
They came to Pherae and pulled up at the house

Of Diocles, son of Ortilochus,
Himself a son of the river Alpheus.
There they spent the night, and Diocles
Gave them the hospitality due to guests.   *205*

When Dawn brushed the pale sky with rose,
They yoked the horses, stepped up into
The inlaid chariot and drove out through the gate
And echoing portico. Peisistratus
Flicked the lash and the horses took off.   *210*
Soon after they reached the high rock of Pylos,
And Telemachus had a word with Nestor's son:

"I wonder if you could do me a favor,
Peisistratus? You and I go back a long way
Because of our fathers' friendship. Moreover,   *215*
We're the same age, and this journey together
Will cement our friendship. This is what I want:
Do not drive me farther than my ship.
Drop me off there. I'm afraid the old man
Will keep me in his house against my will.   *220*
He means well, but I really have to get home."

Nestor's son thought it over, trying to decide
How he could rightfully do Telemachus this favor.
He made up his mind and turned off to the sea
And the ship there. He stowed the beautiful gifts   *225*
From Menelaus—the clothes and the gold—
In the ship's stern and urged his friend on,
Speaking to him words that had wings:

"Get yourself and your crew aboard quickly,
Before I reach home and tell the old man.   *230*
If there's one thing I'm sure of it's this:
Once he has you in his house he won't let you go,
And he'll come here to get you himself
If he has to, and he won't go home empty-handed.
No matter what, he's going to be angry."   *235*

And he drove his horses back to the city

With their beautiful manes flowing in the wind
And quickly reached his father's palace.

Meanwhile, Telemachus was urging on his crew:

"Put all the gear in order on this black ship, men,   *240*
And let's go aboard and get under way."

They carried out his orders and were soon
All on board and sitting on their benches.

Telemachus was busy with all of this,
And was offering sacrifice to Athena   *245*
By the ship's stern, when there came up to him
A traveler from a distant land. He was in exile
From Argos, because he had killed a man,
And he was a seer. He traced his descent
From Melampus, who had lived in Pylos   *250*
In the old days as one of its wealthiest men
But left for other parts, fleeing great Neleus,
That most lordly man, who had seized his wealth
And kept it from him for one full year.
Melampus lay imprisoned in Phylacus' house   *255*
And suffered terribly because of Neleus' daughter
And the delusion which the goddess Erinys
Had laid upon him. He escaped, however,
And drove off the lowing cattle from Phylace
To Pylos, and got even with godlike Neleus,   *260*
And brought Neleus' daughter home
To be his brother's wife. He himself then left
For the horse country of Argos, his destiny being
To live there and rule over many Argives.
There he took a wife and built a lofty house   *265*
And fathered two strong sons. These sons
Were Mantius and Antiphates, and one of them,
Antiphates, sired great-hearted Oicles,
And Oicles was the father of Amphiarus,
Whom Zeus and Apollo showered with love.   *270*
But he did not reach the threshold of old age,
Dying in Thebes because of a woman's gifts.

Melampus' other son, Mantius,
Sired Polypheides and Clytius.
Clytius, because he was so beautiful,   *275*
Was snatched away by gold-stitched Dawn
To live with the immortals. And Apollo
Made Polypheides a seer, a high-hearted man
And the best of men after Amphiaraus was dead.
Eventually, he quarreled with his father   *280*
And moved to Hyperesia, and was the prophet there.

It was his son, Theoclymenus by name,
Who now came up to Telemachus
As he was pouring libations by his black ship
And spoke to him these winged words: *285*

"Friend, since I find you making sacrifice here,
I implore you by your sacrifice and by your god,
Then by your own life and the lives of your crew—
Tell me truly what I ask and do not hide it.
Who are you, and where are you from?   *290*
Where is your city, and where do your parents live?"

Telemachus answered in his clear-headed way:

"Well then, stranger, I will tell you exactly.
I was born in Ithaca, and my father is Odysseus—
If he ever existed. But he has met a grim fate.   *295*
So I have taken my comrades and a black ship
In search of news of my long-absent father."

And godlike Theoclymenus answered:

"I, too, have left my country, because
I killed a man, one of my own clan.   *300*
He has many brothers and kinsmen left
In bluegrass Argos, powerful men,
And I am on the run to escape a black fate
At their hands. It seems I am doomed to be
A wanderer. Take me on your ship, please,   *305*
Since I have taken refuge with you now.

Don't let them kill me. I think they are coming."

And Telemachus, in his cool-headed way:

"I won't push you away if you want to come.
Welcome aboard, and share whatever we have."   310

With that he relieved him of his bronze spear
And slid it onto the deck of the ship.
They went aboard. Telemachus sat down
In the stern, Theoclymenus beside him.
The sailors untied the stern cables   315
And Telemachus called out orders to them
To take hold of the tackling. They fell to,
Raising the firwood mast and setting it
Into its socket. They made it fast with forestays
And hauled up the white sail with rawhide ropes.   320
And Athena, her eyes flashing with sea-light,
Gave them a tailwind that ripped through the sky,
Speeding the ship across the bright salt sea.
Krouni and Chalcis, with its beautiful streams,
Passed by quickly, and then the sun went down   325
And the seaways grew dark. The ship surged on
With Zeus' wind behind it, on to Pheae
And past limewhite Elis, where the Epeans rule.
Then Telemachus steered her out again
To the swiftly passing islands, wondering whether   330
He would dodge death or be caught by the suitors.

Meanwhile, Odysseus and the noble swineherd
Were having supper with the others in the hut.
When they had satisfied their appetite
For food and drink, Odysseus spoke among them,   335
Testing Eumaeus to see whether he would
Still take care of him there on the farmstead
Or send him off to the city:

"Listen now, Eumaeus, and you other men, too.
In the morning I'm off to beg in the city,   340
I don't want to eat you out of house and home.

So tell me what I need to know, and give me a guide
Who can lead me there. Once in the city
I can knock about on my own, as I must,
Hoping for a cup of water and a loaf of bread.   345
And I might go up to Odysseus' house
And bring some news to Penelope.
I might make the rounds of the insolent suitors
And see if they will give me some dinner
From all the good food they have. I might even   350
Start waiting on them, doing whatever they need.
I'll tell you something now. Thanks to Hermes,
The Guide, who lends grace and glory
To all that men do, when it comes to serving
No one can touch me, in splitting firewood,   355
Building a fire, roasting meat and carving it,
Or in pouring wine, or in any of the things
Lesser men do when they wait on nobles."

And the swineherd, greatly troubled, responded:

"Where did you get such a notion, stranger?   360
You must want to die, if you really intend
To go in there with that mob of suitors,
Whose arrogance reaches the iron heavens.
Their serving men are not at all like you.
They're young, well dressed in tunics and cloaks,   365
Handsome and sleek. The tables are polished
And piled high with bread, meat, and wine.
Stay here. You're not bothering anyone,
Not me nor any other man who is here.
But when Odysseus' son comes, he himself   370
Will give you a cloak and tunic to wear,
And will send you wherever your heart desires."

And the enduring, godlike Odysseus answered:

"Eumaeus, may you be as dear to father Zeus
As you are to me, for you have given me a rest   375
From wandering the world in grief and pain.
Nothing is harder on a man than homelessness.

But when it comes to feeding his belly, a man will endure
Whatever hardship and sorrows he must.
But now, since you are keeping me here   380
A while, and asking me to wait for Telemachus,
Tell me about noble Odysseus' mother,
And his father, whom he left behind
On the brink of old age when he went to Troy.
Are they still alive and under the sun,   385
Or are they now dead and in Hades' gloom?"

The noble swineherd made this response:

"I will tell you, stranger, since you ask.
Laertes is still alive, but prays constantly
That his life will dwindle away in his halls.   390
He grieves terribly for his missing son
And for his own lady, his wedded wife.
He took her death hard, and it delivered him
To an unripe old age. She herself died
Of grief for her son, a miserable death   395
That I would wish on no one dear to me.
For as long as she lived, hard as it was for her,
I always enjoyed seeing how she was,
Asking about her health, for she herself
Had brought me up with long-robed Ctimene,   400
Her youngest child. I was brought up with her,
Almost as if I were one of the family.
When we reached that lovely time of our youth,
They sent her to Samê, sent her off to be married,
And got themselves countless gifts in exchange.   405
As for me, my lady clothed me in a cloak and tunic,
Very fine ones, and gave me sandals for my feet,
And sent me off to the fields. But in her heart
She loved me more than that. I do without now,
But the blessed gods make my work prosper.   410
I stay busy with it, and it gives me enough
To eat and drink and give some to beggars.
From my mistress now I get nothing pleasant,
Word or deed. Trouble has come to the house—
These overbearing men. But servants still need   415

To speak to their mistress face to face,
Hear all the gossip, eat and drink,
And afterward take something back to the fields,
The sort of thing that warms a servant's heart."

Odysseus, his mind teeming, responded: 420

"You must have been awfully young, Eumaeus,
When you were forced to travel so far away
From your parents and home. How did it happen?
Did your parents live in a broad-wayed city
That was ransacked in war? Or were you alone   425
Out in the fields with your cattle and sheep
When raiders grabbed you and took you in their ship
And sold you for a good price to your master here?"

Then the swineherd Eumaeus told his story:

"Well, stranger, since you're curious about this,   430
Sit back and relax and drink your wine.
These nights are ungodly long. There's time to sleep
And to enjoy stories both. You shouldn't lie down
Too early. Too much sleep can leave a man tired.
If any of the rest of you would like,   435
You can go sleep outside. Just eat something
At daybreak and go out with our master's swine.
We two are going to stay here in the hut,
Eating and drinking and swapping stories
About each others' hard times. Past sorrows   440
Can comfort a man, especially one
Who has suffered much and wandered far.
But on to what you asked me about.
          There is an island called Syria—
You may have heard of it—above Ortygia   445
And off toward the setting of the summer sun.
It doesn't have many people, but it's good land,
Rich in flocks and herds, full of grapes and wheat.
There's never any famine, and no disease.
When folks grow old, Apollo and Artemis   450
Come to town with their silver bows

And shoot them dead with their gentle arrows.
There are two cities that take up the island,
And my father Ctesius, son of Ormenus,
Ruled over both, a man like a god.   *455*
      One day some Phoenician traders arrived,
Greedy men, with a shipload of baubles.
In my father's house was a Phoenician woman,
Tall and beautiful and skilled at crafts.
One of the craggy Phoenicians seduced her   *460*
As she was washing her clothes, lying with her
In their hollow ship—the sort of thing
That will gull the mind of any woman.
Afterward, he asked her who she was
And where she came from. She promptly pointed   *465*
To the high roof of my father's house:

'I am proud to say I am from bronze-rich Sidon
And am a daughter of Arybas, a wealthy man.
But Taphian pirates abducted me
As I came from the fields, and brought me here   *470*
And sold me to the master of that house over there,
Who paid a small fortune for me.'

"The man who had lain with her in secret said:

'Would you like to return with us to your home
And see your high-roofed house, and your parents, too?   *475*
They are still alive and said to be rich.'

"And the Phoenician woman responded:

'Perhaps, if you sailors will swear an oath
That you will bring me home without harming me.'

"When they had sworn the oath, the woman said: *480*

'Be quiet now, and if any of you sees me
In the street or at the well, don't speak to me,
Or someone may tell the old king in the palace
And he might suspect something and lock me up

In painful bonds and sentence you to death.   485
Don't forget this. Just sell all your merchandise,
And as soon as your ship is laden with goods,
Send a messenger to me up in the palace.
I'll bring whatever gold I can lay my hands on.
And there's something else I can put up for my passage.   490
I'm the nurse of one of my master's children,
A clever boy who always tags along with me.
I'll bring him on board. He'll get a good price
In whatever foreign land you sell him off.'

"And with that she went off to the beautiful palace.   495
The Phoenicians stayed in our land for a full year
And filled their ship through all the trade they did.
When their ship was loaded for their voyage home,
They sent a messenger to tip off the woman.
A cunning man came to my father's house   500
With a golden necklace strung with amber.
While the women in the hall, and my noble mother,
Were looking it over and offering a price,
The man nodded to the woman in silence,
Nodded and went back to his hollow ship.   505
She took me by the hand and led me outside,
Stopping on the porch to scoop up three
Of the golden goblets left on the tables
By retainers of my father who had banqueted there
And then gone off to debate in the council.   510
She tucked these goblets into her bosom
And bore them off. I innocently followed.
The sun went down and the streets grew dark.
We hurried on to the glimmering harbor
Where the Phoenician ship was moored.   515
They had us board, and the ship set sail
Over the water with a following wind.
We sailed on for six solid days and nights,
But when Zeus put a seventh day in the sky,
Artemis came with her showering arrows   520
And shot the woman. She fell with a thud
Into the hold, like a tern plunging down.
They threw her overboard for the seals and fish,

And there I was, with a broken heart.
The wind and the waves bore the ship along   525
To Ithaca, where Laertes bought me.
And that was how I first saw this land."

Then Zeus-bred Odysseus said to him:

"Eumaeus, your story, with its tale
Of your painful ordeal, has touched my heart.   530
But in your case Zeus has set some good
Alongside the evil, since after all your suffering
You wound up at the house of a kindly man
Who gives you food and drink and treats you well.
You have a good life. But as for me, I came here   535
While wandering around from city to city."

They spoke to one another in this way
And then lay down to sleep, but not for long,
For Dawn soon rose in the blossoming sky.

Telemachus and his crew were now near to shore   540
And furling the sails in the early light.
They struck the mast quickly and rowed the ship
Up to her mooring. They threw out the anchor-stones,
Made the stern cables fast, and then disembarked
Onto the beach, where they prepared their meal   545
And mixed the glinting wine. After they had eaten,
Telemachus, clear-headed as ever, spoke to them:

"You men row the black ship to the town
While I go visit the fields and the herdsmen.
Around dusk, after I've looked over my lands,   550
I'll come to the city, and tomorrow morning
I'll set before you, as wages for your journey,
An excellent feast of meat and fine wine."

Then godlike Theoclymenus put in:

"And where shall I go, dear child? To whose house,   555
Of all those who are lords in rocky Ithaca?

Or should I go straight to yours and your mother's house?"

And Telemachus, in his clear-headed way:

"Ordinarily I would say go to our house,
For it has everything needed for hospitality.   560
But it wouldn't work out for you right now
Since I'll be away, and my mother won't see you.
She doesn't appear often before the suitors
But weaves at her loom in an upper chamber.
I'll tell you, though, whom you can go to: 565
Eurymachus, son of Polybus, whom now
The Ithacans look to as if he were a god.
He's the best man and is the most eager
To marry my mother and take over
My father's position. Only Olympian Zeus,   570
High in the air, knows if their doom will come
Crashing down on them before any wedding day."

As he spoke a bird flew by on the right,
A hawk, swift herald of Apollo, clutching
A dove in his talons, plucking her as he flew   575
And shedding her feathers down to the ground
Between the ship and Telemachus himself.
Theoclymenus called him aside
And, clasping his hand, said to him:

"Telemachus, that bird did not fly by on our right   580
Without a god sending it. I knew when I saw it
That it was a bird of omen. Your lineage
Is Ithaca's most royal. You will rule forever."

And Telemachus, clear-headed and calm:

"Would that what you say come true, stranger.   585
Then you would have from me such gifts
That whoever met you would call you blessed."

Then he said to Peiraeus, his trusted companion:

"Peiraeus, you have always come through for me,
And you went with me to Pylos. So now,   *590*
I ask you to show this stranger hospitality
In your house. Take good care of him until I come."

And Peiraeus, a spearman in his own right, said:

"Telemachus, no matter how long you stay out here,
I'll take care of him and give him my hospitality."   *595*

Then Peiraeus boarded the ship and gave the order
For the crew to board and untie the stern cables.
They were soon at their places. Telemachus, though,
Put on his fine sandals, took his bronze-tipped spear
From the ship's deck, and stood by as the crew   *600*
Untied the cables and shoved off.
                                     Then Odysseus' son
Stepped out with swift strides until he reached
The farmstead where his countless swine were kept
By a servant whose heart was loyal and true.

ODYSSEY 16

Meanwhile, in the hut, Odysseus
And the noble swineherd had kindled a fire
And were making breakfast in the early light.
They had already sent the herdsmen out
With the droves of swine.
                              The dogs fawned   5
Around Telemachus and did not bark at him
As he approached. Odysseus noticed
The dogs fawning and heard footsteps.
His words flew fast to Eumaeus:

"Eumaeus, one of your men must be coming,   10
Or at least someone you know. The dogs aren't barking
And are fawning around him. I can hear his footsteps."

His words weren't out when his own son
Stood in the doorway. Up jumped the swineherd
In amazement, and from his hands fell the vessels   15
He was using to mix the wine. He went
To greet his master, kissing his head
And his shining eyes and both his hands.

   And as a loving father embraces his own son
   Come back from a distant land after ten long years,   20
   His only son, greatly beloved and much sorrowed for—

So did the noble swineherd clasp Telemachus
And kiss him all over—he had escaped from death—
And sobbing he spoke to him these winged words:

"You have come, Telemachus, sweet light!   25
I thought I would never see you again
After you left in your ship for Pylos. But come in,
Dear child, let me feast my eyes on you
Here in my house, come back from abroad!
You don't visit the farm often, or us herdsmen,   30
But stay in town. It must do your heart good
To look at that weeviling crowd of suitors."

And Telemachus, in his clear-headed way:

"Have it your way, Papa. But it's for your sake I've come,
To see you with my own eyes, and to hear from you   35
Whether my mother is still in our house,
Or someone else has married her by now,
And Odysseus' bed, with no one to sleep in it,
Has become a nest of spider webs."

The swineherd answered him: 40

"Yes, she's in your house, waiting and waiting
With an enduring heart, poor soul,
Weeping away the lonely days and nights."

He spoke, and took the young man's spear.
Telemachus went in, and as he crossed   45
The stone threshold, Odysseus stood up
To offer him his seat, but Telemachus,
From across the room, checked him and said:

"Keep your seat, stranger. We'll find another one
Around the place. Eumaeus here can do that."   50

He spoke, and Odysseus sat down again.
The swineherd piled up some green brushwood
And covered it with a fleece, and upon this
The true son of Odysseus sat down.
Then the swineherd set out platters of roast meat—   55
Leftovers from yesterday's meal—
And hurried around heaping up bread in baskets

And mixing sweet wine in an ivy-wood bowl.
Then he sat down opposite godlike Odysseus,
And they helped themselves to the fare before them. 60
When they had enough to eat and drink,
Telemachus spoke to the godlike swineherd:

"Where did this stranger come from, Papa?
What kind of sailors brought him to Ithaca?
I don't suppose he walked to our island." 65

And you answered, Eumaeus, my swineherd:

"I'll tell you everything plainly, child.
He says he was born somewhere in Crete
And that it has been his lot to be a roamer
And wander from city to city. But now 70
He has run away from a Thesprotian ship
And come to my farmstead. I put him in your hands.
Do as you wish. He declares he is your suppliant."

And Telemachus, wise beyond his years:

"This makes my heart ache, Eumaeus. 75
How can I welcome this guest in my house?
I am still young, and I don't have the confidence
To defend myself if someone picks a fight.
As for my mother, her heart is torn.
She can't decide whether to stay here with me 80
And keep the house, honoring her husband's bed
And the voice of the people, or to go away
With whichever man among her suitors
Is the best of the Achaeans, and offers the most gifts.
But as to our guest—now that he's come to your house, 85
I will give him a tunic and cloak, fine clothes,
And a two-edged sword, and sandals for his feet,
And passage to wherever his heart desires.
Or keep him here if you wish, at your farmstead
And take care of him. I'll send the clothes 90
And all of his food, so it won't be a hardship
For you or your men. What I won't allow

Is for him to come up there among the suitors.
They are far too reckless and arrogant,
And I fear they will make fun of him, mock him,   *95*
And it would be hard for me to take that.
But what could I do? One man, however powerful,
Can't do much against superior numbers."

Then Odysseus, who had borne much, said:

"My friend—surely it is right for me to speak up—   *100*
It breaks my heart to hear you talk about
The suitors acting like this in your house
And going against the will of a man as great as you.
It is against your will, isn't it? What happened?
Do the people up and down the land all hate you?   *105*
Has a god turned them against you? Or do you blame
Your brothers, whom a man has to rely upon
In a fight, especially if a big fight comes up?
I wish I were as vigorous as I am angry,
Or were a son of flawless Odysseus, or Odysseus himself!   *110*
Then I would put my neck on the chopping block
If I did not give them hell when I came into
The halls of Odysseus, son of Laertes!
But if they overwhelmed me with superior numbers,
I would rather be dead, killed in my own halls,   *115*
Than have to keep watching these disgraceful deeds,
Strangers mistreated, men dragging the women
Through the beautiful halls, wine spilled,
Bread wasted, and all with no end in sight."

Telemachus answered in his clear-headed way: *120*

"Well, stranger, I'll tell you the whole story.
It's not that the people have turned against me,
Nor do I have any brothers to blame. Zeus
Has made our family run in a single line.
Laertes was the only son of Arcesius,   *125*
And Laertes had only one son, Odysseus,
Who only had me, a son he never knew.
And so now our house is filled with enemies,

All of the nobles who rule the islands—
Dulichium, Samê, wooded Zacynthus—　　　　　　　　　　*130*
And all of those with power on rocky Ithaca
Are courting my mother and ruining our house.
She neither refuses to make a marriage she hates
Or is able to stop it. They are eating us
Out of house and home, and will come after me soon.　　*135*
But all of this rests on the knees of the gods.
Eumaeus, go tell Penelope right away
That I'm safe and back from Pylos.
I'll wait for you here. Tell only her
And don't let any of the suitors find out.　　　　　　*140*
Many of them are plotting against me."

And you answered him, Eumaeus, my swineherd:

"I follow you, Telemachus, I understand.
But tell me this. Should I go the same way
To Laertes also, and tell him the news?　　　　　　　*145*
Poor man, for a while he still oversaw the fields,
Although he was grieving greatly for Odysseus,
And would eat and drink with the slaves in the house
Whenever he had a notion. But now, since the very day
You sailed to Pylos, they say he hasn't been　　　　*150*
Eating or drinking as before, or overseeing the fields.
He just sits and groans, weeping his heart out,
And the flesh is wasting away from his bones."

And Telemachus, in his clear-headed way:

"That's hard, but we will let him be, despite our pain.　*155*
If mortals could have all their wishes granted,
We would choose first the day of my father's return.
No, just deliver your message and come back,
And don't go traipsing all through the countryside
Looking for Laertes. But tell my mother　　　　　　　*160*
To send the housekeeper as soon as she can,
Secretly. She could bring the old man the message."

So the swineherd got going. He tied on his sandals

And was off to the city.
                    The swineherd's departure
Was not unnoticed by Athena. She approached   *165*
The farmstead in the likeness of a woman,
Beautiful, tall, and accomplished in handiwork,
And stood in the doorway of Eumaeus' hut,
Showing herself to Odysseus. Telemachus
Did not see her before him or notice her presence,   *170*
For the gods are not visible to everyone.
But Odysseus saw her, and the dogs did, too,
And they did not bark, but slunk away whining
To the other side of the farmstead. The goddess
Lifted her brows, and Odysseus understood.   *175*
He went out of the hut, past the courtyard's great wall,
And stood before her. Athena said to him:

"Son of Laertes in the line of Zeus,
Tell your son now and do not keep him in the dark,
So that you two can plan the suitors' destruction   *180*
And then go into town. As for myself,
I will not be gone long. No, I am eager for battle."

With this, she touched him with her golden wand.
A fresh tunic and cloak replaced his rags,
And he was taller and younger, his skin tanned,   *185*
His jawline firm, and his beard glossy black.
Having worked her magic, the goddess left,
And Odysseus went back into the hut.
His son was astounded. Shaken and flustered,
He turned away his eyes for fear it was a god,   *190*
And words fell from his lips in nervous flurries:

"You look different, stranger, than you did before,
And your clothes are different, and your complexion.
You must be a god, one of the immortals
Who hold high heaven. Be gracious to us   *195*
So we can offer you acceptable sacrifice
And finely wrought gold. And spare us, please."

And godlike Odysseus, who had borne much:

"I am no god. Why liken me to the deathless ones?
No, I am your father, on whose account you have suffered   *200*
Many pains and endured the violence of men."

Saying this, he kissed his son, and let his tears
Fall to the ground. He had held them in until now.
But Telemachus could not believe
That this was his father, and he blurted out: *205*

"You cannot be my father Odysseus.
You must be some spirit, enchanting me
Only to increase my grief and pain later.
No mortal man could figure out how to do this
All on his own. Only a god could so easily   *210*
Transform someone from old to young.
A while ago you were old and shabbily dressed,
And now you are like the gods who hold high heaven."

And Odysseus, from his mind's teeming depths:

"Telemachus, it does not become you to be so amazed   *215*
That your father is here in this house. You can be sure
That no other Odysseus will ever come.
But I am here, just as you see, home at last
After twenty years of suffering and wandering.
So you will know, this is Athena's doing.   *220*
She can make me look like whatever she wants:
A beggar sometimes, and sometimes a young man
Wearing fine clothes. It's easy for the gods
To glorify a man or to make him look poor."

He spoke, and sat down. And Telemachus   *225*
Threw his arms around his wonderful father
And wept. And a longing arose in both of them
To weep and lament, and their shrill cries
Crowded the air

          like the cries of birds—
     Sea-eagles or taloned vultures—   *230*
     Whose young chicks rough farmers have stolen
     Out of their nests before they were fledged.

Their tears were that piteous. And the sun,
Its light fading, would have set on their weeping,
Had not Telemachus suddenly said to his father: 235

"What ship brought you here, Father,
And where did the crew say they were from?
I don't suppose you came here on foot."

And Odysseus, the godlike survivor:

"I'll tell you the truth about this, son.   240
The Phaeacians brought me, famed sailors
Who give passage to all who come their way.
They brought me over the sea as I slept
In their swift ship, and set me ashore on Ithaca
With donations of bronze and clothing and gold,   245
Splendid treasures that are now stored in caves
By grace of the gods. I have come here now
At Athena's suggestion. You and I must plan
How to kill our enemies. List them for me now
So I can know who they are, and how many,   250
And so I can weigh the odds and decide whether
You and I can go up against them alone
Or whether we have to enlist some allies."

Telemachus took a deep breath and said:

"Father, look now, I know your great reputation,   255
How you can handle a spear and what a strategist you are,
But this is too much for me. Two men
Simply cannot fight against such superior numbers
And superior force. There are not just ten suitors,
Or twice that, but many times more. Here's the count: 260
From Dulichium there are fifty-two—
The pick of their young men—and six attendants.
From Samê there are twenty-four,
From Zacynthus there are twenty,
And from Ithaca itself, twelve, all the noblest,   265
And with them are Medon the herald,

The divine bard, and two attendants who carve.
If we go up against all of them in the hall,
I fear your vengeance will be bitter indeed.
Please try to think of someone to help us,   *270*
Someone who would gladly be our ally."

And Odysseus, who had borne much:

"I'll tell you who will help. Do you think
That Athena and her father, Zeus,
Would be help enough? Or should I think of more?"   *275*

Telemachus answered in his clear-headed way:

"You're talking about two excellent allies,
Although they do sit a little high in the clouds
And have to rule the whole world and the gods as well."

And Odysseus, who had borne much: *280*

"Those two won't hold back from battle for long.
They'll be here, all right, when the fighting starts
Between the suitors and us in my high-roofed halls.
For now, go at daybreak up to the house,
And keep company with these insolent hangers-on.   *285*
The swineherd will lead me to the city later
Looking like an old, broken-down beggar.
If they treat me badly in the house,
Just endure it. Even if they drag me
Through the door by my feet, or throw things at me,   *290*
Just bear it patiently. Try to dissuade them,
Try to talk them out of their folly, sure,
But they won't listen to you at all,
Because their day of reckoning is near.
And here's something else for you to keep in mind: *295*
When Athena in her wisdom prompts me,
I'll give you a signal. When you see me nod,
Take all the weapons that are in the hall
Into the lofted storeroom and stow them there.
When the suitors miss them and ask you   *300*

Where they are, set their minds at ease, saying:
'Oh, I have stored them out of the smoke.
They're nothing like they were when Odysseus
Went off to Troy, but are all grimed with soot.
Also, a god put this thought into my head,   305
That when you men are drinking, you might
Start quarreling and someone could get hurt,
Which would ruin your feasting and courting.
Steel has a way of drawing a man to it.'
But leave behind a couple of swords for us,   310
And two spears and oxhide shields—leave them
Where we can get to them in a hurry.
Pallas Athena and Zeus in his cunning
Will keep the suitors in a daze for a while.
          And one more thing before you go.   315
If you are really my son and have my blood
In your veins, don't let anyone know
That Odysseus is at home—not Laertes,
Not the swineherd, not anyone in the house,
Not even Penelope. You and I by ourselves   320
Will figure out which way the women are leaning.
We'll test more than one of the servants, too,
And see who respects us and fears us,
And who cares nothing about either one of us
And fails to honor you. You're a man now."   325

And Odysseus' resplendent son answered:

"You'll soon see what I'm made of, Father,
And I don't think you'll find me lacking.
But I'm not sure your plan will work
To our advantage. Think about it.   330
It'll take forever for you to make the rounds
Testing each man, while back in the house
The high-handed suitors are having a good time
Eating their way through everything we own.
I agree you should find out which of the women   335
Dishonor you, and which are innocent.
But as for testing the men in the fields,
Let's do that afterward, if indeed you know

Something from Zeus, who holds the aegis."

While these two were speaking to each other,   340
The sturdy ship that brought Telemachus
And his crew from Pylos was pulling in
To Ithaca. They sailed into the deep harbor
And hauled the black ship up onto the shore.
Porters in high spirits relieved them of their gear   345
And carried the beautiful gifts to Clytius' house.
They sent a herald ahead to Odysseus' palace
To tell Penelope that Telemachus
Was out in the country and had ordered the ship
To sail on to the city so that she, the queen,   350
Would not fall to weeping with worry.
So it happened that the swineherd and herald
Met while they were bringing the same message
To Odysseus' wife. When they reached the palace,
The herald spoke out in the women's presence: 355

"As of now, Lady, your son has returned."

But the swineherd went up to Penelope
And told her all that her son had asked him to.
His message delivered, he left the hall
And went through the courtyard and back to his swine.   360

This was bad news for the suitors.
They filed out of the hall and past the great wall
Of the courtyard and sat down before the gates.
Eurymachus, Polybus' son, was first to speak:

"Damn it! Telemachus has some nerve,   365
Pulling off this voyage. We never thought
We'd see it happen. Well, let's get a tarred ship
Out on the water, the best we have, and a crew
To man the oars and tell our men out at sea
To get back here as soon as they can."   370

He was still speaking when Amphinomus,
Turning around, saw a ship in the harbor,

Sails being furled, the crew with oars in their hands.
He chuckled softly and said to his companions:

"Well, so much for a message. Here they are.   375
Either some god told them, or they spotted
Telemachus' ship sailing by but couldn't catch her."

They trooped down to the shore and made quick work
Of hauling the black ship onto the beach.
Attendants relieved the crew of their gear,   380
And the whole company went off to the assembly.
They wouldn't allow anyone else, young or old,
To sit with them. Antinous rose to speak:

"Just look at how the gods have saved this man!
Day after day watchmen sat on the windy heights,   385
Relieving each other until the sun went down.
And we never spent the night on the shore
But were out at sea all night, waiting for dawn,
Waiting for Telemachus, out for his blood—
And now some god has delivered him home.   390
We'll have to find a way to do him in here.
We can't let him slip through our hands again.
As long as Telemachus is still alive
I don't like our odds in what we're trying to do.
He's shrewd and he's smart, and the people   395
Aren't on our side at all any more.
We have to act before he calls an assembly.
I don't think he's going to let things slide.
He's going to be angry, and he'll stand up
And tell everyone how we plotted his death   400
But could not catch him. They won't approve
When they hear of our crimes, and there's a danger
They'll do something to us, drive us out
Of our land, and we'll wind up in exile.
No, we have to beat him to it, jump him   405
Out in the fields away from the city,
Or on the road. We'll keep all his possessions,
Dividing them fairly among us. His house, though,
We'll give to his mother and whoever weds her.

But if you don't like this plan, if you'd rather   410
He stay alive and keep his ancestral wealth,
We shouldn't keep gathering here any more
And devouring all this pleasant fare.
Each man will have to court her from his own house,
Sending her gifts and trying to win her hand,   415
And she will marry the man who offers the most
And comes to her as her fated husband."

He spoke, and they all sat there in silence
Until Amphinomus stood up to speak.
Son of Nisus and grandson of Aretias,   420
He led the suitors who came from Dulichium,
With its grassy meadows and rich wheatfields.
Penelope liked him, for the way he spoke
And the good sense he showed, and now
He spoke to the suitors with good will to all: 425

"Friends, I would not willingly choose to kill
Telemachus. It is a serious matter to murder
Someone of royal stock. We should first consult
The will of the gods. If great Zeus ordains it,
I will kill him myself, and urge on others.   430
But if the gods are against it, I urge you to stop."

Amphinomus' speech carried the day. The suitors
Stood up and went back to Odysseus' house,
Entered and sat on their polished chairs.

Penelope now had a notion to come out   435
Among her overbearing, insolent suitors.
She had learned of the plot to kill her son
In his own house—the herald Medon told her
After he overheard the suitors talking—
And so the beautiful lady came   440
Into the hall with her serving women.
When she had come among the suitors
She stood shawled in light by a column
That supported the roof of the great house.

Hiding her cheeks behind her silken veils,   *445*
She spoke these harsh words to Antinous:

"Antinous, you are a haughty and evil man.
They say you are the best of your generation
In all of Ithaca in counsel and in speech,
But you don't measure up to your reputation.   *450*
You must be mad. Plotting Telemachus' death!
Don't you care at all that your father was once
A suppliant here? Zeus witnesses this,
And it is unholy for suppliants and hosts
To harm each other. Or haven't you heard   *455*
Of the time your father came to this house
As a fugitive? The people were angry with him
Because he had joined up with the Taphian pirates
And harassed our allies, the Thesprotians.
The citizens wanted to beat him to death   *460*
And gobble up his large and pleasant estate,
But they were held in check by Odysseus.
It is his house that you are now gobbling up
Without atonement, his wife you are wooing,
His son you are trying to kill—and as for me,   *465*
You are causing me unspeakable distress.
Stop it, I tell you, and tell the others to stop."

Then Eurymachus, son of Polybus, answered:

"Penelope, Icarius' wise daughter,
Cheer up. Don't be so upset by all this.   *470*
There's not a man alive, nor will there ever be,
Who will lay hands on your son, Telemachus,
While I still breathe and look upon this earth.
Anyone who tries, I give you my solemn assurance,
Will spill his black blood around the point of my spear.   *475*
No, I, too, often sat on Odysseus' knees,
And the great hero would put roast meat in my hands
And make me sip red wine. And so Telemachus
Is the dearest of all men to me, and I guarantee
He need have no fear of death—from the suitors,   *480*
That is. From the gods there is no avoiding it."

A heart-warming speech, but he was still planning
To kill her son.
                    Penelope went upstairs
To her softly lit rooms and wept for Odysseus,
Her beloved husband, until grey-eyed Athena   485
Cast sweet sleep upon the woman's eyelids.

Evening fell, and the swineherd came back
To Odysseus and his son, who had slaughtered
A yearling boar and were busy making supper.
Athena drew near to Odysseus and tapped him   490
With her wand, making him into an old man again,
Clothed in rags. She was afraid the swineherd
Would recognize him and, unable to keep the secret,
Go bring the news to Penelope.

Telemachus looked up and said to the swineherd: 495

"You're back, Eumaeus. What news from town?
Have the suitors returned from their ambush,
Or are they still looking for me to sail past?"

And you answered him, Eumaeus, my swineherd:

"It wasn't my business to nose around town   500
Asking about that, and I wanted to come back
As soon as I had delivered my message.
On the way in, though, I met up with a herald
Sent by your shipmates. He was fast
And got there first to tell your mother the news.   505
I know one more thing, for I saw it myself.
I was above the city, by the hill of Hermes,
On my way back, when I saw a sailing ship
Pull into our harbor. She had a large crew
And was loaded with shields and bladed spears.   510
I thought it was them, but I don't really know."

Telemachus smiled, feeling his ancestors' blood,
And glanced at Odysseus, avoiding the swineherd's eye.

When they had finished preparing the meal,
They fell to feasting. There was plenty for everyone,   *515*
And when they all had enough of food and drink,
Their minds turned toward rest, and they took the gift of sleep.

ODYSSEY 17

When Dawn brushed the early sky with rose
Odysseus' son bound on his beautiful sandals
And hefted his spear. He was in a hurry
To get to the city, and he said to his swineherd:

"I'm off to the town, Eumaeus. My mother   5
Won't stop crying until she sees me again,
In person. But this is what I want you to do.
Take this down-and-out stranger into the city
So that he can beg for food. Whoever wants to
Can give him some bread and a cup of water.   10
There's no way I can worry about everyone,
I have too much on my mind. If the stranger
Gets upset about this, it's just too bad.
I'm the sort of person who likes to talk straight."

And Odysseus, his mind teeming, said: 15

"Friend, don't think I'm eager myself
To be left behind here. For a beggar like me,
It's better to beg for food in the town
Than out in the fields, and whoever wants to
Can give me something. I'm past the age   20
Where I can stay on a farm and have to do
Everything some foreman tells me.
You go on. This man here will lead me to town
As soon as I have warmed myself by the fire
And the sun is higher. These clothes I'm wearing   25
Are not so good, and the morning frost

Might do me in. You say the city is pretty far."

Thus Odysseus, and Telemachus strode quickly
Out of the farmstead, sowing death for the suitors
With every step he took.
                  When he came to the house   *30*
He leaned his spear against a tall pillar
And went in over the stone threshold.
                          Eurycleia
Spotted him first, as she was spreading fleeces
Over finely wrought chairs. She burst into tears
And ran straight over to him. The other maids   *35*
Of Odysseus' household gathered around
And kissed his head and shoulders in welcome.

Then from her bedroom came wise Penelope,
Looking like Artemis or golden Aphrodite.
She burst into tears and threw her arms around him   *40*
And kissed his head and both his shining eyes,
And through her sobs spoke these winged words:

"You have come, Telemachus, sweet light!
I thought I would never see you again
After you left in your ship for Pylos—   *45*
Behind my back—for news of your father.
But tell me, what did you find out about him?"

Telemachus answered her coolly:

"Don't make me weep, mother, or get me
All worked up. I barely escaped with my life.   *50*
Now bathe yourself and put on clean clothes,
Then go to your bedroom upstairs with your maids
And vow formal sacrifice to the immortal gods
In the hope that Zeus will grant us vengeance.
I'm going to town so I can invite to our house   *55*
A stranger who came here with me from Pylos.
I sent him on ahead with some of my crew,
And I told Peiraeus to take him home
And show him hospitality until I arrived."

Penelope's response to this died on her lips.   *60*
She bathed, and dressed herself in clean clothes,
And vowed sacrifices to the immortal gods,
Praying that Zeus would grant them vengeance some day.

Telemachus went out through the hall
Holding a spear, two lean hounds at his side.   *65*
Athena shed a silver grace upon him,
And everyone marveled at him as he passed.
The haughty suitors crowded around him,
Fine words on their lips, and evil in their hearts.
Telemachus slipped away from the throng   *70*
And went to sit down over to one side
With Mentor, Antiphus, and Halitherses,
Old friends of his father. They wanted to know
Everything Telemachus had done. And then
Peiraeus came up, leading the stranger, Theoclymenus,   *75*
Up through the city to where the men were gathered.
Telemachus did not keep his back to him long
But went up to the stranger, who was his guest.
It was Peiraeus who spoke first, saying:

"Telemachus, get some women over to my house,   *80*
So I can send you the gifts Menelaus gave you."

And Telemachus, in his clear-headed way:

"Peiraeus, we don't know how things will turn out.
Should the suitors treacherously kill me at home
And divide among them my family's wealth,   *85*
I would rather that you keep all these gifts
And enjoy them, rather than any of that crowd.
But if I manage to sow the seeds of their death,
I'll be glad to have all of it back from you then."

Saying that, Telemachus led the stranger,   *90*
Who had endured much in life, to his house.
They went inside and laid their cloaks on chairs,
And then went into the polished tubs and bathed.
When the maids had bathed them and rubbed them

With oil, and flung upon them fleecy cloaks and tunics,   *95*
They came out of the baths and sat down on chairs.
A maid poured water from a golden pitcher
Into a silver basin for them to wash their hands
And then set up a polished table nearby.
Another serving woman, grave and dignified,   *100*
Set out bread and generous helpings
From the other dishes she had.
                    Penelope
Sat opposite her son by the doorpost of the hall,
Leaning back on a chair and spinning fine yarn.
The two men reached for the good cheer before them,   *105*
And when they had their fill of food and drink,
Penelope was the first to speak:

                    "Telemachus,
I think I will go now to my room upstairs
And lie down on my bed, which has become for me
A sorrowful bed, ever wet with my tears   *110*
Since the day Odysseus left for Troy
With the sons of Atreus. You do not have the heart
To tell me, before the suitors come in,
Whatever you have heard about your father's return."

And Telemachus, in his clear-headed way: *115*

"Rest assured I will tell you now, mother.
We went to Pylos, and Nestor, the king there,
Took me into his house. He welcomed me
As a father might welcome his long-lost son,
And he put me up with his own glorious sons.   *120*
But he said he had heard nothing from anyone
About whether Odysseus was dead or alive.
He sent me in a chariot to visit Menelaus,
Atreus' son, and there I saw Helen,
For whose sake the Greek and Trojan armies   *125*
Suffered so much, by the will of the gods.
Then Menelaus asked me why I had come
To gleaming Lacedaemon. I told him why,
And this is exactly what he told me then:

'Those dogs! Those puny weaklings,   *130*
Wanting to sleep in the bed of a hero!
A doe might as well bed her suckling fawns
In the lair of a lion, leaving them there
In the bush and then going off over the hills
Looking for grassy fields. When the lion   *135*
Comes back, the fawns die an ugly death.
That's the kind of death these men will die
When Odysseus comes back. O Father Zeus,
And Athena and Apollo, bring Odysseus back
With the strength he showed in Lesbos once   *140*
When he wrestled a match with Philomeleides
And threw him hard, making all of us cheer—
That's the Odysseus I want the suitors to meet!
They'd get married all right—to bitter death.
But, as to what you ask me about,   *145*
I will not stray from the point or deceive you.
No, I will tell you all that the infallible
Old Man of the Sea told me, and hide nothing.
He said he saw him on an island, miserable,
In the halls of Calypso, who keeps him there   *150*
Against his will. He has no way to get home
To his native land. He has no ships left,
No crew to row him over the sea's broad back.'
Those were the words of Menelaus, Atreus' son,
The great spearman. When I finished up there,   *155*
I set out for home, and a fair wind from the gods
Brought me back quickly to my native land."

So he spoke, and his words wrung her heart.
Then Theoclymenus made his voice heard:

"Revered lady, wife of Laertes' son, Odysseus,   *160*
Menelaus is in the dark about all this, but now
Hear what I have to say, for I will prophesy
Unerringly to you and conceal nothing.
With Zeus above all gods as my witness,
I swear, by this table of hospitality,   *165*
And by Odysseus' hearth, to which I have come,
That this same Odysseus, mark my words,

Is at this moment in his own native land,
Sitting still or on the move, learning of this evil,
And he is sowing evil for all the suitors.   170
Such is the bird of omen I saw
From the ship, and I cried it out to Telemachus."

And Penelope, calm and circumspect:

"Ah, stranger, may your words come true.
Then you would know my kindness, and my gifts   175
Would make you blessed in all men's eyes."

While they spoke to each other in this way,
The suitors were entertaining themselves
In front of Odysseus' palace again,
Throwing the javelin and discus   180
On the level terrace, arrogant as ever.
When it was time for dinner, and the flocks
Were coming in from the fields, Medon,
Who was the suitors' favorite herald
And was always at their feasts, called out: 185

"Young men, now that you have enjoyed yourselves
On the field, come inside so we can prepare a feast.
Dinner at dinnertime is not a bad thing at all."

It didn't take much to persuade them. Up they rose
And filed into the stately house. They laid their cloaks   190
On the chairs, and some of them got busy
Slaughtering great sheep and plump goats,
Fattened hogs, too, and a heifer of the herd.

While they were making their dinner, Odysseus
And the noble swineherd were getting ready   195
To go up from the fields to the city.
The swineherd started off by saying:

"Well, stranger, since you're eager to go
To the city today, as my master ordered—
Although for my part I'd rather have you here   200

To mind the farm, but I do respect him
And fear him, and I certainly don't want
A tongue-lashing from him, which could go hard—
Anyway, we'd better get going. It's late
In the day, and it'll be colder toward evening."   *205*

And Odysseus, his mind teeming:

"No need to tell me that. I understand.
Let's go. You lead the way, all the way.
But, if you have one cut, give me a staff
To lean on. You said the trail was slippery."   *210*

He spoke, and threw around his shoulders
His ratty pouch, full of holes and slung
By a twisted cord. Eumaeus gave him a staff
That suited him, and the two of them set out.
The dogs and the herdsmen stayed behind   *215*
To guard the farmstead. And so the swineherd
Led his master to the city, looking like
An old, broken-down beggar, leaning
On a staff and dressed in miserable rags.

They were well along the rugged path   *220*
And near to the city when they came to a spring
Where the townspeople got their water.
This beautiful fountain had been made
By Ithacus, and Neritus, and Polyctor.
A grove of poplars encircled it   *225*
And the cold water flowed from the rock above,
On top of which was built an altar to the nymphs,
Where all wayfarers made offerings.
                                        There
Melanthius, son of Dolius, met them
As he was driving his she-goats, the best   *230*
In the herds, into town for the suitors' dinner.
Two herdsmen trailed along behind him.
When he saw Eumaeus and his companion,
He greeted them with language so ugly
It made Odysseus' blood boil to hear it: *235*

"Well, look at this, trash dragging along trash.
Birds of a feather, as usual. Where
Are you taking this walking pile of shit,
You miserable hog-tender, this diseased beggar
Who will slobber all over our feasts?   240
How many doorposts has he rubbed with his shoulders,
Begging for scraps? You think he's ever gotten
A proper present, a cauldron or sword? Ha!
Give him to me and I'll have him sweep out the pens
And carry loads of shoots for the goats to eat,   245
Put some muscle on his thigh by drinking whey.
I'll bet he's never done a hard day's work in his life.
No, he prefers to beg his way through town
For food to stuff into his bottomless belly.
I'll tell you this, though, and you can count on it.   250
If he comes to the palace of godlike Odysseus,
He'll be pelted with footstools aimed at his head.
If he's lucky they'll only splinter on his ribs."

And as he passed Odysseus, the fool kicked him
On the hip, trying to shove him off the path.   255
Odysseus absorbed the blow without even quivering—
Only stood there and tried to decide whether
To jump the man and knock him dead with his staff
Or lift him by the ears and smash his head to the ground.
In the end, he controlled himself and just took it.   260
But the swineherd looked the man in the eye
And told him off, and lifted his hands in prayer:

"Nymphs of the spring, daughters of Zeus,
If Odysseus ever honored you by burning
Thigh bones of lambs and kids wrapped in rich fat,   265
Grant me this prayer:
                        May my master come back,
May some god guide him back!
                                          Then,
He would scatter all that puffery of yours,
All the airs you put on strutting around town
While bad herdsmen destroy all the flocks."   270

Melanthius, the goatherd, came back with this:

"Listen to the dog talk, with his big, bad notions.
I'm going to take him off in a black ship someday
Far from Ithaca, and sell him for a fortune.
You want my prayer? May Apollo with his silver bow   *275*
Strike Telemachus dead today in his halls,
Or may the suitors kill him, as surely as Odysseus
Is lost for good in some faraway land."

He left them with that. They walked on slowly,
While the goatherd pushed ahead and came quickly   *280*
To the palace. He went right in and sat down
Among the suitors, opposite Eurymachus,
Whom he liked best of all. The servers
Set out for him a helping of meat,
And the grave housekeeper brought him bread.   *285*

Odysseus and the swineherd came up to the house
And halted. The sound of the hollow lyre
Drifted out to them, for Phemius
Was sweeping the strings as he began his song.
Odysseus took the swineherd's hand and said: *290*

"Eumaeus, this beautiful house must be Odysseus'.
It would stand out anywhere. Look at all the rooms
And stories, and the court built with wall and coping,
And the well-fenced double gates. No one could scorn it.
And I can tell there are many men feasting inside   *295*
From the savor of meat wafting out from it,
And the sound of the lyre, which rounds out a feast."

And you answered him, swineherd Eumaeus:

"You don't miss a thing, do you? Well,
Let's figure out what we should do here.   *300*
Either you go in first and mingle with the suitors,
While I wait here; or you wait here,
If you'd rather, and I'll go in before you.
But don't wait long, or someone might see you

And either throw something at you or smack you.   *305*
Think it over. What would you like to do?"

And Odysseus, the godlike survivor: ,

"I understand. You don't have to prompt me.
You go in before me, and I'll wait here.
I've had things thrown at me before,   *310*
And I have an enduring heart, Eumaeus.
God knows I've had my share of suffering
At war and at sea. I can take more if I have to.
But no one can hide a hungry belly.
It's our worst enemy. It's why we launch ships   *315*
To bring war to men across the barren sea."

And as they talked, a dog that was lying there
Lifted his head and pricked up his ears.
This was Argus, whom Odysseus himself
Had patiently bred—but never got to enjoy—   *320*
Before he left for Ilion. The young men
Used to set him after wild goats, deer, and hare.
Now, his master gone, he lay neglected
In the dung of mules and cattle outside the doors,
A deep pile where Odysseus' farmhands   *325*
Would go for manure to spread on his fields.
There lay the hound Argus, infested with lice.
And now, when he sensed Odysseus was near,
He wagged his tail and dropped both ears
But could not drag himself nearer his master.   *330*
Odysseus wiped away a tear, turning his head
So Eumaeus wouldn't notice, and asked him:

"Eumaeus, isn't it strange that this dog
Is lying in the dung? He's a beautiful animal,
But I wonder if he has speed to match his looks,   *335*
Or if he's like the table dogs men keep for show."

And you answered him, Eumaeus, my swineherd:

"Ah yes, this dog belonged to a man who has died

Far from home. He was quite an animal once.
If he were now as he was when Odysseus   *340*
Left for Troy, you would be amazed
At his speed and strength. There's nothing
In the deep woods that dog couldn't catch,
And what a nose he had for tracking!
But he's fallen on hard times, now his master   *345*
Has died abroad. These feckless women
Don't take care of him. Servants never do right
When their masters aren't on top of them.
Zeus takes away half a man's worth
The day he loses his freedom."

                So saying,   *350*
Eumaeus entered the great house
And the hall filled with the insolent suitors.
But the shadow of death descended upon Argus,
Once he had seen Odysseus after twenty years.

Godlike Telemachus spotted the swineherd first   ·   *355*
Striding through the hall, and with a nod of his head
Signaled him to join him. Eumaeus looked around
And took a stool that lay near, one that the carver
Ordinarily sat on when he sliced meat for the suitors
Dining in the hall. Eumaeus took this stool   *360*
And placed it at Telemachus' table, opposite him,
And sat down. A herald came and served him
A portion of meat, and bread from the basket.

Soon after, Odysseus came in, looking like
An old, broken-down beggar, leaning   *365*
On a staff and dressed in miserable rags.
He sat down on the ashwood threshold
Just inside the doors, leaning back
On the cypress doorpost, a post planed and trued
By some skillful carpenter in days gone by.   *370*
Telemachus called the swineherd over
And taking a whole loaf from the beautiful basket
And all the meat his hands could hold, said to him:

"Take this over to the stranger, and tell him
To go around and beg from each of the suitors.   375
Shame is no good companion for a man in need."

Thus Telemachus. The swineherd nodded,
And going over to Odysseus, said to him:

"Telemachus gives you this, and he tells you
To go around and beg from each of the suitors.   380
Shame, he says, is not good for a beggar."

And Odysseus, his mind teeming:

"Lord Zeus, may Telemachus be blessed among men
And may he have all that his heart desires."

And he took the food in both his hands   385
And set it down at his feet on his beggar's pouch.
Odysseus ate as long as the bard sang in the hall.
When the song came to an end, and the suitors
Began to be noisy and boisterous, Athena
Drew near to him and prompted him   390
To go among the suitors and beg for crusts
And so learn which of them were decent men
And which were scoundrels—not that the goddess had
The slightest intention of sparing any of them.

Odysseus made his rounds from right to left,   395
Stretching his hands out to every side,
As if he had been a beggar all his life.
They all pitied him and gave him something,
And they wondered out loud who he was
And where he had come from. To which questions   400
Melanthius, the goatherd, volunteered:

"Hear me, suitors of our noble queen.
As to this stranger, I have seen him before.
The swineherd brought him here, but who he is
I have no idea, or where he claims he was born."   405

At this, Antinous tore into the swineherd:

"Swineherd! Why did you bring this man to town?
Don't we have enough tramps around here without him,
This nuisance of a beggar who will foul our feast?
I suppose you don't care that these men are eating away   *410*
Your master's wealth, or you wouldn't have invited him."

The swineherd Eumaeus came back with this:

"You may be a fine gentleman, Antinous,
But that's an ugly thing to say. Who, indeed,
Ever goes out of his way to invite a stranger   *415*
From abroad, unless it's a prophet, or healer,
Or a builder, or a singer of tales—someone like that,
A master of his craft who benefits everyone.
Men like that get invited everywhere on earth.
But who would burden himself with a beggar?   *420*
You're just plain mean, the meanest of the suitors
To Odysseus' servants, and especially to me.
But I don't care, as long as my lady Penelope
Lives in the hall, and godlike Telemachus."

To which Telemachus responded coolly: *425*

"Quiet! Don't waste your words on this man.
Antinous is nasty like that—provoking people
With harsh words and egging them on."

And then he had these fletched words for Antinous:

"Why, Antinous, you're just like a father to me,   *430*
Kindly advising me to kick this stranger out.
God forbid that should ever happen. No,
Go ahead and give him something. I want you to.
Don't worry about my mother or anyone else
In this house, when it comes to giving things away.   *435*
But the truth is that you're just being selfish
And would rather eat more yourself than give any away."

And Antinous answered him:

"What a high and mighty speech, Telemachus!
Look now, if only everyone gave him what I will,   440
It would be months before he darkened your door."

As he spoke he grabbed the stool upon which
He propped his shining feet whenever he dined
And brandished it beneath the table.
But all the rest gave the beggar something   445
And filled his pouch with bread and meat.
And Odysseus would have had his taste of the suitors
Free of charge, but on his way back to the threshold
He stopped by Antinous' place and said:

"Give me something, friend. You don't look like   450
You are the poorest man here—far from it—
But the most well off. You look like a king.
So you should give me more than the others.
If you did, I'd sing your praises all over the earth.
I, too, once had a house of my own, a rich man   455
In a wealthy house, and I gave freely and often
To any and everyone who wandered by.
I had slaves, too, more than I could count,
And everything I needed to live the good life.
But Zeus smashed it all to pieces one day—   460
Who knows why?—when he sent me out
With roving pirates all the way to Egypt
So I could meet my doom.
                              I moored my ships
In the river Nile, and you can be sure I ordered
My trusty mates to stand by and guard them   465
While I sent out scouts to look around.
Then the crews got cocky and overconfident
And started pillaging the Egyptian countryside,
Carrying off the women and children
And killing the men. The cry came to the city,   470
And at daybreak troops answered the call.
The whole plain was filled with infantry,
War chariots, and the glint of bronze.

Thundering Zeus threw my men into a panic,
And not one had the courage to stand and fight   *475*
Against odds like that. It was bad.
They killed many of us outright with bronze
And led the rest to their city to work as slaves.
But they gave me to a friend of theirs, from Cyprus,
To take me back there and give me to Dmetor,   *480*
Son of Iasus, who ruled Cyprus with an iron hand.
From there I came here, with all my hard luck."

Antinous had this to say in reply:

"What god has brought this plague in here?
Get off to the side, away from me,   *485*
Or I'll show you Egypt and Cyprus,
You pushy panhandler! You don't know your place.
You make your rounds and everyone
Hands things out recklessly. And why shouldn't they?
It's easy to be generous with someone else's wealth."   *490*

Odysseus took a step back and answered him:

"It's too bad your mind doesn't match your good looks.
You wouldn't give a suppliant even a pinch of salt
If you had to give it from your own cupboard.
Here you sit at another man's table   *495*
And you can't bear to give me a piece of bread
From the huge pile that's right by your hand."

This made Antinous even angrier,
And he shot back with a dark scowl:

"That does it. I'm not going to let you just   *500*
Breeze out of here if you're going to insult me."

As he spoke he grabbed the footstool and threw it,
Hitting Odysseus under his right shoulderblade.
Odysseus stood there as solid as a rock
And didn't even blink. He only shook his head   *505*
In silence, and brooded darkly.

Then he went back to the threshold and sat down
With his pouch bulging and spoke to the suitors:

"Hear me suitors of our glorious queen,
So I can speak my mind. No one regrets   *510*
Being hit while fighting for his own possessions,
His cattle or sheep. But Antinous struck me
Because of my belly, that vile growling beast
That gives us so much trouble. If there are gods
For beggars, or avenging spirits,   *515*
May death come to Antinous before marriage does."

Antinous, son of Eupeithes, answered:

"Just sit still and eat, stranger—or get the hell out.
Keep talking like this and some of the young men here
Will haul you by the feet all through the house   *520*
And strip the skin right off your back."

Thus Antinous. But the other suitors
Turned on him, one of them saying:

"That was foul, Antinous, hitting a poor beggar.
You're done for if he turns out to be a god   *525*
Come down from heaven, the way they do,
Disguised as strangers from abroad or whatever,
Going around to different cities
And seeing who's lawless and who lives by the rules."

Antinous paid no attention to this.   *530*
Telemachus took it hard that his father was struck
But he kept it inside. Not a tear
Fell from his eye. He only shook his head
In silence, and brooded darkly.

When Penelope, sitting with her maids,   *535*
Heard the stranger had been struck, she said:

"So may you be struck by the Archer God."

And Eurynome, the housekeeper, said to her:

"If our prayers were answered, not one of these men
Would live to see Dawn take her seat in the sky."   *540*

Penelope answered in her circumspect way:

"They're all hateful, nurse, for their evil designs,
But Antinous is like black death itself.
Some poor stranger makes his rounds through the house
Begging alms from the men because he is in need,   *545*
And all the others fill his pouch with gifts,
But Antinous throws a footstool at him
And hits him in the back beneath his shoulder."

Thus Penelope, sitting with her women,
While noble Odysseus ate his dinner.   *550*
Then she called the swineherd to her and said:

"Noble Eumaeus, tell the stranger to come here
So that I can greet him and ask him if perhaps
He has heard anything about Odysseus
Or seen him with his own eyes. By his looks   *555*
He is a man who has wandered the world."

And you, my swineherd, answered her:

"I wish the men would keep quiet, Lady,
For his speech could charm your very soul.
Three nights I had him with me, and three days   *560*
I kept him in my hut, for it was to me he first came
When he jumped ship—but he still did not finish
The long story of all his hard times.
It was just as when men gaze at a bard
Who sings to them songs learned from the gods,   *565*
Bittersweet songs, and they could listen forever—
That's how he charmed me when he sat in my house.
He says he's an ancestral friend of Odysseus,
And that he comes from Crete, the land of Minos.
It was from Crete he came here, on a hard journey   *570*

That gets ever harder as he wanders on
Like a rolling stone. He insists he has news
That Odysseus is near, over in Thesprotia,
Alive and well, and bringing many treasures home."

And Penelope, calm and circumspect: *575*

"Go call him here, so he can tell me face to face.
As for these men, let them play their games outside
Or here in the house. They're in a good mood,
As well they might be, their own possessions
Lying safe at home, their bread and sweet wine   *580*
Feeding only their servants, while they themselves
Mob our house day after day, slaughtering
All our oxen, our sheep and fat goats,
Partying and recklessly drinking our wine,
Ruining everything. For there is no man here   *585*
Like Odysseus to protect this house.
But if Odysseus should ever come home,
He and his son would make them pay for this outrage."

Just as she finished, Telemachus sneezed,
A loud sneeze that rang through the halls.   *590*
Penelope laughed and said to Eumaeus:

"Go ahead and call the stranger for me!
Didn't you see my son sneeze at my words?
That means death will surely come to the suitors,
One and all. Not a single man will escape.   *595*
And one more thing—what do you think of this?
If I find that he speaks everything truly,
I'll clothe him in a handsome tunic and cloak."

The swineherd took this all in. He went over
To Odysseus, and his words flew fast: *600*

"Penelope, Telemachus' mother,
Wants to see you. Her heart urges her,
For all her pain, to ask you about her husband.
If she finds that you speak everything truly,

She will give you a handsome tunic and cloak,   605
Which you really do need. As for your belly,
You'll still have to fill it by public begging."

And Odysseus, who had borne much:

"Eumaeus, I will soon be telling the whole truth
To Penelope, Icarius' wise daughter.   610
For I know Odysseus very well,
And he and I have been through much the same grief.
But I'm leery of this mob of rough suitors,
Whose arrogance grates on the sky's iron dome.
Just now as I was making my way through the hall,   615
Not doing any harm to anyone, this man
Struck me—hard—and neither Telemachus
Nor anyone else did anything to stop him.
So please ask Penelope, for all her eagerness,
To wait in the hall until the sun goes down.   620
Then she can ask me about her husband's return.
And she can seat me nearer the fire. These clothes
I have on are not very good, as you should know,
For it was to you first I came as a suppliant."

When he heard this the swineherd went off,   625
And when he crossed the threshold Penelope said:

"You're not bringing him with you, Eumaeus.
What does he mean by this? Does he fear someone
More than he should, or is there something else here
That makes him hang back? A shy beggar's a poor one."   630

And you answered her, Eumaeus, my swineherd:

"What he says is right, as anyone would agree,
About avoiding the violence of arrogant men.
He asks you to wait until the sun goes down.
And it would be far seemlier for you too, Lady,   635
If you and the stranger had your talk in private."

Penelope answered in her circumspect way:

"Our guest is no fool. He sees what could happen.
These men are bent on senseless violence,
More than any mortal men I can imagine."   *640*

Thus Penelope, and the godlike swineherd,
Having said his piece to her, went off
Into the throng of suitors. He found Telemachus,
And with his head close to him so no one could hear,
He spoke to him these feathered words: *645*

"I am going off now, dear Telemachus,
To guard the swine and all—
Your livelihood and mine. You take charge
Of everything here. Take care of yourself,
First and foremost, and be on the lookout   *650*
So you don't get hurt. Many of these men
Are up to no good. May Zeus destroy them
Utterly, before any harm can come to us."

And Telemachus, in his cool-headed way:

"Amen to that. Go after supper. But at dawn   *655*
Come back with your best boars for sacrifice.
Everything here is up to me, and the gods."

So the swineherd sat down again on a polished chair.
When he had eaten and drunk to his heart's content,
He went off to his swine, leaving the courts and hall   *660*
Full of banqueters. They were singing and dancing
And having a good time, for it was evening now.

ODYSSEY 18

And now there came the town beggar
Making his rounds, known throughout Ithaca
For his greedy belly and endless bouts
Of eating and drinking. He had no real strength
Or fighting power—just plenty of bulk.   5
Arnaeus was the name his mother had given him,
But the young men all called him Irus
Because he was always running errands for someone.
He had a mind to drive Odysseus out of his own house
And started in on him with words like this: 10

"Out of the doorway, geezer, before I throw you out
On your ear! Don't you see all these people
Winking at me to give you the bum's rush?
I wouldn't want to stoop so low, but if you don't
Get out now, I may have to lay hands on you."   15

Odysseus gave him a measured look and said:

"What's wrong with you? I'm not doing
Or saying anything to bother you. I don't mind
If someone gives you a handout, even a large one.
This doorway is big enough for both of us.   20
There's no need for you to be jealous of others.
Now look, you're a vagrant, just like I am.
Prosperity is up to the gods. But if I were you,
I'd be careful about challenging me with your fists.
I might get angry, and old man though I am,   25
I just might haul off and bust you in the mouth.

276

I'd have more peace and quiet tomorrow.
I don't think you'd come back a second time
To the hall of Laertes' son Odysseus."

This got Irus angry, and he answered:					*30*

"Listen to the mangy glutton run on,
Like an old kitchen woman! I'll fix him good—
Hit him with a left and then a right until
I knock his teeth out onto the ground,
The way we'd do a pig caught eating the crops.			*35*
Put 'em up, and everybody will see how we fight.
How are you going to stand up to a younger man?"

That's how they goaded each other on
There on the great polished threshold.
Antinous took this in and said with a laugh:				*40*

"How about this, friends? We haven't had
This much fun in a long time. Thank God
For a little entertainment! The stranger and Irus
Are getting into a fight. Let's have them square off!"

They all jumped up laughing and crowded around			*45*
The two tattered beggars. And Antinous said:

"Listen, proud suitors, to my proposal.
We've got these goat paunches on the fire,
Stuffed with fat and blood, ready for supper.
Whichever of the two wins and proves himself			*50*
The better man, gets the stuffed paunch of his choice.
Furthermore, he dines with us in perpetuity
And to the exclusion of all other beggars."

Everyone approved of Antinous' speech.
Then Odysseus, who knew all the moves, said:				*55*

"Friends, there's no way a broken-down old man
Can fight with a younger. Still, my belly,
That troublemaker, urges me on. So,

I'll just have to get beat up. But all of you,
Swear me an oath that no one, favoring Irus,   60
Will foul me and beat me for him."

They all swore that they wouldn't hit him,
And then Telemachus, feeling his power, said:

"Stranger, if you have the heart for this fight,
Don't worry about the onlookers. If anyone   65
Strikes you, he will have to fight us all.
I guarantee this as your host, and I am joined
By Antinous and Eurymachus,
Lords and men of discernment both."

Everyone praised this speech.
                        Then Odysseus   70
Tied his rags around his waist, revealing
His sculpted thighs, his broad shoulders,
His muscular chest and arms. Athena
Stood near the hero, magnifying his build.
The suitors' jaws dropped open.   75
They looked at each other and said things like:

"Irus is history."
                "Brought it on himself, too."
"Will you look at the thigh on that old man!"

So they spoke. Irus' heart was in his throat,
But some servants tucked up his clothes anyway   80
And dragged him out, his rolls of fat quivering.
Antinous laid into him, saying:

"You big slob. You'll be sorry
You were ever born, if you try to duck
This woebegone, broken-down old man.   85
I'm going to give it to you straight now.
If he gets the better of you and beats you,
I'm going to throw you on a black ship
And send you to the mainland to King Echetus,
The maimer, who will slice off your nose and ears   90

With cold bronze, and tear out your balls
And give them raw to the dogs to eat."

This made Irus tremble even more.
They shoved him out into the middle,
And both men put up their fists. Odysseus,   95
The wily veteran, thought it over.
Should he knock the man stone cold dead,
Or ease up on the punch and just lay him out flat?
Better to go easy and just flatten him, he thought,
So that the crowd won't get suspicious.   100
The fighters stood tall, circling each other,
And as Irus aimed a punch at his right shoulder,
Odysseus caught him just beneath the ear,
Crushing his jawbone. Blood ran from his mouth,
And he fell in the dust snorting like an ox   105
And gnashing his teeth, his heels kicking the ground.
The suitors lifted their hands and died
With laughter. Odysseus took Irus by one fat foot
And dragged him out through the doorway
All the way to the court and the portico's gates.   110
He propped him up against the courtyard's wall,
Stuck his staff in his hand, and said to him:

"Sit there now and scare off the pigs and dogs,
And stop lording it over the other beggars,
You sorry bastard, or things could get worse."   115

And he slung his old pouch over one shoulder,
Walked back to the threshold, and sat down.
The suitors went inside, laughing and joking,
And one of them came up to Odysseus and said:

"May Zeus and the other gods grant you, stranger,   120
Whatever your heart most dearly desires,
Since you have ended this glutton's begging career.
We'll ship him off to Echetus the maimer!"

Odysseus took heart at these auspicious words.
Antinous set before him the huge paunch   125

Stuffed with fat and blood, and Amphinomus
Served him a couple of loaves from the basket,
Toasted him with a golden cup, and said:

"Hail to the revered stranger. May good fortune
Come to you, though you have only bad luck now."   *130*

And Odysseus, from his mind's teeming depths:

"Amphinomus, you come across as a sensible man,
Just as your father was. I have heard of him,
Nisus of Dulichium, a good man, and wealthy,
Known far and wide. They say you are his son,   *135*
And you seem soft-spoken, a good man yourself.
So I'll tell you something you should take to heart.
Of all the things that breathe and move upon it,
Earth nurtures nothing feebler than man.
While the gods favor him and his step is quick,   *140*
He thinks he will never have to suffer in life.
Then when the blessed ones bring evil his way,
He bears it in sorrow with an enduring heart.
Our outlook changes with the kind of day
Zeus our Father decides to give us.   *145*
I, too, once got used to prosperity,
And I did many foolish things in my pride,
Trusting my father and brothers would save me.
So I know a man should never be an outlaw,
But keep in peace the gifts heaven gives him.   *150*
Just look at what the suitors are doing now,
Wasting the wealth and dishonoring the wife
Of a man who, I tell you, will not be gone long
From his family and friends and his native land.
He's very close. Better for you if some god   *155*
Leads you away from here and takes you home
Before you meet him upon his return.
Once he's under this roof, I do not think
The suitors will escape without blood being spilled."

He spoke, poured a libation, drank the sweet wine,   *160*
And then gave the cup back to Amphinomus,

Who went away through the hall with his head bowed
And his heart heavy with a sense of foreboding.
He would not escape death, though. Pallas Athena
Had him pinned, and he would be killed outright   *165*
By a spear from the hand of Telemachus.

And now the Grey-eyed One put into the heart
Of Penelope, Icarius' wise daughter,
A notion to show herself to the suitors.
All of a sudden she wanted to make their blood pound—   *170*
And to make herself more worthy than ever
In the eyes of her son, and of her husband.
With a whimsical laugh she said to the housekeeper:

"Eurynome, my heart longs, though it never has before,
To show myself to the suitors, hateful as they are.   *175*
And I would like to say something to my son,
Something that might help him—he should not
Continually keep the company of the suitors,
Overbearing men who speak politely to his face
And plan all the while to hurt him later."   *180*

And the housekeeper Eurynome said:

"Yes indeed, child, everything you said is right.
Go on then, and speak your mind to your son
And don't hide anything—after you have bathed,
That is, and dabbed your cheeks with ointment.   *185*
Don't go like this, bleary-eyed from crying.
All this grieving only makes you look worse.
Your son is that age, you know. You prayed your heart out
For the gods to let you see him as a bearded man."

And Penelope, in her circumspect way: *190*

"Eurynome, don't try, even though you love me,
To talk me into bathing and putting on makeup.
Any beauty I had the Olympian gods destroyed
On the day my husband left in the hollow ships.
But go tell Autonoë and Hippodameia   *195*

To come stand by my side when I enter the hall.
It would be shameful for me to go alone among men."

She spoke, and the old housekeeper went off
To tell the two women Penelope wanted them.

Athena's eyes glinted. She had another idea.   200
First, she made Penelope so sweetly drowsy
That she leaned back, her whole body limp,
And went to sleep right there on her couch.
Then the shimmering goddess went to work on her,
So that all the men would gape in wonder.   205
First she cleansed her lovely face, using
The pure, distilled Beauty that Aphrodite
Anoints herself with when she goes garlanded
Into the beguiling dance of the Graces.
Then she made her look taller, and filled out her figure,   210
And made her skin whiter than polished ivory.
Her work done, the goddess glimmered away.
Just then, some of the women came by,
Talking noisily, and Penelope woke up.
She rubbed her cheeks with her hands and said: 215

"What a soft, sweet sleep! If only Artemis
Would send as soft a death to me at once
So I would no longer waste away in sorrow,
Longing for my dear husband's winning ways.
He was in all ways the very best of men."   220

She spoke. Light from the upper rooms
Flooded the stairs as Penelope came down,
Not alone, two maids trailed behind—
And when she had come among the suitors
She stood in her glory beside a column   225
That supported the roof of the great house,
Hiding her cheeks behind her silken veils,
Grave handmaidens standing on either side.
The suitors' knees grew weak when they saw her.
They were spellbound, in love, and each man prayed   230
That he would lie beside her in bed. But,

It was to her son, Telemachus, that she spoke:

"Telemachus, what can you be thinking of?
You were intelligent even as a child,
But now that you have reached manhood—   *235*
So handsome and tall that any stranger
Who happened to see you would be able to tell
You're a rich man's son—you're not thinking straight,
Not any more. Just look at what has happened
Here in these halls! How would you like it   *240*
If our guest, sitting as he is in our house,
Were to be treated roughly and come to harm?
It would be a disgrace, and the shame would be yours."

And Telemachus, in his clear-headed way:

"I don't blame you for being angry, Mother,   *245*
But I'm aware of all this myself. I know
Everything that is going on here, good and bad.
I used to think as a child, but not any more.
But I can't think clearly with all these men
Sitting around driving me to distraction.   *250*
They don't mean me any good, and I have
No one to help me. But I can tell you this,
That the fight between the stranger and Irus
Did not go the way the suitors wanted.
Our guest proved to be the better man.   *255*
O Father Zeus, and Athena and Apollo,
If only the suitors were beaten like that,
Their limbs unstrung, nodding their heads,
Some in the courtyard and some in the hall,
Just as Irus now sits by the gate,   *260*
Lolling his head as if he were drunk,
Unable to stand up or get himself home,
Wherever that is, because his limbs are like putty."

Thus mother and son. Then Eurymachus
Addressed Penelope, saying to her: *265*

"Daughter of Icarius, wise Penelope,

If all the Greeks throughout the mainland
Could see you now, even more suitors
Would be here tomorrow, feasting in your hall,
For you are far and away the most beautiful   270
And most intelligent woman in the world."

And wise Penelope answered him:

"Eurymachus, the gods destroyed my beauty
On the day when the Argives sailed for Ilion
And with them went my husband, Odysseus.   275
If he were to come back and be part of my life,
My fame would be greater and more resplendent.
But now I grieve, so many sorrows
Has some spirit visited upon me.
And this much is true: when Odysseus left   280
He clasped my right hand in his and said to me:
'I do not think, my wife, that all the Greeks
Will return from Ilion safe and sound.
They say the Trojans are real warriors,
Spearmen and bowmen, and they drive chariots,   285
Which can turn the tide in any battle.
So I do not know whether the god of war
Will send me back or if I'll go down
There in Troy. So everything here is in your hands.
Take care of my father and of my mother   290
As you do now, or even more, when I am gone.
But when you see our son a bearded man,
Marry whom you will, and leave this house.'
So he spoke, and it's all coming true.
There will come a night when a hateful marriage   295
Will darken my bed, cursed as I am, my happiness
Destroyed by Zeus. And I have more heartache.
This isn't the way suitors usually behave
When men compete for the hand of a lady,
A woman of some worth, a rich man's daughter.   300
They bring cattle, and fat sheep,
To feast the bride's friends, and they give her
Glorious gifts. They do not devour
Another's livelihood without recompense."

She spoke, and Odysseus, the godlike survivor,   *305*
Smiled inwardly to see how she extracted gifts
From the suitors, weaving a spell upon them
With her words, while her mind was set elsewhere.

Then Antinous, Eupeithes' son, said to her:

"Daughter of Icarius, wise Penelope,   *310*
As far as gifts go, take whatever any man
Wishes to give. It's not good to refuse gifts.
But as for us, we're not going back to our lands
Or anywhere else until you marry
Whoever proves to be the best of the Achaeans."   *315*

Everyone approved of what Antinous said,
And each man sent a herald to fetch his gifts.
Antinous' man brought a beautiful robe,
All embroidered. It had twelve golden brooches,
Each of them fitted with hooked clasps.   *320*
Eurymachus' man came back right away
With an intricately crafted golden chain
Strung with amber and bright as the sun.
Eurydamas' attendants brought a pair of earrings,
Three elegant teardrops gleaming from each.   *325*
From the house of Peisander, Polyctor's son,
There came a necklace of exquisite beauty.
And so it went, each man bringing
One lovely gift after another.

                              And Penelope,
A moving silver grace, went up to her chamber,   *330*
Her women behind her bearing the beautiful gifts.

The suitors turned to amusing themselves
With dance and song until evening fell.
When twilight shaded their merrymaking
They set up three braziers in the great hall   *335*
To give them light. They stoked these with kindling,
Seasoned and dry and newly split with the axe.
They set torches between the braziers,

And the household women set about lighting them.
Zeus-bred Odysseus, always thinking,   *340*
Went up to these women and had a word with them:

"Maidservants of Odysseus, your long-absent lord,
Go off now to where your revered queen is sitting
And do your spinning, or card wool, by her side.
Sit with her and keep her company. Cheer her up.   *345*
I'll take care of keeping the torches lit
For these men. Even if they stay up until dawn
They won't outlast me. I can put up with a lot."

The women looked at each other and laughed.
Then Melantho, fair-cheeked and sassy,   *350*
Had some ugly words for him. This Melantho
Was born to Dolius, but Penelope
Had reared her as her very own child,
Spoiling her with toys and whatever she wanted.
Even so she had no feeling for Penelope   *355*
But loved Eurymachus and slept with him.
And now she lit into Odysseus:

"You must be out of your mind, you old wreck,
Unwilling to go to the blacksmith's to sleep
Or anywhere else. You just blabber on here,   *360*
Bold as can be, with all these real men around,
Feeling no fear. Are you drunk, or are you
Always like this, with all your blather?
Pleased with yourself, aren't you, because you beat that bum,
Irus? Someone a lot better than Irus   *365*
Might stand up to you soon and pound you
Bloody with his fists as he drives you outside."

Odysseus shot her a dark look and growled:

"Just let me tell Telemachus what you are saying,
You bitch. He'll cut you to ribbons on the spot."   *370*

His words scattered the women, sending them
Flying through the hall in terror, convinced

That he meant what he said.
                              Odysseus
Took his stand by the torches, keeping them lit
And watching all the men. But his heart seethed   375
With other business, soon to be finished.

Now Athena was not about to let the suitors
Abstain from insults. She wanted pain
To sink deeper into Odysseus' bones.
And so Eurymachus began to jeer   380
At him for his friends' entertainment:

"Hear me, suitors of our glorious queen,
While I speak my mind. It is not without
The will of the gods that this man has come
To Odysseus' palace. We get a nice glow   385
Of torchlight from him—from his head,
That is, since it doesn't have a hair on it!"

And then speaking directly to Odysseus,
Destroyer of cities, Eurymachus said:

"I wonder if you'd like to be a hired hand,   390
Stranger. Should I hire you to work
On one of my outlying farms gathering fieldstones
And planting tall trees? Oh, I'll pay you.
I'll keep you fed the year round out there,
Give you some clothes and sandals to wear.   395
But you've never done a hard day's work
In your life, preferring to beg your way through town
For food to stuff into your bottomless belly."

And Odysseus, his mind teeming:

"Eurymachus, I wish we could have a contest   400
Working in the fields during the summertime,
When the days are long, just you and I
Out in a hayfield with long, curved scythes,
And plenty of grass so we could test our work,
Fasting until late evening.

Or how about this?   405
We could each drive oxen, the best there are,
Big and tawny, both well fed with grass,
The same age, yoked the same way, tireless animals—
And each with four acres of rich soil to plow.
Then you'd see if I could cut a straight furrow   410
Clear to the end.
                        And it would be even better
If Zeus brought war upon us from somewhere,
Today, right now, and I had a shield, two spears,
And a bronze helmet that fit close to my temples.
Then you would see me out in the front ranks,   415
And you wouldn't stand here jeering at me
Because of my belly. But you are insufferable,
And you have a hard heart. No doubt you think
You are some great man, a tough guy,
Because you hang out with puny weaklings.   420
If Odysseus came back home, these doors,
Wide as they are, would be far too narrow
For you to squeeze through as you made for daylight."

This made Eurymachus all the more furious.
Scowling at Odysseus he said to him: 425

"You won't get away with this kind of talk,
Bold as can be with all these real men around,
Feeling no fear. Are you drunk, or are you
Always like this, with all your blather?
Are you all pumped up because you beat that bum, Irus?" 430

And he grabbed a footstool, but Odysseus,
Wary of the man, sat down at the knees
Of Amphinomus, the suitor from Dulichium,
And Eurymachus' missile struck a cupbearer
On the right hand. The wine jug he held   435
Clattered to the ground, and the man groaned
And fell backward into the dust.
                              The suitors
Were in an uproar throughout the shadowy hall.
One man would glance at his neighbor and say:

"Better if the stranger had never made it here;   440
Then he couldn't have brought us all this trouble.
Here we are, brawling about beggars. Our feasts
Will be ruined if we let things turn ugly."

Then Telemachus made his voice heard:

"You are all raving now. Your drunken guzzling   445
Is beginning to show, or some god
Is stirring you up. But now that you have feasted,
Go home and get some rest—whenever you're ready,
Of course. I'm not driving anyone away."

He spoke, and they all bit their lips and marveled   450
At Telemachus for speaking so boldly.
Then Amphinomus addressed the suitors:

"Friends, no man should be angry at a thing
Fairly spoken, or respond by arguing.
Do not mistreat this stranger any longer,   455
Or any of godlike Odysseus' household.
Now let the cupbearer start us off
So we can pour libation and go home to rest.
This stranger we will leave in Odysseus' halls—
Where he landed—and in Telemachus' keeping."   460

Amphinomus' words pleased everyone,
And a bowl was mixed by his herald, Mulius.
He served a cup to each man in turn,
And they poured libations to the blessed gods
And drank sweet wine to their hearts' content.   465
Then they all went home and took their rest.

ODYSSEY 19

So Odysseus was left alone in the hall,
Planning death for the suitors with Athena's aid.
He spoke winged words to Telemachus:

"Telemachus, get all the weapons out of the hall.
When the suitors miss them and ask you   5
Where they are, set their minds at ease, saying:
'Oh, I have stored them out of the smoke.
They're nothing like they were when Odysseus
Went off to Troy, but are all grimed with soot.
Also, a god put this thought into my head,   10
That when you men are drinking, you might
Start quarreling and someone could get hurt,
Which would ruin your feasting and courting.
Steel has a way of drawing a man to it.'"

Thus Odysseus. Telemachus nodded,   15
And calling Eurycleia he said to her:

"Nurse, shut the women inside their rooms
While I put my father's weapons away,
The beautiful weapons left out in the hall
And dulled by the smoke since he went off to war.   20
I was just a child then. But now I want
To store them away, safe from the smoke."

And Eurycleia, his old nurse, said:

"Yes, child, you are right
To care for the house and guard its wealth.   25

But who will fetch a light and carry it for you,
Since you won't let any of the women do it?"

Telemachus coolly answered her:

"This stranger here. I won't let anyone
Who gets rations be idle, even a traveler   30
From a distant land."

                        Telemachus' words sank in,
And the nurse locked the doors of the great hall.
Odysseus and his illustrious son sprang up
And began storing away the helmets, bossed shields,
And honed spears. And before them Pallas Athena,   35
Bearing a golden lamp, made a beautiful light.
Telemachus suddenly blurted out to his father:

"Father, this is a miracle I'm seeing!
The walls of the house, the lovely panels,
The beams of fir, and the high columns   40
Are glowing like fire. Some god is inside,
One of the gods from the open sky."

Odysseus, his mind teeming, replied:

"Hush. Don't be too curious about this.
This is the way of the gods who hold high heaven.   45
Go get some rest. I'll remain behind here
And draw out the maids—and your mother,
Who in her grief will ask many questions."

And Telemachus went out through the hall
By the light of blazing torches. He came   50
To his room, lay down, and waited for dawn.
Odysseus again was alone in the hall,
Planning death for the suitors with Athena's aid.

Penelope, wary and thoughtful,
Now came from her bedroom, and she was like   55
Artemis or golden Aphrodite.

They set a chair for her by the fire
Where she always sat, a chair inlaid
With spiraling ivory and silver
Which the craftsman Icmalius had made long ago.   60
It had a footstool attached, covered now
With a thick fleece.
                Penelope sat down,
Taking everything in. White-armed maids
Came out from the women's quarters
And started to take away all of the food,   65
Clearing the tables and picking up the cups
From which the men had been drinking.
They emptied the braziers, scattering the embers
Onto the floor, and then stocked them up
With loads of fresh wood for warmth and light.   70

Then Melantho started in on Odysseus again:

"Are we going to have to put up with you all night,
Roaming though the house and spying on the women?
Go on outside and be glad you had supper,
Or you'll soon stagger out struck with a torch."   75

And Odysseus answered from his teeming mind:

"What's wrong with you, woman? Are you mean to me
Because I'm dirty and dressed in rags
And beg through the land? I do it because I have to.
That's how it is with beggars and vagabonds.   80
You know, I too once lived in a house in a city,
A rich man in a wealthy house, and I often gave
Gifts to wanderers, whatever they needed.
I had servants, too, countless servants,
And plenty of everything else a man needs   85
To live the good life and be considered wealthy.
But Zeus crushed me. Who knows why?
So be careful, woman. Someday you may lose
That glowing beauty that makes you stand out now.
Or your mistress may become fed up with you.   90
Or Odysseus may come. We can still hope for that.

But even if, as seems likely, he is dead
And will never return, his son, Telemachus,
Is now very much like him, by Apollo's grace,
And if any of the women are behaving loosely   *95*
It won't get by him. He's no longer a child."

None of this was lost on Penelope,
And she scolded the maidservant, saying:

"Your outrageous conduct does not escape me,
Shameless whore that you are, and it will be   *100*
On your own head. You knew very well,
For you heard me say it, that I intended
To question the stranger here in my halls
About my husband; for I am sick with worry."

Then to Eurynome, the housekeeper, she said: *105*

"Bring a chair here with a fleece upon it
So that the stranger can sit down and tell his tale
And listen to me. I have many questions for him."

So Eurynome brought up a polished chair
And threw a fleece over it, and upon it sat   *110*
Odysseus, patient and godlike.
Penelope, watchful, began with a question:

"First, stranger, let me ask you this:
Who are you and where are you from?"

Odysseus, his mind teeming, answered her: *115*

"Lady, no one on earth could find fault with you,
For your fame reaches the heavens above,
Just like the fame of a blameless king,
A godfearing man who rules over thousands
Of valiant men, upholding justice.   *120*
His rich, black land bears barley and wheat,
The trees are laden with fruit, the flocks
Are always with young, and the sea teems with fish—

Because he rules well, and so his people prosper.
Ask me, therefore, about anything else,   *125*
But not about my birth or my native land.
That would fill my heart with painful memories.
I have many sorrows, and it wouldn't be right
To sit here weeping in another's house,
Nor is it good to be constantly grieving.   *130*
I don't want one of your maids, or you yourself,
To be upset with me and say I am awash with tears
Because the wine has gone to my head."

And Penelope, watching, answered him:

"Stranger, the gods destroyed my beauty   *135*
On the day when the Argives sailed for Ilion
And with them went my husband, Odysseus.
If he were to come back and be part of my life,
My fame would be greater and more resplendent so.
But now I ache, so many sorrows   *140*
Has some spirit showered upon me.
All of the nobles who rule the islands—
Dulichium, Samê, wooded Zacynthus—
And all those with power on rocky Ithaca
Are courting me and ruining this house.   *145*
So I pay no attention to strangers
Or to suppliants or public heralds. No,
I just waste away with longing for Odysseus.
My suitors press on, and I weave my wiles.
First some god breathed into me the thought   *150*
Of setting up a great loom in the main hall,
And I started weaving a vast fabric
With a very fine thread, and I said to them:

'Young men—my suitors, since Odysseus is dead—
Eager as you are to marry me, you must wait   *155*
Until I finish this robe—it would be a shame
To waste my spinning—a shroud for the hero
Laertes, when death's doom lays him low.
I fear the Achaean women would reproach me
If he should lie in death shroudless for all his wealth.'   *160*

"So I spoke, and their proud hearts consented.
Every day I would weave at the great loom,
And every night unweave the web by torchlight.
I fooled them for three years with my craft.
But in the fourth year, as the seasons rolled by,   165
And the moons waned, and the days dragged on,
My shameless and headstrong serving women
Betrayed me. The men barged in and caught me at it,
And a howl went up. So I was forced to finish the shroud.
Now I can't escape the marriage. I'm at my wit's end.   170
My parents are pressing me to marry,
And my son agonizes over the fact
That these men are devouring his inheritance.
He is a man now, and able to preside
Over a household to which Zeus grants honor.   175
But tell me of your birth, for you are not sprung,
As the saying goes, from stock or stone."

And Odysseus, from his mind's teeming depths:

"Honored wife of Laertes' son, Odysseus,
Will you never stop asking about my lineage?   180
All right, I will tell you, but bear in mind
You are only adding to the sorrows I have.
For so it is when a man has been away from home
As long as I have, wandering from city to city
And bearing hardships. Still, I will tell you.   185
              Crete is an island that lies in the middle
Of the wine-dark sea, a fine, rich land
With ninety cities swarming with people
Who speak many different languages.
There are Achaeans there, and native Cretans,   190
Cydonians, Pelasgians, and three tribes of Dorians.
One of the cities is great Cnossus,
Where Minos ruled and every nine years
Conversed with great Zeus. He was the father
Of my father, the great hero Deucalion.   195
Deucalion had another son, Idomeneus,
Who sailed his beaked ships to Ilion
Following the sons of Atreus. I was the younger,

And he the better man. My name is Aethon.
     It was in Crete that I saw Odysseus   *200*
And gave him gifts of hospitality.
He had been blown off course rounding Malea
On his way to Troy. He put in at Amnisus,
Where the cave of Eileithyia is found.
That is a difficult harbor, and he barely escaped   *205*
The teeth of the storm. He went up to the city
And asked for Idomeneus, claiming to be
An old and honored friend. But Idomeneus' ships
Had left for Troy ten days before, so I
Took him in and entertained him well,   *210*
Drawing on the ample supplies in the house.
I gathered his men and distributed to them
Barley meal, wine, and bulls for sacrifice
From the public supplies, to keep them happy.
They stayed for twelve days. A norther so strong   *215*
You could barely stand upright in it
Had them corraled—some evil spirit had roused it.
On the thirteenth day the wind dropped, and they left."

All lies, but he made them seem like the truth,
And as she listened, her face melted with tears.   *220*

> *Snow deposited high in the mountains by the wild West Wind*
> *Slowly melts under the East Wind's breath,*
> *And as it melts the rivers rise in their channels.*

So her lovely cheeks coursed with tears as she wept
For her husband, who was sitting before her.   *225*
Odysseus pitied her tears in his heart,
But his eyes were as steady between their lids
As if they were made of horn or iron
As he concealed his own tears through guile.
When Penelope had cried herself out,   *230*
She spoke to him again, saying:

"Now I feel I must test you, stranger,
To see if you really did entertain my husband
And his godlike companions, as you say you did.

Tell me what sort of clothes he wore, and tell me   235
What he was like, and what his men were like."

And Odysseus, from his mind's teeming depths:

"Lady, it is difficult for me to speak
After we've been apart for so long. It has been
Twenty years since he left my country.   240
But I have an image of him in my mind.
Odysseus wore a fleecy purple cloak,
Folded over, and it had a brooch
With a double clasp, fashioned of gold,
And on the front was an intricate design: 245
A hound holding in his forepaws a dappled fawn
That writhed to get free. Everyone marveled
At how, though it was all made of gold,
The hound had his eye fixed on the fawn
As he was strangling it, and the fawn   250
Twisted and struggled to get to its feet.
And I remember the tunic he wore,
Glistening like onionskin, soft and shiny
And with a sheen like sunlight. There were
Quite a few women who admired it.   255
But remember, now, I do not know
Whether Odysseus wore this at home,
Or whether one of his men gave it to him
When he boarded ship, or someone else,
For Odysseus was a man with many friends.   260
He had few equals among the Achaeans.
I, too, gave him gifts—a bronze sword,
A beautiful purple cloak, and a fringed tunic,
And I gave him a ceremonious send-off
In his benched ship. And one more thing: 265
He had a herald, a little older than he was,
And I will tell you what he looked like.
He was slope-shouldered, with dark skin
And curly hair. His name was Eurybates,
And Odysseus held him in higher esteem   270
Than his other men, because they thought alike."

These words stirred up Penelope's grief.
She recognized the unmistakeable tokens
Odysseus was giving her. She wept again,
And then composed herself and said to him: 275

"You may have been pitied before, stranger,
But now you will be loved and honored
Here in my halls. I gave him those clothes.
I folded them, brought them from the storeroom,
And pinned on the gleaming brooch,   280
To delight him. But I will never welcome him
Home again, and so the fates were dark
When Odysseus left in his hollow ship
For Ilion, that curse of a city."

And Odysseus, from his mind's teeming depths: 285

"Revered wife of Laertes' son, Odysseus,
Do not mar your fair skin with tears any more,
Or melt your heart with weeping for your husband.
Not that I blame you. Any woman weeps
When she has lost her husband, a man with whom   290
She has made love and whose children she has borne—
And the husband you've lost is Odysseus,
Who they say is like the immortal gods.
Stop weeping, though, and listen to my words,
For what I am about to tell you is true.   295
I have lately heard of Odysseus' return,
That he is near, in the rich land of Thesprotia,
Still alive. And he is bringing home treasures,
Seeking gifts, and getting them, throughout the land.
But he lost his trusty crew and his hollow ship   300
On the wine-dark sea. As he was sailing out
From the island of Thrinacia, Zeus and Helios
Hit him hard because his companions had killed
The cattle of the Sun. His men went under,
But he rode his ship's keel until the waves   ·   305
Washed him ashore in the land of the Phaeacians,
Whose race is closely akin to the gods'.
They treated him as if he were a god,

Gave him many gifts, and were more than willing
To escort him home. And he would have been here   *310*
By now, but he thought it more profitable
To gather wealth by roaming the land.
No one is as good as Odysseus
At finding ways to gain an advantage.
I had all this from Pheidon, the Thesprotian king.   *315*
And he swore to me, as he poured libations
There in his house, that a ship was already launched,
And a crew standing by, to take him home.
He sent me off first, since a Thesprotian ship
Happened to be leaving for Dulichium,   *320*
But before I left, Pheidon showed me
All the treasure Odysseus had amassed,
Bronze, gold, and wrought iron, enough to feed
His children's children for ten generations,
All stored there for him in the halls of the king.   *325*
Odysseus, he said, had gone to Dodona
To consult the oak-tree oracle of Zeus
And ask how he should return to Ithaca—
Openly or in secret—after being gone so long.
So he is safe, and will come soon.   *330*
He is very near, and will not be away long
From his dear ones and his native land.
I will swear to this. Now Zeus on high
Be my witness, and this hospitable table,
And the hearth of flawless Odysseus himself—   *335*
That everything will happen just as I say:
Before this month is out Odysseus will come,
In the dark of the moon, before the new crescent."

And Penelope, watching him carefully:

"Ah, stranger, may your words come true.   *340*
Then you would know my kindness, and my gifts
Would make you blessed in all men's eyes.
But I know in my heart that Odysseus
Will never come home, and that you will never
Find passage elsewhere, since there is not now   *345*
Any master in the house like Odysseus—

If he ever existed—to send honored guests
Safely on their way, or to welcome them.
But still, wash our guest's feet, maidens,
And prepare a bed for him. Set up a frame   *350*
And cover it with cloaks and lustrous blankets
To keep him cozy and warm. When golden Dawn
Shows her first light, bathe him and anoint him,
So he can sit side by side with Telemachus
And share in the feast here in the hall.   *355*
And anyone who causes this man any pain
Will regret it sorely and will accomplish nothing
Here in this house, however angry he gets.
For how would you ever find out, stranger,
Whether or not I surpass all other women   *360*
In presence of mind, if you sit down to dinner
Squalid and disheveled here in my hall?
Our lives are short. A hard-hearted man
Is cursed while he lives and reviled in death.
But a good-hearted man has his fame spread   *365*
Far and wide by the guests he has honored,
And men speak well of him all over the earth."

And Odysseus, his mind teeming, answered her:

"Revered wife of Odysseus, Laertes' son,
I lost all interest in cloaks and blankets   *370*
On the day I left the snowy mountains of Crete
In my long-oared ship. I will lie down tonight,
As I have through many a sleepless night,
On a poor bed, waiting for golden-throned Dawn.
Nor do I have any taste for foot-baths,   *375*
And none of the serving women here in your hall
Will touch my feet, unless there is some old,
Trustworthy woman who has suffered as I have.
I would not mind if she touched my feet."

And Penelope, watching him carefully: *380*

"Of all the travelers who have come to my house,
None, dear guest, have been as thoughtful as you

And none as welcome, so wise are your words.
I do have an old and trustworthy woman here,
Who nursed and raised my ill-starred husband,   385
Taking him in her arms the day he was born.
She will wash your feet, frail as she is.
Eurycleia, rise and wash your master's—that is,
Wash the feet of this man who is your master's age.
Odysseus' feet and hands are no doubt like his now,   390
For men age quickly when life is hard."

At this, the old woman hid her face in her hands.
Shedding warm tears, she spoke through her sobs:

"My lost child, I can do nothing for you.
Zeus must have hated you above all other men,   395
Although you were always godfearing. No one
Burned more offerings to the Lord of Lightning,
So many fat thighbones, bulls by the hundreds,
With prayers that you reach a sleek old age
And raise your glorious son. And now the god has   400
Deprived you alone of your day of return.
        And I suppose, stranger, women mocked him, too,
When he came to some man's gloried house
In a distant land, just as these cheeky bitches
All mock you here. It is to avoid their insults   405
That you will not allow them to wash your feet.
But Penelope, Icarius' wise daughter,
Has asked me to do it, and I will,
For her sake and for yours,
For my heart is throbbing with sorrow.   410
But listen now to what I have to say.
Many road-weary strangers have come here,
But I have never seen such a resemblance
As that between you and Odysseus,
In looks, voice—even the shape of your feet."   415

And Odysseus, from his mind's teeming depths:

"Oh, everyone who has seen us both says that,
Old woman, that we are very much alike,

Just as you yourself have noticed."

And the old woman took the shining basin   *420*
She used for washing feet, poured
Cold water into it, and then added the hot.
Odysseus, waiting, suddenly sat down at the hearth
And turned away toward the shadows. The scar!
It flashed through his mind that his old nurse   *425*
Would notice his scar as soon as she touched him,
And then everything would be out in the open.
She drew near and started to wash her master,
And knew at once the scar from the wound
He had gotten long ago from a boar's white tusk   *430*
When he had gone to Parnassus to visit Autolycus,
His mother's father, who was the best man on earth
At thieving and lying, skills he had learned
From Hermes. He had won the god's favor
With choice burnt offerings of lambs and kids.   *435*

Autolycus had visited Ithaca once
When his grandson was still a newborn baby.
After he finished supper, Eurycleia
Put the child in his lap and said to him:

"Autolycus, now name the child   *440*
Of your own dear child. He has been much prayed for."

Then Autolycus made this response:

"Daughter and son-in-law of mine,
Give this child the name I now tell you.
I come here as one who is odious, yes,   *445*
Hateful to many for the pain I have caused
All over the land. Let this child, therefore,
Go by the name of Odysseus.
For my part, when he is grown up
And comes to the great house of his mother's kin   *450*
In Parnassus, where my possessions lie,
I will give him a share and send him home happy."

In due time, Odysseus came to get these gifts
From Autolycus. His grandfather
And his uncles all welcomed him warmly,   *455*
And Amphithea, his mother's mother,
Embraced Odysseus and kissed his head
And beautiful eyes. Autolycus told his sons
To prepare a meal, and they obeyed at once,
Leading in a bull, five years old,   *460*
Which they flayed, dressed, and butchered.
They skewered the meat, roasted it skillfully,
And then served out portions to everyone.
All day long until the sun went down
They feasted to their hearts' content.   *465*
But when the sun set and darkness came on
They went to bed and slept through the night.
When Dawn brushed the early sky with rose,
They went out to hunt—Autolycus' sons
Running their hounds—and with them went   *470*
Godlike Odysseus. They climbed the steep wooded slopes
Of Mount Parnassus and soon reached
The windy hollows. The sun was up now,
Rising from the damasked waters of Ocean
And just striking the fields, when the beaters came   *475*
Into a glade. The dogs were out front,
Tracking the scent, and behind the dogs
Came Autolycus' sons and noble Odysseus,
His brandished spear casting a long shadow.
Nearby, a great boar was lying in his lair,   *480*
A thicket that was proof against the wild wet wind
And could not be pierced by the rays of the sun,
So dense it was. Dead leaves lay deep
Upon the ground there. The sound of men and dogs
Pressing on though the leaves reached the boar's ears,   *485*
And he charged out from his lair, back bristling
And his eyes spitting fire. He stood at bay
Right before them, and Odysseus rushed him,
Holding his spear high, eager to thrust.
The boar was too quick. Slashing in,   *490*
He got Odysseus in the thigh, right above the knee,
His white tusk tearing a long gash in the muscle

Just shy of the bone. Even so, Odysseus
Did not miss his mark, angling his spear
Into the boar's right shoulder. The gleaming point   *495*
Went all the way through, and with a loud grunt
The boar went down and gasped out his life.
Autolycus' sons took care of the carcass
And tended the wound of the flawless Odysseus,
Skillfully binding it and staunching the blood   *500*
By chanting a spell. Then they quickly returned
To their father's house. When Odysseus
Had regained his strength, Autolycus and his sons
Gave him glorious gifts and sent him home happy,
Home to Ithaca. His mother and father   *505*
Rejoiced at his return and asked him all about
How he got his scar; and he told them the story
Of how a boar had gashed him with his white tusk
As he hunted on Parnassus with Autolycus' sons.

This was the scar the old woman recognized   *510*
When the palm of her hand ran over it
As she held his leg. She let the leg fall,
And his foot clanged against the bronze basin,
Tipping it over and spilling the water
All over the floor. Eurycleia's heart   *515*
Trembled with mingled joy and grief,
Tears filled her eyes, and her voice
Was choked as she reached out
And touched Odysseus' chin and said:

"You are Odysseus, dear child. I did not know you   *520*
Until I laid my hands on my master's body."

She spoke, and turned her eyes toward Penelope,
Wanting to show her that her husband was home.
But Penelope could not return her gaze
Or understand her meaning, for Athena   *525*
Had diverted her mind. Odysseus reached
For the old woman's throat, seized it in his right hand
And drawing her closer with his other, he said:

"Do you want to destroy me? You yourself
Nursed me at your own breast, and now   530
After twenty hard years I've come back home.
Now that some god has let you in on the secret,
You keep it to yourself, you hear? If you don't,
I'll tell you this, and I swear I'll do it:
If, with heaven's help, I subdue the suitors,   535
I will not spare you—even if you are my nurse—
When I kill the other women in the hall."

And Eurycleia, the wise old woman:

"How can you say that, my child? You know
What I'm made of. You know I won't break.   540
I'll be as steady as solid stone or iron.
And I'll tell you this, and you remember it:
If, with heaven's help, you subdue the proud suitors,
I'll list for you all the women in the house,
Those who dishonor you and those who are true."   545

And Odysseus, his mind teeming:

"Nurse, you don't have to tell me about them.
I'll keep an eye out and get to know each one.
Don't say a thing. Just leave it up to the gods."

At this, the old woman went off for more water   550
To wash his feet, since it had all been spilled.
When she had washed him and rubbed on oil,
Odysseus pulled his chair close to the fire again
To keep warm, and hid the scar with his rags.

Penelope now resumed their talk: 555

"There's one more thing I want to ask you about,
And then it will be time to get some sleep—
At least for those to whom sweet sleep comes
Despite their cares. But some god has given me
Immeasurable sorrow. By day   560
I console myself with lamentation

And see to my work and that of my women.
But at night, when sleep takes hold of others,
I lie in bed, smothered by my own anxiety,
Mourning restlessly, my heart racing.   565
Just as the daughter of Pandareus,
The pale nightingale, sings sweetly
In the greening of spring, perched in the leaves,
And trills out her song of lament for her son,
Her beloved Itylus, whom she killed unwittingly,   570
Itylus, the son of Zethus her lord—
So too my heart is torn with dismay.
Should I stay here with my son
And keep everything safe and just as it is,
My goods, my slaves, my high-gabled house,   575
Honoring my husband's bed and public opinion—
Or should I go with whoever is best
Of all my suitors, and gives me gifts past counting?
And then there's my son. While he was young
And not yet mature, he kept me from leaving   580
My husband's house and marrying another.
But now that he's grown and come into manhood,
He begs me to leave, worried because
These Achaean men are devouring his goods.
      But listen now to a dream I had   585
And tell me what it means. In my dream
I have twenty geese at home. I love to watch them
Come out of the water and eat grains of wheat.
But a huge eagle with a hooked beak comes
Down from the mountain and breaks their necks,   590
Killing them all. They lie strewn through the hall
While he rides the wind up to the bright sky.
I weep and wail, still in my dream,
And Achaean ladies gather around me
As I grieve because the eagle killed my geese.   595
Then the eagle comes back and perches upon
A jutting roofbeam and speaks to me
In a human voice, telling me not to cry:

'Take heart, daughter of famed Icarius.
This is no dream, but a true vision   600

That you can trust. The geese are the suitors,
And I, who was once an eagle, am now
Your husband come back, and I will deal out doom,
A grisly death for all of the suitors.'

"So he spoke, and I woke up refreshed.   605
Looking around I saw the geese in the house,
Feeding on wheat by the trough, as before."

And Odysseus, his mind teeming:

"Lady, there is no way to give this dream
Another slant. Odysseus himself has shown you   610
How he will finish this business. The suitors' doom
Is clear. Not one will escape death's black birds."

And Penelope, in her circumspect way:

"Stranger, you should know that dreams
Are hard to interpret, and don't always come true.   615
There are two gates for dreams to drift through,
One made of horn and the other of ivory.
Dreams that pass through the gate of ivory
Are deceptive dreams and will not come true,
But when someone has a dream that has passed   620
Through the gate of polished horn, that dream
Will come true. My strange dream, though,
Did not come from there. If it had,
It would have been welcome to me and my child.
            One more thing, and, please, take it to heart.   625
Dawn is coming, the accursed dawn of the day
Which will sever me from the house of Odysseus.
I will announce a contest. Odysseus
Used to line up axes inside his hall,
Twelve of them, like the curved chocks   630
That prop up a ship when it is being built,
And he would stand far off and send an arrow
Whizzing through them all. I will propose
This contest to my suitors, and whoever
Can bend that bow and slip the string on its notch   635

And shoot an arrow through all twelve axes,
With him will I go, leaving behind this house
I was married in, this beautiful, prosperous house,
Which I will remember always, even in my dreams."

And Odysseus, from the depths of his teeming mind: *640*

"Revered wife of Laertes' son, Odysseus,
Do not put off this contest any longer,
For Odysseus will be here, with all his cunning,
Handling that polished bow, before these men
Could ever string it and shoot through the iron."   *645*

Then Penelope, still watching him:

"If you were willing, stranger, to sit here
Beside me in my halls and give me joy,
Sleep would never settle upon my eyes.
But we cannot always be sleepless,   *650*
For every thing there is a season, and a time
For all we do on the life-giving earth.
I will go now to my room upstairs
And lie on my bed, which has become
A sorrowful bed, wet with my tears   *655*
Since the day Odysseus left
For Ilion, that accursed city.
I will lie there, but you can lie here
In the hall. Spread some blankets on the floor,
Or have the maids make up a bed for you."   *660*

Saying this, Penelope went upstairs
To her softly lit room, not alone,
For her women went up with her.
Once in her room she wept for Odysseus,
Her beloved husband, wept until Athena   *665*
Let sweet sleep settle upon her eyelids.

ODYSSEY 20

Odysseus lay down to sleep
On the outer porch. He spread out
An uncured oxhide, and on top of that
He layered fleeces from the many sheep
That were always being slaughtered
There in his house. Eurynome   5
Covered him with a cloak, and there he lay,
Sleepless, his mind racing with thoughts
Of how to punish the suitors.
                             And then the women
Came from the house, on their way,
As usual, to sleep with the suitors,   10
Laughing with each other and giggling.
Odysseus felt his chest tighten. He brooded
For a long time over what he should do—
Rush out and kill every last one of them,
Or let them sleep with the arrogant bastards   15
This one last time. He growled under his breath

   The way a dog standing over her pups growls
   When she sees a stranger and digs in to fight—

So Odysseus growled at their iniquity,
But he slapped his chest hard and scolded his heart: 20

"Endure, my heart. You endured worse than this
On that day when the invincible Cyclops
Ate our comrades. You bore it until your cunning
Got you out of the cave where you thought you would die."

In this way Odysseus scolded his heart,   25
And his heart in obedience beat steady and strong.
But the great hero himself tossed and turned.

> *It was like a man roasting a paunch*
> *Stuffed with fat and blood over a fire.*
> *He can't wait for it to be done*   30
> *And so keeps turning it over and over—*

Odysseus tossing and turning as he pondered how
To get his hands on the shameless suitors,
One man against many.
                              And then Athena came
Down from the sky, and stood above his head   35
In the form of a woman, and spoke to him:

"Why are you sleepless, most ill-fated of men?
This is your house, and in this house are your wife
And child, a son any father would hope for."

And Odysseus, his mind teeming: 40

"Yes, Goddess, all that you say is true,
But my heart is brooding over this—
How to get my hands on the shameless suitors,
Alone as I am, against the whole pack of them.
And worse, even if I were to kill them   45
By your will and the will of Zeus, how
Would I get out of it? Think about that."

And Athena, eyes flashing in the dark:

"Let it go, Odysseus. Some people trust
Their puny human friends more than you trust me.   50
And here I am, a goddess, protecting you
In all your trials. To put it plainly,
Even if there were fifty squadrons of armed men
All around us, doing their mortal best to kill us,
You would still be able to run off their cattle!   55
Now get some sleep. Staying up all night

Will only sap your strength. All your troubles,
Odysseus, will soon be over."
                              Athena spoke
And shed sleep on his eyelids, and then
She was off to Olympus, a being of light.   *60*

While Odysseus slept, his cares melting away
Under the spell of sleep, his wife awoke,
And she wept as she sat upon her soft bed.
When her heart had its fill of weeping,
The godlike woman prayed to Artemis: *65*

"Artemis, mighty daughter of Zeus—please,
Shoot an arrow into my breast and take my life
This very moment. This is my wish,
Or that a storm wind snatch me away
And bear me off over the gloomy passes   *70*
And cast me down at the mouth of Ocean,
As winds once bore off Pandareus' daughters.
The gods had slain their parents, and they were left
Orphans in their halls. Aphrodite fed them
Cheese, sweet honey, and mellow wine;   *75*
Hera made them wise and beautiful
Beyond all women; holy Artemis made them tall;
And Athena taught them glorious handiwork.
But while Aphrodite was off to high Olympus
To arrange their marriages, on her way to Zeus,   *80*
The high lord of thunder, who knows all,
All the good and bad fortune of mortal men—
The storm spirits snatched the girls away
And gave them as slaves to the hateful Furies.
So may the Olympians blot me out,   *85*
Or Artemis, in her tall headdress, shoot me,
That I may pass beneath the hateful earth
With Odysseus in my mind's eye, never
To gratify the heart of a lesser man.
Grief is endurable when one weeps by day   *90*
But can sleep at night. Sleep makes us forget
All things, both the good and the bad,
Once it enshrouds our eyelids. But some spirit

Keeps sending me bad dreams. This very night
There slept with me again someone who looked   *95*
Just like Odysseus when he left with the army,
And my heart was glad, because I did not think
It was a dream, but the waking truth at last."

She spoke, and Dawn came, seated on gold.
Odysseus heard Penelope's voice as she wept   *100*
And in that moment between sleep and waking
He felt in his heart that she knew him already
And was standing beside his head.
                                    He picked up
The cloak and fleeces on which he had slept
And put them on a chair in the hall. Then he took   *105*
The oxhide outside and set it down, and,
Lifting his palms to the sky, he prayed to Zeus:

"Father Zeus, if it was the gods' will
To bring me home over land and sea
After afflicting me, show me a sign.   *110*
Let someone of those stirring inside the house
Speak for me a word of good omen,
And send me a sign also from the open sky."

Zeus in his wisdom heard his prayer
And thundered from snow-capped Olympus   *115*
High above the clouds. Odysseus was glad.
And a woman uttered a word of omen
As she ground at a mill nearby in the house.
Twelve women in all worked the mills there,
Grinding barley and wheat into flour,   *120*
The marrow of men. The other women,
Their wheat ground, were sleeping now,
But she, the weakest of them, was still at it.
Stopping her mill, she spoke these words:

"Father Zeus, lord of gods and men.   *125*
That was a loud thunderclap out of a clear sky!
You must be showing someone a sign.
Will you answer an old woman's prayer?

Let this be the last and final day
The suitors feast in Odysseus' hall.   *130*
I've broken my back grinding their grain.
Let this meal be their last."

Odysseus smiled at this omen, and at the thunder
From Zeus. He would have his vengeance.

The other women were up now, huddled together   *135*
As they kindled the day's fire on the hearth.
Telemachus rose from bed, a godlike man,
And got dressed. He slung his sharp sword
Around one shoulder, tied fine leather sandals
Onto his supple feet, and, spear in hand,   *140*
Went to the threshold and spoke to Eurycleia:

"Dear nurse, have you looked after our guest,
Given him a bed and food, or is he lying uncared for?
That's my mother's style, wise as she is,
Honoring one man outrageously   *145*
And sending a better man away neglected."

And Eurycleia, with all her wits about her:

"Don't blame her, child, when she is blameless.
He sat and drank wine as long as he wanted,
But he said he wasn't hungry. She asked him.   *150*
When he got tired and wanted to sleep,
She told the women to make up a bed,
But he, like many who are down on their luck,
Wouldn't sleep on a bed, or under blankets.
He lay on an undressed oxhide and some fleeces   *155*
Out on the porch, and we threw a cloak over him."

Thus Eurycleia, and Telemachus went out,
Spear in hand and two hounds at his heels,
To join the other men in the public square.
Then Eurycleia, Peisenor's granddaughter,   *160*
A noble woman, called to her maids:

"Some of you get busy and sweep the hall
And sprinkle it, and put the purple coverlets
On the good chairs. And we'll need some others,
To sponge down the tables, and wash the bowls   165
And goblets. The rest of you go down
And fetch water from the spring, quickly.
The suitors will be here early today.
It's a feast day, a holiday for everyone."

She spoke, and they did as she said. Twenty   170
Went down to the spring with its dark water,
And the rest did their house work skillfully.

Then in came the town's serving men. They started
Splitting logs, doing a good job of it. The women
Came back from the spring, and behind them   175
Came the swineherd, driving three prime boars,
The herd's finest. He let them feed in the courtyard
And then turned to Odysseus with a pleasant manner:

"Stranger, are you getting any more respect yet,
Or are they still insulting you in the hall?"   180

And Odysseus, his mind teeming:

"Eumaeus, it is outrageous the way these men
Carry on in another man's house. May the gods
Punish them! They have no sense of shame."

After this exchange, Melanthius came up,   185
The goatherd, leading the best she-goats
From all the herds for the suitors' feast.
Two herdsmen followed him. He tethered the goats
In the echoing portico, and then taunted Odysseus:

"Are you still here, pestering everyone?   190
Why don't you get the hell outside?
You and I are going to have to settle this
With our fists. I don't like your way of begging.
There are other feasts you can go to, you know."

Odysseus made no response, but sat   195
Shaking his head and brooding darkly.

And then a third herdsman came, Philoetius,
Driving for the suitors a barren heifer
And fat she-goats. This livestock had been brought over,
Along with Philoetius, by ferrymen   200
Who ply the straits with all sorts of passengers.
He tethered the animals in the echoing portico
And then went up to the swineherd and asked:

"Who's the new arrival, swineherd?
Where does he say he comes from,   205
And who are his parents and kinsmen?
Poor guy! He looks like some kind of king,
But the gods can make it tough
For wanderers, even if they're royalty."

He spoke, then came up to Odysseus,   210
Stretched out his right hand, and said:

"Welcome, stranger, and may good luck
Come your way, hard as things are for you now.
Father Zeus, no god curses us worse than you!
You have no pity for men. You beget them,   215
Then plunge them into misery and pain.
Stranger, I broke into a sweat when I saw you,
And my eyes are full of tears. You remind me
Of Odysseus. He too is clothed in rags like this,
I suppose, and is a wanderer like you,   220
If he is still alive, that is, and still sees the sunlight.
But if he is already dead and has gone to Hades,
Then I weep for noble Odysseus.
He put me in charge of his cattle when I was a boy
In the land of the Cephallenians, and now   225
Those cattle are past counting. No breed
Ever flourished like that for any mortal man.
But now other men order me to drive them
So they can eat them, with no regard at all
For the son in the house, or the gods' wrath.   230

No, they're hot to divide among themselves
All the property of our long-absent master.
As for myself, I go around and around in my heart,
Trying to decide. It would be very bad of me,
While my master's son still lives, to go off   *235*
To some other place with my cattle,
To a foreign land. But it is worse still
To stay here and suffer, in charge of herds
Handed over to others. I would have fled
Long ago, believe me, to some powerful lord,   *240*
Because things here are no longer bearable,
Except that I still imagine, still have some hope
That my unfortunate master will someday return
And scatter the suitors out of this house."

And Odysseus, his great mind teeming: *245*

"You're a good man, cowherd, and smart,
And I see that you understand things,
So I will say something and seal it with an oath.
With Zeus and all the gods above as witnesses,
And by Odysseus' hearth, and this table   *250*
Of hospitality to which I have come,
I swear that while you are here, Odysseus
Will come home, and you will see, if you wish,
The death of the suitors, who lord it over this hall."

To which the cowherd responded: *255*

"May Zeus bring what you say to pass, stranger.
Then you would see what these hands can do."

And Eumaeus, too, prayed to all the gods
That wise Odysseus might return to his home.

So went their talk.
                    The suitors, meanwhile,   *260*
Were laying plans for Telemachus' death,
But as they talked a bird appeared on their left,
A high-flying eagle with a dove in its talons.

This prompted Amphinomus to say to them:

"This plan of ours isn't going to work, friends—   *265*
Killing Telemachus. We might as well just eat."

The suitors all agreed with Amphinomus.
Going into the house of godlike Odysseus,
They laid their cloaks on chairs and got busy
Slaughtering big sheep and plump goats   *270*
And fatted swine, and the herd's prize heifer.
They roasted the entrails, served them, and mixed wine
In the bowls. The swineherd passed out the cups,
Philoetius handed out bread from a beautiful basket,
And Melanthius poured for them. They reached out   *275*
To all the tasty dishes spread before them.

Telemachus, pressing his advantage,
Showed Odysseus to a seat
Inside the great hall by the stone threshold,
Giving him a shabby stool beside a little table.   *280*
He served him a portion of the entrails
And a cup of wine, and he said to him:

"Sit here among these heroes and sip your wine.
I myself will protect you from their insults
And keep their hands from you. This house   *285*
Is not a public inn, but the palace of Odysseus,
Who inherited it to pass on to me.
So, all you suitors, control yourselves.
I don't want any fights breaking out here."

They bit their lips at this and wondered   *290*
At Telemachus. It had been a bold speech.
Then Antinous, Eupeithes' son, said:

"Hard as it is, we'd better listen to him, men.
Telemachus really means business now.
If Zeus had allowed it, we'd have shut his mouth   *295*
By now, here in these halls, fine speaker or not."

But Telemachus paid no attention to Antinous.

Meanwhile, down in the town, heralds
Were leading a sacrifice of one hundred bulls
Through the streets, and Achaean men,   300
Their long hair flowing, were gathering
In a shady grove sacred to Apollo,
The god whose arrows strike from afar.

In Odysseus' palace they were now drawing
The roasted meat from the spits and dividing it up   305
For a glorious feast. The servers set out
A portion for Odysseus equal to the others,
This at the command of Telemachus,
Godlike Odysseus' own true son.

But Athena was not about to let the suitors   310
Abstain from insults. She wanted the pain
To sink deeper into Odysseus' bones.
There was a particularly arrogant suitor
From the island of Samê—Ctessipus by name.
This man, relying on his enormous wealth,   315
Courted the wife of the long-absent Odysseus.
He spoke now among the insolent crowd:

"Hear me, suitors. I have something to say.
The stranger here has been served a portion
Equal to ours. This is all as it should be.   320
It would not be right to deprive any guest
Telemachus entertains here in these halls.
So I'd like to give him a gift myself,
A little gratuity he might want to pass on
To the bath woman or one of the other slaves   325
Who live in the house of godlike Odysseus."

So saying, he picked up an ox's hoof
From a basket and threw it hard. Odysseus
Snapped his head aside and dodged it,
Smiling to himself, a grim and bitter smile.   330
The ox's hoof crashed into the solid wall,

And Telemachus tore into Ctessipus:

"You're damned lucky you missed him,
Ctessipus—or rather that he dodged your throw—
Or I would have rammed my spear into your gut,   335
And your father would have been busy
With your funeral instead of making plans for a wedding.
No more of this ugliness in my house—from anyone!
I understand now what's going on around here,
The good and the bad. I was a child before.   340
But we still have to put up with all this,
Seeing the sheep slaughtered, the wine drunk,
The bread—one man can't stop many.
You don't have to be hostile to me,
But if you are determined to cut me down,   345
Well, I'd rather be killed in cold blood
Than have to watch this disgusting behavior—
Guests mistreated and men dragging the women
Shamefully through these beautiful halls."

Dead silence reigned in those beautiful halls   350
Until Agelaus, son of Damastor, said:

"Friends, no one should get angry at a speech
Justly spoken, or respond to it harshly.
We should stop mistreating the stranger
And all of the servants in Odysseus' house.   355
But I would like to offer to Telemachus,
And to his mother, some friendly advice,
And I hope that it gets through to both of them.
As long as you still held hope in your hearts
That Odysseus would find his way back home,   360
No one could blame you for waiting for him
And restraining the suitors—clearly the better course
Had he ever come back and returned to his home.
But now it is clear he will never return.
Sit down with your mother and tell her this.   365
Tell her to marry the best of her suitors,
Whoever that is, whoever gives her the most.
Then you can enjoy what your father has left you,

And she can keep another man's house."

Telemachus answered in his cool-headed way: *370*

"I swear by Zeus and by my poor father,
Who has either perished far from Ithaca
Or is wandering still, that I do not, Agelaus,
Delay my mother's marriage. On the contrary,
I encourage her to marry the man of her choice,   *375*
And I offer her a dowry of gifts past counting.
But it would be shameful for me to order her to leave—
May the gods forbid it—against her own will."

Thus Telemachus. And Pallas Athena
Touched the suitors' minds with hysteria.   *380*
They couldn't stop laughing, and as they laughed
It seemed to them that their jaws were not theirs,
And the meat that they ate was dabbled with blood.
Tears filled their eyes, and their hearts raced.
Then the seer Theoclymenus spoke among them: *385*

"Wretches, what wicked thing is this that you suffer?
You are shrouded in night from top to toe,
Lamentation flares, your cheeks melt with tears,
And the walls of the house are spattered with blood.
The porch and the court are crowded with ghosts   *390*
Streaming down to the undergloom. The sun is gone
From heaven, and an evil mist spreads over the land."

Thus the seer, and they just giggled at him.
Eurymachus was the first to actually speak:

"This newly arrived stranger has lost his mind!   *395*
Quick, get him outside, since he thinks it's night in here."

To which the seer Theoclymenus replied:

"I don't need any escorts, Eurymachus.
I have eyes, ears, and my own two feet,
And a mind in good working order.   *400*

I'll leave under my own power, for I can see
Evil coming upon you, inescapable evil
For every last one of you who in your blind pride
Do violence to the house of Odysseus."

And with that he left the great hall   *405*
And went to Peiraeus, who took him in gladly.
The suitors stood there smirking at each other
And tried to provoke Telemachus
By ridiculing his guests with comments like these:

"Hey, Telemachus, you don't have much luck   *410*
With the kind of guests you keep around.
You've got this filthy vagabond here
Who always wants a handout of bread and wine
And can't help out with anything, a useless load.
Then this other one posing as a prophet.   *415*
If you ask me we ought to throw them on a ship
And send them off to the Sicilians.
At least then you would turn a little profit."

So went their talk. But Telemachus ignored them,
Watching his father in silence, waiting for the moment   *420*
When he would lay his hands on the shameless suitors.

By now Penelope, Icarius' wise daughter,
Had set her chair across from the suitors
And heard the words of each man in the hall.
During all their laughter they had been busy   *425*
Preparing their dinner, a tasty meal
For which they had slaughtered many animals.
But no meal could be more graceless than the one
A goddess and a hero would serve to them soon.
After all, they started the whole ugly business.   *430*

ODYSSEY 21

Owl-eyed Athena now prompted Penelope
To set before the suitors Odysseus' bow
And the grey iron, implements of the contest
And of their death.
               Penelope climbed
The steep stairs to her bedroom and picked up   *5*
A beautiful bronze key with an ivory handle
And went with her maids to a remote storeroom
Where her husband's treasures lay—bronze, gold,
And wrought iron. And there lay the curved bow
And the quiver, still loaded with arrows,   *10*
Gifts which a friend of Odysseus had given him
When they met in Lacedaemon long ago.
This was Iphitus, Eurytus' son, a godlike man.
They had met in Messene, in the house of Ortilochus.
Odysseus had come to collect a debt   *15*
The Messenians owed him: three hundred sheep
They had taken from Ithaca in a sea raid,
And the shepherds with them. Odysseus
Had come to get them back, a long journey
For a young man, sent by his father and elders.   *20*
Iphitus had come to search for twelve mares
He had lost, along with the mules they were nursing.
These mares turned out to be the death of Iphitus
When he came to the house of Heracles,
Zeus' tough-hearted son, who killed him,   *25*
Guest though he was, without any regard
For the gods' wrath or the table they had shared—
Killed the man and kept the strong-hoofed mares.

It was while looking for these mares that Iphitus
Met Odysseus and gave him the bow   *30*
Which old Eurytus had carried and left to his son.
Odysseus gave him a sword and spear
To mark the beginning of their friendship
But before they had a chance to entertain each other
Zeus' son killed Iphitus, son of Eurytus,   *35*
A man like the gods. Odysseus did not take
The bow with him on his black ship to Troy.
It lay at home as a memento of his friend,
And Odysseus carried it only on Ithaca.

Penelope came to the storeroom   *40*
And stepped onto the oak threshold
Which a carpenter in the old days had planed,
Leveled, and then fitted with doorposts
And polished doors. Lovely in the half-light,
She quickly loosened the thong from the hook,   *45*
Drove home the key and shot back the bolts.
The doors bellowed like a bull in a meadow
And flew open before her. Stepping through,
She climbed onto a high platform that held chests
Filled with fragrant clothes. She reached up   *50*
And took the bow, case and all, from its peg,
Then sat down and laid the gleaming case on her knees
Her eyes welling with tears. Then she opened the case
And took out her husband's bow. When she had her fill
Of weeping, she went back to the hall   *55*
And the lordly suitors, bearing in her hands
The curved bow and the quiver loaded
With whining arrows. Two maidservants
Walked beside her, carrying a wicker chest
Filled with the bronze and iron gear her husband   *60*
Once used for this contest. When the beautiful woman
Reached the crowded hall, she stood
In the doorway flanked by her maidservants.
Then, covering her face with her shining veil,
Penelope spoke to her suitors: *65*

"Hear me, proud suitors. You have used this house

For an eternity now—to eat and drink
In its master's absence, nor could you offer
Any excuse except your lust to marry me.
Well, your prize is here, and this is the contest.   70
I set before you the great bow of godlike Odysseus.
Whoever bends this bow and slips the string on its notch
And shoots an arrow through all twelve axes,
With him will I go, leaving behind this house
I was married in, this beautiful, prosperous house,   75
Which I will remember always, even in my dreams."

Penelope said this, and then ordered Eumaeus
To set out for the suitors the bow and grey iron.
All in tears, Eumaeus took them and laid them down,
And the cowherd wept, too, when he saw   80
His master's bow. Antinous scoffed at them both:

"You stupid yokels! You can't see farther than your noses.
What a pair! Disturbing the lady with your bawling.
She's sad enough already because she's lost her husband.
Either sit here in silence or go outside to weep,   85
And leave the bow behind for us suitors. This contest
Will separate the men from the boys. It won't be easy
To string that polished bow. There is no man here
Such as Odysseus was. I know. I saw him myself
And remember him well, though I was still a child."   90

So Antinous said, hoping in his heart
That he would string the bow first and shoot an arrow
Through the iron. But the only arrow
He would touch first would be the one shot
Into his throat from the hands of Odysseus,   95
The man he himself was dishonoring
While inciting his comrades to do the same.

And then Telemachus, with a sigh of disgust:

"Look at me! Zeus must have robbed me of my wits.
My dear mother declares, for all her good sense,   100
That she will marry another and abandon this house,

And all I do is laugh and think it is funny.
Well, come on, you suitors, here's your prize,
A woman the likes of whom does not exist
In all Achaea, or in sacred Pylos,   *105*
Nowhere in Argos or in Mycenae,
Or on Ithaca itself or on the dark mainland.
You all know this. Why should I praise my mother?
Let's get going. Don't start making excuses
To put off stringing the bow. We'll see what happens.   *110*
And I might give that bow a try myself.
If I string it and shoot an arrow through the axeheads,
It won't bother me so much that my honored mother
Is leaving this house and going off with another,
Because I would at least be left here as someone   *115*
Capable of matching his father's prowess."

With that he took off his scarlet cloak, stood up,
And unstrapped his sword from his shoulders.
Then he went to work setting up the axeheads,
First digging a long trench true to the line   *120*
To hold them in a row, and then tamping the earth
Around each one. Everyone was amazed
That he made such a neat job of it
When he had never seen it done before.
Then he went and took his stance on the threshold   *125*
And began to try the bow. Three times
He made it quiver as he strained to string it,
And three times he eased off, although in his heart
He yearned to draw that bow and shoot an arrow
Through the iron axeheads. And on his fourth try   *130*
He would have succeeded in muscling the string
Onto its notch, but Odysseus reined him in,
Signaling him to stop with an upward nod.
So Telemachus said for all to hear:

"I guess I'm going to be a weakling forever!   *135*
Or else I'm still too young and don't have the strength
To defend myself against an enemy.
But come on, all of you who are stronger than me—
Give the bow a try and let's settle this contest."

And he set the bow aside, propping it against   *140*
The polished, jointed door, and leaning the arrow
Against the beautiful latch. Then Telemachus
Sat down on the chair from which he had risen.

Antinous, Eupeithes' son, then said:

"All right. We go in order from left to right,   *145*
Starting from where the wine gets poured."

Everyone agreed with Antinous' idea.
First up was their soothsayer, Leodes,
Oenops' son. He always sat in the corner
By the wine-bowl, and he was the only one   *150*
Who loathed the way the suitors behaved.
He now carried the bow and the arrow
Onto the threshold, took his stance,
And tried to bend the bow and string it,
But his tender, unworn hands gave out,   *155*
And he said for all the suitors to hear:

"Friends, I'm not the man to string this bow.
Someone else can take it. I foresee it will rob
Many a young hero of the breath of life.
And that will be just as well, since it is far better   *160*
To die than live on and fall short of the goal
We gather here for, with high hopes day after day.
You might hope in your heart—you might yearn—
To marry Penelope, the wife of Odysseus,
But after you've tried this bow and seen what it's like,   *165*
Go woo some other Achaean woman
And try to win her with your gifts. And Penelope
Should just marry the highest bidder,
The man who is fated to be her husband."

And he set the bow aside, propping it against   *170*
The polished, jointed door, and leaning the arrow
Against the beautiful latch. Then
He sat down on the chair from which he had risen.
And Antinous heaped contempt upon him:

"What kind of thing is that to say, Leodes?   *175*
I'm not going to stand here and listen to this.
You think this bow is going rob some young heroes
Of life, just because you can't string it?
The truth is your mother didn't bear a son
Strong enough to shoot arrows from bows.   *180*
But there are others who will string it soon enough."

Then Antinous called to Melanthius, the goatherd:

"Get over here and start a fire, Melanthius,
And set by it a bench with a fleece over it,
And bring out a tub of lard from the pantry,   *185*
So we can grease the bow, and warm it up.
Then maybe we can finish this contest."

He spoke, and Melanthius quickly rekindled the fire
And placed by it a bench covered with a fleece
And brought out from the pantry a tub of lard   *190*
With which the young men limbered up the bow—
But they still didn't have the strength to string it.

Only Antinous and godlike Eurymachus,
The suitors' ringleaders—and their strongest—
Were still left in the contest.

                    Meanwhile,   *195*
Two other men had risen and left the hall—
The cowherd and swineherd—and Odysseus himself
Went out, too. When the three of them
Were outside the gates, Odysseus said softly:

"Cowherd and swineherd, I've been wondering   *200*
If I should tell you what I'm about to tell you now.
Let me ask you this. What would you do
If Odysseus suddenly showed up here
Out of the blue, just like that?
Would you side with the suitors or Odysseus?   *205*
Tell me how you stand."

And the cattle herder answered him:

"Father Zeus, if only this would come true!
Let him come back. Let some god guide him.
Then you would see what these hands could do."   *210*

And Eumaeus prayed likewise to all the gods
That Odysseus would return.

                   When Odysseus
Was sure of both these men, he spoke to them again:

"I am back, right here in front of you.
After twenty hard years I have returned to my home.   *215*
I know that only you two of all my slaves
Truly want me back. I have heard
None of the others pray for my return.
So this is my promise to you. If a god
Beats these proud suitors down before me,   *220*
I will give you each a wife, property,
And a house built near mine. You two shall be
Friends to me and brothers to Telemachus.
And look, so you can be sure of who I am,
Here's a clear sign, that scar from the wound   *225*
I got from a boar's tusk when I went long ago
To Parnassus with the sons of Autolycus."

And he pulled his rags aside from the scar.
When the two men had examined it carefully,
They threw their arms around Odysseus and wept,   *230*
And kept kissing his head and shoulders in welcome.
Odysseus kissed their heads and hands,
And the sun would have gone down on their weeping,
Had not Odysseus stopped them, saying:

"No more weeping and wailing now. Someone might come   *235*
Out of the hall and see us and tell those inside.
We'll go back in now—not together, one at a time.
I'll go first, and then you. And here's what to watch for.
None of the suitors will allow the bow and quiver

To be given to me. It'll be up to you, Eumaeus,   240
To bring the bow over and place it in my hands.
Then tell the women to lock the doors to their hall,
And if they hear the sound of men groaning
Or being struck, tell them not to rush out
But to sit still and do their work in silence.   245
Philoetius, I want you to bar the courtyard gate
And secure it quickly with a piece of rope."

With this, Odysseus entered his great hall
And sat down on the chair from which he had risen.
Then the two herdsmen entered separately.   250

Eurymachus was turning the bow
Over and over in his hands, warming it
On this side and that by the fire, but even so
He was unable to string it. His pride hurt,
Shoulders sagging, he groaned and then swore: 255

"Damn it! It's not just myself I'm sorry for,
But for all of us—and not for the marriage either.
That hurts, but there are plenty of other women,
Some here in Ithaca, some in other cities.
No, it's that we fall so short of Odysseus'   260
Godlike strength. We can't even string his bow!
We'll be laughed at for generations to come!"

Antinous, son of Eupeithes, answered him:

"That'll never happen, Eurymachus,
And you know it. Now look, today is a holiday   265
Throughout the land, a sacred feast
In honor of Apollo, the Archer God.
This is no time to be bending bows.
So just set it quietly aside for now.
As for the axes, why don't we leave them   270
Just as they are? No one is going to come
Into Odysseus' hall and steal those axes.
Now let's have the cupbearer start us off
So we can forget about the bow

And pour libations. Come morning,   275
We'll have Melanthius bring along
The best she-goats in all the herds,
So we can lay prime thigh-pieces
On the altar of Apollo, the Archer God,
And then finish this business with the bow."   280

Antinous' proposal carried the day.
The heralds poured water over everyone's hands,
And boys filled the mixing bowls up to the brim
And served out the wine, first pouring
A few drops into each cup for libation.   285
When they had poured out their libations
And drunk as much as they wanted, Odysseus
Spoke among them, his heart full of cunning:

"Hear me, suitors of the glorious queen—
And I address Eurymachus most of all,   290
And godlike Antinous, since his speech
Was right on the mark when he said that for now
You should stop the contest and leave everything
Up to the gods. Tomorrow the Archer God
Will give the victory to whomever he chooses.   295
But come, let me have the polished bow.
I want to see, here in this hall with you,
If my grip is still strong, and if I still have
Any power left in these gnarled arms of mine,
Or if my hard traveling has have sapped all my strength."   300

They seethed with anger when they heard this,
Afraid that he would string the polished bow,
And Antinous addressed him contemptuously:

"You don't have an ounce of sense in you,
You miserable tramp. Isn't it enough   305
That we let you hang around with us,
Undisturbed, with a full share of the feast?
You even get to listen to what we say,
Which no other stranger, much less beggar, can do.
It's wine that's screwing you up, as it does   310

Anyone who guzzles it down. It was wine
That deluded the great centaur, Eurytion,
In the hall of Peirithous, the Lapith hero.
Eurytion got blind-drunk and in his madness
Did a terrible thing in Peirithous' house.   315
The enraged Lapiths sliced off his nose and ears
And dragged him outside, and Eurytion
Went off in a stupor, mutilated and muddled.
Men and centaurs have been at odds ever since.
Eurytion hurt himself because he got drunk.   320
And you're going to get hurt, too, I predict,
Hurt badly, if you string the bow. No one
In all the land will show you any kindness.
We'll send you off in a black ship to Echetus,
Who maims them all. You'll never get out alive.   325
So just be quiet and keep on drinking,
And don't challenge men who are younger than you."

It was Penelope who answered Antinous:

"It is not good, or just, Antinous,
To cheat any of Telemachus' guests   330
Who come to this house. Do you think
That if this stranger proves strong enough
To string Odysseus' bow, he will then
Lead me to his home and make me his wife?
I can't imagine that he harbors this hope.   335
So do not ruin your feast on that account.
The very idea is preposterous."

Eurymachus responded to this:

"Daughter of Icarius, wise Penelope,
Of course it's preposterous that this man   340
Would marry you. That's not what we're worried about.
But we are embarrassed at what men—and women—will say:
'A bunch of weaklings were wooing the wife
Of a man they couldn't touch—they couldn't even string
His polished bow. Then along came a vagrant   345
Who strung it easily and shot through the iron.'

That's what they'll say, to our lasting shame."

And Penelope, her eyes narrowing:

"Eurymachus, men who gobble up
The house of a prince cannot expect   *350*
To have a good reputation anywhere.
So there isn't any point in bringing up honor.
This stranger is a very well-built man
And says he is the son of a noble father.
So give him the bow and let us see what happens.   *355*
And here is my promise to all of you.
If Apollo gives this man the glory
And he strings the bow, I will clothe him
In a fine cloak and tunic, and give him
A javelin to ward off dogs and men,   *360*
And a double-edged sword, and sandals
For his feet, and I will give him passage
To wherever his heart desires."

This time it was Telemachus who answered:

"As for the bow, Mother, no man alive   *365*
Has a stronger claim than I do to give it
To whomever I want, or to deny it—
No, none of the lords on rocky Ithaca
Nor on the islands over toward Elis,
None of them could force his will upon me,   *370*
Not even if I wanted to give this bow
Outright, case and arrows and all,
As a gift to the stranger.
                          Go to your rooms,
Mother, and take care of your work,
Spinning and weaving, and have the maids do theirs.   *375*
This bow is men's business, and my business
Especially, since I am the master of this house."

Penelope was stunned and turned to go,
Her son's masterful words pressed to her heart.
She went up the stairs to her room with her women   *380*

And wept for Odysseus, her beloved husband,
Until grey-eyed Athena cast sleep on her eyelids.

Downstairs, the noble swineherd was carrying
The curved bow across the hall. The suitors
Were in an uproar, and one of them called out: 385

"Where do you think you're going with that bow,
You miserable swineherd? You're out of line.
Go back to your pigsties, where your own dogs
Will wolf you down—a nice, lonely death—
If Apollo and the other gods smile upon us."   390

Afraid, the swineherd stopped in his tracks
And set the bow down. Men were yelling at him
All through the hall, and now Telemachus weighed in:

"Keep going with the bow. You'll regret it
If you try to obey everyone. I may be   395
Younger than you, but I'll chase you back
Into the country with a shower of stones.
I am stronger than you. I wish I were as strong
When it came to the suitors. I'd throw more than one
Out of here in a sorry state. They're all up to no good."   400

This got the suitors laughing hilariously
At Telemachus. The tension in the room eased,
And the swineherd carried the bow
Across to Odysseus and put it in his hands.
Then he called Eurycleia aside and said: 405

"Telemachus says you should lock the doors to the hall,
And if the women hear the sound of men groaning
Or being struck, tell them not to rush out
But to sit still and do their work in silence."

Eumaeus' words sank in, and Eurycleia   410
Locked the doors to the crowded hall.

Meanwhile, Philoetius left without a word
And barred the gates to the fenced courtyard.

Beside the portico there lay a ship's hawser
Made of papyrus. Philoetius used this   415
To secure the gates, and then he went back in,
Sat down on the chair from which he had risen,
And kept his eyes on Odysseus.

He was handling the bow, turning it over and over
And testing its flex to make sure that worms   420
Had not eaten the horn in its master's absence.
The suitors glanced at each other
And started to make sarcastic remarks:

"Ha! A real connoisseur, an expert in bows!"

"He must have one just like it in a case at home."   425

"Or plans to make one just like it, to judge by the way
The masterful tramp keeps turning it in his hands."

"May he have as much success in life
As he'll have in trying to string that bow."

Thus the suitors, while Odysseus, deep in thought,   430
Was looking over his bow. And then, effortlessly,

> *Like a musician stretching a string*
> *Over a new peg on his lyre, and making*
> *The twisted sheep-gut fast at either end,*

Odysseus strung the great bow. Lifting it up,   435
He plucked the string, and it sang beautifully
Under his touch, with a note like a swallow's.
The suitors were aghast. The color drained
From their faces, and Zeus thundered loud,
Showing his portents and cheering the heart   440
Of the long-enduring, godlike Odysseus.
One arrow lay bare on the table. The rest,
Which the suitors were about to taste,
Were still in the quiver. Odysseus picked up
The arrow from the table and laid it upon   445

The bridge of the bow, and, still in his chair,
Drew the bowstring and the notched arrow back.
He took aim and let fly, and the bronze-tipped arrow
Passed clean through the holes of all twelve axeheads
From first to last. And he said to Telemachus: *450*

"Well, Telemachus, the guest in your hall
Has not disgraced you. I did not miss my target,
Nor did I take all day in stringing the bow.
I still have my strength, and I'm not as the suitors
Make me out to be in their taunts and jeers.   *455*
But now it is time to cook these men's supper,
While it is still light outside, and after that,
We'll need some entertainment—music and song—
The finishing touches for a perfect banquet."

He spoke, and lowered his brows. Telemachus,   *460*
The true son of godlike Odysseus, slung on
His sharp sword, seized his spear, and gleaming in bronze
Took his place by his father's side.

ODYSSEY 22

And now Odysseus' cunning was revealed.
He stripped off his rags and leapt with his bow
To the great threshold. Spreading the arrows
Out before his feet, he spoke to the suitors:

"Now that we've separated the men from the boys,   5
I'll see if I can hit a mark that no man
Has ever hit. Apollo grant me glory!"

As he spoke he took aim at Antinous,
Who at that moment was lifting to his lips
A golden cup—a fine, two-eared golden goblet—   10
And was just about to sip the wine. Bloodshed
Was the farthest thing from his mind.
They were at a banquet. Who would think
That one man, however strong, would take them all on
And so ensure his own death? Odysseus   15
Took dead aim at Antinous' throat and shot,
And the arrow punched all the way through
The soft neck tissue. Antinous fell to one side,
The cup dropped from his hands, and a jet
Of dark blood spurted from his nostrils.   20
He kicked the table as he went down,
Spilling the food on the floor, and the bread
And roast meat were fouled in the dust.
                                        The crowd
Burst into an uproar when they saw
Antinous go down. They jumped from their seats   25
And ran in a panic through the hall,

336

Scanning the walls for weapons—
A spear, a shield. But there were none to be had.
Odysseus listened to their angry jeers:

"You think you can shoot at men, you tramp?"   30

"That's your last contest—you're as good as dead!"

"You've killed the best young man in Ithaca!"

"Vultures will eat you on this very spot!"

They all assumed he had not shot to kill,
And had no idea how tightly the net   35
Had been drawn around them. Odysseus
Scowled at the whole lot of them, and said:

"You dogs! You thought I would never
Come home from Troy. So you wasted my house,
Forced the women to sleep with you,   40
And while I was still alive you courted my wife
Without any fear of the gods in high heaven
Or of any retribution from the world of men.
Now the net has been drawn tight around you."

At these words the color drained from their faces,   45
And they all looked around for a way to escape.
Only Eurymachus had anything to say:

"If you are really Odysseus of Ithaca,
Then what you say is just. The citizens
Have done many foolish things in this house   50
And many in the fields. But the man to blame
Lies here dead, Antinous. He started it all,
Not so much because he wanted a marriage
Or needed one, but for another purpose,
Which Zeus did not fulfill: he wanted to be king   55
In Ithaca, and to kill your son in ambush.
Now he's been killed, and he deserved it.
But spare your people. We will pay you back

For all we have eaten and drunk in your house.
We will make a collection; each man will put in   *60*
The worth of twenty oxen; we will make restitution
In bronze and gold until your heart is soothed.
Until then no one could blame you for being angry."

Odysseus fixed him with a stare and said:

"Eurymachus, not even if all of you   *65*
Gave me your entire family fortunes,
All that you have and ever will have,
Would I stay my hands from killing.
You courted my wife, and you will pay in full.
Your only choice now is to fight like men   *70*
Or run for it. Who knows, one or two of you
Might live to see another day. But I doubt it."

Their blood turned milky when they heard this.
Eurymachus now turned to them and said:

"Friends, this man is not going to stop at anything.   *75*
He's got his arrows and bow, and he'll shoot
From the threshold until he's killed us all.
We've got to fight back. Draw your swords
And use the tables as shields. If we charge him
In a mass and push him from the doorway   *80*
We can get reinforcements from town in no time.
Then this man will have shot his last shot."

With that, he drew his honed bronze sword
And charged Odysseus with an ear-splitting cry.
Odysseus in the same instant let loose an arrow   *85*
That entered his chest just beside the nipple
And spiked down to his liver. The sword fell
From Eurymachus' hand. He spun around
And fell on a table, knocking off dishes and cups,
And rolled to the ground, his forehead banging   *90*
Up and down against it and his feet kicking a chair
In his death throes, until the world went dark.

Amphinomus went for Odysseus next,
Rushing at him with his sword drawn,
Hoping to drive him away from the door.   95
Telemachus got the jump on him, though,
Driving a bronze-tipped spear into his back
Square between his shoulder blades
And through to his chest. He fell with a thud,
His forehead hammering into the ground.   100
Telemachus sprang back, leaving the spear
Right where it was, stuck in Amphinomus,
Fearing that if he tried to pull it out
Someone would rush him and cut him down
As he bent over the corpse. So he ran over   105
To his father's side, and his words flew fast:

"I'll bring you a shield, Father, two spears
And a bronze helmet—I'll find one that fits.
When I come back I'll arm myself
And the cowherd and swineherd. Better armed than not."   110

And Odysseus, the great tactician:

"Bring me what you can while I still have arrows
Or these men might drive me away from the door."

And Telemachus was off to the room
Where the weapons were stored. He took   115
Four shields, eight spears, and four bronze helmets
With thick horsehair plumes and brought them
Quickly to his father. Telemachus armed himself,
The two servants did likewise, and the three of them
Took their stand alongside the cunning warrior,   120
Odysseus. As long as the arrows held out
He kept picking off the suitors one by one,
And they fell thick as flies. But when the master archer
Ran out of arrows, he leaned the bow
Against the doorpost of the entrance hall   125
And slung a four-ply shield over his shoulder,
Put on his head a well-wrought helmet
With a plume that made his every nod a threat,

And took two spears tipped with heavy bronze.

Built into the higher wall of the main hall   *130*
Was a back door reached by a short flight of stairs
And leading to a passage closed by double doors.
Odysseus posted the swineherd at this doorway,
Which could be attacked by only one man at a time.
It was just then that Agelaus called to the suitors: *135*

"Let's one of us get up to the back door
And get word to the town. Act quickly
And this man will have shot his last."

But the goatherd Melanthius answered him:

"That won't work, Agelaus.   *140*
The door outside is too near the courtyard—
An easy shot from where he is standing—
And the passageway is dangerously narrow.
One good man could hold it against all of us.
Look, let me bring you weapons and armor   *145*
From the storeroom. That has to be where
Odysseus and his son have laid them away."

So saying, Melanthius clambered up
To Odysseus' storerooms. There he picked out
Twelve shields and as many spears and helmets   *150*
And brought them out quickly to give to the suitors.
Odysseus' heart sank, and his knees grew weak
When he saw the suitors putting on armor
And brandishing spears. This wasn't going to be easy.
His words flew out to Telemachus: *155*

"One of the women in the halls must be
Waging war against us—unless it's Melanthius."

And Telemachus, cool-headed under fire:

"No, it's my fault, Father, and no one else's.
I must have left the storeroom door open,   *160*

And one of them spotted it.
                    Eumaeus!
Go close the door to the storeroom,
And see whether one of the women is behind this,
Or Melanthius, son of Dolius, as I suspect."

As they were speaking, Melanthius the goatherd   *165*
Was making another trip to the storeroom
For more weapons. The swineherd spotted him
And was quick to point him out to Odysseus:

"There he goes, my lord Odysseus—
The sneak—just as we thought, on his way   *170*
To the storeroom! Tell me what to do.
Kill him if I prove to be the better man,
Or bring him to you, so he can pay in full
For all the wrongs he has done here in your house?"

Odysseus brought his mind to bear on this: *175*

"Telemachus and I will keep the suitors busy
In the hall here. Don't worry about that.
Tie him up. Bend his arms and legs behind him
And lash them to a board strapped onto his back.
Then hoist him up to the rafters in the store room   *180*
And leave him there to twist in the wind."

This was just what Eumaeus and the cowherd
Wanted to hear. Off they went to the storeroom,
Unseen by Melanthius, who was inside
Rooting around for armor and weapons.   *185*
They lay in wait on either side of the door,
And when Melanthius crossed the threshold,
Carrying a beautiful helmet in one hand
And in the other a broad old shield,
Flecked with rust—a shield the hero Laertes   *190*
Had carried in his youth but that had long since
Been laid aside with its straps unstitched—
Eumaeus and the cowherd Philoetius
Jumped him and dragged him by the hair

Back into the storeroom. They threw him   *195*
Hard to the ground, knocking the wind out of him,
And tied his hands and feet behind his back,
Making it hurt, as Odysseus had ordered.
Then they attached a rope to his body
And hoisted him up along the tall pillar   *200*
Until he was up by the rafters, and you,
Swineherd Eumaeus, you mocked him:

"Now you'll really be on watch, Melanthius,
The whole night through, lying on a feather bed—
Just your style—and you're sure to see   *205*
The early dawn come up from Ocean's streams,
Couched in gold, at the hour when you drive your goats
Up to the hall to make a feast for the suitors."

So Melanthius was left there, racked with pain,
While Eumaeus and the cowherd put on their armor,   *210*
Closed the polished door, and rejoined Odysseus,
The cunning warrior. So they took their stand
There on the threshold, breathing fury,
Four of them against the many who stood in the hall.

And then Athena was with them, Zeus' daughter   *215*
Looking just like Mentor and assuming his voice.
Odysseus, glad to see her, spoke these words:

"Mentor, old friend, help me out here.
Remember all the favors I've done for you.
We go back a long way, you and I."   *220*

He figured it was Athena, the soldier's goddess.
On the other side, the suitors yelled and shouted,
Agelaus' voice rising to rebuke Athena:

"You there, Mentor, don't let Odysseus
Talk you into helping him and fighting us.   *225*
This is the way I see it turning out.
When we have killed these men, father and son,
We'll kill you next for what you mean to do

In this hall. You'll pay with your life.
And when we've taken care of all five of you,   230
We'll take everything you have, Mentor,
Everything in your house and in your fields,
And add it to Odysseus' property.
We won't let your sons stay in your house
Or let your daughters or even your wife   235
Go about freely in the town of Ithaca."

This made Athena all the more angry,
And she turned on Odysseus and snapped at him:

"I can't believe, Odysseus, that you,
Of all people, have lost the guts you had   240
When you fought the Trojans for nine long years
To get Helen back, killing so many in combat
And coming up with the plan that took wide Troy.
How is it that now, when you've come home,
You get all teary-eyed about showing your strength   245
To this pack of suitors? Get over here
Next to me and see what I can do. I'll show you
What sort of man Mentor, son of Alcimus, is,
And how he repays favors in the heat of battle."

Athena spoke these words, but she did not yet   250
Give Odysseus the strength to turn the tide.
She was still testing him, and his glorious son,
To see what they were made of. As for herself,
The goddess flew up to the roofbeam
Of the smoky hall, just like a swallow.   255

The suitors were now rallied by Agelaus
And by Damastor, Eurynomus, and Amphimedon,
As well as by Demoptolemus and Peisander,
Son of Polyctor, and the warrior Polybus.
These were the best of the suitors lucky enough   260
To still be fighting for their lives. The rest
Had been laid low by the showers of arrows.
Agelaus now made this speech to them:

"He's had it now. Mentor's abandoned him
After all that hot air, and the four of them   265
Are left alone at the outer doors.
All right, now. Don't throw your spears all at once.
You six go first, and hope that Zeus allows
Odysseus to be hit and gives us the glory.
The others won't matter once he goes down."   270

They took his advice and gave it their best,
But Athena made their shots all come to nothing,
One man hitting the doorpost, another the door,
Another's bronze-tipped ash spear sticking
Into the wall. Odysseus and his men   275
Weren't even nicked, and the great hero said to them:

"It's our turn now. I say we throw our spears
Right into the crowd. These bastards mean to kill us
On top of everything else they've done to wrong me."

He spoke, and they all threw their sharp spears   280
With deadly aim. Odysseus hit Demoptolemus;
Telemachus got Euryades; the swineherd, Elatus;
And the cattle herder took out Peisander.
They all bit the dirt at the same moment,
And the suitors retreated to the back of the hall,   285
Allowing Odysseus and his men to run out
And pull their spears from the dead men's bodies.

The suitors rallied for another volley,
Throwing their sharp spears with all they had.
This time Athena made most of them miss,   290
One man hitting the doorpost, another the door,
Another's bronze-tipped ash spear sticking
Into the wall. But Amphimedon's spear
Grazed Telemachus' wrist, breaking the skin,
And Ctessipus' spear clipped Eumaeus' shoulder   295
As it sailed over his shield and kept on going
Until it hit the ground. Then Odysseus and his men
Got off another round into the throng,
Odysseus, sacker of cities, hitting Eurydamas;

Telemachus getting Amphimedon; the swineherd, Polybus;   *300*
And lastly the cattle herder striking Ctessipus
Square in the chest. And he crowed over him:

"Always picking a fight, just like your father.
Well, you can stop all your big talk now.
We'll let the gods have the last word this time.   *305*
Take this spear as your host's gift, fair exchange
For the hoof you threw at godlike Odysseus
When he made his rounds begging in the hall."

Thus the herder of the spiral-horned cattle.

Odysseus, meanwhile, had skewered Damastor's son   *310*
With a hard spear-thrust in hand-to-hand fighting,
And Telemachus killed Leocritus, Evenor's son,
Piercing him in the groin and driving his bronze spear
All the way through. Leocritus pitched forward,
His forehead slamming onto the ground.

                            Only then   *315*
Did Athena hold up her overpowering aegis
From her high perch, and the minds of the suitors
Shriveled with fear, and they fled through the hall

> *Like a herd of cattle that an iridescent gadfly*
> *Goads along on a warm spring afternoon,*   *320*

With Odysseus and his men after them

> *Like vultures with crooked talons and hooked beaks*
> *Descending from the mountains upon a flock*
> *Of smaller birds, who fly low under the clouds*
> *And over the plain. The vultures swoop down*   *325*
> *To pick them off; the smaller birds cannot escape,*
> *And men thrill to see the chase in the sky.*

Odysseus and his cohorts were clubbing the suitors
Right and left all through the hall; horrible groans
Rose from their lips as their heads were smashed in,   *330*
And the floor of the great hall smoked with blood.

It was then that Leodes, the soothsayer, rushed forward,
Clasped Odysseus' knees, and begged for his life:

"By your knees, Odysseus, respect me
And pity me. I swear I have never said or done   *335*
Anything wrong to any woman in your house.
I tried to stop the suitors when they did such things,
But they wouldn't listen, wouldn't keep their hands clean,
And now they've paid a cruel price for their sins.
And I, their soothsayer, who have done no wrong,   *340*
Will be laid low with them. That's the gratitude I get."

Odysseus scowled down at the man and said:

"If you are really their soothsayer, as you boast you are,
How many times must you have prayed in the halls
That my sweet homecoming would never come,   *345*
And that you would be the one my wife would go off with
And bear children to! You're a dead man."

As he spoke his strong hand reached for a sword
That lay nearby—a sword Agelaus had dropped
When he was killed. The soothsayer was struck   *350*
Full in the neck. His lips were still forming words
When his lopped head rolled in the dust.

All this while the bard, Phemius, was busy
Trying not to be killed. This man, Terpes' son,
Sang for the suitors under compulsion.   *355*
He stood now with his pure-toned lyre
Near the high back door, trying to decide
Whether he should slip out from the hall
And crouch at the altar of Zeus of the Courtyard—
The great altar on which Laertes and Odysseus   *360*
Had burned many an ox's thigh—
Or whether he should rush forward
And supplicate Odysseus by his knees.
Better to fall at the man's knees, he thought.
So he laid the hollow lyre on the ground   *365*
Between the wine-bowl and silver-studded chair

And ran up to Odysseus and clasped his knees.
His words flew up to Odysseus like birds:

"By your knees, Odysseus, respect me
And pity me. You will regret it someday   *370*
If you kill a bard—me—who sings for gods and men.
I am self-taught, and a god has planted in my heart
All sorts of songs and stories, and I can sing to you
As to a god. So don't be too eager
To slit my throat. Telemachus will tell you   *375*
That I didn't come to your house by choice
To entertain the suitors at their feasts.
There were too many of them; they made me come."

Telemachus heard him and said to his father:

"He's innocent; don't kill him.   *380*
And let's spare the herald, Medon,
Who used to take care of me when I was a child,
If Philoetius hasn't already killed him—
Or the swineherd—or if he didn't run into you
As you were charging through the house."   *385*

Medon heard what Telemachus said.
He was under a chair, wrapped in an oxhide,
Cowering from death. Now he jumped up,
Stripped off the oxhide, ran to Telemachus
And fell at his knees. His words rose on wings: *390*

"I'm here, Telemachus! Hold back, and ask your father
To hold back too, or he might kill me with cold bronze,
Strong as he is and as mad as he is at the suitors,
Who ate away his house and paid you no honor."

Odysseus smiled at this and said to him: *395*

"Don't worry, he's saved you. Now you know,
And you can tell the world, how much better
Good deeds are than evil. Go outside, now,
You and the singer, and sit in the yard

Away from the slaughter, until I finish   *400*
Everything I have to do inside the house."

So he spoke, and the two went out of the hall
And sat down by the altar of great Zeus,
Wide-eyed and expecting death at any moment.
Odysseus, too, had his eyes wide open,   *405*
Looking all through his house to see if anyone
Was still alive and hiding from death.
But everyone he saw lay in the blood and dust,
The whole lot of them,

> *like fish that fishermen*
> *Have drawn up in nets from the grey sea*   *410*
> *Onto the curved shore. They lie all in heaps*
> *On the sand beach, longing for the salt waves,*
> *And the blazing sun drains their life away.*

So too the suitors, lying in heaps.

Then Odysseus called to Telemachus: *415*

"Go call the nurse Eurycleia for me.
I want to tell her something."

> So Telemachus went
To Eurycleia's room, rattled the door, and called:

"Get up and come out here, old woman—you
Who are in charge of all our women servants.   *420*
Come on. My father has something to say to you."

Eurycleia's response died on her lips.
She opened the doors to the great hall,
Came out, and followed Telemachus
To where Odysseus, spattered with blood and grime
Stood among the bodies of the slain.   *425*

> *A lion that has just fed upon an ox in a field*
> *Has his chest and cheeks smeared with blood,*
> *And his face is terrible to look upon.*

So too Odysseus,
Smeared with gore from head to foot.

When Eurycleia   *430*
Saw all the corpses and the pools of blood,
She lifted her head to cry out in triumph—
But Odysseus stopped her cold,
Reining her in with these words:

"Rejoice in your heart, but do not cry aloud.   *435*
It is unholy to gloat over the slain. These men
Have been destroyed by divine destiny
And their own recklessness. They honored no one,
Rich or poor, high or low, who came to them.
And so by their folly they have brought upon themselves   *440*
An ugly fate.
                Now tell me, which of the women
Dishonor me and which are innocent?"

And Eurycleia, the loyal nurse:

"Yes indeed, child, I will tell you all.
There are fifty women in your house,   *445*
Servants we have taught to do their work,
To card wool and bear all the drudgery.
Of these, twelve have shamed this house
And respect neither me nor Penelope herself.
Telemachus has only now become a man,   *450*
And his mother has not allowed him
To direct the women servants.
                        May I go now
To the upstairs room and tell your wife?
Some god has wrapped her up in sleep."

Odysseus, his mind teeming, answered her: *455*

"Don't wake her yet. First bring those women
Who have acted so disgracefully."

While the old woman went out through the hall
To tell the women the news—and to summon twelve—

Odysseus called Telemachus and the two herdsmen   *460*
And spoke to them words fletched like arrows:

"Start carrying out the bodies,
And have the women help you.
                              Then sponge down
All of the beautiful tables and chairs.
When you have set the whole house in order,   *465*
Take the women outside between the round house
And the courtyard fence. Slash them with your swords
Until they have forgotten their secret lovemaking
With the suitors. Then finish them off."

Thus Odysseus, and the women came in,   *470*
Huddled together and shedding salt tears.
First they carried out the dead bodies
And set them down under the courtyard's portico,
Propping them against each other. Odysseus himself
Kept them at it. Then he had them sponge down   *475*
All of the beautiful tables and chairs.
Telemachus, the swineherd, and the cowherd
Scraped the floor with hoes, and the women
Carried out the scrapings and threw them away.
When they had set the whole house in order,   *480*
They took the women out between the round house
And the courtyard fence, penning them in
With no way to escape. And Telemachus,
In his cool-headed way, said to the others:

"I won't allow a clean death for these women—   *485*
The suitors' sluts—who have heaped reproaches
Upon my own head and upon my mother's."

He spoke, and tied the cable of a dark-prowed ship
To a great pillar and pulled it about the round house,
Stretching it high so their feet couldn't touch the ground.   *490*

   Long-winged thrushes, or doves, making their way
   To their roosts, fall into a snare set in a thicket,
   And the bed that receives them is far from welcome.

So too these women, their heads hanging in a row,
The cable looped around each of their necks. *495*
It was a most piteous death. Their feet fluttered
For a little while, but not for long.

Then they brought Melanthius outside,
And in their fury they sliced off
His nose and ears with cold bronze
And pulled his genitals out by the root— *500*
Raw meat for the dogs—and chopped off
His hands and feet.

                    This done,
They washed their own hands and feet
And went back into their master's great hall. *505*

Then Odysseus said to Eurycleia:

"Bring me sulfur, old woman, and fire,
So that I can fumigate the hall.
And go tell Penelope to come down here,
And all of the women in the house as well." *510*

And Eurycleia, the faithful nurse:

"As you say, child. But first let me bring you
A tunic and a cloak for you to put on.
You should not be standing here like this
With rags on your body. It's not right." *515*

Odysseus, his mind teeming, answered her:

"First make a fire for me here in the hall."

He spoke, and Eurycleia did as she was told.
She brought fire and sulfur, and Odysseus
Purified his house, the halls and the courtyard. *520*

Then the old nurse went through Odysseus'
Beautiful house, telling the women the news.

They came from their hall with torches in their hands
And thronged around Odysseus and embraced him.
And as they kissed his head and shoulders and hands   525
He felt a sudden, sweet urge to weep,
For in his heart he knew them all.

ODYSSEY 23

The old woman laughed as she went upstairs
To tell her mistress that her husband was home.
She ran up the steps, lifting her knees high,
And, bending over Penelope, she said:

"Wake up, dear child, so you can see for yourself   5
What you have yearned for day in and day out.
Odysseus has come home, after all this time,
And has killed those men who tried to marry you
And who ravaged your house and bullied your son."

And Penelope, alert now and wary: 10

"Dear nurse, the gods have driven you crazy.
The gods can make even the wise mad,
Just as they often make the foolish wise.
Now they have wrecked your usually sound mind.
Why do you mock me and my sorrowful heart,   15
Waking me from sleep to tell me this nonsense—
And such a sweet sleep. It sealed my eyelids.
I haven't slept like that since the day Odysseus
Left for Ilion—that accursed city.
Now go back down to the hall.   20
If any of the others had told me this
And wakened me from sleep, I would have
Sent her back with something to be sorry about!
You can thank your old age for this at least."

And Eurycleia, the loyal nurse: 25

"I am not mocking you, child. Odysseus
Really is here. He's come home, just as I say.
He's the stranger they all insulted in the great hall.
Telemachus has known all along, but had
The self-control to hide his father's plans   30
Until he could pay the arrogant bastards back."

Penelope felt a sudden pang of joy. She leapt
From her bed and flung her arms around the old woman,
And with tears in her eyes she said to her:

"Dear nurse, if it is true, if he really has   35
Come back to his house, tell me how
He laid his hands on the shameless suitors,
One man alone against all of that mob."

Eurycleia answered her:

"I didn't see and didn't ask. I only heard the groaning   40
Of men being killed. We women sat
In the far corner of our quarters, trembling,
With the good solid doors bolted shut
Until your son came from the hall to call me,
Telemachus. His father had sent him to call me.   45
And there he was, Odysseus, standing
In a sea of dead bodies, all piled
On top of each other on the hard-packed floor.
It would have warmed your heart to see him,
Spattered with blood and filth like a lion.   50
And now the bodies are all gathered together
At the gates, and he is purifying the house
With sulfur, and has built a great fire,
And has sent me to call you. Come with me now
So that both your hearts can be happy again.   55
You have suffered so much, but now
Your long desire has been fulfilled.
He has come himself, alive, to his own hearth,
And has found you and his son in the hall.
As for the suitors, who did him wrong,   60
He's taken his revenge on every last man."

And Penelope, ever cautious:

"Dear nurse, don't gloat over them yet.
You know how welcome the sight of him
Would be to us all, and especially to me   65
And the son he and I bore. But this story
Can't be true, not the way you tell it.
One of the immortals must have killed the suitors,
Angry at their arrogance and evil deeds.
They respected no man, good or bad,   70
So their blind folly has killed them. But Odysseus
Is lost, lost to us here, and gone forever."

And Eurycleia, the faithful nurse:

"Child, how can you say this? Your husband
Is here at his own fireside, and yet you are sure   75
He will never come home! Always on guard!
But here's something else, clear proof:
The scar he got from the tusk of that boar.
I noticed it when I was washing his feet
And wanted to tell you, but he shrewdly clamped   80
His hand on my mouth and wouldn't let me speak.
Just come with me, and I will stake my life on it.
If I am lying you can torture me to death."

Still wary, Penelope replied:

"Dear nurse, it is hard for you to comprehend   85
The ways of the eternal gods, wise as you are.
Still, let us go to my son, so that I may see
The suitors dead and the man who killed them."

And Penelope descended the stairs, her heart
In turmoil. Should she hold back and question   90
Her husband? Or should she go up to him,
Embrace him, and kiss his hands and head?
She entered the hall, crossing the stone threshold,
And sat opposite Odysseus, in the firelight
Beside the farther wall. He sat by a column,   95

Looking down, waiting to see if his incomparable wife
Would say anything to him when she saw him.
She sat a long time in silence, wondering.
She would look at his face and see her husband,
But then fail to know him in his dirty rags.   *100*
Telemachus couldn't take it any more:

"Mother, how can you be so hard,
Holding back like that? Why don't you sit
Next to father and talk to him, ask him things?
No other woman would have the heart   *105*
To stand off from her husband who has come back
After twenty hard years to his country and home.
But your heart is always colder than stone."

And Penelope, cautious as ever:

"My child, I am lost in wonder   *110*
And unable to speak or ask a question
Or look him in the eyes. If he really is
Odysseus come home, the two of us
Will be sure of each other, very sure.
There are secrets between us no one else knows."   *115*

Odysseus, who had borne much, smiled,
And his words flew to his son on wings:

"Telemachus, let your mother test me
In our hall. She will soon see more clearly.
Now, because I am dirty and wearing rags,   *120*
She is not ready to acknowledge who I am.
But you and I have to devise a plan.
When someone kills just one man,
Even a man who has few to avenge him,
He goes into exile, leaving country and kin.   *125*
Well, we have killed a city of young men,
The flower of Ithaca. Think about that."

And Telemachus, in his clear-headed way:

"You should think about it, Father. They say
No man alive can match you for cunning.   *130*
We'll follow you for all we are worth,
And I don't think we'll fail for lack of courage."

And Odysseus, the master strategist:

"Well, this is what I think we should do.
First, bathe yourselves and put on clean tunics   *135*
And tell the women to choose thir clothes well.
Then have the singer pick up his lyre
And lead everyone in a lively dance tune,
Loud and clear. Anyone who hears the sound,
A passerby or neighbor, will think it's a wedding,   *140*
And so word of the suitors' killing won't spread
Down through the town before we can reach
Our woodland farm. Once there we'll see
What kind of luck the Olympian gives us."

They did as he said. The men bathed   *145*
And put on tunics, and the women dressed up.
The godlike singer, sweeping his hollow lyre,
Put a song in their hearts and made their feet move,
And the great hall resounded under the tread
Of men and silken-waisted women dancing.   *150*
And people outside would hear it and say:

"Well, someone has finally married the queen,
Fickle woman. Couldn't bear to keep the house
For her true husband until he came back."

But they had no idea how things actually stood.   *155*

Odysseus, meanwhile, was being bathed
By the housekeeper, Eurynome. She
Rubbed him with olive oil and threw about him
A beautiful cloak and tunic. And Athena
Shed beauty upon him, and made him look   *160*
Taller and more muscled, and made his hair
Tumble down his head like hyacinth flowers.

Imagine a craftsman overlaying silver
With pure gold. He has learned his art
From Pallas Athena and Lord Hephaestus,   *165*
And creates works of breathtaking beauty.

So Athena herself made his head and shoulders
Shimmer with grace. He came from the bath
Like a god, and sat down on the chair again
Opposite his wife, and spoke to her and said: *170*

"You're a mysterious woman.
                    The gods
Have given to you, more than to any
Other woman, an unyielding heart.
No other woman would be able to endure
Standing off from her husband, come back   *175*
After twenty hard years to his country and home.
Nurse, make up a bed for me so I can lie down
Alone, since her heart is a cold lump of iron."

And Penelope, cautious and wary:

"You're a mysterious man.
                    I am not being proud   *180*
Or scornful, nor am I bewildered—not at all.
I know very well what you looked like
When you left Ithaca on your long-oared ship.
Nurse, bring the bed out from the master bedroom,
The bedstead he made himself, and spread it for him   *185*
With fleeces and blankets and silky coverlets."

She was testing her husband.
                    Odysseus
Could bear no more, and he cried out to his wife:

"By God, woman, now you've cut deep.
Who moved my bed? It would be hard   *190*
For anyone, no matter how skilled, to move it.
A god could come down and move it easily,
But not a man alive, however young and strong,

Could ever pry it up. There's something telling
About how that bed's built, and no one else   *195*
Built it but me.
         There was an olive tree
Growing on the site, long-leaved and full,
Its trunk thick as a post. I built my bedroom
Around that tree, and when I had finished
The masonry walls and done the roofing   *200*
And set in the jointed, close-fitting doors,
I lopped off all of the olive's branches,
Trimmed the trunk from the root on up,
And rounded it and trued it with an adze until
I had myself a bedpost. I bored it with an auger,   *205*
And starting from this I framed up the whole bed,
Inlaying it with gold and silver and ivory
And stretching across it oxhide thongs dyed purple.
So there's our secret. But I do not know, woman,
Whether my bed is still firmly in place, or if   *210*
Some other man has cut through the olive's trunk."

At this, Penelope finally let go.
Odysseus had shown he knew their old secret.
In tears, she ran straight to him, threw her arms
Around him, kissed his face, and said: *215*

"Don't be angry with me, Odysseus. You,
Of all men, know how the world goes.
It is the gods who gave us sorrow, the gods
Who begrudged us a life together, enjoying
Our youth and arriving side by side   *220*
To the threshold of old age. Don't hold it against me
That when I first saw you I didn't welcome you
As I do now. My heart has been cold with fear
That an imposter would come and deceive me.
There are many who scheme for ill-gotten gains.   *225*
Not even Helen, daughter of Zeus,
Would have slept with a foreigner had she known
The Greeks would go to war to bring her back home.
It was a god who drove her to that dreadful act,
Or she never would have thought of doing what she did, *230*

The horror that brought suffering to us as well.
But now, since you have confirmed the secret
Of our marriage bed, which no one has ever seen—
Only you and I and a single servant, Actor's daughter,
Whom my father gave me before I ever came here   *235*
And who kept the doors of our bridal chamber—
You have persuaded even my stubborn heart."

This brought tears from deep within him,
And as he wept he clung to his beloved wife.

> *Land is a welcome sight to men swimming*   *240*
> *For their lives, after Poseidon has smashed their ship*
> *In heavy seas. Only a few of them escape*
> *And make it to shore. They come out*
> *Of the grey water crusted with brine, glad*
> *To be alive and set foot on dry land.*   *245*

So welcome a sight was her husband to her.
She would not loosen her white arms from his neck,
And rose-fingered Dawn would have risen
On their weeping, had not Athena stepped in
And held back the long night at the end of its course   *250*
And stopped gold-stitched Dawn at Ocean's shores
From yoking the horses that bring light to men,
Lampus and Phaethon, the colts of Dawn.

Then Odysseus said to his wife:

"We have not yet come to the end of our trials.   *255*
There is still a long, hard task for me to complete,
As the spirit of Tiresias foretold to me
On the day I went down to the house of Hades
To ask him about my companions' return
And my own. But come to bed now,   *260*
And we'll close our eyes in the pleasure of sleep."

And Penelope calmly answered him:

"Your bed is ready for you whenever

You want it, now that the gods have brought you
Home to your family and native land.   265
But since you've brought it up, tell me
About this trial. I'll learn about it soon enough,
And it won't be any worse to hear it now."

And Odysseus, his mind teeming:

"You are a mystery to me. Why do you insist   270
I tell you now? Well, here's the whole story.
It's not a tale you will enjoy, and I have no joy
In telling it.
                   Tiresias told me that I must go
To city after city carrying a broad-bladed oar,
Until I come to men who know nothing of the sea,   275
Who eat their food unsalted, and have never seen
Red-prowed ships or the oars that wing them along.
And he told me that I would know I had found them
When I met another traveler who thought
The oar I was carrying was a winnowing fan.   280
Then I must fix my oar in the earth
And offer sacrifice to Lord Poseidon,
A ram, a bull, and a boar in its prime.
Then at last I am to come home and offer
Grand sacrifice to the immortal gods   285
Who hold high heaven, to each in turn.
And death shall come to me from the sea,
As gentle as this touch, and take me off
When I am worn out in sleek old age,
With my people prosperous around me.   290
All this Tiresias said would come true."

Then Penelope, watching him, answered:

"If the gods are going to grant you a happy old age,
There is hope your troubles will someday be over."

While they spoke to one another,   295
Eurynome and the nurse made the bed
By torchlight, spreading it with soft coverlets.

Then the old nurse went to her room to lie down,
And Eurynome, who kept the bedroom,
Led the couple to their bed, lighting the way.   *300*
When she had led them in, she withdrew,
And they went with joy to their bed
And to their rituals of old.

      Telemachus and his men
Stopped dancing, stopped the women's dance,
And lay down to sleep in the shadowy halls.   *305*

After Odysseus and Penelope
Had made sweet love, they took turns
Telling stories to each other. She told him
All that she had to endure as the fair lady
In the palace, looking upon the loathsome throng   *310*
Of suitors, who used her as an excuse
To kill many cattle, whole flocks of sheep,
And to empty the cellar of much of its wine.
Odysseus told her of all the suffering
He had brought upon others, and of all the pain   *315*
He endured himself. She loved listening to him
And did not fall asleep until he had told the whole tale.

He began with how he overcame the Cicones
And then came to the land of the Lotus-Eaters,
And all that the Cyclops did, and how he   *320*
Paid him back for eating his comrades.
Then how he came to Aeolus,
Who welcomed him and sent him on his way,
But since it was not his destiny to return home then,
The stormwinds grabbed him and swept him off   *325*
Groaning deeply over the teeming saltwater.
Then how he came to the Laestrygonians,
Who destroyed his ships and all their crews,
Leaving him with only one black-tarred hull.
Then all of Circe's tricks and wiles,   *330*
And how he sailed to the dank house of Hades
To consult the spirit of Theban Tiresias
And saw his old comrades there

And his aged mother who nursed him as a child.
Then how he heard the Sirens' eternal song,   335
And came to the Clashing Rocks,
And dread Charybdis and Scylla,
Whom no man had ever escaped before.
Then how his crew killed the cattle of the Sun,
And how Zeus, the high lord of thunder,   340
Slivered his ship with lightning, and all his men
Went down, and he alone survived.
And he told her how he came to Ogygia,
The island of the nymph Calypso,
Who kept him there in her scalloped caves,   345
Yearning for him to be her husband,
And how she took care of him, and promised
To make him immortal and ageless all his days
But did not persuade the heart in his breast.
Then how he crawled out of the sea in Phaeacia,   350
And how the Phaeacians honored him like a god
And sent him on a ship to his own native land
With gifts of bronze and clothing and gold.

He told the story all the way through,
And then sleep, which slackens our bodies,   355
Fell upon him and released him from care.

The Grey-eyed One knew what to do next.
When she felt that Odysseus was satisfied
With sleep and with lying next to his wife,
She roused the slumbering, golden Dawn,   360
Who climbed from Ocean with light for the world.
Odysseus got up from his rose-shadowed bed
And turned to Penelope with these instructions:

"My wife, we've had our fill of trials now,
You here, weeping over all the troubles   365
My absence caused, and I, bound by Zeus
To suffer far from the home I yearned for.
Now that we have both come to the bed
We have long desired, you must take charge
Of all that is mine in the house, while I   370

See to replenishing the flocks and herds
The insolent suitors have depleted.
I'll get some back on raids, some as tribute,
Until the pens are full again. But now,
I want you to know I am going to our farm   *375*
To see my father, who has suffered terribly
On my account. You don't need me to tell you
That when the sun rises the news will spread
That I have killed the suitors in our hall. So,
Go upstairs with your women and sit quietly.   *380*
Don't look outside or speak to anyone."

Odysseus spoke and put on his beautiful armor.
He woke Telemachus, and the cowherd
And swineherd, and had them arm also.
They strapped on their bronze, opened the doors   *385*
And went out, Odysseus leading the way.
It was light by now, but Athena hid them
In darkness, and spirited them out of the city.

ODYSSEY 24

Hermes, meanwhile, was calling forth
The ghosts of the suitors. He held the wand
He uses to charm mortal eyes to sleep
And make sleepers awake; and with this beautiful,
Golden wand he marshaled the ghosts,   5
Who followed along squeaking and gibbering.

> *Bats deep inside an eerie cave*
> *Flit and gibber when one of them falls*
> *From the cluster clinging to the rock overhead.*

So too these ghosts, as Hermes led them   10
Down the cold, dank ways, past
The streams of Ocean, past the White Rock,
Past the Gates of the Sun and the Land of Dreams,
Until they came to the Meadow of Asphodel,
Where the spirits of the dead dwell, phantoms   15
Of men outworn.

                Here was the ghost of Achilles,
And those of Patroclus, of flawless Antilochus,
And of Ajax, the best of the Achaeans
After Achilles, Peleus' incomparable son.
These ghosts gathered around Achilles   20
And were joined by the ghost of Agamemnon,
Son of Atreus, grieving, he himself surrounded
By the ghosts of those who had died with him
And met their fate in the house of Aegisthus.
The son of Peleus was the first to greet him: 25

"Son of Atreus, we believed that you of all heroes
Were dear to thundering Zeus your whole life through,
For you were the lord of the great army at Troy,
Where we Greeks endured a bitter campaign.
But you too had an early rendezvous with death,   30
Which no man can escape once he is born.
How much better to have died at Troy
With all the honor you commanded there!
The entire Greek army would have raised you a tomb,
And you would have won glory for your son as well.   35
As it was, you were doomed to a most pitiable death."

And the ghost of Agamemnon answered:

"Godlike Achilles, you did have the good fortune
To die in Troy, far from Argos. Around you fell
Some of the best Greeks and Trojans of their time,   40
Fighting for your body, as you lay there
In the howling dust of war, one of the great,
Your horsemanship forgotten. We fought all day
And would never have stopped, had not Zeus
Halted us with a great storm. Then we bore your body   45
Back to the ships and laid it on a bier, and cleansed
Your beautiful flesh with warm water and ointments,
And the men shed many hot tears and cut their hair.
Then your mother heard, and she came from the sea
With her saltwater women, and an eerie cry   50
Rose over the deep. The troops panicked,
And they would have run for the ships, had not
A man who was wise in the old ways stopped them,
Nestor, whose counsel had prevailed before.
Full of concern, he called out to the troops: 55

'Argives and Achaeans, halt! This is no time to flee.
It is his mother, with her immortal nymphs,
Come from the sea to mourn her dead son.'

"When he said that the troops settled down.
Then the daughters of the Old Man of the Sea   60
Stood all around you and wailed piteously,

And they dressed you in immortal clothing.
And the Muses, all nine, chanted the dirge,
Singing responsively in beautiful voices.
You couldn't have seen a dry eye in the army,   65
So poignant was the song of the Muses.
For seventeen days we mourned you like that,
Men and gods together. On the eighteenth day
We gave you to the fire, slaughtering sheep
And horned cattle around you. You were burned   70
In the clothing of the gods, with rich unguents
And sweet honey, and many Greek heroes
Paraded in arms around your burning pyre,
Both infantry and charioteers,
And the sound of their marching rose to heaven.   75
When the fire had consumed you,
We gathered your white bones at dawn, Achilles,
And laid them in unmixed wine and unguents.
Your mother had given us a golden urn,
A gift of Dionysus, she said, made by Hephaestus.   80
In this urn lie your white bones, Achilles,
Mingled with those of the dead Patroclus.
Just apart lie the bones of Antilochus
Whom you honored most after Patroclus died.
Over them all we spearmen of the great army   85
Heaped an immense and perfect barrow
On a headland beside the broad Hellespont
So that it might be seen from far out at sea
By men now and men to come.
                                    Your mother, Thetis,
Had collected beautiful prizes from the gods   90
And now set them down in the middle of the field
To honor the best of the Achaean athletes.
You have been to many heroes' funeral games
Where young men contend for prizes,
But you would have marveled at the sight   95
Of the beautiful prizes silver-footed Thetis
Set out for you. You were very dear to the gods.
Not even in death have you lost your name,
Achilles, nor your honor among men.
But what did I get for winding up the war?   100

Zeus worked out for me a ghastly death
At the hands of Aegisthus and my murderous wife."

As these two heroes talked with each other,
Quicksilver Hermes was leading down
The ghosts of the suitors killed by Odysseus.   *105*
When Hermes and these ghosts drew near,
The two heroes were amazed and went up to see
Who they were. The ghost of Agamemnon
Recognized one of them, Amphimedon,
Who had been his host in Ithaca, and called out: *110*

"Amphimedon! Why have you come down
Beneath the dark earth, you and your company,
All men of rank, all the same age? It's as if
Someone had hand-picked the city's best men.
Did Poseidon sink your ships and drown you   *115*
In the wind-whipped waves? Was it that, or
Did an enemy destroy you on land
As you cut off their cattle and flocks of sheep—
Or as they fought for their city and women?
Tell me. Remember who is asking—   *120*
An old friend of your house. I came there
With godlike Menelaus to urge Odysseus
To sail with the fleet to Ilion. A full month
That journey to Ithaca took us—hard work
Persuading Odysseus, destroyer of cities."   *125*

The ghost of Amphimedon responded:

"Son of Atreus, most glorious Agamemnon,
I remember all that, just as you tell it,
And I will tell you exactly what happened to us,
And how it ended in our bitter death.   *130*
We were courting the wife of Odysseus,
Long gone by then. She loathed the thought
Of remarrying, but she wouldn't give us a yes or no.
Her mind was bent on death and darkness for us.
Here is one of the tricks she dreamed up: *135*
She set up a loom in the hall and started weaving—

A huge, fine-threaded piece—and then came out and said:

'Young men—my suitors, since Odysseus is dead—
Eager as you are to marry me, you must wait
Until I finish this robe—it would be a shame   140
To waste my spinning—a shroud for the hero
Laertes, when death's doom lays him low.
I fear the Achaean women would reproach me
If he should lie shroudless for all his wealth.'

"We went along with this appeal to our honor.   145
Every day she would weave at the great loom,
And every night she would unweave by torchlight.
She fooled us for three years with her craft.
But in the fourth year, as the seasons rolled by,
And the moons waned, and the days dragged on,   150
One of her women who knew all about it
Told us, and we caught her unweaving
The gloried shroud. Then we forced her to finish it.
When it was done she washed it and showed it to us,
And it shone like the sun or the moon.
                                        It was then   155
That some evil spirit brought Odysseus
From who knows where to the border of his land,
Where the swineherd lived. Odysseus' son
Put in from Pylos in his black ship and joined him.
These two, after they had plotted an ugly death   160
For the suitors, came up to the town, first Telemachus
And then later Odysseus, led by the swineherd,
Who brought his master wearing tattered clothes,
Looking for all the world like a miserable old beggar,
Leaning on a staff, his rags hanging off him.   165
None of us could know who he was, not even
The older men, when he showed up like that.
We threw things at him and gave him a hard time.
He just took it, pelted and taunted in his own house,
Until, prompted by Zeus, he and Telemachus   170
Removed all the weapons from the hall
And locked them away in a storeroom.
Then he showed all his cunning. He told his wife

To set before the suitors his bow and grey iron—
Implements for a contest, and for our ill-fated death.   *175*
None of us were able to string that bow.
We couldn't even come close. When it came
Around to Odysseus, we cried out and objected,
'Don't give the bow to that beggar,
No matter what he says!' Telemachus alone   *180*
Urged him on and encouraged him to take it.
And he did. The great Odysseus
Took the bow, strung it easily, and shot an arrow
Straight through the iron. Then he stood on the threshold,
Poured the arrows out, and glaring around him   *185*
He shot Lord Antinous. And then he shot others,
With perfect aim, and we fell thick and fast.
You could see that some god was helping them,
The way they raged through the hall, cutting us down
Right and left; and you could hear   *190*
The hideous groans of men as their heads
Were bashed in. The floor smoked with blood.
        That's how we died, Agamemnon. Our bodies
Still lie uncared for in Odysseus' halls.
Word has not yet reached our friends and family,   *195*
Who could wash the black blood from our wounds
And lay us out with wailing, as is due the dead."

And the ghost of Agamemnon responded:

"Well done, Odysseus, Laertes' wily son!
You won a wife of great character   *200*
In Icarius' daughter. What a mind she has,
A woman beyond reproach! How well Penelope
Kept in her heart her husband, Odysseus.
And so her virtue's fame will never perish,
And the gods will make among men on earth   *205*
A song of praise for steadfast Penelope.
But Tyndareus' daughter was evil to the core,
Killing her own husband, and her song will be
A song of scorn, bringing ill-repute
To all women, even the virtuous."   *210*

That was the drift of their talk as they stood
In the Dark Lord's halls deep under the earth.

Odysseus and the others went from the town
And made good time getting down to Laertes'
Well-kept fields. The old man had worked hard   215
Reclaiming the land from the wilderness.
His farmhouse was there with a row of huts around it
Where the field hands ate and rested and slept.
These were his slaves, and they did as he wished.
There was an old Sicilian woman, too,   220
Who took good care of the old man out in the country.

Odysseus had a word with the herdsmen and his son:

"Go into the farmhouse and make yourselves busy.
Sacrifice the best pig and roast it for dinner.
I am going to test my father. Will he recognize me?   225
Will he know who I am after all these years?"

He disarmed and gave his weapons to the herdsmen.
They hurried off indoors, leaving Odysseus
To search through the rows of fruit trees and vines.
He did not find Dolius, or any of his sons   230
Anywhere in the orchard. Old Dolius had taken them
To gather fieldstones for a garden wall.
But he found his father, alone, on a well-banked plot,
Spading a plant. He had on an old, dirty shirt,
Mended and patched, and leather leggings   235
Pieced together as protection from scratches.
He wore gloves because of the bushes, and on his head
He had a goatskin cap, crowning his sorrow.
Odysseus, who had borne much, saw him like this,
Worn with age and a grieving heart,   240
And wept as he watched from a pear tree's shade.
He thought it over. Should he just throw his arms
Around his father, kiss him and tell him all he had done,
And how he'd returned to his homeland again—
Or should he question him and feel him out first?   245
Better that way, he thought, to feel him out first

With a few pointed remarks. With this in mind,
Godlike Odysseus walked up to his father,
Who kept his head down and went on digging.
His illustrious son stood close by him and said: 250

"Well, old-timer, you certainly know how to garden.
There's not a plant, a fig tree, a vine or an olive,
Not a pear tree or leek in this whole garden untended.
But if I may say so without getting you angry,
You don't take such good care of yourself. Old age   255
Is hard, yes. But unwashed, scruffy and dressed in rags?
It can't be that your lord is too lax to care for you,
And anyway there's nothing in your build or looks
To suggest you're a slave. You look more like a king,
The sort of man who after he has bathed and eaten   260
Sleeps on a soft bed, as is only right for elders.
Come on now and give me a straight answer.
Whose slave are you? Whose orchard is this?
And tell me this, too, so that I can be sure:
Is this really Ithaca I've come to, as I was told   265
By that man I ran into on my way over here?
He wasn't very polite, couldn't be bothered
To tell me what I wanted, or even to hear me out.
I've been trying to find out about an old friend
I entertained at my house once, whether he's still alive   270
Or is dead by now and gone down to Hades.
So I'll ask you, if you'll give me your attention.
I was host to a man once back in my own country,
A man who means more to me than anyone else
Who has ever visited my home from abroad.   275
He claimed his family was from Ithaca, and he said
His father was Laertes, son of Arcesius.
I took him into my home, and entertained him
In a style befitting the wealth in my house,
And gave him suitable gifts to seal our friendship: 280
Seven ingots of fine gold, a silver mixing bowl
Embossed with flowers, twelve cloaks, as many
Carpets, mantles and tunics, and his choice of four
Beautiful women superbly trained in handicrafts."

A tear wet his father's cheek as he answered: 285

"You've come to the land you're looking for, stranger,
But it's in the hands of haughty and violent men.
You've given all those generous gifts in vain.
If you were to find him alive here in Ithaca
He would send you off with the beautiful gifts   290
And fine hospitality you deserve as his friend.
But tell me this now, and tell me the truth:
How many years has it been since you hosted
Your ill-fated guest, my son—if I ever had a son?
Born for sorrow he was, and now far from home,   295
Far from his loved ones, his bones are picked clean
By fish undersea; or on some wild shore
His body is feeding the scavenging birds,
Unburied, unmourned by his mother and me,
Who brought him into this world. Nor has his wife,   300
Penelope, patient and wise, who brought him so much,
Lamented her husband on a funeral bier
Or closed his eyelids, as is due the dead.
And tell me this, too, so that I will know.
Who are you?   305
What city are you from? Who are your parents?
And where have you moored the sailing ship
That brought you and your crew of heroes here?
Or did you come as a passenger on another's ship
That put you ashore and went on its way?"   310

And Odysseus, his great mind teeming:

"I'll tell you everything point by point.
I come from Alybas and have my home there.
I'm the son of Apheidas and Polypemon's grandson.
My name is Eperitus. Some storm spirit drove me   315
Off course from Sicily and, as luck had it, here.
My ship stands off wild country far from the town.
As for Odysseus, it's been five years now
Since he left my land, ill-fated maybe,
But the birds were good when he sailed out—   320
On the right. This cheered me as I sent him off,

And he was cheered, too, our hearts full of hope
We would meet again and exchange splendid gifts."

A black mist of pain shrouded Laertes.
He scooped up fistfuls of shimmering dust   *325*
And groaned as he poured it upon his grey head.
This wrung Odysseus' heart, and bitter longing
Stung his nostrils as he watched his father.
With a bound he embraced him, kissed him and said:

"I'm the one that you miss, Father, right here,   *330*
Back in my homeland after twenty years.
But don't cry now. Hold back your tears.
I'm telling you, we really have to hurry.
I've killed the suitors in our house and avenged
All of the wrongs that have grieved your heart."   *335*

But Laertes' voice rang out in answer:

"If you are really Odysseus and my son come back,
Give me a sign, a clear sign I can trust."

And Odysseus, the master strategist:

"First, here's the scar I got on Parnassus   *340*
From that boar's bright tusk. Mother and you
Had sent me to my grandfather Autolycus
To collect some presents he had promised me
When he had visited us here. And let me count off
All of the trees in the orchard rows   *345*
You gave me one day when I was still a boy.
You gave me thirteen pear trees, ten apple trees,
Forty fig trees, and fifty vine rows
That ripened one by one as the season went on
With heavy clusters of all sorts of grapes."   *350*

He spoke, and the old man's knees went slack
As he recognized the signs Odysseus showed him.
He threw his arms around his beloved son
And gasped for breath. And godly Odysseus,

Who had borne much, embraced him.   355
When he had caught his breath and his spirit returned,
Laertes' voice rang out to the sky:

"Father Zeus, there are still gods on high Olympus,
If the suitors have really paid the price!
But now I have a terrible fear   360
That all of Ithaca will be upon us soon,
And word will have gone out to Cephallenia, too."

And Odysseus, his mind teeming:

"We don't have to worry about that right now.
Let's go to the cottage near the orchard.   365
I sent Telemachus there, and the cowherd
And swineherd, to prepare a meal for us."

And they went together to the house
With its comfortable rooms and found
Telemachus and the two herdsmen there   370
Carving huge roasts and mixing wine.
While they were busy with these tasks,
The old Sicilian woman bathed great Laertes
In his own house and rubbed him down
With olive oil and threw about his shoulders   375
A handsome cloak. And Athena came
And made the shepherd of the people
Taller than before and added muscle to his frame.
When he came from the bath, his son marveled
At his deathless, godlike appearance,   380
And his words rose to his father on wings:

"Father, surely one of the gods eternal
Has made you larger, and more handsome, too."

And Laertes, feeling the magic, answered him:

"I wish by Zeus and Athena and Apollo   385
That I could have stood at your side yesterday
In our house, armor on my shoulders,

As the man I was when I took Nericus,
The mainland town, commanding the Cephallenians!
I would have beaten the daylights out of them   390
There in our halls, and made your heart proud."

While they were talking, the others
Had finished preparing the meal.
They all sat down on benches and chairs
And were just serving themselves food   395
When old Dolius came in with his sons,
Weary from their work in the fields.
Their mother, the old Sicilian woman,
Had gone out to call them. It was she
Who made their meals and took care   400
Of Dolius, now that old age had set in.
When they saw Odysseus, and realized
Who he was, they stood there dumbfounded.
Odysseus spoke to them gently and said:

"Old man, sit down to dinner, and all of you,   405
You can stop being amazed. Hungry as we are,
We've been waiting a long time for you."

He spoke, and Dolius ran up to him
With arms outstretched, and clasped
Odysseus' hand and kissed him on the wrist.   410
Trembling with excitement, the old man said:

"My dear Odysseus, you have come back home.
We missed you so much but never hoped
To see you again. The gods themselves
Have brought you back. Welcome, welcome,   415
And may the gods grant you happiness.
But tell me this—I have to know—
Does Penelope know that you have returned,
Or should we send her a messenger?"

And Odysseus, his mind teeming: 420

"She knows, old man. You don't have to worry."

He spoke, and Dolius sat down in a polished chair.
His sons then gathered around glorious Odysseus
And greeted him and clasped his hands
And then sat down in order next to their father.   *425*

While they were busy with their meal,
Rumor, that swift messenger, flew
All through the city, telling everyone
About the grim fate the suitors had met.
Before long a crowd had gathered   *430*
Outside Odysseus' palace, and the sound
Of their lamentation hung in the air.
They carried their dead out of the hall
And buried them. Those from other cities
They put aboard ships to be brought home by sea.   *435*
Then they all went to the meeting place,
Sad at heart. When they were assembled,
Eupeithes rose and spoke among them,
Upon his heart an unbearable grief
For his son Antinous, the first man   *440*
Whom Odysseus killed. Weeping for him
He addressed the assembly and said:

"My friends, it is truly monstrous—
What this man has done to our city.
First, he sailed off with many of our finest men   *445*
And lost the ships and every man aboard.
Now he has come back and killed many others,
By far the best of the Cephallenians.
We must act now, before he runs off to Pylos
Or takes refuge with the Epean lords of Elis.   *450*
We will be disgraced forever if we don't avenge
Our sons' and brothers' deaths, and if we don't,
I see no point in living. I'd rather be dead.
Let's move now, before they cross the sea!"

He wept as he spoke, and they all pitied him.   *455*
Then up came Medon and the godlike bard
From Odysseus' halls. They had just woken up
From a long sleep and stood now in the midst

Of the wondering crowd. Medon had this to say:

"Hear me, men of Ithaca. It was not without the will   *460*
Of the deathless gods that Odysseus managed this.
I myself saw one of the immortals
Close to Odysseus. He looked just like Mentor
But was a god, now appearing in front of Odysseus,
Urging him on, then raging through the hall   *465*
Terrifying the suitors, who fell thick and fast."

He spoke, and they all turned pale with fear.
Then the old hero Halitherses, son of Mastor,
Rose to speak. He alone looked ahead and behind,
And spoke with the best of intentions to them: *470*

"Now hear what I have to say, men of Ithaca.
You have only yourselves to blame, my friends,
For what has happened. You would not obey me
Nor Mentor, shepherd of the people, when we told you
To make your sons stop their foolishness.   *475*
It was what your sons did that was truly monstrous,
Wasting the wealth and dishonoring the wife
Of a great man, who they said would never return.
Now listen to me and keep your peace. Some of you
Are asking for trouble—and you just might find it."   *480*

Less than half of them took his advice
And stayed in their seats. Most of them
Jumped up with a whoop and went with Eupeithes.
They rushed to get weapons, and when the mob
Had armed themselves in glowing bronze,   *485*
They put the city behind them, following Eupeithes,
Who in his folly thought he would avenge
His son's death, but met his own fate instead.
Eupeithes would never return home again.

Athena, meanwhile, was having a word with Zeus: *490*

"Father of us all, Son of Cronus most high,
Tell me what is hidden in that mind of yours.

Will you let this grim struggle go on?
Or will you establish peace on Ithaca?"

And Zeus in his thunderhead responded: *495*

"Why question me, Daughter? Wasn't this
Your plan, to have Odysseus pay them back
With a vengeance? Do as you will,
But I will tell you what would be fitting.
Now that Odysseus has paid the suitors back,   *500*
Let all parties swear a solemn oath,
That he will be king on Ithaca all of his days.
We, for our part, will have them forget
The killing of their sons and brothers.
Let them live in friendship as before,   *505*
And let peace and prosperity abound."

This was all Athena needed to hear,
And she streaked down from Olympus' peaks.

The meal was over. Seeing that his company
Had satisfied their hunger, Odysseus said: *510*

"Someone should go out to see if they're coming."

One of Dolius' sons went to the doorway,
Looked out, and saw the mob closing in.
His words flew fast to Odysseus:

"They're almost here. We'd better arm quickly."   *515*

They jumped up and put on their gear,
Odysseus and his three men and Dolius' six sons.
Laertes and Dolius armed themselves, too,
Warriors in a pinch despite their white hair.
When they had strapped on their bronze   *520*
They opened the doors and headed out
Behind Odysseus.

            Athena joined them,

Looking for all the world like Mentor,
And Odysseus was glad to see her. He turned
To his son Telemachus and said: *525*

"Telemachus, now you will see firsthand
What it means to distinguish yourself in war.
Don't shame your ancestors. We have been
Strong and brave in every generation."

And Telemachus coolly answered him: *530*

"The way I feel now, I don't think you'll see me
Shaming my ancestors, as you put it, Father."

Laertes was delighted with this and exclaimed:

"What a day, dear gods! My son and grandson
Going head to head to see who is best."   *535*

The Grey-eyed One stood next to him and said:

"Son of Arcesius, my dearest comrade,
Say a prayer to Zeus and his grey-eyed daughter,
And then cast your long-shadowed spear."

Pallas Athena breathed great strength into him,   *540*
And with a prayer to Zeus' grey-eyed daughter,
Laertes cast his long-shadowed spear
And hit Eupeithes square in the helmet.
Bronze bored through bronze, and Eupeithes
Thudded to the ground, his armor clattering.   *545*
Odysseus and his glorious son
Charged the front lines, thrusting hard
With their swords and spears. They would have killed
Every last man—not one would have gone home—
Had not Athena, daughter of the Storm Cloud,   *550*
Given voice to a cry that stopped them all cold:

"ITHACANS!
          Lay down your arms now,
And go your ways with no more bloodshed."

Thus Athena, and they turned pale with fear.
The weapons dropped from their trembling hands   *555*
And fell to the ground as the goddess' voice
Sent shock waves through them. They turned
Back toward the city and ran for their lives.
With a roar, the great, long-suffering Odysseus
Gathered himself and swept after them   *560*

    Like a soaring raptor.

          At that moment
Zeus, Son of Cronus, hurled down
A flaming thunderbolt that landed at the feet
Of his owl-eyed daughter, who said:

"Son of Laertes in the line of Zeus,   *565*
Cunning Odysseus—restrain yourself.
End this quarrel and cease from fighting
Lest broad-browed Zeus frown upon you."

Thus Athena. The man obeyed and was glad,
And the goddess made both sides swear binding oaths—   *570*
Pallas Athena, daughter of the Storm Cloud,
Who looked like Mentor and spoke with his voice.

Translator's Postscript

If you do this practice, you can lock eyebrows with the masters of old, seeing through their eyes and hearing with their ears. Wouldn't you like to do that? Thus Wu Men, the great Sung Dynasty Ch'an master. For the last decade I have attempted locking eyebrows with Homer, the great master of European poetry. We know so little about him. "A blind man who lives on rugged Chios" is as much as we are told (this almost an aside at the end of the Homeric "Hymn to Delian Apollo"). I can well believe that the poet was blind. Jacques Lusseyran, the French Resistance leader, tells us that after he lost his eyesight as a young boy he found that the whole world was filled with light, and that the light came from his mind and was the core of his being. Homer's mind, too, and his world, are filled with light. In the *Iliad* the light is intense, the light of noon, searing and white. In the *Odyssey* it is a softer light, the roselight of dawn—or of the setting sun, as the ancient critic Longinus says: "The grandeur remains apart from the intensity." Penelope waits and dreams in that quiet light; Telemachus wakes to it; and Odysseus, in the dark of the moon, returns to it and becomes himself again.

The light in the *Odyssey* casts an enchantment over the most ordinary actions in the poem. Penelope walks across a room, Telemachus gets dressed—and these actions are as magical as any of the marvelous adventures Odysseus has. The poem, again as Longinus puts it, is like the sea at low tide, withdrawn into its solitude, greatness ebbing and flowing, and the poet wanders along the shore where there are many curious things, and into the mythical and incredible: "What else can we call all this but the dreaming of a Zeus?" But it is not only then that we are entranced. Everywhere the poet turns his mind there is a sense of seeing things as if for the first time, and seeing their essential wholeness. The spell that we are under is an enlightening enchantment, not the drowsiness of the Lotus-Eaters, who become forgetful of home, but a waking realization that every moment of experience is our luminous, original home. This is the true *nostos* of the *Odyssey*, and the completion of the poetic vision that begins in the raw, brilliant radiance of the *Iliad*.

§

In spite of the difference, or development, in tone between the two Greek epics, their poetics are fundamentally the same, and the poetics of my translation of the *Odyssey* are largely the same as enunciated in the preface to my *Iliad* translation: rhythms and language drawn from natural speech; emphasis on the physicality, rapidity, and suppleness of the verse; varied treatment of epithets and formulae, often heightening their effect as poetic events; treatment of similes as partially independent poetic moments; close attention to presentation of the text on the page; commitment to the poetic line, Above all, and like my *Iliad* translation, this translation of the *Odyssey* reflects the oral nature of the original; it began as scripts for performance, and it has been shaped by the complementary pressures of poetic composition and oral performance. I owe all the audiences and their conveners a debt of gratitude.

The opening phrase of this translation,

S_PEAK, M_EMORY—

in place of the more literal "Tell me, Muse," recalls the title of Nabokov's memoir, who himself was recalling Homer as he recalled his own life. This is the way of translation as art, a kind of anamnesis in which we remember our own voice as the poet's. This process began for me when I first encountered the *Odyssey* in Greek—under the tutelage of Emmett Bienvenu, S. J., at Loyola University in New Orleans, in an introductory course designed to prepare students to read Homer as soon as possible. The power of Homer's verse and its sheer physical beauty were transformative for me. Poetry was the stream of my life, but this was an immortal river of poetry, and I knew as soon as we had construed and scanned the opening lines of the *Odyssey*, which I immediately memorized and recited over and over, that I wanted to translate Homer, to meet his poetry with my own, to merge our voices. That has been done now, as well as I could, after a long apprenticeship and long practice—and with the considerable help of colleagues past and present.

W. B. Stanford's commentary on the *Odyssey* has been my constant companion in this work; and I have made extensive use of the Oxford commentary by Heubeck, S. West, Hainsworth, Hoekstra, Russo, and Fernández-Galiano. These are indispensable scholarly resources. I find myself returning again and again to the works of Paolo Vivante for his perspectives on Homer's poetic qualities.

Sheila Murnaghan's scholarship and sensitive understanding of a broad range of Homeric and Odyssean issues are available to all in her Introduction. I am personally grateful to her for her careful reading of the manuscript and the hundreds of suggestions she made to improve the translation, as well as for her friendship and encouragement.

Brian Rak, the editor at Hackett Publishing Company, has kept the work on course with a keen eye for every detail and with unfailing good humor. My gratitude to him deepens with every project we do together. I would like to acknowledge the entire staff at Hackett, and in particular Meera Dash, Managing Editor.

Susan Warden, with her dancer's understanding of line and rhythm and her choreographer's instinctive ability to spot and restructure awkward passages, has had a pervasive influence on the movement and tone of this translation. She has my deepest gratitude.

William Levitan provided invaluable guidance when I began work on this translation, as he has on many other occasions. Jonathan Shay's insights into the language and behavior of combat veterans have helped shaped my translation of many of Odysseus' speeches. Clyde Curry Smith has made numerous acute and useful observations and found ways to improve the translation and glossary. The glossary itself was compiled by Linda Mann, Allen Lubben, and Melissa Chiang, all graduate students at the University of Kansas; Melissa Chiang also worked on the bibliography. The index of speeches was compiled by Josh Baruth, an undergraduate classics major. My thanks to all these, and to all my colleagues and students in the University of Kansas classics department for their support, particularly to Tara Welch, who used the translation in manuscript form in one of her classes, and to Christina Arnold for her patient, competent help with preparation of the manuscript.

Judy Roitman has provided the support that only a wife of twenty years could.

Work on this translation was supported by the University of Kansas General Research Fund and by a Creative Work Fellowship from the Hall Center for the Humanities.

Stanley Lombardo
University of Kansas

Glossary of Names

(First appearance noted by book and line number.)

Achaeans (A-kee´-unz): General term used by Homer to refer to Greeks. 2.139

Acheron (A´-ker-on): River in the Underworld, land of the dead. 10.537

Achilles (A-kil´-eez): Son of Peleus and Thetis. He is the heroic leader of the Myrmidons in the Trojan War and is slain by Paris. Odysseus consults him in the Underworld. 3.117

Aeaea (Ee-ee´-a): Island on which Circe lives. 9.34

Aegisthus (Ee-jis´-thus): Son of Thyestes and Pelopia. He seduces Clytemnestra, wife of Agamemnon, while Agamemnon is away fighting the Trojan War and helps her slay Agamemnon when he returns. Orestes avenges this action years later by murdering both Clytemnestra and Aegisthus. 1.35

Aegyptus (Ee-jip´-tus): The Nile River. 4.511

Aeolus (Ee´-oh-lus): King of the island Aeolia and keeper of the winds. 10.2

Aeson (Ee´-son): Son of Cretheus and Tyro; father of Jason, leader of the Argonauts. 11.262

Aethon (Ee´-thon): One of Odysseus' aliases used in his conversation with Penelope. 19.199

Agamemnon (A-ga-mem´-non): Son of Atreus and Aerope; brother of Menelaus; husband of Clytemnestra. He commands the Greek forces in the Trojan War. He is killed by his wife and her lover when he returns home; his son, Orestes, avenges this murder. 1.36

Agelaus (A-je-lay´-us): One of Penelope's suitors; son of Damastor; killed by Odysseus. 20.351

Ajax (1) (Ay´-jax): Son of Telamon and Perioboea; also called Great Ajax or Telamonian Ajax. He contends with Odysseus for the prize of Achilles' arms, given in honor of service to the Greek cause in the Trojan War. When Ajax loses, he temporarily takes leaves of his wits and commits suicide when he regains his senses. 3.120

Ajax (2) (Ay´-jax): Son of Oileus and Eriopes; also called Little Ajax or Oilean Ajax. He survives the Trojan War, but his boasting angers Poseidon, who kills Ajax on his return home. 4.525

Alcinous (Al-si´-no-us): Grandson of Poseidon; king of the Phaeacians; husband of Arete and father of Nausicaa. He graciously entertains Odysseus and gives him riches and safe transport to Ithaca. 6.12

Alcmene (Alk-mee´-ee): Wife of Amphitryon; mother of Heracles (by Zeus). 2.131

Amphimedon (Am-fi´-me-don): One of Penelope's suitors. He is killed by Telemachus. In the Underworld he tells Agamemnon about the slaughter of the suitors. 22.257

Amphinomus (Am-fi´-no-mus): Son of Nisus. A leader of Penelope's suitors, he convinces other suitors not to slay Telemachus on his return from Pylos unless the gods give a sign of favor. Although warned by Odysseus, Amphinomus is slain with the other suitors. 16.371

Amphion (Am-feye´-on): Son of Zeus and Antiope; husband of Niobe. 11.266

Amphithea (Am-fi´-the-a): Wife of Autolycus; grandmother of Odysseus. 19.456

Amphitryon (Am-fi´-tri-on): King of Tiryns; husband of Alcmene; mortal father of Heracles. 11.270

Anticleia (An-ti-klay´-a): Daughter of Autolycus; wife of Laertes and mother of Odysseus. She is able to speak to Odysseus when he visits her in the Underworld. 11.82

Anticlus (An´-ti-klus): One of the Greek warriors who hides in the wooden horse at Troy. Odysseus restrains him from responding when Helen imitates the voices of Greek wives. 4.306

Antinous (An-ti´-no-us): Son of Eupeithes; an Ithacan noble and the primary leader of Penelope's suitors. He is the first suitor slain by Odysseus. 1.404

Antiphates (An-ti´-fa-teez): King of the Laestrygonians. 10.120

Antiphus (An´-ti-fus): Name given to two of Odysseus' companions, one of whom is the son of Aegyptius, the last of Odysseus' companions eaten by the Cyclops. 2.17

Aphrodite (A-fro-deye´-tee): Goddess of love and beauty. Daughter of Zeus and Dione; wife of Hephaestus. During a sexual liaison, Aphrodite and Ares are caught in a trap set by Hephaestus and exposed to the laughter of the gods. 4.17

Apollo (A-pol´-oh): Patron god of music and the arts. Son of Zeus and Leto; brother of Artemis. Also called Phoebus Apollo, he is associated with the lyre and archery. It is on the day of his festival that the suitors are murdered. 3.309

Arcesius (Ar-ke´-si-us): Father of Laertes and grandfather of Odysseus. 4.808

Ares (Ai´-reez): God of War. Son of Zeus and Hera; lover of Aphrodite. 3.120

Arete (A-ree´-tee): Wife of Alcinous; mother of Nausicaa. Queen of the Phaeacians, to whom Odysseus, shipwrecked on the island, kneels as a suppliant first, rather than to Alcinous. 7.57

Argives (Ar´-geyvz): The Greeks who fight at Troy under the leadership of Agamemnon. 1.228

Argo (Ar´-goh): The ship of the Argonauts. 12.72

Argos (Ar´-gos): City or district in the northeastern Peloponnese, Greek region of the Achaeans. 1.364

Argus (Ar´-gos): Odysseus' dog, the only creature to recognize Odysseus on his return to Ithaca. Argus dies almost immediately thereafter. 17.319

Ariadne (A-ri-ad´-nee): Daughter of Minos, king of Crete, and Pasiphae. She helps Theseus overcome the Minotaur, is killed by Artemis, and is seen by Odysseus in the Underworld. 11.329

Artemis (Ar´-te-mis): Goddess of the hunt and the moon. Daughter of Zeus and Leto; sister of Apollo. Like her brother, Artemis brings natural death to mortals, but she is the slaughterer of female mortals in particular. 4.127

Athena (A-thee´-na): Goddess of wisdom, crafts, and battle. Daughter of Zeus; usually said to have sprung from his head. She is also called Pallas Athena and the Grey-eyed One. She frequently appears to Odysseus and helps him return home. 1.49

Atlas (At´-las): Titan who holds up the pillars of the sky; father of Calypso. 1.58

Atreus (Ay´-tryoos): Son of Pelops and Hippodameia; brother of Thyestes; father of Agamemnon and Menelaus. 3.147

Autolycus (Aw-to´-li-kus): Father of Anticleia; maternal grandfather of Odysseus. He gives Odysseus his name. 11.82

Boreas (Bo´-re-as): The North Wind. Husband of Oreithyia and father of Calais and Zetes. 5.297

Cadmus (Kad´-mus): Founder and king of Cadmea (Thebes). Married to Harmonia; father of Polydorus, Autonoë, Semele, Ino, and Agave. 5.335

Calypso (Ka-lip´-soh): Goddess, daughter of Atlas. Her name is a play on a Greek word meaning "to conceal." She detains Odysseus for seven years on her island, Ogygia, offering him immortality if he remains. 1.17

Cassandra (Ka-san´-dra): Trojan princess and prophetess, daughter of Priam and Hecuba. Taken as a war prize by Agamemnon, she is murdered with him by Clytemnestra and Aegisthus on his return home. 11.436

Castor (Kas´-tor): Son of Tyndareus and Leda; brother of Polydeuces, Clytemnestra, and Helen. 11.307

Cephallenians (Se-fa-lee´-ni-unz): Inhabitants of a much larger island near Ithaca under Odysseus' command. 20.225

Charybdis (Ka-rib´-dis): Whirlpool situated opposite Scylla. 12.107

Cicones (Si-koh´-neez): Allies of Troy, the first people Odysseus encounters (and raids) on his return home. Maron, the priest, gives Odysseus some excellent wine in return for sparing his and his family's lives. 9.42

Circe (Sir´-see): Goddess and sorceress; daughter of Helius and Perse. When Odysseus lands on her island, Aeaea, she turns many of his men into swine, but Odysseus (with Hermes' help) resists her magic and convinces her to undo her spell. He and his men remain on her island for one year. 8.485

Clytemnestra (Kleye-tem-nes´-tra): Daughter of Tyndareus and Leda; married first to Tantalus and then to Agamemnon, to whom she bore Iphigeneia, Electra, Chrysothemis, and Orestes. She killed her husband and his concubine Cassandra with the aid of her lover, Aegisthus. Years later Orestes avenged his father's death by murdering his mother. 3.293

Cnossus (Knos´-os): Principal city on the island of Crete. 19.192

Cocytus (Ko-kee´-tos): River forming one of the boundaries of Hades. 10.538

Crete: Island in the Aegean Sea south of the Peloponnese, ruled by Idomeneus. 3.210

Ctessipus (Kte-si´-pus): Wealthy suitor of Penelope. He throws a cowfoot at Odysseus' head when Odysseus is disguised as a beggar. He is killed by Philoetius. 20.314

Ctimene (Kti-mee´-nee): Daughter of Laertes and Anticleia; sister of Odysseus. 15.400

Cyclopes (Seye´-klops): One-eyed, man-eating giants. Their occupation of Hyperia forces the Phaeacians to relocate. The term in the singular (Cyclops) also refers to Polyphemus. 1.76

Cytherean (Si-thee-ree´-an): Epithet of Aphrodite, perhaps from the name of the island Cythera, where some claim the goddess was born. 8.312

Danaans (Da-nay´-unz): One of three general names Homer uses when referring to Greeks. The other two are Achaeans and Argives. 1.371

Deiphobus (Dee-i´-fo-bus)): Prince of Troy, son of Priam and Hecuba. He marries Helen after Paris' death and is killed at Troy by Menelaus. 4.293

Demeter (Dee-mee´-tur): Goddess of crops and the harvest. Daughter of Cronus and Rhea; mother of Persephone. 5.125

Demodocus (Dee-mo´-do-kus): Blind singer of tales at Phaeacia. 8.46

Demoptolemus (Dee-mop-to´-le-mus): One of Penelope's suitors. 22.258

Diocles (Deye´-o-kleez): Inhabitant of Pherae who receives Telemachus on his trip to Sparta and on his return. 3.537

Diomedes (Deye-o-mee´-deez): Son of Tydeus and Deipyle; king of Argos. He accompanies Odysseus at night around the city and is one of the few Greeks to return home quickly after the destruction of Troy. 3.184

Dodona (Doh-doh´-na): City in northwestern Greece; home to a famous oracle of Zeus. 14.356

Dolios (Do´-li-us): Old servant of Odysseus who remains faithful during Odysseus' absence. He later defends Odysseus against the relatives of the slain suitors. 4.787

Dorians (Doh´-ri-unz): Greek-speaking inhabitants of Crete. 19.191

Echephron (E-ke´-fron): Son of Nestor. 3.454

Echetus (E´-ke-tus): King of Eperius who acquires a reputation for cruelty. 18.89

Egypt: Country in Africa or its king. 3.332

Eidothea (Eye-do´-the-a): Daughter of Proteus who advises Menelaus on his journey home with Helen. 4.389

Elatus (E´-la-tus): One of Penelope's suitors; slain by Eumaeus. 22.282

Elpenor (El-pee´-nor): Member of Odysseus' crew who dies when he falls asleep on a roof on Circe's island and falls off. When Odysseus visits the Underworld, Elpenor's shade asks Odysseus for a proper funeral. 10.574

Epeius (E-pee´-us): Son of Panopeus. With Athena's help, he builds the Trojan Horse. 8.533

Epicaste (E-pi-kas´-tee): Also known as Jocasta. Daughter of Menoeceus; wife of Laius and mother of Oedipus. 11.275

Erebus (E´-re-bus): Another name for Hades; sometimes refers to an especially dark place within the Underworld. 10.551

Eriphyle (E-ri-feye´-lee): Daughter of Talaus and Lysimache; wife and betrayer of Amphiaraus. Her shade appears to Odysseus in the Underworld. 11.335

Eumaeus (Yoo-may´-us): Odysseus' loyal swineherd who generously hosts Odysseus, disguised as a beggar upon his return to Ithaca. Eumaeus later assists Odysseus in the slaughter of the suitors. 14.63

Eupeithes (Yoo-pay´-theez): Father of Antinous. He rallies the relatives of the slain suitors against Odysseus and is killed by Laertes. 1.404

Euryades (Yoo-reye´-a-deez): One of Penelope's suitors. He is killed by Telemachus. 22.282

Eurybates (Yoo-ri´-ba-teez): Round-shouldered, swarthy, and curly haired herald whom Odysseus values for his quick mind. 19.269

Eurycleia (Yoo-ri-klay´-a): Daughter of Ops; nurse to Odysseus and later to Telemachus. She recognizes Odysseus' scar on his thigh but at his request does not reveal his identity. 1.452

Eurydamas (Yoo-ri´-da-mas): One of Penelope's suitors killed by Odysseus. 18.324

Eurylochus (Yoo-ri´-lo-kus): Leading member of Odysseus' crew. He tells Odysseus that Circe transformed several crew members, and he incites the crew to slaughter Helios' cattle. 10.220

Eurymachus (Yoo-ri´-ma-kus): One of Penelope's suitors. 1.421

Eurynome (Yoo-ri´-no-mee): Penelope's housekeeper. 17.538

Eurynomus (Yoo-ri´-no-mus): Son of Antiphus; suitor to Penelope. 2.21

Hades (Hay´-deez): God of the Underworld. Son of Cronus and Rhea. His name probably means "Unseen One." Also refers to the dwelling place of the dead, named for its ruler. 3.450

Halitherses (Ha-li-thur´-seez): Son of Mastor; Ithacan soothsayer. He predicts Odysseus' return to Ithaca. 2.175

Helen (He´-len): Daughter of Leda and Zeus or Tyndareus; wife of Menelaus. She is the most beautiful woman in the world and is given to Paris by Aphrodite. Menelaus' efforts to regain Helen are the basis of the Trojan War. 4.15

Helios (Hee´-li-os): The Sun God. 8.294

Hephaestus (He-feyes´-tus): God of fire and patron of metalworkers and crafts. Son of Zeus and Hera. He marries Aphrodite, who is not always faithful. He forges Achilles' armor. 4.652

Hera (Hee´-ra): Queen of the Olympian gods. Daughter of Cronus and Rhea; Zeus' sister and wife. Goddess of childbirth and marriage. 4.538

Hermes (Hur´-meez): Divine messenger of the gods and guide to mortal travelers. Son of Zeus and Maia. 1.43

Hermione (Hur-meye´-o-nee): Daughter of Menelaus and Helen. 4.16

Hypereia (Hi-pe-reye´-a): First homeland of the Phaeacians whence they are driven by the Cyclopes. 6.4

Icarius (I-ka´-ri-us): Father of Penelope; brother of Menelaus. 1.347

Ilion (Il´-i-on): Troy. 9.42

Ino (Eye´-noh): Daughter of Cadmus and Harmonia. She disguises and rears her nephew Dionysus to protect him from Hera's wrath. She becomes a nereid and is renamed Leucothea, meaning "White Goddess." 5.336

Iphitus (I´-fi-tus): Son of Eurytus, king of Oechalia. He gives Odysseus his bow. 21.13

Irus (Eye´-rus): Ithacan beggar who frequents the gatherings of Penelope's suitors at the palace. He loses a boxing match to the disguised Odysseus. 18.7

Ithaca (Ith´-a-ka): Rocky island home of Odysseus. 1.22

Jason (Jay´-son): Son of Aeson and leader of the Argonauts. 12.74

Lacedaemon (La-ke-deye´-mon): Sparta. City and kingdom of Menelaus. 3.363

Laertes (Lay-er´-teez): Son of Arcesius; husband of Anticleia and father of Odysseus and Ctimene. 1.204

Laestrygonians (Leye-stri-goh´-ni-unz): Giant cannibals who eat part of Odysseus' crew and destroy all the ships but Odysseus'. 10.95

Lampetië (Lam-pe´-ti-ee): Daughter of Helios and Neaera. When Odysseus' men slaughter Helios' cattle, the nymph tells her father. 12.138

Leda (Lee´-da): Wife of Tyndareus; mother of Castor, Polydeuces, Clytemnestra, and Helen. 11.305

Leocritus (Lee-o´-kri-tus): Suitor killed by Telemachus. 2.264

Leodes (Lee-oh´-deez): Suitor with prophetic gifts, killed by Odysseus. 21.148

Leto (Lee´-toh): Titan goddess. Daughter of Coeus and Phoebe; mother of Artemis and Apollo. 6.105

Malea (Ma-lay´-a): Cape on the southeast tip of the Peloponnese known for its difficulty in navigation. 3.317

Marathon (Ma´-ra-thon): Attic city northeast of Athens. 7.87

Maron (May´-ron): Priest of Apollo at Ismarus who gives Odysseus the wine that is used to intoxicate the Cyclops. 9.189

Medon (Mee´-don): Ithacan herald who remains faithful to his lord, Odysseus, and is spared when the suitors are killed. 4.722

Megapenthes (Me-ga-pen´-theez): Son of Menelaus by a slave woman. His name means "great sorrow," presumably because Menelaus was unable to have children with Helen after the birth of

Hermione. He marries the daughter of Alector on the day that Telemachus arrives in Sparta. 4.14

Megara (Me´-ga-ra): Daughter of Creon and the wife of Heracles. 11.273

Melanthius (Me-lan´-thi-us): Odysseus' goatherd; son of Dolius. He aligns himself with the suitors while Odysseus is away and insults his master disguised as a beggar. He is killed for his disloyalty. 17.229

Melantho (Me-lan´-thoh): Daughter of Dolius; sister of Melanthius; handmaid of Penelope. She becomes the mistress of Eurymachus during Odysseus' absence and a deceitful antagonist. Telemachus hangs her for her betrayal. 18.350

Memnon (Mem´-non): Son of Dawn and Tithonus; nephew of Priam. He kills Nestor's son Antilochus and in turn is killed by Achilles. Zeus grants him immortality when he dies. 4.199

Menelaus (Me-ne-lay´-us): Son of Atreus and Aerope; brother of Agamemnon; ruler of Lacedaemon; husband of Helen. 1.303

Mentes (Men´-teez): Taphian captain, son of Anchialus, in whose form Athena first appears to Telemachus. 1.112

Mentor (Men´-tor): Close friend of Odysseus who is to look after the household during Odysseus' absence. Athena often appears in his form. 2.244

Minos (Meye´-nos): Son of Zeus and Europa; king of Crete; husband of Pasiphae; father of Ariadne, Phaedra, and Deucalion; brother of Rhadamanthus. After his death he becomes a judge of the dead in Hades. 11.596

Muses (Mu´-zez): Goddesses of the arts who inspire poets and musicians. Daughters of Zeus and Mnemosyne. 8.67

Mycenae (Meye-see´-nee): Ancient city in Argos ruled by Agamemnon. 3.339

Mycene (Meye-see´-neh): Legendary daughter of Inachus. The namesake of Mycenae. 2.131

Myrmidons (Mur´-mi-donz): A people inhabiting southern Thessaly. Achilles' crack troops in the *Iliad*. 3.207

Nausicaa (Naw-si´-kay-a): Phaeacian princess; daughter of Alcinous and Arete. 6.17

Nausithous (Naw-si´-tho-us): Son of Poseidon and Periboea; father of Alcinous. He leads the Phaeacians to Schería where they find a peaceful existence. 6.7

Neleus (Neel´-yoos): Son of Poseidon and Tyro; brother of Pelias; father of Nestor. 3.86

Neoptolemus (Nee-op-to´-le-mus): Son of Achilles and Deidameia. 11.530

Nericus (Nee´-ri-cus): A coastal town in western Greece once conquered by Laertes. 24.388

Neriton (Nee´-ri-ton): A thickly forested mountain on Ithaca. 9.25

Nestor (Nes´-tor): Son of Neleus and Chloris; king of Pylos. He fights in the Trojan War, although already an old man, and is known for his valuable counsel. Father of Peisistratus, Thrasymedes, and Antilochus. 1.302

Noemon (No-ee´-mon): Wealthy Ithacan who, inspired by Athena, lends Telemachus a ship to sail to Pylos. His name means "thoughtful." 2.410

Ocean: The river encircling the earth. Son of Uranus and Earth; husband of Tethys. 4.597

Odysseus (O-dis´-yoos): Son of Laertes and Anticlea; husband of Penelope; father of Telemachus. *Odysseus* may mean either "giver of woe" or "woeful one." 1.15

Oedipus (Ee´-di-pus): Son of Laius and Epicaste who unknowingly kills his father and marries his mother. 11.275

Ogygia (Oh-gi´-ja): Mythical island where the nymph Calypso resides. 1.92

Olympus (O-lim´-pus): Mount Olympus, the tallest mountain in Greece, believed to be the abode of the gods. 1.109

Ops (Ops): Father of Eurycleia, nurse to Odysseus and Telemachus. 1.452

Orestes (O-res´-teez): Son of Agamemnon and Clytemnestra. He avenges his father's murder by killing his mother and her lover, Aegisthus. 1.36

Orion (O-reye´-on): Mythical hunter famed for his size and handsome looks. The goddess Dawn falls in love with him and bears him away to her island, Ortygia. The other gods become envious of the love affair and urge Artemis to slay the hunter. 5.121

Pallas (Pal´-as): Epithet of the goddess Athena that may mean "maiden" or "weapon-brandishing." 1.134

Pandareus (Pan-dar´-yoos): A king of Miletas in Crete; father of Aedon. He steals a golden dog from the temple of Zeus in Crete, and consequently both he and his wife are killed. 19.566

Paphos (Pa´-fos): A city on the southern coast of Cyprus and an important center for the cult of Aphrodite. 8.390

Patroclus (Pa-tro´-klus): Son of Menoetius. Greek warrior of the Myrmidon contingent at Troy and dear friend of Achilles. He rallies his Achaean comrades by donning Achilles' armor but is then killed by Hector. 3.121

Peirithous (Peye-ri´-tho-us): Son of Ixion and king of the Lapiths. The centaur Eurytion becomes drunk and attempts to abduct his fiancée Hippodamia during their wedding. This causes the war between the Lapiths and the Centaurs. 11.665

Peisander (Peye-sand´-er): One of Penelope's suitors. 22.258

Peisistratus (Peye-sis´-tra-tus): Youngest son of Nestor who accompanies Telemachus to Sparta. 3.40

Peleus (Pee´-li-as): Husband of the sea-goddess Thetis and father of the hero Achilles. 11.486

Penelope (Pe-ne´-lo-pee): Daughter of Icarius and Periboea; wife of Odysseus; mother of Telemachus. 1.240

Perse (Pur´-see): Daughter of Oceanus and mother of Circe by Helios. 10.155

Persephone (Pur-se´-fo-nee): Daughter of Demeter and Zeus; wife of Hades; queen of the Underworld. 10.513

Perseus (Purs´-yoos): A son of Nestor (not to be confused with the son of Zeus and Danae, the hero who beheads Medusa). 3.454

Phaeacians (Fee-ay´-shunz): The people who inhabit Phaeacia (sometimes called Schería). As descendants of Poseidon they are loved by the gods and have remarkable seafaring abilities. According to legend, they have ships that move without the aid of rudder or sail. 5.37

Phaedra (Fay´-dra): Daughter of Minos and Pasiphae. Wife of Theseus but falls in love with his son Hippolytus and hangs herself. Odysseus is visited by her ghost in the Underworld. 11.328

Pharos (Fa´-ros): An island off the coast of Egypt where Proteus and his seals reside. 4.380

Phemius (Fee´-mi-us): Son of Terpius; a bard in Ithaca. Although he is forced to entertain the suitors, he remains faithful to the house of Laertes. Odysseus spares him because of his fidelity. 1.165

Pherae (Feh´-ree): Town between Pylos and Sparta where Telemachus and Peisistratus stay on their way to Sparta. 3.536

Philoctetes (Fi-lok-tee´-teez): Son of Poias and great archer hero. On his way to Troy a serpent bites him. The smell of the festering wound is so foul that the Greeks abandon him on the island of Lemnos. However, it was predetermined that Troy would not fall without his help. 3.209

Philoetius (Fi-lee´-tee-us): Cowherd who remains faithful to Odysseus. 20.197

Phoebus (Fee´-bus): An epithet of Apollo meaning "bright," identifying him with the sun. 3.309

Phoenicia (Fee-ni´-sha): A country on the Mediterranean coast in Syria. The Phoenicians were known for being skilled seafarers and traders. 4.87

Phorcys (For´-kis): Sea-god; father of Thoösa; grandfather of Polyphemus. 1.78

Pleiades (Plee´-a-deez): A constellation of seven stars used by ancient seamen for nocturnal navigation. The Pleiades were originally the seven daughters of Atlas and Pleione. 5.272

Polybus (Pol´-i-bus): Father of Eurymachus, 1.421; Theban man visited by Menelaus and Helen, 4.131; Phaeacian craftsman, 8.412; one of Penelope's suitors killed by Eumaeus. 22.259

Polydamna (Po-li-dam´-na): Egyptian wife of Thon who supplies Helen with herbal somnifers. 4.242

Polydeuces (Po-li-dyoo´-seez): Son of Leda and Tyndareus; brother of Helen; twin brother of Castor. He is known for his skill as a boxer. 11.307

Polyphemus (Po-li-fee´-mus): One of the Cyclopes, son of Poseidon and Thoösa. This one-eyed giant consumes some of Odysseus' men after he traps them in his cave. To escape from the cave, Odysseus and his men drive a heated pole into Polyphemus' only eye. As punishment for his son's blinding, Poseidon torments Odysseus until he reaches Ithaca. 1.76

Poseidon (Po-seye´-don): God of the sea. Son of Cronus and Rhea; brother of Zeus, Hades, and Hera; father of the Cyclops Polyphemus. 1.25

Priam (Preye´-am): King of Troy; son of Laomedon and Strymo; husband of Hecuba; father of Hector and Paris. He is killed by Neoptolemus as Troy falls to the Greeks. 3.118

Proteus (Proh´-tyoos): A shape-shifting sea-god; son of Oceanus and Tethys; father of Eidothea. Also known as the "Old Man of the Sea." He is generally associated with the island of Pharos. 4.390

Pylos (Peye-los): City on the southwest coast of the Peloponnese ruled by Nestor. 1.100

Pyriphlegethon (Peye-ri-fle´-gey-thon): One of the three rivers near the entrance to Hades. 10.537

Rhadamanthus (Ra-da-man´-thus): A son of Europa and Zeus and brother of Minos. Because he is a fair king, he is granted eternal life in the Elysian fields. 4.594

Rhexenor (Rex-ee´-nor): Son of Nausithous; brother of Alcinous; father of Arete. 7.68

Schería (Ske-ri´-a): The island inhabited by the Phaeacians. 6.8

Scylla (Sil´-a): The cave-dwelling monster possessing female attributes from the waist up but six dog heads and a dozen canine feet from the waist down. *Scylla* is Greek for "she-pup." She inhabits the cliff across the strait from Charybdis. 12.88

Scyros (Skeye´-ros): Island in the Aegean where Achilles is hidden to prevent him from going to the Trojan War. 11.532

Sirens (Seye´-rens): Singing creatures with female heads and breasts, and large birdlike bodies. They lure sailors to their island with an irresistible song. 12.41

Sisyphus (Si´-si-fus): Son of Aeolus, and a king of Corinth. He was condemned to spend eternity in Hades perpetually pushing a huge stone up a hill. 11.622

Sparta (Spar´-ta): City in the southwest Peleponnese that was ruled by Menelaus. 1.100

Styx (Stix): One of the rivers that flows near Hades. When gods swear by this river their oaths are irretractable. 5.184

Tantalus (Tan´-ta-lus): Father of Pelops and Niobe; mythical king of Phrygia. He was forced to suffer in Hades with everlasting hunger and thirst for trying to serve the gods the mortal flesh of his son Pelops. 11.611

Taphians (Ta´-fi-unz): The inhabitants of Taphos, a seafaring people ruled by Mentes. Taphos is a city on the west coast of Greece. 1.112

Telamon (Tel´-a-mon): Father of the hero Ajax. 11.569

Telemachus (Te-lem´-a-kus): Son of Odysseus and Penelope. His name means "battle from afar." 1.121

Telemos (Te´-le-mus): A seer among the Cyclopes who had warned Polyphemus that he would lose his eye to a mortal named Odysseus. 9.507

Telepylus (Te-le´-pi-lus): The fortress of the Laestrygonians. 10.94

Tenedos (Te´-ne-dos): A small island off the coast of Asia Minor. 3.175

Themis (The´-mis): Titan goddess of law and order. Daughter of Uranus and Gaia. 2.73

Theseus (Thees´-yoos): Athenian hero; son of Aegeus. He slays the Minotaur with the help of Minos' daughter Ariadne, who had fallen in love with Theseus. 11.329

Thetis (Thee´-tis): A sea-goddess, one of the Nereids. Daughter of Nereus and Doris; wife of Peleus; mother of Achilles. 24.89

Thoösa (Tho-oh´-sa): A nymph; mother of Polyphemus by Poseidon. 1.77

Thrinacia (Thri-nay´-sha): Island where Helios' cattle pastured. 11.105

Thyestes (Theye-es´-teez): Father of Aegisthus and brother of Atreus. 4.541

Tiresias (Teye-ree´-si-as): The blind seer from Thebes whose shade counsels Odysseus in the Underworld. 10.514

Tithonus (Ti-thoh´-nus): Son of Laomedon and husband of Dawn. 5.2

Tityus (Ti´-ti-yus): A giant and son of Gaia. He attempted to rape Leto. He was killed and was eternally punished by two vultures that tore at his liver. 7.347

Tritogeneia (Tri-to-ge-nee´-a): Epithet of Athena meaning "third born." 3.416

Trojans (Troh´-junz): The inhabitants of Troy. 3.94

Troy (Troy): City in northwestern Asia Minor; ruled by Priam; conquered by the Greeks in the Trojan War. Site at which the *Iliad* takes place. 1.3

Tyndareus (Tin-da´-ri-us): Husband of Leda; father of Castor, Polydeuces, and Clytemnestra; foster father of Helen. 11.305

Zeus (Zyoos): The supreme god of Olympus, known as the father of gods and men. Son of Cronus and Rhea; husband and brother of Hera; father of Athena, Aphrodite, Ares, Apollo, Artemis, Hephaestus, and others. 1.33

Index of Speeches

* Denotes a speech within a speech.

Antinous   17.407; to Telemachus 17.439; to Odysseus 17.484,
(continued)   17.500, 17.518; to the Suitors 18.41, 18.47; to Irus
                    18.83; to Penelope 18.310; to the Suitors 20.293; to
                    Eumaeus and Philoetius 21.82; to fellow archers
                    21.145; to Leodes 21.175; to Melanthius 21.183; to
                    Eurymachus 21.264; to Odysseus 21.304

Apollo   to Hermes (Demodocus' song) 8.361

Ares   to Aphrodite (Demodocus' song) 8.315

Arete   to Odysseus 7.253, 8.479; to the Phaeacians 11.345

Athena   to Zeus 1.50, 1.88; to Telemachus 1.193, 1.239,
                    1.271, 1.332; (as Mentor) to Telemachus 2.293,
                    2.427, 3.15, 3.28; (as Mentor) to Poseidon 3.61; (as
                    Mentor) to Telemachus 3.255; (as Mentor) to
                    Nestor 3.368, 3.394; to Zeus 5.9; (as Dymas' daugh-
                    ter) to Nausicaa 6.25; (as a young girl) to Odysseus
                    7.30, 7.52; (as Pontonous) to the Phaeacian leaders
                    and counselors 8.11; (as the discus marker) to Odys-
                    seus 8.215; (as a shepherd) to Odysseus 13.246; (as a
                    beautiful woman) to Odysseus 13.299, 13.341,
                    13.376, 13.389, 13.408, 13.436; to Telemachus 15.9;
                    to Odysseus 16.178; (as a woman) to Odysseus
                    20.37, 20.49; (as Mentor) to Odysseus 22.239; to
                    Zeus 24.491; (as Mentor) to Laertes 24.537; (as
                    Mentor) to the Ithacans 24.552; (as Mentor) to Od-
                    ysseus 24.565

Autolycus   to Eurycleia 19.443

Calypso   to Hermes 5.89, 5.118; to Odysseus 5.159, 5.181,
                    5.202

Circe   to Odysseus *10.341, *10.346, *10.403, *10.426; to
                    Odysseus and his crew *10.478; to Odysseus *10.509,
                    *10.527; to Odysseus and his crew *12.22; to Odys-
                    seus *12.38, *12.120

Ctessipus   to the Suitors 20.318

Eurymachus	to Telemachus 1.422; to Halitherses 2.196; to the Suitors 16.365; to Penelope 16.469, 18.266; to the Suitors 18.382; to Odysseus 18.390, 18.426; to the Suitors 20.395, 21.256; to Penelope 21.339; to Odysseus 22.48; to the Suitors 22.75
Eurynome	to Penelope 17.539, 18.182
Olympian god	to another Olympian god (Demodocus' song) 8.355
Halitherses	to the men of Ithaca 2.179, 24.471
Helen	to Menelaus 4.144; to Telemachus, Menelaus, and Peisistratus 4.252; to Telemachus 15.135; to Telemachus, Menelaus, and Peisistratus (a prophecy) 15.186
Helios	to the gods *12.388
Hephaestus	to the gods (Demodocus' song) 8.329; to Poseidon (Demodocus' song) 8.377, 8.385
Heracles	(from Underworld) to Odysseus *11.648
Herald	(random herald) to Penelope 16.356
Hermes	to Calypso 5.97, 5.145; to Apollo (Demodocus' song) 8.365; to Odysseus *10.301
Ino	to Odysseus 5.341
Irus	to Odysseus 18.11, 18.31
Ithacans	(listening to Phemius) among themselves 23.152
Laertes	to Odysseus 24.286, 24.337; to Zeus (a prayer) 24.358; to Odysseus 24.385; to the gods 24.534
Laodamas	to his friends 8.146; to Odysseus 8.158

Index of Speeches   407

Leocritus   to Mentor 2.265

Leodes   to the Suitors 21.157; to Odysseus 22.334

Arete's maids   to Odysseus 7.361

Medon   to Penelope 4.745, 4.761; to the Suitors 17.186; to
                 Telemachus 22.391; to the men of Ithaca 24.460

Melanthius   to Eumaeus and Odysseus 17.236, (a prayer) 17.272;
                 to the Suitors 17.402; to Odysseus 20.190; to Age-
                 laus 22.140

Melantho   to Odysseus 18.358, 19.72

Menelaus   to Eteoneus 4.34; to Telemachus and Peisistratus
                 4.64, 4.82; to Helen 4.154; to Telemachus, Helen,
                 and Peisistratus 4.176; to Peisistratus 4.215; to
                 Helen 4.285; to Telemachus 4.333, 4.357; to Eido-
                 thea *4.401, *4.421; to Proteus *4.493, *4.512, *4.579;
                 to Telemachus 4.646, 15.70, 15.120; to Telemachus
                 and Peisistratus 15.164; to Telemachus *17.130

Mentor   to the men of Ithaca 2.249

Miller   to Zeus (a prayer) 20.125

Nausicaa   to Alcinous 6.58; to Odysseus 6.191; to the ringleted
                 girls 6.204, 6.247; to Odysseus 6.262, 8.498

Nestor   to his guests 3.76; to Telemachus 3.113, 3.235,
                 3.280; to Telemachus and Athena (as Mentor)
                 3.385; to Telemachus 3.413; to his sons 3.459,
                 3.522; to his troops *24.56

Noemon   to Antinous 4.670, 4.690

Odysseus   to Calypso 5.172, 5.215; to his soul 5.300, 5.358,
                 5.411; to the god flowing in him 5.448; to his soul
                 5.471; to himself 6.118; to Nausicaa 6.149; to the

Odysseus
(continued)

ringleted girls 6.224; to Athena (a prayer) 6.332; to Athena (as a young girl) 7.24; to Arete (a prayer) 7.155; to Alcinous 7.221; to Arete 7.258; to Alcinous 7.324; to Zeus (a prayer) 7.352; to Laodamas 8.167; to Euryalus 8.181; to the Phaeacians 8.222; to Alcinous 8.413; to Euryalus 8.447; to Nausicaa 8.501; to a herald 8.514; to Demodocus 8.524; to Alcinous 9.2; to his crew *9.167; to Polyphemus *9.252, *9.275, *9.343, *9.360, *9.475, *9.500; to Aeolus' family *10.77; to his crew *10.193, *10.208; to Eurylochus *10.291; to Circe *10.359, *10.408; to his crew *10.446; to Circe *10.503, *10.524; to his crew *10.570, *10.585; to Elpenor (dead) *11.53, *11.77; to Tiresias (dead) *11.138; to Anticleia (dead) *11.163, *11.211; to Alcinous 11.365, 11.388; to Agamemnon (dead) *11.407, *11.452, *11.481; to Achilles (dead) *11.498, *11.529; to Ajax (dead) *11.580; to Circe *12.116; to his crew *12.161, *12.216, *12.279; to Eurylochus *12.304; to his crew *12.328; to the gods *12.382; to the Phaeacians 13.39; to Arete 13.61; to himself 13.208; to Athena (as a shepherd) 13.237, 13.265; to Athena (as a beautiful woman) 13.323; to the Nymphs, Naiades, and daughters of Zeus (a prayer) 13.369; to Athena (as a beautiful woman) 13.398, 13.432; to Eumaeus 14.61, 14.130, 14.165, 14.214, 14.423, 14.474, 14.500, 15.339, 15.374, 15.421, 15.529, 16.10; to Telemachus 16.100, 16.199, 16.215, 16.240, 16.273, 16.281, 17.16; to Eumaeus 17.207, 17.291, 17.308, 17.333, (a prayer) 17.383; to Antinous 17.450, 17.492; to the Suitors 17.509; to Eumaeus 17.609; to Irus 18.17; to the Suitors 18.56; to Irus 18.113; to Amphinomus 18.132; to Penelope *18.282; to maidservants 18.342; to Melantho 18.369; to Eurymachus 18.400; to Telemachus 19.4, 19.44; to Melantho 19.77; to Penelope 19.116, 19.179, 19.238, 19.286, 19.369; to Eurycleia 19.417, 19.529, 19.547; to Penelope 19.609, 19.641; to his heart 20.21; to Athena 20.41; to Zeus (a prayer) 20.108; to Eumaeus 20.182; to Philoetius 20.246; to Philoetius and

Eumaeus 21.200, 21.214, 21.235; to the Suitors 21.289; to Telemachus 21.451; to the Suitors 22.5, 22.38; to Eurymachus 22.65; to Telemachus 22.112, 22.156; to Eumaeus and Philoetius 22.176; to Athena (as Mentor) 22.218; to Telemachus, Eumaeus, and Philoetius 22.277; to Leodes 22.343; to Medon 22.396; to Telemachus 22.416; to Eurycleia 22.435, 22.456; to Telemachus, Eumaeus, and Philoetius 22.462; to Eurycleia 22.507, 22.517; to Telemachus 23.118, 23.134; to Penelope 23.171, 23.189, 23.255, 23.270, 23.364; to Telemachus, Eumaeus, and Philoetius 24.223; to Laertes 24.251, 24.312, 24.330, 24.340, 24.364, 24.382; to Dolius and his sons 24.405; to Dolius 24.421; to his guests 24.511; to Telemachus 24.526

Odysseus' crew   to Odysseus *9.493; among themselves *10.45; to Odysseus *10.442, *10.465, *10.493

Peiraeus   to Telemachus 15.594, 17.80

Peisistratus   to Athena (as Mentor) 3.48; to Menelaus 4.162, 4.201; to Telemachus 15.51; to Menelaus 15.181; to Telemachus 15.229

Penelope   to Phemius 1.356; to the Suitors 2.105; to Medon 4.728, 4.755; to the women of the house 4.774; to Athena (a prayer) 4.817; to Iphthime (as a phantom in slumber) 4.868, 4.890; to Antinous 16.447; to Telemachus 17.43, 17.107; to Theoclymenus 17.174; to herself 17.537; to Eurynome 17.542; to Eumaeus 17.552, 17.576, 17.592, 17.627, 17.638; to Eurynome 18.174, 18.191; to herself 18.216; to Telemachus 18.233; to Eurymachus 18.273; to Melantho 19.99; to Eurynome 19.106; to Odysseus 19.113, 19.135; to the Suitors *19.154; to Odysseus 19.232, 19.276, 19.340; to Odysseus and Eurycleia 19.381; to Odysseus 19.556, 19.614, 19.647; to Artemis (a prayer) 20.66; to the Suitors 21.66; to Antinous 21.329; to Eurymachus 21.349; to Eurycleia

Penelope (continued)	23.11, 23.35, 23.63, 23.85; to Telemachus 23.110; to Odysseus 23.180, 23.216, 23.263, 23.293; to the Suitors *24.138
Phaeacians	among themselves 13.173; (a Phaeacian sailor) to Nausicaa (hypothetical) *6.284
Phantom	(as Iphthime) to Penelope (in slumber) 4.862, 4.884, 4.895
Phemius	to Odysseus 22.369
Philoetius	to Eumaeus 20.204; to Odysseus 20.212, 20.256; to Zeus and Odysseus (a prayer) 21.208; to Ctessipus 22.303
Phoenicians	(daughter of Arybas) to Phoenician trader *15.467; (a Phoenician trader) to the daughter of Arybas *15.474; (daughter of Arybas) to Phoenician traders *15.478, *15.481
Polites	to part of Odysseus' crew *10.243
Polyphemus	to the Greeks 9.246; to Odysseus *9.265, *9.352, *9.367; to fellow Cyclopes *9.407; to ram *9.445; to Odysseus *9.505; to Poseidon (a prayer) *9.522
Poseidon	to himself 5.286, 5.380; to Hephaestus (Demodocus' song) 8.374, 8.382; (as Enipeus) to Tyro *11.252; to Zeus 13.132, 13.152
Proteus	to Menelaus *4.490, *4.500, *4.518, *4.571, *4.584
Sirens	to Odysseus (song) *12.192
Suitors	to Telemachus 2.347; among themselves 4.826; one of them to Antinous 17.524; among themselves 18.77; to Odysseus 18.120; among themselves 18.440; to Telemachus 20.410; one of them to Eumaeus 21.386; among themselves 21.424

Suggestions for Further Reading

Homeri Opera. Ed. by T. W. Allen. 2nd ed., Vols. III and IV. Oxford Classical Texts. London and New York, 1917.

The Odyssey. Ed. with Introduction, Commentary and Indexes by W. B. Stanford. 2nd ed., 2 vols. London and New York, 1967.

A Commentary on Homer's Odyssey. Vol. I: Books I–VIII, A. Heubeck, S. West, J. B. Hainsworth. Vol. II: Books IX–XVI, A. Heubeck, A. Hoekstra. Vol. III: Books XVII–XXIV, J. Russo, M. Fernández-Galiano, A. Heubeck. New York and Oxford, 1988–92.

Homer, *The Odyssey*. Ed. with English translation by A. T. Murray, revised by George E. Dimock. 2 vols. The Loeb Classical Library. Cambridge, Mass., and London, 1995.

Ahl, Frederick, and Hanna M. Roisman. *The Odyssey Re-Formed*. Ithaca, 1996.

Arnold, Matthew. "On Translating Homer." In *On the Classical Tradition*, ed. by R. H. Super. Michigan University Press. Ann Arbor and London, 1960.

Auerbach, Erich. *Mimesis: The Representation of Reality in Western Literature*. Trans. by Willard Trask. Chapter 1, "Odysseus' Scar." Princeton, 1953.

Austin, Norman. *Archery at the Dark of the Moon: Poetic Problems in Homer's Odyssey*. University of California Press. Berkeley, Los Angeles, and London, 1975.

Beye, Charles R. *The Iliad, the Odyssey, and the Epic Tradition*. New York and London, 1966.

Bloom, Harold, ed. *Homer's Odyssey*. New York, 1996.

Buitron, Diana, and Beth Cohen, eds. *The Odyssey and Ancient Art: An Epic in Word and Image*. The Edith C. Blum Art Institute, Bard College, Annandale-on-Hudson, New York, 1992.

Carter, Jane B., and Sarah P. Morris, eds. *The Ages of Homer: A Tribute to Emily Townsend Vermeule*. Austin, 1995.

Clarke, Howard. *The Art of the Odyssey*. Prentice-Hall. Englewood Cliffs, N.J., 1967.

———. *Homer's Readers: A Historical Introduction to the Iliad and the Odyssey*. Newark, Del., 1981.

Clay, Jenny Strauss. *The Wrath of Athena: Gods and Men in the Odyssey*. Princeton, 1983.

Cohen, Beth, ed. *The Distaff Side: Representing the Female in Homer's Odyssey.* New York and London, 1995.

Cook, Erwin F., *The Odyssey in Athens: Myths of Cultural Origins.* Cornell University Press. Ithaca, N.Y., 1995.

Dawe, R. D. *The Odyssey: Translation and Analysis.* Sussex, 1993.

Doherty, Lillian Eileen. *Siren Songs: Gender, Audiences, and Narrators in the Odyssey.* University of Michigan Press. Ann Arbor, 1995

Felson, Nancy. *Regarding Penelope: From Character to Poetics,* revised paperback edition. University of Oklahoma Press. Norman, 1997.

Finley, M. I. *The World of Odysseus.* 2nd rev. ed. Harmondsworth, 1979.

Frame, Douglas. *The Myth of Return in Early Greek Epic.* New Haven, 1978.

Griffin, Jasper. *Homer on Life and Death.* Clarendon Press. Oxford, 1980.

Katz, Marilyn A. *Penelope's Renown: Meaning and Indeterminancy in the Odyssey.* Princeton, 1991.

Kirk, G. S. *The Songs of Homer.* Cambridge University Press. Cambridge, England, 1962.

Lamberton, R., and J. J. Keaney, eds. *Homer's Ancient Readers: The Hermeneutics of Greek Epic's Earliest Exegetes.* Princeton University Press, 1992.

Lord, Albert. *The Singer of Tales.* Harvard University Press. Cambridge, Mass., 1960.

———. *The Singer Resumes the Tale.* Ed. by M. L. Lord. Cornell University Press. Ithaca, N.Y., 1995.

Morris, Ian, and Barry Powell, eds. *A New Companion to Homer.* Brill. Leiden, Netherlands, 1997.

Moulton, Carroll. *Similes in the Homeric Poems.* Vandenhoeck und Ruprecht. Göttingen, Germany, 1977.

Murnaghan, Sheila. *Disguise and Recognition in the Odyssey.* Princeton, 1987.

Myrsiades, Kostas, ed. *Approaches to Teaching Homer's Iliad and Odyssey.* New York, 1987.

Nagy, Gregory. *The Best of Achaeans: Concepts of the Hero in Archaic Greek Poetry,* rev. ed. Baltimore and London. Johns Hopkins University Press, 1999.

Page, Denys. *Folktales in Homer's Odyssey.* Cambridge, Mass. Harvard University Press, 1973.

———. *The Homeric Odyssey.* Oxford. Clarendon Press, 1955.

Parry, Milman. *The Making of Homeric Verse: The Collected Papers of Milman Parry.* Ed. by Adam Parry. Clarendon Press. Oxford, 1971.

Peradotto, John. *Man in the Middle Voice: Name and Narration in the Odyssey.* Martin Classical Lectures, New Series, Vol. 1. Princeton, 1990.

Pucci, Pietro. *Odysseus Polutropos: Intertextual Readings in the Odyssey and the Iliad.* 2nd ed. Ithaca, N.Y., 1995.

Reece, Steve. *The Stranger's Welcome: The Aesthetics of the Homeric Hospitality Scene.* University of Michigan Press. Ann Arbor, 1993.

Rubens, Beaty, and Oliver Taplin. *An Odyssey Round Odysseus: The Man and His Story Traced Through Time and Place.* London, 1989.

Rutherford, R. B. *Homer.* Greece and Rome. New surveys in the classics, no. 26. Oxford University Press, 1994.

Schein, Seth, ed. *Reading the Odyssey: Selected Interpretive Essays.* Princeton University Press. Princeton, 1996.

Scully, Stephen. *Homer and the Sacred City.* Ithaca and London, 1990.

Segal, Charles. *Singers, Heroes, and Gods in the Odyssey.* Cornell University Press. Ithaca, N.Y., 1994.

Stanford, W. B. *The Ulysses Theme: A Study in the Adaptability of the Homeric Hero.* Oxford, 1983.

Steiner, George, and Robert Fagles, eds. *Homer: A Collection of Critical Essays.* Ed. by Maynard Mack. Twentieth Century Views. Englewood Cliffs, N. J., 1962.

Thalmann, William G. *The Odyssey: Poem of Return.* Twayne. NewYork. 1992.

———. *The Swineherd and the Bow: Representations of Class in the Odyssey.* Cornell University Press. Ithaca, N.Y., 1998.

Tracy, Stephen W. *The Story of the Odyssey.* Princeton. Princeton University Press, 1990.

Vivante, Paolo. *Homer.* Yale University Press. New Haven and London, 1985.

———. *Homeric Rhythm: A Philosophical Study.* Greenwood Press. Westport, Conn., 1997.

Wace, Alan J. B., and Frank Stubbings. *A Companion to Homer.* London, 1962.

Whitman, Cedric H. *Homer and the Heroic Tradition.* Harvard University Press. Cambridge, Mass., and London, 1958.